PROGRESS
PROGRESS
PROGRESSIONS
PROGRESSIONS
PROGRESSIONS
PROGRESSIONS
PROGRESSIONS
PROGRESSIONS
PROGRESSIONS

PROGRESSIONS
PROGRESSIONS
PROGRESSIONS
PROGRESSIONS
PROGRESSIONS
PROGRESSIONS
PROGRESSIONS
PROGRESSIONS

Third Edition

BARBARA FINE CLOUSE

Allyn and Bacon
Boston   London   Toronto   Sydney   Tokyo   Singapore

Vice President, Editor in Chief, Humanities: Joe Opiela
Editorial Assistant: Susannah Davidson
Cover Coordinator: Linda Knowles
Manufacturing Buyer: Aloka Rathnam
Marketing Manager: Lisa Kimball
Editorial-Production Service: Electronic Publishing Services Inc.
Cover Designer: Studio Nine

Copyright © 1996, 1993 by Allyn & Bacon
A Simon & Schuster Company
Needham Heights, Massachusetts 02194

Library of Congress Cataloging-in-Publication Data

Clouse, Barbara Fine.
    Progressions / Barbara Fine Clouse. — 3rd ed.
        p. cm.
    Includes index.
    ISBN 0-205-17522-8
    1. English language—Rhetoric. 2. English language—Grammar.
I. Title.
PE1408.C5355 1995
808'.042—dc20   95-6301
                                                                          CIP

Printed in the United States of America

10 9 8 7 6 5 4 3 2   99 98 97 96

For Betty Fine Shepherd and Lee Fine

Contents

Preface

Progressions helps underprepared writers achieve the competence and confidence to write effectively in and out of the classroom. To achieve this goal, the text has two primary thrusts: it explains and illustrates the conventions of effective writing, and it presents a range of procedures students can follow as they move from idea generation to drafting to revising to editing and on to proofreading. In short, students learn both the characteristics of effective writing *and* procedures to generate such writing.

To support the student working toward proficiency, *Progressions* includes the following features:

- *Jargon-free prose* Students are given clear, concise, jargon-free explanations of the conventions of effective writing. Each consideration—whether at the sentence, paragraph, or essay level—is presented and illustrated. The illustrations are predominantly from student papers, so they represent attainable goals.

- *Frequently appearing exercises* Exercises appear after each concept presented, providing frequent opportunities for practice.

- *Detailed coverage of the writing process* The text describes a number of procedures for handling each stage of the writing process: idea generation, ordering, drafting, revising, editing, and proofreading. Students can sample procedures until they discover techniques that work well for them.

- *Emphasis on revision* To help students appreciate the recursive nature of writing, the need for revision, and the stages writers work through, Chapter 2 presents a student essay as it developed from idea generation through three drafts to finished copy. Annotations explain the changes in each stage of the essay and what prompted them. Revision is emphasized throughout the text, with a range of revision strategies, including reader response and revision checklists, presented.

- *Practical procedures* All writing assignments are accompanied by procedures students can easily follow. These procedures are an important support system for the student. Also, checklists appear after discussion of each mode, after discussion of paragraph structure, and after discussion of essay structure, to aid students as they revise.

- *Collaborative activities* There is an emphasis on collaboration, including collaborative learning activities, in sections labeled "Working Together."

- *Complete coverage of the paragraph* Students can hone rhetorical and editing skills at this level and move on to longer essays when they are more skilled and confident.

- *Description of editing techniques* Considerable emphasis is given to sentence-level concerns. Particularly helpful are specific strategies for finding and correcting errors with fragments, comma splices, run-ons, agreement, and pronoun reference. The pre- and post-tests accompanying each discussion of a grammar or usage point help students assess their strengths and weaknesses and how much they have learned.

- *Comprehension aids* For reading support, effort was made to keep the prose at an appropriate level and to avoid condescension. To aid comprehension and to provide easier access, main points are highlighted in the margins or grouped in short lists. Also, chapter goals are given as a form of prereading.

- *Reading instruction accompanied by professional essays* A chapter on reading and writing in response to reading (including writing summaries and taking essay examinations) is provided because these are vital academic survival skills and because of the strong reading–writing link. This chapter includes 11 previously published essays, many of which are followed by questions and writing assignments (at both the paragraph and the essay level). Earlier sections of the text treating methods of development are cross-referenced to the essays so students can study professional pieces in addition to student models.

- *Accessible resource material* The appendices offer valuable support to the student.
- *Personal Editing Profile* Appendix I helps students construct personal editing profiles so they become sensitive to their patterns of error and thus edit more effectively.
- *Problem-Solving Guide* Appendix II, which offers suggestions for working through writing problems, is a ready reference for students who get stuck along the way.
- *Answers to Pretests* Appendix III provides answers to the pretests, so students can determine their level of competence with each point of grammar discussed.

FEATURES NEW TO THIS EDITION

The third edition of *Progressions* includes many important new features, providing increased support for the developing writer:

- Information on writing with a word processor or computer
- New material on using listing as an idea generation technique
- An expanded discussion of audience and purpose
- An expanded discussion of writing conclusions
- An expanded discussion of pronoun reference problems
- An improved discussion of kinds of verbs (action verbs, helping verbs, and linking verbs)
- An explanation of comma splices
- A discussion of idiomatic expressions, which should be particularly helpful to students who speak English as a second language

Other changes were made to further strengthen the text:

- To freshen the text, many of the exercises and reading selections are new.
- The organization has been improved: material on identifying subjects and verbs appears earlier and is highlighted in its own chapter. The material on sentence fragments is highlighted in its own chapter, as is the material on run-ons and comma splices. These chapters now appear in the unit on effective sentences.

- More of the exercises call for students to edit paragraphs rather than sentences.
- All the professional essays now have headnotes and definitions of potentially difficult vocabulary.
- More professional essays are multicultural.

ORGANIZATION OF THE BOOK

Progressions is organized to provide students with a logical and comfortable sequence of instruction. At the same time, effort was made to organize so that instructors could easily work out of sequence should they desire.

The writing process is treated first in Chapters 1 and 2 so students begin with an awareness of the stages of writing and procedures they can follow. Paragraph structure is treated in Chapter 3. Here students learn about the topic sentence; adequate, specific, relevant detail; and supporting generalizations. Chapter 4 treats methods of development at the paragraph level. For each method of development—narration, description, illustration, process analysis, definition, comparison and contrast, cause-and-effect analysis, classification, and persuasion—the following features appear: student samples, discussion of rhetorical and structural features, a checklist to use during revision, a writing assignment, and prewriting tips.

Chapter 5 treats the essay. It explains essay structure and describes a way to plan the essay. Also, a checklist is provided to aid students as they revise. Ten student essays are included, several of which are expansions of student paragraphs that appeared earlier. These essays illustrate the methods of development described in Chapter 4. A writing assignment and tips for handling the essay appear as well.

Chapters 6, 7, 8, 9, and 10 deal with effective sentences. Discussions are jargon-free, but enough terminology is provided that students become familiar with key terms. Exercises occur frequently to provide ample practice.

Chapters 11–14 treat grammar and usage. Discussions are preceded by pretests and followed by post tests. Explanations are kept as simple and jargon-free as possible; however, enough terminology appears that students become familiar with key terms. Exercises occur frequently for ample practice, and students are often given specific strategies for finding and correcting errors.

Writing in response to reading is the focus of Chapter 15. Here students learn active reading; steps are presented and explained so students learn specific reading techniques. A published essay that has been annotated is provided as an example of how to mark a text during active reading. Six previously published essays appear, so students can practice active reading. Each of these is preceded by headnotes and glosses of difficult vocabulary and followed by questions on content and structure. Each reading is also followed by three paragraph-length writing assignments and three essay-length writing assignments. Chapter 15 also treats summary writing. The characteristics of a summary are explained and followed by a sample summary. Specific procedures for writing a summary are given, so students have a specific strategy for approaching this task. Three published essays appear, which students are to summarize for practice. Finally, Chapter 15 teaches students how to write effective essay examination answers.

ACKNOWLEDGMENTS

For their help with revising the third edition, I gratefully acknowledge the following reviewers: Peter Ashley, Baltimore Community College; Nancy Culberson, Georgia College; Victoria Ford, Seattle Central Community College; Clarence Hundley, Thomas Nelson Community College; Karen Levy, Sierra Community College; Violet O'Valle, Tarrant County Junior College; Pat Richardson, Tidewater Community College; and Rachel Shaffer, MSU-Billings. Their sensitive reading of the manuscript and their informed counsel provided substantial aid.

And to Denny, Greg, and Jeff: thank you, guys, for your understanding and support; you're the best.

A Letter to the Students Who Use This Book

Dear Students:

   With the right resources, *everyone* can learn to write clearly and effectively. The right resources are *language experience, a supportive teacher, a supportive textbook, opportunities to practice,* and *a desire to learn.*

- *language experience*—Because you have been speaking, reading, hearing, and writing English for many years, you know a great deal about its workings. This knowledge will serve you well as a solid base on which to build.

- *a supportive teacher*—Throughout the term, your writing teacher will provide instruction, guidance, and advice. He or she will be rooting for you, taking pleasure in each step forward you make. Rely on this person. Take your instructor's suggestions to heart and follow all instructions carefully—they are meant to help you. If you have questions, ask them immediately. Your instructor wants to help and wants you to succeed.

- *a supportive textbook*—For best results, study each assigned lesson carefully. Underline the main points and review them often. If you have questions, write them down (so you do not forget them) and ask your instructor. Do the best job you can on the exercises and study the ones you miss so you can learn from your mistakes. If you do not understand your errors, ask your instructor for help.

   I am certain that by the end of the term you will be a more confident, effective writer. When that happens, please let me hear from you. Write to me, to the attention of the English Editor, Allyn and Bacon Publishing Company, 160 Gould Street, Needham Heights, MA 02194, and tell me about your success.

Sincerely,

Barbara Fine Clouse

Barbara Fine Clouse

CHAPTER

1

The Writing Process: Planning—Writing—Rewriting

Successful writers rarely produce their work in one quick sitting. Instead, most successful writers (even professional ones) work through three stages. Stage one is the *planning stage,* when writers consider what they want to say and the order they want to say it in. Stage two is the *writing stage,* when writers first put their ideas down in composition form. (Another name for this stage is *drafting.*) Stage three is the *rewriting stage,* when writers shape and refine the draft they produced during stage two.

You too should learn to work through several stages. Do not expect your writing to roll off your pen or pop off the keys in perfect form. Instead, expect to work and rework a piece as you gradually shape it to a satisfying finished product. Remember, this gradual shaping in a series of stages is how the writing process works.

> The stages of writing are
>
> 1. planning
> 2. writing
> 3. rewriting

The rest of this chapter will discuss the planning, writing and rewriting stages writers work through. You will learn:

1. how to use five techniques (listing, brainstorming, clustering, freewriting, and journal writing) to discover ideas to include in your writing
2. how to order your ideas
3. how to use linking words and phrases (called *transitions*) so your reader can follow your order of ideas
4. how to write a first draft
5. how to refine your draft into a finished piece of writing

PLANNING YOUR WRITING: GENERATING IDEAS

All writers get stuck sometimes. When they do, listing, brainstorming, clustering, freewriting, and journal writing can help.

Occasionally, a writer gets lucky and all the right ideas spill onto the page in a burst of inspiration. However, that is extremely rare. Usually, writers work for their ideas, so do not spend too much time staring at a blank page. Go after the ideas you need by listing, brainstorming, clustering, freewriting, and journal writing. *Listing, brainstorming, clustering, freewriting,* and *journal writing* are techniques described in this chapter for discovering writing topics and ideas.

Listing

When listing, do not evaluate how good your ideas are; write everything that occurs to you.

Listing can supply topics and ideas. To list, spill out every idea that occurs to you, without evaluating how good the ideas are. Just record everything you think of. You will find that one idea leads to another until you have a list of useful and not-so-useful thoughts. You may need to pause at times to think of ideas, but if you let yourself write every thought that comes to mind without restraining yourself, you will develop a helpful list.

Here is a list developed by a student who wanted to write about athletics:

football   player salaries
baseball   player strikes
basketball   what sports mean to boys
coaching   betting

training   athletic scholarships

college   opportunities for women

professional   recruiting violations

when I was cut from the basketball
team

great athletes (Michael Jordan, etc.)

preventing injuries

Little League

When you run out of ideas, review your list and decide on a topic. The student who wrote the above list decided to write about the time he was cut from the basketball team.

Next, list again—this time to discover ideas for writing about your topic. Here is the student's second list. Notice that he crossed out the ideas he decided not to include, the ones not closely enough related to his topic.

> Study your list to find a writing topic.

went to every practice-played well

really wanted it bad

was sure I made the team

~~my father wanted it bad too~~

after school, checked list- didn't see
my name

~~it was like the time I struck out in~~
~~Little League~~

cried all the way home

was embarrassed – all my friends made the team

Luis didn't talk to me anymore

~~Jerrold also didn't make the team~~

felt like a failure

lost friends because they were always at practice, etc.

felt sorry for myself and stupid

An idea-generation list can be turned into a scratch outline.

   After crossing out ideas, some writers determine a suitable order for their ideas and number them to reflect this order. The result is a *scratch outline*, a guide that tells the writer what ideas will appear in the first draft and what order they will appear in. Here is the student writer's list turned into a scratch outline.

2 went to every practice – played well

1 really wanted it bad

3 was sure I made the team

~~my father wanted it bad too~~

4 after school, checked list – didn't see my name

~~it was like the time I struck out in Little League~~

5 cried all the way home

8 was embarrassed – all my friends made
the team

10 Luis didn't talk to me anymore

~~Gerrold also didn't make the team~~

6 felt like a failure

9 lost friends because they were always
at practice, etc.

7 felt sorry for myself and stupid

Practice 1.1

Assume you will write about a person you admire. The person can be a famous person, a friend, a relative, a teacher, a coach, or anyone you regard highly. To decide whom you will write about, use the space below to list the names of everyone you can think of that you admire for any reason at all, no matter how small. (Try to list at least five people.)

Study your list and select the person you wish to write about. Using a separate sheet of paper, spend about ten minutes listing to discover the reasons you admire this person. Write three of these reasons in the spaces provided. Number your ideas to show which will appear first, second, and third.

_____

_____

_____

Brainstorming

Brainstorming is asking questions about your topic. The answers can supply ideas to include in your writing.

> To brainstorm, ask questions about your topic.

Some of the following questions will be suited to your topic, and some of them will not be. Each time you brainstorm, select the appropriate questions and disregard the rest. Also, you will probably think of additional questions suited to your particular topic.

Who was involved?	Why is it important?
What happened?	What can be learned?
When did it happen?	What is it like? (or different from?)
Why did it happen?	What does it mean?
Where did it happen?	What is (was) the cause?
How did it happen?	What is (was) the effect?
How is it done?	How is it made?

Here is a list of brainstorming questions and answers a student used when she wrote about getting married right out of high school. Notice that the writer used some of the questions in the preceding list but not others; also notice that she added questions she thought of that were especially suited to her particular topic.

What happened?

I got married right after high school graduation.

Why did it happen?

I was pregnant. I felt I had to get married.

What was it like?

At first very exciting because I felt mature and more sophisticated than my friends. I was glad to be away from my parents.

Then what happened?

My husband joined the service. I was alone most of the time and missed out on what my friends were doing. It was lonely and scary.

What was the effect?

The marriage lasted seven years and then we divorced. I felt cheated out of some very good years. Now I must raise my son alone. It's hard.

What can be learned?

Teen marriages are difficult. They are no solution to an unplanned pregnancy. I was stupid to get married. If you're pregnant, think about all your choices.

After brainstorming, study your answers to find a specific writing topic. When the student writer studied her brainstorming, she decided to write about why teen marriages are a problem, using her own experience as an example. Select your topic on the basis of which answers interest you or on the basis of what you have the most information on.

> Study your brainstorming to find a specific topic.

Practice 1.2

Assume you will write about a difficult decision you made. If you cannot think of a decision you want to write about, do some listing on another sheet of paper. After settling on the decision, on a separate page, brainstorm for about fifteen minutes to develop ideas that might appear in the writing. When your brainstorming is complete, study your answers and decide on a specific writing topic. Write it here:

_____

Now, in the spaces provided, record five ideas that could appear in your writing about a difficult decision.

1. _____

   _____

2. _____

   _____

3. _____

   _____

4. _____

   _____

5. _____

   _____

Clustering

> Clustering helps you see how your ideas relate to each other.

Clustering is an excellent idea-generation technique because it helps you see how your ideas connect to each other. To cluster, write one general idea down in the center of a large sheet of paper and circle it:

Next, around the circled general idea write related ideas and connect them to the central circle.

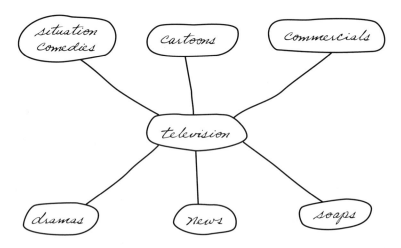

As you think of more ideas, write them down, circle them, and connect them to the ideas they are the most closely related to:

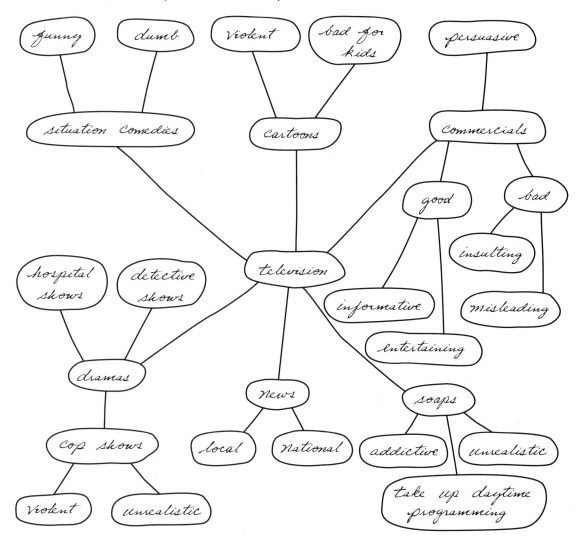

Continue writing, circling, and connecting ideas until you can think of nothing more. As with all idea-generation techniques, do not censor yourself or evaluate the worth of your ideas—just write down everything you can think of.

Sometimes one clustering gives you enough to get underway. If not, study what you have and settle on a topic for your writing. For example, the writer of the preceding clustering decided to write about television commercials. Once you have settled on a topic, do a second clustering with your topic circled in the middle.

A second clustering can be done to discover ideas for developing a topic.

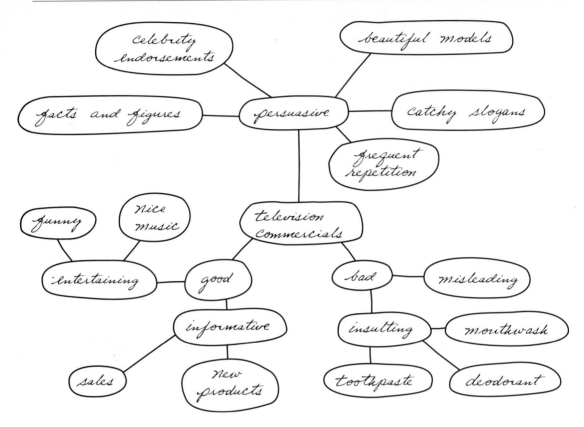

The student writer of this second clustering decided to write about the techniques used in television commercials to persuade people to buy products. She used the ideas clustering around the "persuasive" circle in her writing.

Practice 1.3

Assume you have been asked to write about education reform. On a separate sheet, develop a clustering with "education reform" circled in the center. When you discover a topic, write that topic here.

_____

Now, on a separate sheet, develop a second clustering. Place your topic in the center. When you can think of nothing more to add to the clustering, record four of the ideas you thought of here.

1. _____

2. _____

3. _____

4. _____

Freewriting

Freewriting is nonstop writing that works like this: for ten to fifteen minutes, write anything and everything that comes to mind. Do not decide whether your ideas are "good" or "bad." Just record everything, even the silly ideas. Also, do not worry about grammar, spelling, or neatness. If you cannot think of anything to write, then write "I don't know what to write." Write the alphabet, the names of your family members, or your feelings at the moment. Eventually, more ideas will occur to you, and you can record them. Continue in this fashion, without lifting your pen from the page.

When time is up, read your freewriting. Most people find they have discovered at least one good idea. Many people find more than one good idea. These ideas will require shaping, but they can get you started.

The following freewriting was done by a student searching for ideas about college life. Notice that the writer was not concerned about grammar, spelling, and correctness. Also, notice the free flow of thought; the author did not eliminate silly or irrelevant ideas but used them as a springboard to more serious and relevant ones.

> When freewriting, do not stop, do not censor yourself, and do not worry about grammar, spelling, or neatness.

How has college affected me, that's a loaded question. I'm 42 so coming here was really scary. I didn't think I could keep up with the kids, I thought I was too rusty and out of practice. I was so insecure that I overdid it, studying ridiculous amounts of time for even little quizzes. Well when I started getting grades on things I realized that I was doing better than the people younger than me and that really boosted my confidence. The first time I had to write a paper I was a basket case, I didn't do so good, but now I'm getting better thanks to the writing center. It's lonely sometimes cause its hard to talk to eighteen year olds about my divorce or the kids or money problems, but their sweet and they see me as a mother so I help them alot. The best effect is that for the first time in years since Dan walked out I feel like I have a future. I know I'll get my degree and go on to make a living and support myself and the kids. Its an awful lot of work. Did I say that already? I think I'm running out of things to say. Running. I do alot of that. With school, the job, the kids stuff, all I do is run, run, run. No wonder I'm exhausted all the time. I'll bet none of these kids here could keep up with me. I guess I feel pretty proud of myself. What else can I say? I can't think I can't think Oh am I tired now I can't think because I'm tired. One other effect is that my kids think its cool that moms in school, sometimes we even study together. I think I feel older being around so many young people, but I do feel like I can do anything they do and that's a good feeling.

In her freewriting, the student discovered several ideas she could write about: the insecurity she felt when she returned to college, how the Writing Center helped her become a better writer, acting like a mother to younger students, feeling as if she has a future, her exhaustion, her pride in herself, and what it is like to be around younger people in school. The student decided that she wanted to write about her exhaustion, so she made that idea her writing topic.

Often, one freewriting gets the writer started. Other times, a second freewriting is needed, which focuses on the idea or ideas that surfaced in the first freewriting. Here is the student's second freewriting, which focuses on her exhaustion:

> A second freewriting focusing on an idea discovered in the first freewriting can be helpful.

I don't know if I can even explain the exhaustion I feel. No matter how hard I work there's always more to do. I get up at 5:00, make lunch and throw in a load of laundry, and straighten the house. But that's a joke because the house always looks like a disaster area no matter how much straightening I do. <u>I cant ever get to the real cleaning.</u> You should see the inside of my refrigerator, its disgusting. I get the kids off to school by 8 and then I leave to be at my job by 9. <u>I work as a bookkeeper all day and then race home at five, throw supper on the table and leave for class. Class goes until 9 and then I come home to the kids and all their homework and problems. I can't even start my homework until they are in bed at 11 so sometimes I'm up way past midnight and then it all starts over.</u> That pretty much sums it up, no there's more. <u>The exhaustion is mental more than physical. All the planning and worrying.</u> Dance lesson, soccer practice, doctor appointments, teacher conferences its so hard to fit it all in. Now what do I say. I guess there's the exhaustion that comes from being on my own and not having anyone to help or count on. I guess I can count on Jeannie, but she has her own problems and I hate to bother her too much. <u>My biggest worry is that I'm not spending time with the kids. And I worry about all the bills. The worrying exhausts me too.</u>

After your second freewriting, read your work and underline useful ideas the way the student writer did. Remember, do not expect polished thoughts; just find raw material that can be shaped. Perhaps the second freewriting will provide enough ideas to get you started. If not, try some brainstorming, clustering, or listing. Idea-generation techniques are often used in combination.

Practice 1.4

Assume you plan to write about ways you have changed in the past three to five years. On a separate paper, freewrite for ten or fifteen minutes to discover ideas for this writing. Remember, do not stop writing for any reason, do not reject any ideas, and do not worry about grammar, spelling, or neatness. If necessary, freewrite a second time until you have at least four ideas. Record these ideas below.

1. _____

_____

2. _____

_____

3. _____

_____

4. _____

_____

Keeping a Journal

> By keeping a journal, writers can explore how they think and feel. They can also develop a storehouse of ideas to use in their writing.

In a journal, writers explore their ideas and feelings about things. However, a journal is *not* a diary, a place to record what happened during the day. Journal writing can be very rewarding because it helps writers solve problems, get in touch with their feelings, vent anger, and discover what they think about issues. Furthermore, a journal can be an excellent source of ideas for writing.

To keep a journal, buy a notebook, and write in it every day, at the same time every day if you can manage it. Date each entry before you write and then take off—write anything that you are moved to write. Do not get hung up on spelling, handwriting, or grammar. This writing is for you.

Journal entries can be about anything, but here are some possibilities:

1. Write about something that happened during the day that angered you, surprised you, cheered you, or moved your emotions in some way.

2. Write about a person you admire, love, hate, respect, or do not understand.

3. Write about how school is going.

4. Write about your goals.

5. Write about your family relationships.

6. Write about possible solutions to a problem you are having.

7. Write about changes you would like to make.

8. Write about your childhood.

9. Write about your classmates.

10. Freewrite about the first thing that comes to your mind.

11. Write about something you recently read or watched on TV.

12. List everything you like and dislike about school or work.

13. Write about what makes you happy or sad.

14. Write about how you feel about your writing.

15. Write about what is important to you.

Make regular entries in your journal, and you will soon have a considerable body of material. When you need ideas for writing, paging through your journal may turn up what you need to get started or keep going.

Working Together: Generating Ideas

When writers need ideas, other people can help because they often think of things we overlook, or they say something that triggers our thinking.

Working together can be as simple as approaching someone and asking what he or she thinks about a particular subject. Just say, "I have to write a paper on _____; do you have any ideas?" The response you get may be enough to get you started.

Working together can also involve sitting down with one or more people and working in a more formal way. Listing, brainstorming, and clustering, in particular, lend themselves to this approach.

> Other people can help a writer who needs ideas.

To list with one or more people, assign a person to write down what everyone says. Then group members begin saying any and all ideas that occur to them while the recorder gets them down in list form. Listing with others can be helpful because one person usually says something that prompts someone else to get an idea.

Brainstorming can also be done with more than one person. Take turns asking questions while the person who needs the ideas answers the questions and records those answers.

To use clustering in a group, assign one group member to do the writing. All group members speak their ideas as they occur to them, and the group decides where on the clustering to connect each idea. Clustering in a group has the same advantage as listing in a group: one person's ideas stimulate the thinking of other people.

□   TIPS FOR GENERATING IDEAS   □

1. Don't wait for inspiration. If ideas do not occur to you right away, go to work with the idea-generation techniques.

2. Write about what you know. Even the idea-generation techniques cannot help you come up with ideas if you do not know very much about the subject.

3. Try each idea-generation technique to learn what works best for you. Even if you do not think a technique will work for you, give it a try. You may be surprised to discover what it can do.

4. Use more than one technique. Sometimes combining techniques yields more ideas than using one technique by itself.

5. Keep your writing topic in mind as you go about your activities. Ideas can occur while you are walking across campus, washing the car, eating lunch, or engaging in other routines.

6. Give yourself enough time. If you wait until the last minute to begin your writing project, you will not allow sufficient time for ideas to surface.

7. Accept rough ideas. Idea generation is the earliest stage of writing, so things are bound to be rough. Don't reject ideas just because they are not polished; you can improve things during revision.

8. Force yourself to write. Writing stimulates thinking, so sit down and fill a page with whatever occurs to you, and you may hit upon a brainstorm.

PLANNING YOUR WRITING: AUDIENCE AND PURPOSE

Typically, writers write for any one or more of these purposes:

> to share something with the reader
>
> to inform the reader of something
>
> to persuade the reader to think or act a particular way
>
> to entertain the reader

Your purpose is important because *why* you are writing influences the *nature* of your writing. For example, let's say you are writing about Thanksgiving. If you want to share with your reader, you might tell about your family celebrations at your grandparents' house. If you want to inform your reader, you might compare modern Thanksgiving celebrations with those of the nineteenth century. If you want to convince your reader of something, you can argue that Thanksgiving should be a day of mourning because of our treatment of Native Americans. Finally, if you want to entertain, you could tell an amusing story about the time you made a fool of yourself at your first Thanksgiving dinner at your in-laws' house.

Like purpose, your audience (the reader) will affect the nature of a piece. Your reader's age, sex, socioeconomic standing, political views, religion, family background, and so forth can influence the detail you include. In addition, how much your reader knows about your topic and how much your reader cares about your topic will affect what you do. Let's say, for example, that you are writing to convince your reader to pass a school levy. If your audience has children, you can discuss improving education. However, if your reader has no children, you may want to mention the improved property values that result from better schools.

You may be thinking that all this talk about audience is unnecessary because your audience will be your writing teacher. However, to prepare you for writing outside the classroom, your writing teacher can assume the identity of any reader you have in mind.

To appreciate how audience and purpose affect writing, consider the options for writing about VCRs. Possibilities include:

1. explaining how to program a VCR (a manufacturer might write this in the owner's manual for the purchaser)

2. convincing someone to purchase a particular brand of VCR (a store owner might write this in an advertising brochure for a potential customer)

3. writing an entertaining article on the trials and tribulations of owning a VCR (a newspaper columnist might write this for the readers of a daily newspaper)

4. explaining how the VCR has affected family life (a psychologist might write this for the readers of *Family Circle* magazine)

5. explaining how the VCR has affected the movie industry (a studio executive might write this for the readers of an industry trade magazine)

The character of each of these pieces will be different because the audience and purpose will be different for each. Specifically, the differences will be in the kinds of details, the vocabulary, and the approach. Let's look at each of these elements.

KINDS OF DETAILS—Purpose will help dictate the kinds of details a writer uses. The piece about how to program a VCR will include all the steps, but the piece convincing a reader to buy a particular brand will only mention that programming is uncomplicated. Similarly, audience affects the details chosen. If the reader of the piece about how to program the VCR is knowledgeable about electronics, then it may not be necessary to explain where buttons are located, but this information would be needed for a reader who knows nothing about the equipment.

VOCABULARY—Your audience will determine the level of vocabulary you use. For example, let's say that you are writing about the effects of the VCR on family life. For an audience of psychologists, you can use the term *projection* but for the average parent, you may need to say "attributing your own faults to someone else."

APPROACH—Audience and purpose will also affect the approach you take. For example, humor would be appropriate in the piece on the trials and tribulations of using a VCR that is meant to entertain the readers of a newspaper. However, the same humor would be misplaced in the owner's manual that explains how to program the device.

☐ TIPS FOR IDENTIFYING AUDIENCE ☐ AND PURPOSE

Part of the planning you should do involves identifying your audience and purpose. Asking the following questions can help with this:

1. Do I want to entertain my reader?
2. Do I want to inform my reader? If so, of what?
3. Do I want to convince my reader to think or act in a certain way? If so, in what way?
4. Do I want to share something with my reader? If so, what?
5. Who will my reader be? (Your instructor can assume the identity of any reader you want.)
6. What does my reader already know about my topic?
7. What strong feelings does my reader hold about my topic?
8. How interested will my reader be?

9. Will my reader's age, sex, race, economic level, political beliefs, or religion influence the response to my topic?

Practice 1.5: Working Together

Each member of your group should find a piece of writing. Possibilities include a newspaper article, a recipe, a magazine article, a business letter, an advertisement, an editorial, an owner's manual, a book or movie review, a textbook chapter, and so on. As a group, analyze each piece of writing and determine the intended audience and purpose and the effect of these factors on the kind of detail, the amount of detail, the vocabulary, and the approach.

PLANNING YOUR WRITING: ORDERING IDEAS

Writers arrange their ideas in a way that helps explain or prove the central idea. Often an effective arrangement is a movement from *general to specific*. In this arrangement, a sentence presents the central idea, which is a general point. The detail that follows provides specific ideas that explain or prove the central idea. Although other effective arrangements are possible, for now we will concern ourselves with general-to-specific order.

> Part of a writer's planning is finding a suitable order for ideas. Often a general-to-specific order is effective.

Three common general-to-specific arrangements are *chronological order, spatial order,* and *emphatic order.*

> In chronological order, events are arranged in the order they occurred.

Chronological Order

Chronological order is time order: events are arranged in the order they occurred. Chronological order is used most frequently when a story is told and the writer arranges details according to what happened first, second, and so forth. In the paragraph that follows, details are arranged chronologically:

The seven ten-year-olds arrived within minutes of each other. I explained that Gregory would be back in a half hour, so they all raced through the downstairs looking for the best hiding places. Julio and Brian hid behind the couch, while Heath and Tod crouched between the end table and wall. Jordan crawled under the dining room table, and Josh scrambled in behind him. Jeffrey found a perfect spot behind the front door. Soon we heard the slam of a car door, and we knew Greg was home. After he walked in the front door, the boys jumped out from their hiding places and yelled, "Surprise!"

Spatial Order

With a spatial order, details are arranged according to their location.

With a *spatial order,* details are arranged according to their location in a particular area. Spatial order is especially useful when you are describing some location. A spatial order often involves moving through space in some sequence: top to bottom, front to back, near to far, inside to outside, and so forth. The paragraph that follows has details arranged in a spatial order:

When I entered the living room, I was appalled by what I saw. Empty potato chip and pretzel bags littered the coffee table and couch; their contents formed a layer of crumbs on the carpet. The antique, crystal lamp on the table next to the couch was resting on its side, and the table itself held at least ten beer cans, all of them squashed in the middle. Beneath the table, the once-beige carpet was stained with a dark splotch that I knew would be permanent. Worst of all was the sight of my teenage son, who had been left in charge. There he was, sprawled across the couch asleep or unconscious—I wasn't sure which.

Emphatic Order

To arrange detail in an emphatic order, begin with your least important point and move to your most important. Also, you can begin with your second most important point and end with your most important.

A writer who uses an *emphatic order* begins with the least important detail and moves gradually to the most important detail. Think of emphatic order as saving the best for last: an emphatic order gives the writer a big finish.

A variation on emphatic order is to begin with your second most important point, end with your most important, and sandwich your other points in between. This gives you the strongest possible opening and closing.

The following paragraph arranges details in an emphatic order:

For several reasons, voters should pass the school levy when it is placed on the ballot during the August special election. First, the additional funds will allow the senior class to take a trip to Washington. More important, passage of the levy means the elementary schools can add computer instruction to the curriculum. Without this instruction, our students will lag behind others in the country. Finally, if the levy passes, our school system can pay its debts and avoid a state loan that will jeopardize its financial well-being for years to come.

Combining Orders

A writer can use any combination of chronological, spatial, and emphatic orders.

A writer can use any combination of chronological, spatial, and emphatic orders in the same piece. For example, look back at the paragraph that illustrates chronological order on p. 19. Notice that for the most part the ideas are arranged according to what happened first, second, third, and so forth. However, notice that a spatial order is also used when the paragraph explains where the children hid (between the end table and the wall, behind the front door, and so forth).

Now look again at the paragraph illustrating spatial order on p. 20. For the most part, ideas are arranged according to their location, but some emphatic order is also apparent. You can tell this because the second to the last sentence begins, "Worst of all." This phrase suggests that the most important detail is at the end.

Deciding on an Effective Order

Many times your instinct will suggest the best order for your ideas. For example, when you are telling a story, you will sense that a time order is called for; when you are describing a scene, you will feel the need for a spatial order; when you are arguing a point, you will realize an emphatic order will be effective.

When you do not sense the best order for your ideas, outlining can help. Try outlining your ideas, using different arrangements, and then study your outlines to determine which seems best. You already learned about the scratch outline in this chapter. Later you will learn about another outlining technique (see p. 155).

> When a writer's instincts do not suggest an effective order, drawing up more than one outline can help the writer decide on the best arrangement.

☐   TIPS FOR ORDERING IDEAS   ☐

1. Do not resist outlining. It can save you time in the long run by making the draft go more smoothly. Try a scratch outline (p. 4) or outline map (p. 155) to order your ideas.

2. Outline more than once. If you are having trouble ordering your ideas, try two or more different arrangements to see what works best.

3. Try different kinds of outlines to see what works best for you.

4. Decide whether spatial, chronological, or emphatic order will work the best before you begin ordering your ideas.

Practice 1.6

1. For each of the following paragraphs, indicate whether the order of ideas is chronological, spatial, or emphatic. In one paragraph, a combination of orders is used.

A. The exasperated mother explained to her son for the fourth time why he could not get a puppy. First, she said, paper training the animal would be too much trouble, especially since no one was home during the day. Then there was the fact that puppies are expensive and their budget was too tight to allow for dog food purchases and veterinarian bills. Most important, she said that they live in an apartment and their lease expressly prohibits all pets except birds.

The ideas are arranged in _____ order.

B. Paper recycling is an interesting process. First, the paper is put into a vat of water with chemicals that remove the ink and turn the paper into soft pulp. This vat is called a pulper. From the pulper, the pulp goes to a machine that removes staples, clips, and anything else that is not paper. Next, the pulp is cleaned and mixed with water to form a thick paste that is spread on a metal sheet where it is heated, dried, and smoothed. When the paste dries, it is crisp, new paper.

The ideas are arranged in _____ order.

C. When I walked into the sixty-dollar-a-night hotel room, I was outraged by what I saw. Directly in front of me was an unmade bed, its sheets a dingy gray. The wall behind the bed was stained with a brown splotch that looked alarmingly like dried blood. There were no drapes on the window; instead, a tattered blind partially blocked the sun. I turned to check the bathroom to my right. There the situation was just as bad: dirty towels were on the floor; the sink was rust-stained, and the mirror above it was opaque with dust and lint. Furious, I stormed out of the room to find the manager and get a full refund.

The ideas are arranged in _____ order.

2. Assume that each of the following sentences is the first sentence of a paragraph, the sentence that presents the writer's central idea. On the space provided, indicate whether the order of ideas is likely to be spatial, chronological, emphatic, or some combination of these.

A. It would be a serious mistake to zone Fifth Avenue to allow the construction of a shopping plaza.

The order of ideas is likely to be _____.

B. The kitchen of the model home is the most efficient one I have seen.

The order of ideas is likely to be _____.

C. The military should not be responsible for the development of experimental spacecraft.

The order of ideas is likely to be _____.

D. My first day of college did not go well.

The order of ideas is likely to be _____.

E. Anyone can learn to change the oil in a car.

The order of ideas is likely to be _____.

3. For each of the following writing topics, use the idea-generation technique of your choice to develop at least four ideas. Do this on a separate sheet. Then, in the space provided, write the ideas in the order they are likely to appear in the writing.

A. Topic: Changes I'd Most Like to Make in Myself

First idea _____

Second idea _____

Third idea _____

Fourth idea _____

The order of my ideas is _____.

The idea-generation technique I used is _____.

B. Topic: A Time When Something Did Not Go as Expected

First idea _____

Second idea _____

Third idea _____

Fourth idea _____

The order of my ideas is _____.

The idea-generation technique I used is _____.

C. Topic: Why X-Rated Movies Should (or Should Not) Be Banned

First idea _____

Second idea _____

Third idea _____

Fourth idea _____

The order of my ideas is _____.

The idea-generation technique I used is _____.

USING TRANSITIONS

Transitions are words and phrases that help a reader follow the order of ideas. Some transitions are a clue that chronological order has been used, some transitions are a clue that spatial order has been used, and some transitions are a clue that emphatic order has been used.

Take another look at the paragraph illustrating chronological order on p. 19. Notice that the transitions *soon* and *after* suggest a time sequence. Now look at the paragraph illustrating spatial order on p. 20. Notice that transitions like *next to, beneath,* and *across* indicate that ideas are arranged according to location. Finally, reread the paragraph illustrating emphatic order on p. 20. In this case, the transition *more important* provides the clue that emphatic order has been used.

Transitions are being discussed now because they help writers clarify the order of ideas for the reader. However, checking for effective use of transitions is part of revising, not part of the early planning stages of writing.

The chart that follows notes some common transitions used to signal chronological, spatial, and emphatic orders. (A more complete discussion of transitions begins on p. 96.)

> Transitions are words and phrases that help the reader understand the order of ideas.

Transition Chart

Transitions that Signal Chronological Order	first, second, third . . ., next, then, after, before, in the meantime, finally, at the same time, during, meanwhile, at first, when, as soon as

Before the shortstop could make the play at second, the runner slid into the bag.

Transitions that Signal Spatial Order	nearby, near to, beside, over, far from, next to, under, around, through, in front of, behind, surrounding, alongside, away from, on top of, around, toward, at

Behind the sofa I found the black leather glove I lost last January.

Transitions that Signal Emphatic Order	more important, most important, most of all, best of all, of greatest significance, least of all, even better

The tax proposal will burden the poor. *More important,* it will cause industry to relocate to other areas.

Practice 1.7

1. Read the following paragraph and circle every transition that signals chronological, spatial, or emphatic order. (You will circle five transitions in all.)

> All children who swim should be taught a number of important safety rules. First, they should be taught to swim only where there is supervision. Next, they should be cautioned to dive only in designated areas. Even better, they should be told not to dive at all, since each year hundreds of people suffer permanent, crippling injuries as a result of diving. If caught in a strong current, a child should know to swim across that current or parallel to shore. Once free of the current, the child should head for shore at once. Most important, all children should be taught never, ever to swim alone.

2. In the following sentences, fill in the blanks with transitions according to the directions given. If you need help selecting a transition, refer to the chart beginning on p. 24.

   A. Use transitions that signal chronological order:

   Paula and Eric began a new financial program. _____ they refinanced their home mortgage, and _____ they began a regular savings program.

   B. Use a transition that signals emphatic order:

Contrary to popular belief, regular exercise decreases a person's appetite. _____ exercise helps prevent bone loss, which is vital in preventing osteoporosis.

C. Use transitions that signal spatial order:

Lee spent weeks redecorating Rosa's room to make it more suitable for a five-year-old. _____ the bed she stenciled nursery rhyme characters on the wall, and _____ the closet she built shelves to hold toys. _____ the windows she hung yellow curtains.

3. *Working Together:* with two or three of your classmates, write sentences according to the directions. Use a separate sheet.

A. Write two sentences that describe the location of some of the things in your writing classroom. Begin the second sentence with a transition that signals a spatial order.

B. Write two sentences about what you did this morning. Begin the second sentence with a transition that signals a chronological order.

C. Write two sentences that tell why foreign languages should (or should not) be taught in high school. Begin the second sentence with a transition that signals emphatic order.

WRITING YOUR FIRST DRAFT

A first draft is the first version of a piece of writing. It is also known as a rough draft because it is likely to have problems the writer will solve later, when the draft is refined.

After generating ideas and deciding on a suitable order, writers usually consider most of their planning complete, and they are ready to put their plan in action by writing a first draft. A *first draft* is the earliest version of a piece of writing.

You should understand what a first draft is and what it is not. A first draft is *not* a finished piece of writing; it is *not* something the writer is completely satisfied with; it is *not* something that can be copied over and handed to a reader. Instead, a first draft *is* a first effort. It has problems, mistakes, and areas the writer is unsure about. Thus, a first draft is often called a *rough draft.*

☐   TIPS FOR WRITING THE FIRST DRAFT   ☐

1. Write your draft from beginning to end in one sitting. The sooner you get your draft down, the sooner you will know what kind of raw material you have to work with.

2. Forget perfection. You can improve the draft later. For now, just get your ideas down the best way you can.

3. If you get stuck, skip the troublesome part and push on. Later you can work out the problem.

4. Do not spend much time making changes as you go. Save most of your changes for later, when you revise the draft.

5. As you draft, refer often to your list of generated ideas so that you do not lose sight of the plan you have for your writing.

6. If you have trouble getting started, write your draft as if you were speaking to a close friend.

7. Above all, remember that a first draft is supposed to be rough. Do not feel frustrated if your draft is nowhere near as strong as you want your final version to be.

Practice 1.8

When you completed number 3A for Practice 1.6, you generated and ordered ideas for a composition about things you would like to change about yourself. Using those ordered ideas as a guide, write a first draft for a paragraph. The first sentence of your draft should be one of these:

The change I'd most like to make in myself is _____.
(You fill in the blank.)

or

The changes I'd most like to make in myself are _____ and _____. (You fill in the blanks.)

Develop your paragraph by explaining why you want to make the change or changes.

Follow the suggestions described in "Tips for Writing the First Draft," and remember that the draft is supposed to be rough. (Save your draft because you will use it in a later activity.)

REWRITING: REVISING YOUR FIRST DRAFT

Once the first draft is complete, a writer makes changes to improve the writing and make it suitable for a reader. The process of making changes is *revision*. Revision is an important aspect of any writing project, and frequently the most time-consuming.

> When writers revise, they make changes in their first draft to improve it. This revision process is very important and often time-consuming.

Revision Concerns

When writers shape their drafts during revision, they try to see their work from a reader's viewpoint. As a result, they are concerned with several things, noted for you here:

1. adding detail where necessary to prove or explain a point
2. deleting detail that is not clearly related to the central idea
3. making sure detail is arranged in a logical order
4. making changes necessary for clarity
5. eliminating problems with word choice
6. adding transitions where needed
7. improving the flow of sentences, if necessary
8. making sure everything is suited to the audience and purpose

> During revision, a writer is concerned with detail and sentence effectiveness, not with grammar and usage.

You may have noticed from the list that during revision the writer does not attend to matters of correctness such as spelling, punctuation, subject-verb agreement, and so forth. Does this surprise you? If so, you are not alone, for many people think that revising means "fixing up" a piece of writing by correcting the mistakes. However, this is not the case. Mistakes in grammar, spelling, punctuation, and such are attended to *after* revising—during editing. During revision, the writer works to improve detail and sentence effectiveness.

□   TIPS FOR REVISING   □

1. Before revising, leave your work for a day. This time-out lets you rest and clear your head so you can view your draft objectively. You are more likely to notice problems in your draft if you leave it for awhile than if you do not get away from it.

2. Before revising, type your first draft. You will be amazed at the number of problems you notice when your work is no longer in your own handwriting.

3. At least once, read your draft out loud *very slowly.* Sometimes writers hear problems they fail to see. (Be careful to read what is actually on the page—not what you *meant* to write.)

4. Revise in stages so you do not attempt too much at once. For example, the first time through, check to be sure everything is related to the point you are making. The second time through, be sure you have enough detail. The third time through, study word choice and clarity (word choice is discussed on p. 264).

The fourth time through, check for flow and transitions. (Flow is discussed on p. 234.)

5. Many changes can be made directly on the draft. Do not be afraid to scratch out, draw arrows, and write in margins. Revision is often a "messy" process.

6. Periodically, leave your work for a few hours to refresh yourself. You will be more productive when you return.

Working Together: Reader Response

Successful writers know that they can get valuable advice if they share their drafts with others during revision. For this reason, successful writers are always handing a draft to someone and saying, "Read this and tell me what you think." When we let others read our work in progress, we can get a clearer sense of its strengths and weaknesses so we can make effective revisions.

The Reader Response Sheet on p. 31 can be copied and given to people who will evaluate your drafts. First, review the following suggestions.

If You Are the Writer Seeking Information

1. Give your readers a legible draft; recopy or retype if necessary.

2. If you want information not covered by the questions on the response sheet, write out additional questions.

3. Get the opinion of at least two readers. (Make copies of your draft so each reader is evaluating an unmarked writing.)

4. Do not automatically accept the responses. Instead, weigh them out carefully and make thoughtful decisions about which responses to accept and which to reject.

5. If your readers disagree or if you are unsure if a response is reliable, ask your instructor for advice.

6. After you study the completed response sheets, talk to your readers to learn why they responded as they did. Ask them any questions you have and make notes about their responses.

If You Are the Reader Evaluating a Draft

1. Read the entire draft before writing any comments.

2. Respond as specifically as possible. Rather than saying, "Paragraph 2 is unclear," say, "Paragraph 2 is unclear because I don't understand why you believe more men should become elementary education majors." In other words, explain *why* you react as you do.

3. Give specific suggestions for revision. Rather than saying, "Add more detail," say, "Add more detail about why you were so angry when you did not make the team so I understand what caused the emotion." In other words, suggest a revision strategy.

Practice 1.9

Reread the list of revision concerns on p. 28 and then proceed with this *Practice* exercise.

1. Reread the draft you wrote for *Practice* 1.8. As you do, place a check mark beside anything you wish to revise. (Remember, do not be concerned with grammar and usage at this point.)

   A. Did you notice problems with the draft that you did not notice when you wrote it? _____

   If you did, you have seen how leaving your work can help you become more objective.

   B. How many check marks did you place? _____

2. Take a few moments and type your draft; then reread it. On the typed copy place a square beside anything you would like to change. (Remember, do not be concerned with grammar and usage at this point.)

   A. Did you notice problems on the typed copy that you did not notice before? _____

   If you did, you have seen how typing a draft can help a writer.

   B. How many squares did you place?_____

3. Read your draft out loud very slowly. Each time you hear a problem that you did not notice previously, place an X by the problem.

   A. Did you hear any problems that you did not notice before?

   _____

   If you did, you have seen how reading a draft aloud can help a writer.

   B. Did reading your draft out loud give you a fresh slant on your work? _____

Continued on page 32

READER RESPONSE SHEET

Writer's Name _____

Reader's Name   _____

1. In a sentence, state the writer's main point.

2. What do you like best about the draft? Be specific.

3. Do all the details clearly relate to the main point? Place parentheses around unrelated details.

4. Underline any unclear points. What can be done to clarify?

5. Place brackets around any points that need more explanation. What detail should be added?

6. Are ideas arranged in an easy-to-follow order? If not, what changes should be made?

7. Place an ! next to any particularly effective word choice; circle any ineffective word choice.

8. Does the draft hold your interest? Explain why or why not.

4. Go over your draft one more time and answer the following questions:

    A. Do you need to eliminate points that are not related to the main point you want to make?_____

    B. Do you need to add details so your point is well established?_____

    C. Do you need to make changes to improve word choice?

    _____

    D. Do you need to make changes to increase clarity?_____

    E. Do you need to add transitions?_____

    F. Do you need to improve the flow of your writing because it sounds choppy? _____

(Save your draft because you will need it for a later activity.)

5. *Working Together:* Copy the Reader Response Sheet on p. 31 and trade drafts with a classmate. Each of you should fill out a response sheet and then answer the following question:

What did you learn about your draft as a result of getting reader response?

REWRITING: EDITING YOUR DRAFT

> Writers edit to find and correct errors in grammar and usage that detract from the effectiveness of writing.

While revising, you may work through several drafts before you are satisfied with the detail, organization, and wording. Once you are satisfied, you can turn your attention to grammar and usage. The process of finding and correcting errors in grammar and usage is *editing*. Careful editing is important because mistakes distract a reader. Also, a reader who encounters errors in spelling, sentence structure, punctuation, and such may doubt your ability.

Editing Concerns

During editing, a writer has a great deal to consider. The following is a list of many of these editing concerns, which are explained on the pages in parentheses.

    eliminating sentence fragments (p. 239)

    eliminating run-on sentences and comma splices (p. 254)

    using correct verb forms (p. 305)

avoiding inappropriate tense shifts (p. 342)

achieving agreement between subjects and verbs (p. 330)

achieving agreement between pronouns and antecedents (p. 347)

eliminating faulty pronoun reference (p. 361)

avoiding person shifts (p. 372)

eliminating misplaced and dangling modifiers (p. 387 and p. 388)

using comparative and superlative forms correctly (p. 383)

capitalizing correctly (p. 392)

punctuating correctly (p. 398)

spelling correctly (p. 296)

□ TIPS FOR EDITING □

1. Look for the mistakes you are likely to make. For example, if you have a history of writing sentence fragments, look especially for fragments. To help you become aware of the kinds of errors you make, Appendix I contains a Personal Editing Profile. Now is a good time to look at this editing tool.

2. Edit in stages. The first time through, look for one kind of mistake you are in the habit of making. The second time through, look for another kind of mistake you are in the habit of making. Continue this way and then edit one more time for any other errors that may be in your draft.

3. Read your draft out loud to hear errors that you overlooked visually. (Be careful to read *exactly* what is on the page.)

4. Edit very slowly, using a pen to point to each word and punctuation mark as you go. Make sure you read what the pen is pointing to. If you are reading ahead of your pen, you are going too fast to do an effective job. Also, be sure to read *exactly* what is on the page—not what you meant to write.

5. Place a ruler under the line you are editing. This will help you focus and prevent you from building up too much speed. EDITING CANNOT BE DONE QUICKLY.

6. When in doubt, ask your instructor or another reliable person, or check chapters of this book. Do not guess about a grammar rule.

7. Trust your instincts. If something inside tells you there is a problem, the chances are good there really *is* a problem. Even if you cannot name the problem, better pause and deal with the section of your writing that seems troublesome.

8. Learn the grammar and usage rules. Also, pay careful attention to the errors your instructor notes on your papers. Be sure you understand the nature of each error and how to correct it. If you do not, ask your teacher for help.

9. Spend time away from your work before you begin to edit to clear your head and improve your chances of finding mistakes.

Practice 1.10

1. Review the list of editing concerns on pp. 32–33. Which of these concerns have you had trouble with in the past? _____

   _____

2. What pages of this text cover the concerns you noted in your answer to number 1? _____

   _____

3. Look again at the list of editing concerns. Is there anything in that list that you have never heard of before? Anything that you do not know the meaning of? If so, what?_____

   _____

4. What pages of this text cover the concerns you noted in your answer to number 3? _____

   _____

5. When you completed *Practice* 1.9, exercise number 2, you typed a copy of a draft. Using a pen to point to each word and punctuation mark in that typed draft, edit very slowly, looking for errors in grammar and usage. Make sure you read what you actually wrote—not what you meant to write. Make corrections directly on the page, referring to later chapters as necessary. How many errors did you find? _____

   _____

6. Check the draft one separate time for each kind of mistake you have a habit of making. Place a ruler under each line as you go. If you are unsure how to correct any errors that you find, consult later chapters. How many errors did you find?_____

   _____

7. What pages of later chapters do you think you should study first? _____ What pages do you think you should study second? _____

REWRITING: PROOFREADING YOUR FINAL COPY

After careful editing, copy or type your writing into its final form, the one you will give your reader. You will then be tempted to consider your work complete and go off to reward yourself with a movie or chocolate shake. DON'T. Your writing is not complete until you have run a final check for errors you may have made while copying or typing. This final check is *proofreading*. Proofreading is important because all of us make copying or typing errors, particularly at the end when we may speed up to cross the finish line a little sooner.

> Writers proofread their final copy to check for careless errors made while recopying or typing.

☐   TIPS FOR PROOFREADING   ☐

1. Before proofreading, leave your work for a few hours to refresh yourself and increase your chances of finding errors.

2. Proofread very slowly. Go too quickly and you will overlook errors because you will see what you wanted to write instead of what you actually did write. Point to each word and linger over it for a second to be sure you are not letting mistakes get by you.

3. Place a ruler under each line to keep the pace slow.

4. Ink in minor corrections neatly if your instructor permits. A page with many corrections should be retyped or recopied in the interest of neatness. (Neatness *does* impress a reader.)

WRITING WITH A COMPUTER OR WORD PROCESSOR

If you have not yet tried writing with a computer or word processor, take the plunge. Most writers find that composing is much more efficient with one of these machines. If you do not own your own computer or word processor, your school is likely to have a computer lab open to students.

Whether you already write with a computer or word processor or are new to the process, consider the following tips.

1. Take the time to learn your word processing program thoroughly. If you must learn your school's program, do not hesitate to ask a lab assistant for help. Write some practice pieces so that when you have an assignment, you are comfortable with

all the commands and can concentrate on your writing without worrying about how the machine functions.

2. Work through the entire writing process at the computer, if you like. Whatever planning, writing, and rewriting techniques you customarily do on paper, you can also do at the machine.

3. To generate ideas, try freewriting with the screen dark. You are likely to make more keystroke errors, but you will be less likely to censor yourself, so ideas may flow more readily.

4. When you outline and revise, use your block and move functions to try rearranging things.

5. Revise and edit both on the screen and on print copy. Looking at a screen gives you a different perspective from looking at print copy. If you consider both, you will do a thorough job.

6. When you edit, make full use of spelling and grammar checks that accompany your program, but remember, these are not foolproof, and they are not complete. Thus, you must still edit your work carefully on your own.

7. Do not be fooled by appearance—revise and edit carefully. Because the machine copy looks so good, you may think a draft is in better shape than it really is.

8. Back up your work frequently in case a power failure or other "catastrophic" event causes your work to disappear. In addition, at the end of every session, print out everything you have written for extra insurance.

CHAPTER
2

An Essay from Start to Finish

In Chapter 1 you learned that writers work through stages of planning, writing, and rewriting. In this chapter you will again consider the writing process, only this time you will do so by observing the various stages of a student writer's work in progress. You will follow the work of Madelaine, who wrote about marrying at an early age.

As you see how Madelaine moved from idea generation through proofreading, you will notice the following:

1. A writer often works through several drafts.
2. Effective writing has a central point.
3. Effective writing does not move away from its central point.
4. Effective writing has details in a logical order.
5. Effective writing is free of grammar and usage errors.

PLANNING: GENERATING IDEAS

In Chapter 1 you learned that writers cannot sit around waiting for inspiration. Instead, they must go after the ideas they need by using one or more idea-generation techniques.

Here is the brainstorming Madelaine did when she worked to generate ideas for her essay about getting married right out of high school. Notice that Madelaine did not ask herself very many questions. Also, she did not answer the questions in very much detail. Some people, like Madelaine, do fine with sketchy idea-generation material; if necessary, they add detail when they draft and revise. Most people, however, do better if they generate ideas in more detail. Which kind of writer are you? Try both ways and see which works better for you.

Madelaine's Brainstorming

What happened?

I got married right after high school graduation.

Why did it happen?

I was pregnant. I felt I had to get married.

What was it like?

At first very exciting because I felt mature and more sophisticated than my friends. I was glad to be away from my parents.

Then what happened?

My husband joined the service. I was alone most of the time and missed out on what my friends were doing. It was lonely and scary.

What was the effect?

The marraige lasted seven years and then we divorced. I felt cheated out of some very good years. Now I must raise my son alone. It's hard.

What can be learned?

Teen marraiges are difficult. They are no solution to an unplanned pregnancy.

I was stupid to get married. If you're pregnant, think about all your choices.

PLANNING: ORDERING IDEAS

When Madelaine studied the ideas she generated, she realized that she would be telling the story of her own teenage marriage. Because she would be telling a story, her ideas would be arranged in a chronological order for the most part.

WRITING THE FIRST DRAFT

In Chapter 1 you learned that a first draft is usually rough because it is only a first effort. The following is Madelaine's first, rough draft. (The sentences are numbered as a study aid.) If you compare it to her brainstorming, you will notice that to some extent the author departed from the ideas in the brainstorming. This is not unusual. Writers often find their first drafts going into unexpected areas.

Madelaine's First Draft

¹Teen marraiges are trouble. ²I know cause I've been there, I got married right after high school graduation when I was seventeen. ³It was the logical thing to do since I was "with child" as my grandma would say.

⁴At first it was all exciting cause it was all new to me and I felt mature and more sophisticated than my friends. ⁵But then the trouble part started, my husband joined the service for steady work. ⁶That left me alone to have our child and too be a wife too a man who was so far away. ⁷Than my son was born and things got really bad.

⁸For awhile things went pretty smooth. ⁹Until I began to miss out on all the things kids my age were doing. ¹⁰That presented a problem for me that I couldnt cope with. ¹¹Our marraige lasted for seven years and it ended in divorce.

¹²It was very hard for me to cope with getting a divorce.

[13]I believed in our wedding vows. [14]I wanted so much too make our marraige work. [15]However, Gil had other plans. [16]I finally decided to let him have his freedom, this brought about a change in my life. [17]I had to learn to live my life without Gil. [16]Until one day I realized that I have a whole lot to live for. [19]Than I began to go on to better things, like going back to school.

1. Madelaine's central point is that her own experience proves that teen marriages do not work. However, some of her detail moves away from this idea. Which sentences create a problem because they are not related to the matter at hand?

   _____

   _____

2. At some points, more detail is needed to clarify and prove a point. Which sentences should be followed by more detail?

   _____

   _____

3. Where do you notice a problem with the time sequence?

   _____

   _____

Reader Response to Madelaine's First Draft   Madelaine's writing instructor read Madelaine's first draft and gave her the following written response to consider as she revised. As you read it, consider whether you reacted to the draft the way Madelaine's instructor did.

Madelaine,

I like your opening; it's strong and direct. But I am puzzled about why it was "logical" to get married. Lots of pregnant, unmarried teens make other arrangements. Can you explain?

Also, you say things got bad when your son was

born and you missed out on things. How about some specific examples to explain this? I'm having trouble seeing how your last eight sentences are related to your central idea. Remember, the problem of teen marriage is your central point—not divorce. If you do not want to change your focus, find a way to make this material more related or replace it with something else. You use chronological order well, but the time sequence gets confused when you move from paragraph 2 to paragraph 3. I'm looking forward to your revision. Your draft shows promise. There's a power in it that comes from your honesty and willingness to share a significant experience.

1. Which of the instructor's reactions to Madelaine's draft are the same as your reactions?

   _____

   _____

   _____

2. Do you disagree with any of the instructor's reactions? Which ones? Why do you disagree?

   _____

   _____

   _____

3. Do you have any reactions to Madelaine's draft that are not noted in the instructor's comments? What are they?

   _____

   _____

   _____

REWRITING: REVISING THE FIRST DRAFT

Writers take the raw material of a first draft and gradually shape it into a finished product. In the following pages, you will observe the changes Madelaine made as she went from first to third draft.

¹Teen marraiges are trouble. ²I know cause I've been there, I got married right after high school graduation when I was seventeen. ³It was the logical thing to do since I was "with child" as my grandma would say. ∧ *In the small town I lived in, pregnant girls had only one choice, get married.*

(A) Explains why the decision to marry was logical

(B) Repetitious

⁴At first it was all exciting cause it was all new to me and I felt mature and more sophisticated than my friends.

(C) Unnecessary

⁵But then the trouble part started, my husband joined the service for steady work. ⁶That left me alone to have our child and too be a wife too a man who was so far away. ⁷Than my son was born and things got really bad.

(D) Solves problem with time sequence

⁸~~For awhile things went pretty smooth.~~ ⁹Until I began to miss out on all the things kids my age were doing. ¹⁰That presented a problem for me that I couldnt cope with. ∧ *Housework and laundry weren't fun anymore, they were hard work. My friends were partying and going to the beach.* ¹¹Our marraige lasted for seven years and it ended in divorce.

(E) Reference to omitted sentence 8

(F) Added detail to help reader understand

¹²It was very hard for me to cope with getting a divorce.

make last eight sentences relevant.

¹³I believed in our wedding vows. ¹⁴I wanted so much to make our marraige work. ¹⁵However, Gil had other plans.

(G) Writer needs more time to think of how to handle something; the note will remind her of what she wants to do.

¹⁶I finally decided to let him have his freedom, this brought

about a change in my life. ¹⁷I had to learn to live my life

(H) *Can I include this?*

without Gil. ¹⁸Until one day I realized that I have a whole

lot to live for. ¹⁹Than I began to go on to better things, like

going back to school.

> (H) Writer is unsure, so she asks herself a question. She will think about this and ask her instructor.

Notice that changes were made directly on the first draft. Revising on the draft works very well, unless you must make extensive additions. In this case, you may want to rewrite on separate pages. Also notice that Madelaine's draft has become messy as a result of revising. This is normal, so expect your revisions to be equally messy or even more so. Draw arrows, write in margins, cross out, write above lines—do whatever feels comfortable.

To understand better the kinds of changes made during revision, answer the following questions.

1. Give the letters of the revisions Madelaine made to add necessary detail.

   _____

2. Why did Madelaine make revision D (eliminating sentence 8)?

   _____

   _____

3. Why did Madelaine make revision B?

   _____

   _____

4. Why did Madelaine make revision C?

   _____

   _____

5. Did Madelaine make any ineffective revisions? Explain.

   _____

   _____

   _____

Madelaine's Second Draft   Using the revisions noted on her first draft, Madelaine wrote a second draft. This draft is given for you here, along with an explanation of the changes. Notice that Madelaine did more than incorporate the changes noted on her first draft. She also made other changes. When you write a second draft, you too may make changes that you had not thought of before.

② *Cause* becomes the more formal *because*.

⑦ Sentence added to explain that Gil joined service for more steady work.

⑪ *Tiring* added to show difficulty of her life.

⑬ Added to show the problem she experienced; sentence 10 of first draft can now be omitted.

⑮–⑲ Helps solve relevance problem in first draft; writer has used idea that she has a lot to live for. She questioned whether this idea would be suitable on first draft.

¹Teen marraiges are trouble. ²I know because I've been there, I got married right after high school graduation when I was seventeen. ³It was the logical thing to do since I was "with child" as my grandmother would say. ⁴In the small town I lived in, pregnant girls had only one choice, get married.

⁵At first it was exciting because it was all new to me and I felt more mature and sophisticated than my friends. ⁶But then the trouble started, my husband joined the service for steady work. ⁷(Before that we had been living off money Gil got painting houses and doing yard work.) ⁸That left me alone to have our child and too be a wife too a man who was so far away. ⁹Than my son was born and things got really bad.

¹⁰I began to miss out on all the things kids my age were doing. ¹¹Housework and laundry weren't fun anymore, they were hard, tiring work. ¹²My friends were partying and bar-hopping and going to the beach. ¹³Which made me jealous. ¹⁴Our marraige lasted for seven years and it ended in divorce. ¹⁵For a long time I felt cheated out of some good years and good times. ¹⁶Which gave me a bad attitude.

¹⁷One day, though, I looked at my son and realized I had to get it together to give him a decent life. ¹⁸That's when I enrolled in college to become a medical assistant. ¹⁹Even though I have a lot to live for now, I believe that marraige is not the answer to teen pregnancies.

To understand what can happen when a writer develops a second draft, answer the questions that follow.

1. What new changes did Madelaine make in the second draft?

   _____

   _____

   _____

2. What problem with word choice did Madelaine solve when she wrote her second draft?

   _____

3. Do you think the addition of sentence 7 was a good idea? Explain.

   _____

   _____

4. Do you think the addition of word group 13 was a good idea? Explain.

   _____

   _____

5. Did Madelaine solve the relevance problem that existed in her first draft (the last eight sentences did not seem related to her central point)? Explain.

   _____

   _____

6. Did Madelaine improve the ending of her essay? Explain.

   _____

   _____

Reader Response to Madelaine's Second Draft   Madelaine's writing instructor read her second draft and gave her the following written response. Consider whether you had any of the same reactions to Madelaine's draft.

Your second draft is much improved, Madelaine. Your detail is more satisfying because it is more specific and more related to your central idea. When you revise again, consider explaining your "bad attitude." That phrase is vague and unclear, so I'm not sure what you mean. In what way was your attitude bad? Also, the first part of your last sentence detracts from your central idea—it suggests that teen marriages aren't such a problem after all, since you got your life back on track. When you edit watch out for comma splices and sentence fragments. Also check spellings and look up the difference between to and too.

REWRITING: EDITING THE DRAFT

On the basis of her instructor's reactions to her second draft, Madelaine did some additional revising. After revising, she edited her work to eliminate errors in grammar and usage, the ones her instructor referred to in her response to the second draft. The result was Madelaine's third draft, which appears for you here.

Madelaine's Third Draft

2 - 3 Comma splice
corrected. (See
p. 255)

[1]Teen marraiges are trouble. [2]I know because I've been there. [3]I got married right after high school graduation when I was seventeen. [4]It was the logical thing to do since I was "with child" as my grandmother would say. [5]In the small town I lived in, pregnant girls had only one choice, get married.

[6]At first it was exciting because it was all new to me and I felt more mature and sophisticated than my friends. [7]But then the trouble started. [8]My husband joined the service for steady work. [9](Before that we had been living off money Gil

7 - 8 Comma splice
corrected. (See
p. 255)

got painting houses and doing yard work.) ¹⁰That left me alone to have our child and to be a wife to a man who was so far away. ¹¹Then my son was born and things got really bad.

⑪ *Than* changed to *then*. (See p. 282)

¹²I began to miss out on all the things kids my age were doing. ¹³Housework and laundry weren't fun anymore. ¹⁴They were hard, tiring work. ¹⁵My friends were partying and bar-hopping and going to the beach, which made me jealous. ¹⁶Our marriage lasted for seven years and it ended in divorce. ¹⁷For a long time I felt cheated out of some good years and good times. ¹⁸This feeling gave me a bad attitude. ¹⁹I became lazy because I felt sorry for myself. ²⁰I just sat around all day watching TV and eating. ²¹Some days I never even got out of my nightgown.

⑬–⑭ Comma splice corrected. (See p. 255)

⑮ Fragment eliminated (See p. 239)

⑱ Fragment eliminated (See p. 239)

⑲ ⑳ ㉑ Added to clarify nature of her bad attitude.

²²One day, though, I looked at my son and realized I had to get it together to give him a decent life. ²³That's when I enrolled in college to become a medical assistant. ²⁴Because of all the trouble I went through, I believe that marraige is not the answer to teen pregnancies.

㉔ Sentence is better related to central point. Writer unable to include idea that she has a lot to live for (detail she was unsure of in earlier draft).

REWRITING: PROOFREADING THE FINAL COPY

After editing, Madelaine typed her work for submission to her reader. This final version appears here for you to study. Notice that Madelaine neatly inked in corrections of typographical errors she found when she proofread her work. Also, she corrected the spelling of *marriage*. Finally, notice the title on the final version.

Teen Marriage Is Not the Answer

Teen marriages are trouble. I know because I've been there. I got married right after high school graduation when I was seventeen. It ᵂas the logical thing to do since I was "with child" as my grandmother would say. In the small town I lived in, pregnant girls had only one choice, get married.

At first it was exciting because it was all new to me and I felt more mature and sophisticated than my friends. But then the trouble started. My husband joined the service for steady work. (Before that we had been living off money Gil got p~~ø~~inting^a houses and doing yard work.) That left me alone to have our child and to be a w~~x~~feⁱ to a man who was so far away. Then my son was born and things got really bad.

I began to miss out on all the things kids my age were doing. Housework and laundry weren't fun anymore. ~~t~~hey^T were hard, tiring work. My friends were partying and bar-hopping and going to the beach, which made me jealous. Our marriage lasted for seven years and it ended in divorce. For a long time I felt cheated out of some good years and good times. This feeling gave me a bad attitude. I became lazy because I felt sorry for myself. I just sat around all day watching TV and eating. Some days I never even got out of my nightgown.

One day, though, I looked at my son and realized I had to get it together to give him a decent life. That's when I enrolled in college to become a medical assistant. Because of all the trouble I went through, I believe that marriage is not the answer to teen pregnancies.

Writing Assignment

You now understand that writers do not sit around waiting for inspiration. Instead, they work for their ideas using idea-generation techniques. Also, you know that writers expect to write and rewrite drafts until the composition is ready for a reader.

In addition to understanding how writers operate, you have also learned about some of the qualities of effective writing:

1. Effective writing has a central point.
2. Effective writing does not move away from its central point.
3. Effective writing has enough detail.

4. Effective writing has details in a logical order.

5. Effective writing is free of grammar and usage errors.

Clearly, you have already learned a great deal. Now it is time to put your knowledge into practice—it is time to write a paragraph of your own. To develop a central point for this paragraph, fill in the blanks in this sentence:

The best way to _____ is _____.

You may fill in the blanks any way you wish. Here are some examples:

A. The best way to make friends on campus is to join the ski club.

B. The best way to shop is through a catalog.

C. The best way to impress a date is to plan the perfect picnic.

D. The best way to stay fit is to take up bicycling.

If you are unsure how to proceed, some or all of the following procedures may help.

Planning

1. Freewrite for 10–15 minutes and then list three reasons to support your view. (For other ways to generate ideas, see p. 2.)

2. Review your idea-generation material and make a list of the ideas you want to include.

3. Study your list of ideas. Do they lend themselves to a chronological (time) order, spatial (across space) order, or emphatic (from least important point to most important point) arrangement? Number the ideas in your list to correspond to the order you would like to have in your paragraph. Now you have a scratch outline.

Writing

4. Using your scratch outline as a guide, write through your first draft in one sitting. Allow this draft to be rough. If you get stuck, skip the troublesome part and push on. To ensure a clear statement of your central point, begin your draft with the sentence with the filled-in blanks.

5. Leave your work and take a break for at least several hours (a day would be even better). Getting away will clear your head so you can do a better job of revising.

Rewriting

6. Check each sentence in your draft against the first sentence. Be sure each sentence is directly related to your central point. If the relevance of a sentence is unclear, strike it or find a way to establish the relationship to your central idea.

7. Give your draft to someone whose judgment you trust. Ask that person to mark where more detail is needed. However, you have the final say. Do not add detail unless you decide the reader is correct in calling for more.

8. Leave your work for at least a few hours to clear your head. Then type your draft and reread it to see if problems you overlooked in your own handwriting are apparent in typed copy. Check especially to make sure the meaning of all your sentences is clear. Note: Reader response can be very helpful during revision. Refer now to p. 29.

9. What kinds of grammar and usage mistakes do you make? Edit one separate time for each kind of error. Then leave your work for at least a few hours. When you return, read your draft aloud to listen for errors. Place a ruler under each line as you go so you do not build speed.

10. Check spellings of any words that look misspelled.

11. Copy or type your paragraph into its final form. If you are tired after this, take a break before you proofread.

12. Proofread by pointing to each word and reading what you are pointing to. To ensure that you read exactly what is on the page, force yourself to linger over each word momentarily.

TWO

THE PARAGRAPH

CHAPTER
3

Paragraph Basics

A *paragraph* is a group of sentences developing one central point. Most paragraphs have two parts: the sentence that presents the central point of the paragraph (the *topic sentence*) and the sentences that develop a central point (the *supporting details*). In addition, some paragraphs will have a *closing,* a sentence or two to tie things off neatly.

This chapter will help you learn how to write an effective paragraph. You will learn about

1. the structure of a paragraph
2. the need for adequate detail
3. the need for specific detail
4. the need for relevant detail

> The two main parts of a paragraph are the topic sentence and the supporting details. A closing may also appear.

A SAMPLE PARAGRAPH

As you read the following sample paragraph, decide which sentence presents the central point. That is the topic sentence. Also decide which sentences develop the central point. Those sentences are the supporting details.

A Lounge for Women Over Thirty

The topic sentence presents the central point of the paragraph, and the supporting details develop the central point.

Because so many women in their thirties, forties, and fifties are returning to school, our university should set up a special lounge area for these students. Women in this age group are often uncomfortable in the student union because they are surrounded by students no older than twenty-two or so. They aren't interested in the upcoming rock concert or fraternity party, so often they find they have little to discuss with their younger counterparts. A special lounge would provide a meeting place for the older women. It would be someplace they could go knowing they would find others who share the same interests and concerns. Also this lounge would be a place these students could come together to help each other with their unique problems, the ones they face as a result of returning to school after a long absence. It would also provide a place for group study. Also, because many returning to school after an absence need some brushing up, the lounge could also be a place for tutoring activities. If the university provided this facility, this special, important group of students would feel more comfortable as they pursued their degrees.

1. Which sentence presents the central point of the paragraph? That is, which sentence is the topic sentence?

   _____

2. Most of the sentences after the topic sentence are the

   _____

3. The last sentence is the _____

If you identified the first sentence of the paragraph as the topic sentence, you were correct. This sentence provides the central point of the paragraph (the university should provide a lounge for female students over thirty). The remaining sentences (except the last) are the supporting details (they develop the central point). The last sentence is the closing (it ties the paragraph off neatly).

Practice 3.1

Each group of sentences could be part of a paragraph. One sentence could be a topic sentence, and the others could be part of the supporting details. Write *TS* if the sentence could be a topic sentence, and *SD* if it could be part of the supporting details. Number 1 is done as an example.

1. *SD* He humiliates players by yelling at them in front of the fans.

   TS My nephew's baseball coach should be fired.

   SD The coach allows pitchers to give up too many runs before he pulls them out.

2. ____ Delays in arrivals and departures are at an all-time high.

   ____ Baggage is routinely lost.

   ____ Deregulation of the airlines has created several problems.

   ____ Overbooking of flights is commonplace.

3. ____ Giant toads may weigh three pounds and grow to twelve inches.

   ____ Giant toads have glands that secrete a poison strong enough to kill a dog.

   ____ The number of giant toads in Florida is increasing.

   ____ If you go to Florida, watch out for the giant toads.

4. ____ People can learn to manage their stress.

   ____ Regular exercise helps control stress.

   ____ Focusing on successes rather than defeats keeps stress in check.

   ____ Talking things out with a sympathetic friend relieves stressful feelings.

5. ____ The eleven-month school year saves school districts money.

____ The eleven-month school year will be commonplace in twenty years.

____ The eleven-month school year keeps students from forgetting important concepts over a long summer recess.

____ The eleven-month school year makes efficient use of staff and facilities.

6. ____ Saline is injected into the blood vessel.

____ The procedure is quick, taking only a few moments.

____ Sclerotherapy eliminates spider veins in the legs.

____ Sclerotherapy involves only minor discomfort in most cases.

THE TOPIC SENTENCE

> A topic sentence includes the writer's topic and the writer's view of the topic.

The topic sentence presents the central point of the paragraph. An effective topic sentence usually has two parts: a part that presents the writer's topic and a part that presents the writer's view of that topic. Here are some examples (the topic is underlined once, and the writer's view is underlined twice):

A. Property taxes are an ineffective way to finance public education.

B. Eleven-month school years are becoming increasingly popular.

C. I greatly admire my Aunt Hattie.

D. Changing my major from engineering to computer science proved to be a smart move.

E. Warrick Inn's best feature is its country charm.

Practice 3.2

For each topic sentence, underline once the words that present the topic and underline twice the words that present the view of the topic. Number 1 is done as an example.

1. If you plan to purchase a new car, proceed cautiously.

2. Considering its size and location, the house is overpriced.

3. The aging shopping mall is exceptionally dreary.

4. The new state law requiring high school proficiency testing was not carefully thought out.

5. A stress management course should be taught on all college campuses.

6. If you ask me, nurses are the most underappreciated healthcare providers.

7. The auto workers' strike will have serious consequences throughout the economy.

8. Psychologists are coming to understand that birth order significantly affects personality.

9. Carlos Morales is the most qualified candidate for student government.

10. After the party, the living room looked like a war zone.

11. The effects of depression can be devastating.

Writing Effective Topic Sentences

In addition to including both a topic and your view of that topic, there are other points to remember about topic sentences.

1. **Avoid Statements of Fact.** A topic sentence that states a fact leaves you with nothing to say in the supporting detail. Consider these factual statements:

   I wake up every morning at 6:30.

   Education is very important.

   Soap operas are on in the daytime.

   These are narrow statements of fact that offer no room for the writer's views. What can you say after noting that you wake up at 6:30? Who doesn't agree that education is important? How can you develop a whole paragraph about the fact that daytime TV includes soap operas?

   Statements of fact can be rewritten to be more effective by including the writer's view:

   I highly recommend waking up early each day.

   Because we need more good teachers, we should pay teachers more.

   The number of daytime soap operas should be reduced.

2. **Avoid Very Broad Statements.** They are impossible to treat adequately in a single paragraph. Consider these statements:

   The Vietnam War affected our country profoundly.

   Our educational system must be revamped.

These topic sentences could not be managed in one paragraph. Broader statements like these require treatment in essays made up of several paragraphs.

3. **Be Careful of Vague Words.** Words such as *nice, interesting, great, good,* and *bad,* may not give your reader a clear enough sense of your view.

vague: Being a camp counselor last summer was great.

clearer: Being a camp counselor last summer helped me decide to become a teacher.

vague: Playing in piano recitals was awful.

clearer: Playing in piano recitals made me feel self-conscious.

4. **Avoid Formal Announcements.** Topic sentences like these are generally considered poor style:

This paragraph will discuss how to interview for a job.

I plan to explain why this university should offer a major in hotel management.

The following sentences will describe my first day of college.

Topic sentences like these are far more appealing:

Two points should be remembered when you interview for a job.

A major in hotel management is needed at this university.

My first day of college was hectic.

5. **Avoid Using a Pronoun to Refer to Something in the Title.** If your title is "The Need for Computer Education," avoid a topic sentence like this: "It is needed for a variety of reasons." Instead, write this: "Computer education is needed for a variety of reasons."

6. **Place the Topic Sentence First.** The topic sentence can actually appear anywhere in the paragraph. However, placing it first is convenient. You can try other placements as you become more experienced.

> Avoid topic sentences that are statements of fact or too broad. Also, avoid the formal announcement, vague language, and reference to the title.

Practice 3.3

If the topic sentence is acceptable, write *OK* on the blank; if it is too broad, write *broad* on the blank; if it is a statement of fact, write *fact* on the blank; if the language is vague, write *vague* on the blank;

if the sentence is a formal announcement, write *announcement* on the blank.

1. _____ The time I spent working as a hospital orderly was great.

2. _____ Saturday night I had a blind date.

3. _____ Living in a dorm is a miserable existence.

4. _____ The most pressing problems facing us today are world hunger and unemployment.

5. _____ I will explain here why I believe grading on the curve is unfair.

6. _____ Children need lots of attention.

7. _____ Professor Wiley's group dynamics class is interesting.

8. _____ My paragraph will describe the campus commons at sundown.

9. _____ Two tricks will help a dieter maintain willpower.

10. _____ The Cameron triplets are very different: Jud is an optimist; Jake is a pessimist; and Judy is apathetic.

Practice 3.4: Working Together

With the members of your group, pick three of the unacceptable topic sentences from *Practice 3.3* and rewrite them to make them acceptable. Use a separate sheet.

Practice 3.5

If the statement includes both the topic and view, write *OK* on the blank; if the topic is missing, write *topic;* if the view is missing, write *view.*

1. _____ It was so unexpected I wasn't sure what to do.

2. _____ In my senior year, a championship basketball game taught me the true meaning of sportsmanship.

3. _____ Time-sharing has benefits for an employer.

4. _____ I began my student teaching in a seventh grade study hall.

5. _____ It was very depressing to be there.

6. _____ The governor's tax bill will be voted on in November.

Practice 3.6: Working Together

With the members of your group, select two of the unacceptable topic sentences in *Practice 3.5* and rewrite them on a separate sheet to make them acceptable.

Practice 3.7

For each subject given, write an acceptable topic sentence. Remember to include both a topic and view. Also, avoid writing topic sentences that are too broad, that are statements of fact, or that have vague language or formal announcements. The first one is done as an example. (If you are stuck for ideas, try listing, brainstorming, clustering, or freewriting.)

1. pets *My calico cat, Cali, has an annoying habit.* _____

2. your favorite holiday _____

3. a childhood memory _____

4. a favorite teacher _____

5. your first day of college _____

6. television _____

Practice 3.8

For each list of supporting details, write a topic sentence that would be acceptable. Avoid broad statements, statements of fact, vague language, and formal announcements.

1. topic sentence _____

_____

    A. Check local fashions and be sure your child dresses to conform to them.

    B. Ask the new teacher to assign a friendly classmate as a lunch or gym partner.

C. Instruct your child to strike up conversations and not just wait for others to introduce themselves first.

D. After a week, have your child invite one of his or her new classmates over after school.

2. topic sentence_____

_____

   A. I wanted to study criminal justice.

   B. I was offered a scholarship to play football.

   C. I wanted to move away from home.

   D. My girlfriend was attending college.

3. topic sentence_____

_____

   A. walls covered with grease stains

   B. pieces of cereal, cat food, and dried food all over the floor

   C. dried jelly and other, unidentified matter caked on the refrigerator door

   D. the smell of rotting garbage

4. topic sentence_____

_____

   A. Running improves cardiovascular fitness.

   B. It helps manage stress.

   C. It helps maintain desired weight.

   D. It can be competitive or noncompetitive, whichever the runner prefers.

5. topic sentence_____

_____

   A. Professor Rios involves students in class discussions.

   B. She gives extra help to those who need it.

   C. She never criticizes anyone who makes an error.

   D. She gives fascinating lectures.

THE SUPPORTING DETAILS

The *supporting details* develop the topic sentence. They are all the ideas (facts and opinions) you present to show why you have your

> Supporting details develop the topic sentence by explaining why the writer has the particular view of the topic. Supporting details should be adequate, specific, and relevant.

particular view of your topic. Turn back to p. 52 and reread "A Lounge for Women Over Thirty." Notice that the first sentence presents the writer's topic and view: the university should set up a lounge for female students over thirty. The sentences after the topic sentence are the supporting details, which explain why the university should set up the lounge.

To be effective, supporting details should be *adequate, specific,* and *relevant.* These characteristics are discussed next.

Adequate Detail

To be effective, a paragraph must have enough supporting details so that the reader understands why the writer has his or her view of the topic. Thus, *adequate detail* means enough supporting details (facts and opinions) to develop the writer's topic sentence.

Read and think about this paragraph:

My high school biology teacher changed my life. He saw I was heading for trouble and straightened me out. He also helped me improve my grades so I could play basketball. In fact, he even helped me get into college. I will always be grateful to Mr. Friedman for being there when I needed help the most.

The paragraph begins with a fine topic sentence that includes both topic and view: the topic is the biology teacher, and the view is that he changed the writer's life. However, you probably came away from the paragraph feeling unsatisfied because the supporting details are not adequate. Too few points are made to satisfy the reader that the topic sentence idea is true. The reader still needs information. How did the teacher straighten the writer out? How did he help the writer improve his grades? How did he help the writer get into college?

Now read and think about this revised paragraph:

> Supporting details must be adequate; the writer must supply enough information so that the reader understands why the writer has his or her view.

My high school biology teacher changed my life. He saw I was heading for trouble and called me in after school one day. He explained that he cared what happened to me and wanted to help if he could. When I told him how depressed I was, he arranged counseling at the local mental health center. He also helped me improve my grades by showing me how to take notes and study efficiently. As a result, I regained my basketball eligibility. In fact, Mr. Friedman even helped me get into college by talking to admissions counselors on my behalf. I will always be grateful to Mr. Friedman for being there when I needed help the most.

You probably feel more satisfied after reading the revised version because necessary details have been added. The supporting details in the paragraph are now *adequate*.

Practice 3.9

One of the following paragraphs has adequate detail. The others lack necessary information, so the reader feels unsatisfied at the end. If the paragraph has adequate detail, write *OK* on the blank; if it does not have adequate detail, write *X* on the blank.

Darlene, the Practical Joker

_____ 1. My sister, Darlene, is a practical joker. She drives everybody crazy with her jokes. Once she played this amazing joke on my father. She spent months planning it so everything would work just right. Even though the joke only lasted a moment, Darlene felt it was worth the effort. However, I'm not sure Dad saw it that way. Another time Darlene almost lost her best friend because of a joke she played on her. The problem was that she embarrassed her friend in the school cafeteria. Last April Fool's Day Darlene hired a male stripper to crash my grandmother's seventy-fifth birthday party. What a scene that was! I sure wish someone would play a practical joke on Darlene so she could get a taste of her own medicine.

What a Bargain!

_____ 2. When I bought the '75 Mustang for $1800 I was sure I got a bargain until everything started going wrong. First, I had to pay a lot of money to have the engine repaired, and then I noticed how much body work was needed. Last week the suspension system was diagnosed as terminal, so there's more money I'll have to fork over for this four-wheeled "bargain." I'll never buy another used car again.

Adjusting to College

_____ 3. A new college student can expect to make several adjustments before the freshman year is over.

First, the student must learn to cope with more freedom. Mom and Dad are not around to set a curfew or limit activities. This means the student has only a conscience to guide behavior. With this freedom comes more responsibility to adjust to. Mom and Dad may not be limiting activities, but they are also not around to wash clothes, remind the student of appointments, and force the student to study. This means the student better learn to take care of things or things just won't be taken care of. Finally, the student must learn to adjust to pressure. Exams, crazy roommates, registration hassles, and book lines are just some of what can cause tension. The student must learn to take the pressure of college life or forget that degree. Fortunately, most students make the necessary adjustments before the sophomore year begins.

Practice 3.10: Working Together

Two of the paragraphs in *Practice 3.9* lack adequate detail. With some classmates, list details that could be added to help make the supporting details adequate.

A. Darlene, the Practical Joker

_____

_____

_____

_____

_____

B. What a Bargain!

_____

_____

_____

_____

_____

Specific Detail

Adequate supporting details are specific. Specific detail helps a reader form a clear, detailed understanding of the writer's meaning. The opposite of specific detail is general statement, which gives the reader only a vague sense of the writer's meaning. The following examples show the difference between general and specific.

general statement: The car went down the street.

specific detail: The 1962 Impala sedan rattled down Oak Street, dragging its tail pipe.

You probably formed a clearer picture in your mind when you read the sentence with specific detail. Also, you probably found the specific detail more satisfying than the general statement. Because specific detail is more satisfying and helps the reader form a clearer mental picture, strive for specific supporting details.

> Specific details help ensure adequate detail. Specific details are more satisfying because they help the reader form a clear picture in the mind.

Use Specific Words

One way to provide specific detail is to use specific words. *Specific words* are more exact than general words, so they help the reader form a clearer mental picture. Study the following lists of specific and general words to appreciate the difference between the two.

> Use specific words to help your supporting details be specific enough.

General Words	Specific Words
dog	collie
song	"Home on the Range"
book	*Jurassic Park*
music	jazz
run	sprint
TV show	*Star Trek*
said	shouted
take	grab

Now consider these two sentences to appreciate the difference specific words can make.

A. The young child was on the floor.

B. Ten-year-old Bobby was sprawled across the living room floor.

Sentence B is more interesting because it gives the reader a clearer mental picture. This clearer mental picture comes from replacing the general words *young, child,* and *was on* with the more specific *ten-year-old, Bobby,* and *sprawled across.* Also, the words *living room* are added to identify where Bobby was.

To be sure your words are specific, choose specific nouns and verbs; also, use modifiers.

Specific Nouns:	Nouns are words for people, places, ideas, emotions, and things. Instead of general nouns like *movie, car,* and *restaurant,* choose specific nouns like *Top Gun, Camaro,* and *Perkins' Pancake House.*
Specific Verbs:	Verbs are words that show action. Instead of general verbs like *went, spoke,* and *looked,* choose specific verbs like *raced, shouted,* and *glanced.*
Specific Modifiers:	Modifiers are words that describe nouns and verbs. Often you can use modifiers to make your detail more specific. Add the modifier *pounding* to describe the noun *rain,* and you get the specific *pounding rain.* Add the modifier *carefully* to the verb *stepped,* and you get the specific *stepped carefully.* When you use modifiers, be sure they are specific ones. Rather than the general "sang *badly,*" choose the more specific "sang *off-key*"; rather than the general "*nice* house," choose the more specific "*roomy* house"

Practice 3.11

Next to each general noun or verb, write a more specific alternative. The first two are done as examples.

1. shoes *penny loafers*

2. walk *stroll*

3. drink _____

4. hit_____

5. college course_____

6. looking _____

7. house_____

8. said _____

9. flower _____

10. took _____

Practice 3.12

Use one or more specific modifiers with each noun and verb. The first two are done as examples.

1. the sweater _the pink angora sweater_

2. study _study diligently_

3. the commercial _____

4. drive _____

5. the rose _____

6. barking _____

7. the kitten_____

8. sang _____

9. the apartment_____

10. sleep _____

Practice 3.13

Rewrite each sentence by using a more specific alternative for each underlined word and by following the directions in parentheses. The first one is done as an example.

1. The dog went down the street. (Add a specific modifier after the substitute for *went*.) _The German Shepherd dashed excitedly down Laurel Ave._

2. The man left his tools on the floor. Add a specific modifier before *floor*.) _____

   _____

   _____

3. Several items of clothing were scattered across the floor in Ralph's bedroom. (Add a specific modifier before *bedroom*.)

   _____

   _____

4. A number of things were good bargains at the garage sale. (Add a specific modifier before *garage sale*.) _____

_____

5. Jan decided to buy the car that Stavros was selling, even though it had so much wrong with it. (Add a specific modifier either before or after *decided*.) _____

_____

_____

6. The scouts went away from the campsite because it smelled bad. (Add a specific modifier before *scouts*.) _____

_____

_____

Practice 3.14

Rewrite the sentences to make them more specific. Change general nouns, verbs, and modifiers to specific ones, and add specific modifiers where you wish. The first one is done as an example.

1. A variety of people were at the convention. *Executives, laborers, students, and parents attended the third annual ham radio convention in Morgantown.*

2. Rhoda and I worked hard in the yard. _____

_____

_____

3. The dish I ordered at the restaurant tasted terrible. _____

_____

_____

4. The baby cried in the middle of the night. _____

_____

_____

5. The smell in Jim's apartment was awful. _____

_____

_____

6. The view from the window was very nice. _____

_____

_____

7. The heat made me miserable. _____

_____

_____

8. The teacher helped the girl feel good. _____

_____

_____

9. The dog made so much noise that he kept me awake all night.

_____

_____

10. The desk was in terrible condition. _____

_____

_____

Follow General Statements with Specific Statements

Another way to make your supporting details specific is to follow general statements with specific ones. Here is a paragraph with general statements that are *not* followed by specific ones.

Myrtle Beach, South Carolina, is the perfect summertime family vacation spot. First, there is something for everyone to do. Also, there is a range of excellent accommodations, all reasonably priced. For those who like to take side trips, there are a number of places a person can see in just a day.

The detail in this paragraph is not adequate—there is not enough of it, so you probably come away feeling unsatisfied. To make the detail adequate, follow each general statement with one or more specific ones, as in the following revision. (The specific statements are italicized to make studying the paragraph easier.)

Myrtle Beach, South Carolina, is the perfect summertime family vacation spot. First, there is something for everyone to do. *In addition to miles of beautiful beach and warm ocean to swim in, over three dozen fine golf courses are available. Fishing is possible from rental boats, off piers, and from the shore. For the kids, water slides, grand prix car and boat rides, a dozen beautiful miniature golf courses, and an amusement park provide hours of fun. For the confirmed shoppers, an outlet park with 98 stores, two shopping malls, several plazas, and numerous specialty shops provide more than ample shopping.* Also, there is a range of excellent accommodations, all reasonably priced. *Hotel rooms are available and so are efficiency apartments. One-, two-, and three-bedroom condominiums are plentiful. In fact, you can stay in a beautiful three-bedroom condominium right on the beach for as little as $95.00 a night.* For those who like to take side trips, there are a number of places a person can see in just a day. *Picturesque Conway, beautiful Brookgreen Gardens, quaint Pawley's Island and Murrells Inlet, and historic Georgetown all make comfortable day trips.*

Practice 3.15

Follow each general statement with a specific statement. The first one is done as an example.

1. Six-year-old Jan and five-year-old Juanita were not getting along at all.

   They refused to share their toys and spent the afternoon arguing about everything from the best cartoon show to what game to play.

2. Suddenly the weather turned threatening. _____

   _____

   _____

3. Some television commercials insult the viewer's intelligence.

   _____

   _____

4. The cost of textbooks is outrageous. _____

   _____

   _____

5. Dr. Stone is a dedicated teacher. _____

   _____

   _____

6. The service at Harry's New York Deli is excellent. _____

   _____

   _____

Practice 3.16: Working Together

With the members of your group, write three specific points that could be made after each of the following general statements. The first one is done as an example.

1. The students in third period history class were out of control.

    The students in the back were talking loudly among themselves.

    Two boys were roaming around the room.

    When the teacher called for order, the students talked back to him.

2. Dave treats people badly.

    _____

    _____

    _____

3. Driving with Crystal is a frightening experience.

    _____

    _____

    _____

4. To succeed in college, students need effective study habits.

    _____

    _____

    _____

5. Baby-sitting for the Hernandez twins aged me ten years.

    _____

    _____

    _____

6. The gale force winds caused extensive damage to the coastal town.

    _____

    _____

    _____

•

Practice 3.17: Working Together

The following paragraphs lack specific details because general statements are not followed by specific ones. On a separate sheet, revise these paragraphs with some classmates by following general statements with specific ones.

A. Don't Eat at Joe's

Joe's Eatery on Third Avenue is the worst restaurant in town. When I was there last Tuesday, I was appalled by the condition of the dining room. Also the service could not have been worse. When my food finally arrived, I had to send it back because it was so poorly prepared. Things at Joe's are so bad that I would not be surprised if the place was forced to go out of business soon.

B. How to Protect Your Health in College

College students should be conscious of how to take care of their health. First, they should choose carefully what they eat in the dining hall. Also, they should schedule a regular exercise session. Equally important is building in some recreation time because too much work will lead to stress. Finally, students should know what to do in the event they do become ill on campus.

Relevant Detail

Relevant detail means that the supporting details are directly related to the topic and view presented in the topic sentence. Details that stray from the topic and view create a *relevance problem* (sometimes called a problem with *unity.*)

The following paragraph has two relevance problems. As you read it, look for the supporting details that are not directly related to the topic sentence.

> Supporting details must be relevant. This means they must be clearly related to the topic and view presented in the topic sentence.

The Left-Handed Advantage

Left-handed people have the advantage in baseball and tennis. For one thing, left-handed batters are in a better position to run to first base. Left-handed first basemen also have an edge. At first base players often field balls hit to the right side of the infield. Of course, left-handed basemen wear their gloves on their right hands, so they can catch balls without moving around, the way right-handed players have to. Unfortunately, the left-handed third baseman does not enjoy the same advantage. In tennis, too, a left-handed player is fortunate. A right-handed player generally has little experience playing a lefty, but a lefty has considerable experience playing a righty. Thus, right-handed players will be more confused playing left-handed players than left-handed players will be playing right-handed players. This fact alone helps explain the large number of left-handed tennis champions. Outside of sports, lefties still face problems with door handles and radio knobs meant to be used with the right hand, with right-handed scissors, and with writing from left to right. Still, in sports, the left-handed athlete has an advantage.

You probably noticed two relevance problems in the paragraph. First, the sentence that says the third baseman does not have an advantage is not relevant because it does not relate to the point presented in the topic sentence: that left-handed people *do* have an advantage. Second, the sentence that discusses the problems lefties have outside of tennis and baseball with knobs, doors, scissors, and writing is not relevant because it does not discuss the advantage in tennis and baseball.

You should eliminate supporting details that are not relevant to your topic sentence, or alter the details to make them relevant.

Practice 3.18

The following are topic sentences followed by ideas for supporting details. In each case one idea is not relevant enough to the topic sentence to be included. Draw a line through the detail that creates the relevance problem. The first one is done as an example.

1. Robert Martinez is the best candidate for mayor.

    A. He's an experienced city manager.

    B. His budget proposals are sound.

    C. ~~He would also make an excellent governor.~~

    D. He understands the problems of our city.

2. New York need not be an expensive city to visit.

    A. A number of quality hotels offer reasonable weekend rates.

    B. Inexpensive food is served up by street vendors.

    C. The best entertainment, walking and people watching, costs nothing.

    D. However, a trip to Washington, DC is always expensive.

3. An antipasto salad can be satisfying and healthful if you use the right ingredients.

    A. Substitute low-fat meat and cheese for the high-fat varieties.

    B. Avoid eating the salad with high-calorie pasta smothered in sauce.

    C. Use only the egg white, not the high-cholesterol yolk.

    D. Top the salad with lemon juice rather than fattening salad dressing.

4. For some people, term life insurance is a wiser purchase than whole life insurance.

    A. Term insurance is cheaper.

    B. Term insurance provides maximum coverage when it is needed most.

    C. The insured cannot borrow money against term life insurance, but he or she can borrow money against a whole life policy.

    D. A person with a poor health record may find it easier to get term insurance than whole life.

5. After years of travel, I have learned how to pack efficiently for a trip.

    A. Pack only small, travel-size bottles of toiletries to save space.

    B. Take only color-coordinated clothes to mix and match; this reduces the number of garments needed.

    C. Place tissue paper between layers of clothes to prevent wrinkles.

    D. Invest in good quality luggage so you do not need to replace it after only a few years.

6. Dana Gross is the best candidate for governor.

    A. She knows state government because she served in the state senate for eight years.

    B. She is a strong advocate of a balanced budget.

    C. She has a teaching degree.

    D. She has an excellent working relationship with community leaders.

Practice 3.19

In the following paragraphs, draw a line through the details that are not relevant.

A. Not Necessarily

It is said that the squeaky wheel gets the grease, but my experience proved otherwise. I had been working at Gas City for three years. I began ten hours a week as a regular gas jockey, but soon I was working thirty hours a week. Each of those hours was at minimum wage. I liked this job much better than the one I used to have making fries at Hot Dog House. Mr. Stanko, the boss, said I was one of the best kids who has ever worked for him. He said he trusted me; he said I was a hard worker. About six months ago, he started asking me to open and close the station on occasion. I knew this was a real vote of confidence and decided the time was right to ask for a raise. I worked up my courage and politely made my request—which was not so politely refused. Then I decided to be a squeaky wheel. I asked once a week for a fifty-cent-an-hour raise. After my fourth request, Mr. Stanko said it was obvious I was very unhappy so he was going to let me go. I was too proud to ask him not to, so I was out of work. I was an unemployed squeaky wheel, and there was no grease in sight.

B. Hank

My friend Hank is a remarkable person. Although he was abused by his parents until he was sixteen and placed in a foster home, Hank is a kind, gentle guy. Studies show that abused children often become abusive adults, but Hank is different. He is a Big Brother to a fatherless child and treats this boy with love and compassion. He also works summers as a swim instructor at a local day camp, where he is a favorite among all the campers. He plans to major in math. Hank underwent three years of therapy to work through the problems that his parents caused. Clearly he has beaten the odds because he shows no signs of becoming abusive the way his parents were.

THE CLOSING

Many times a final sentence is needed to bring the paragraph to a satisfying finish. This sentence is the *closing*.

Often an appropriate closing suggests itself. However, if you are unsure how to handle your closing, write a sentence that refers to the topic and/or view presented in your topic sentence. For example, look at the closing of "The Left-Handed Advantage" on p. 71. Notice that this final sentence mentions the left-handed athlete; this refers to the topic noted in the topic sentence (left-handed people). Also notice that the closing mentions that left-handed people have an advantage in sports; this refers to the view in the topic sentence (having an advantage in baseball and tennis).

Another way to handle the closing is to answer the question "So what?" about your topic sentence. The final sentence of "A Lounge for Women Over Thirty" on p. 52 takes this approach.

> A separate closing may be needed to give a paragraph a satisfying finish. This closing sentence can refer to the topic or the view presented in the topic sentence. It can also answer the question "So what?"

Practice 3.20: Working Together

The following paragraph lacks a closing. Work with some classmates to add a closing sentence that provides a satisfying finish. Use any approach you like, including the ones that have been described.

A Safer Aerobics

Low-impact aerobics is safer than traditional aerobics. Traditional aerobics involves a great deal of jumping and jogging. Recently, findings have shown that this jumping and jogging causes shin splints, stress fractures, and injuries to ankles and knees. In low-impact aerobics, one foot is on the floor most of the time, so fragile joints suffer little stress. Some people think that low-impact aerobics does not give the same cardiovascular benefits as traditional aerobics. However this is not true. In low-impact aerobics, vigorous arm movements get the heart rate up into the same target range as that achieved in traditional aerobics.

_____

_____

_____

A PARAGRAPH CHECKLIST _____

Before submitting your paragraph to a reader, be sure you can answer yes to the questions in the following list:

1. Do you have a topic sentence with your topic and view?

2. Is your detail adequate? Check each general noun, verb, and modifier. Are these appropriate, or should you find more specific alternatives? Do you have enough specific details?

3. Is all your detail relevant? Compare each sentence, one at a time, to your topic sentence and ask yourself if each is directly related to the topic and view.

4. Does your paragraph end in a satisfying way?

5. Have you edited carefully, more than once? Follow the editing procedures on p. 33. Leave nothing to chance—if you are unsure about a spelling, grammar, or usage point, consult Chapters 7–14 or your instructor.

6. Did you leave your work whenever you needed to rest and clear your head?

7. Did you proofread slowly and carefully, one word and punctuation mark at a time?

Writing Assignment

Write a paragraph that explains *one* influence a person has had on you. Before you begin this assignment, read the sample student paragraph and the tips that follow.

Megen

Because of a nine-year-old named Megen, I decided to major in physical therapy. I met Megen last quarter, when I worked as an orderly at St. Joseph's Hospital. She was only nine, but she had experienced more pain in those nine years than most people experience in a full lifetime. Megen was paralyzed, but she never used that as an excuse to stop trying. Each day I would wheel Megen down for her grueling physical therapy sessions. I would watch and encourage her as she worked through exercises that brought beads of sweat to her forehead and upper lip. Sometimes the pain was so great she cried, but she never stopped working as long as there was the slightest chance it would help. More than anything, Megen wanted to go to school and play with the other nine-year-olds, and she was willing to work as hard as she could for her dream. But it wasn't to be, for Megen died October 19th. I will never forget Megen's courage, for it showed me what

I wanted to do with the rest of my life. It showed me that I wanted to be a physical therapist and help others strive for their dreams.

The paragraph about Megen illustrates the kind of paragraph you will be writing. Like this sample paragraph, your paragraph will explain who influenced you, what that influence was, and how the influence occurred. Also, your topic sentence should name the person who influenced you (this will be your topic) and note what the influence is or was (this will be your view of the topic).

Before beginning your paragraph, read the following tips. One or more of them may prove helpful to you.

□ TIPS FOR WRITING YOUR PARAGRAPH □

Planning

1. To select a person and influence, think about your teachers, parents, coaches, clergy, friends, relatives, teammates, and neighbors. Do not limit yourself to the recent past, but think all the way back to your childhood. Consider your fears, wishes, ambitions, successes, failures, talents, and career plans. Did someone influence one of them? If you need help discovering ideas, try listing, brainstorming, clustering, journal writing, or freewriting. Once you have decided on the person and influence, fill in the blanks in the following sentence:

   Because of_____, I _____.

   Put the person's name in the first blank and the influence in the second blank to get something like this:

   Because of Uncle Harry, I am no longer afraid of high places.

   The sentence will remind you of your topic and view.
2. Answering these questions should prove helpful:

What happened?	Why is it important?
Who was involved?	How did it happen?
When did it happen?	What was the effect?
Why did it happen?	Will the effect continue?
Where did it happen?	Are you happy about the effect?

   See p. 2 for additional idea-generation techniques.

3. Review the ideas you generated and make a list of the ones you would like to use. Check every point on your list against the sentence you developed when you filled in the blanks. Is each of your ideas directly relevant?

4. Study your list of ideas and decide on an appropriate order. Number the ideas in your list to reflect this order.

Writing

1. Begin with a topic sentence that names the person and the influence he or she has or had on you. This topic sentence can be a version of the planning sentence you developed when you filled in the blanks.

2. Using your list of numbered ideas as a guide, write through your first draft in one sitting. Do not worry about word choice, spelling, grammar, and punctuation. When you revise and edit, you can attend to these. If you get stuck, skip the difficult parts for now and go on.

3. After drafting, take a break for as long as you can—a day would be best—so you can be more objective when you revise.

Rewriting

1. Check your topic sentence to be sure it includes your topic (the person who influenced you) and your view of the topic (how that person influenced you). To do this, place one wavy line under the mention of the person and two wavy lines under the mention of how the person influenced you.

2. Circle every general noun, verb, and modifier. If the circled words are too vague, find more specific alternatives.

3. Underline each general statement. Put parentheses around the specific statements that follow the general ones. Decide whether you have enough specific statements.

4. This might be a good time to take a break. When you return, check each sentence in your draft against the topic sentence to be sure all of your supporting details are relevant.

5. Give your draft to someone with good judgment about writing. Ask that person to mark where more detail is needed, where relevance is unclear, or where meaning is unclear. (See p. 27 for additional revision procedures, and p. 29 for more on using reader response.)

6. Take a break if you need one. When you return, type your draft. Problems you overlooked in your own handwriting may be apparent in type.

7. Edit one separate time for each kind of mistake you are in the habit of making.

8. Read your draft out loud to listen for errors. Be sure you read *exactly* what is on the page, not what you *meant* to write. To avoid building too much speed, point with a pen to each word as you read and do not let your eyes move ahead of what you are pointing to.

9. Check the spelling of any word that might be misspelled. (See p. 32 for additional editing procedures.)

10. Copy or type your paragraph into its final form, and take a break before proofreading.

11. Proofread by pointing to each word on the page and reading what you are pointing to. Don't let your eyes move ahead and be very careful to read exactly what is on the page.

Note: Before submitting your paragraph, be sure you can answer yes to all the questions in the paragraph checklist on p. 76.

CHAPTER
4

Ways to Develop Paragraphs

People write in a variety of situations for a variety of purposes. In college, you write lab reports, essay examination answers, and book reviews. On the job, you may write business letters, memos, and reports. At home, you write letters to friends, business correspondence, and committee reports for organizations you belong to. To write successfully in a range of situations, you must understand the forms in which ideas can be presented—that is what this chapter is about.

It is customary to classify writing into four types: narration, description, exposition, and persuasion. *Narration* is story telling. If you write to a friend to explain what happened when you went on a job interview, you would use narration. *Description* is using words to paint a mental picture. Travel brochures use description to paint mental pictures of sandy beaches, picturesque mountains, and scenic countrysides. *Exposition* is explaining. We encounter exposition every day: the owner's manual of the compact disc player explains how to operate the machine (this is *process analysis*); newspaper articles explain why the budget deficit is high and how it will affect our economy (this is *cause and effect analysis*); psychology textbooks give examples of abnormal behavior (this is *illustration*); magazine articles explain the characteristics of modern men and women (this is *definition*); editorials present the similarities and differences between two candidates for president (this is *comparison and contrast*); biology textbooks group living things according to their characteristics (this is *classification*). In addition to narration, description, and exposition, one other kind of writing exists: *persuasion.* The persuasive writer tries to move the

> The kinds of writing are narration, description, exposition (illustration, process analysis, definition, comparison and contrast, cause and effect analysis, and classification), and persuasion.

reader to think or act a particular way. The campaign literature you receive in the mail is persuasive writing.

To help you learn to write in a variety of situations and for a variety of purposes, this chapter will explain how to develop paragraphs using narration, description, exposition (illustration, process analysis, definition, comparison and contrast, cause and effect analysis, and classification), and persuasion. For each of these ways to develop paragraphs, the chapter includes the following:

1. sample paragraphs written by students for you to study
2. information about how to structure the paragraph
3. information about the kind of supporting details that develop the paragraph
4. a checklist of the characteristics of the paragraph
5. a writing assignment with tips for handling the assignment

NARRATION

> Narration is story-telling.

You tell, hear, and read stories often. When you explain to your roommate what happened on your date last night, you tell a story. When your friend writes to you about the minor car accident she was in, you read a story. When you listen to a classmate tell what happened during the third quarter of the football game, you hear a story.

Another name for story telling is *narration.* When you tell a story, either orally or in writing, you are *narrating.* (For an example of narration in a published essay, see "On Being 17, Bright, and Unable to Read" on p. 441.)

A Sample Narrative Paragraph

The following narrative paragraph, written by a student, will be used to illustrate several points about narration:

Able-bodied but Addle-brained

I became very angry the day I saw an able-bodied woman get out of a car she had just parked in a handicapped space. Last Thursday I had just gotten out of my car in K-Mart's parking lot when a woman in a beat-up Ford Fairlane swerved into a spot clearly marked for handicapped parking. She emerged with three children, all under six, and headed for the entrance. If she had a handicap, I saw no sign of it. I caught up with her and said, "Excuse me, but you parked in a handicapped spot." She just looked at me as if I had beamed down from Mars, and then she said that she was handicapped because she had three kids. That made me furious. I yelled at her that if she considered her children handicaps, she should be investigated. Then I told her that I would report her to store security and ask that her car be towed. When I told the security police officer what happened, he said there was nothing he could do because she had not broken a law. I was so angry at the insensitive woman that I stormed out of the store without doing my shopping. If you ask me, any able-bodied person who parks in a handicapped space should have to spend a week in a wheelchair. I guarantee the person would be more careful about parking after that.

The Topic Sentence

A topic sentence includes the writer's topic and the writer's view of the topic. In the topic sentence of a narrative paragraph, the topic is the event to be narrated. The view is how the writer feels about the event. Let's look again at the topic sentence of "Able-bodied but Addle-brained":

> The topic sentence of a narrative paragraph includes the event to be narrated and how the writer feels about the event.

I became very angry the day I saw an able-bodied woman get out of a car she had just parked in a handicapped space.

Here the topic (the event to be narrated) is the day the able-bodied woman parked in a handicapped space. The view of the topic is that it made the writer angry.

Practice 4.1

The sentences that follow could be topic sentences for narrative paragraphs. Underline the topic (the event to be narrated) once and the writer's view of the topic (how the writer feels about the event) twice. The first one is done as an example.

1. The day my dog was killed I learned the importance of leash laws.
2. My most frightening experience occurred on a Boy Scout hike.
3. One of my happiest moments was when Dad taught me how to fish.
4. I felt like a hero when the Rayen Tigers won the City Series basketball championship.

5. My first day as a college student was hectic.

6. Getting my ham radio license was the high point of my year.

Practice 4.2: Working Together

   Working with some classmates, write a topic sentence that could begin a narrative paragraph about each of the subjects given. Remember to include the event narrated and your view of the event. The first one is done as an example.

1. a first experience *My first baby-sitting job was a nightmare.*

2. a childhood memory _____

_____

3. a school experience _____

_____

4. a time spent with a friend _____

_____

5. a holiday celebration _____

_____

6. a time when you were disappointed (or pleasantly surprised)

_____

_____

Supporting Details

   To develop supporting details for a narrative paragraph, you can answer these questions:

Who was involved?   Where did it happen?

What happened?   Why did it happen?

When did it happen?   How did it happen?

Notice that the answers to most of these questions make up the supporting details for "Able-bodied but Addle-brained."

> Supporting details for a narrative paragraph answer most or all of the questions, who? what? when? where? why? how?

1. Who was involved?

   the writer and a woman

2. What happened?

   The writer became angry and had a confrontation with a woman who parked in a handicapped space.

3. When did it happen?

   last Thursday

4. Where did it happen?

   K-Mart's parking lot

5. Why did it happen?

   The woman was insensitive.

6. How did it happen?

   This question is not answered. (A narrative paragraph sometimes answers most, but not all, of the questions.)

Supporting details in a narrative paragraph are arranged in a chronological (time) order. This means the details are arranged in the order that they occurred, so what happened first is written first, what happened second is written second, and so forth. (Chronological order is also discussed on p. 19.) Reread "Able-bodied but Addle-brained" and notice the chronological order.

Practice 4.3

We have all had our embarrassing moments. Pick one of yours, and assume you will write a paragraph narrating what happened. To develop supporting details, on a separate sheet answer the who? what? when? where? why? and how? questions.

Practice 4.4

> Supporting details for a narrative paragraph are arranged in chronological order.

To practice arranging details in chronological order, list on a separate sheet the first ten things you did today. Be sure to list the activities in the order they occurred.

Transitions That Signal Chronological Order

Transitions are words that help the reader identify the order of ideas. Because you use chronological order when you write narration, now is a good time to review the transitions that signal this order in the chart on p. 24.

Practice 4.5

Read the following narrative paragraph written by a student and answer the questions after it:

A Costly Lesson

A car accident two years ago taught me the dangers of drinking and driving. It was about 11:30 p.m., the night before Easter. My buddies and I were driving around, and we decided to go to the drive-in. Someone suggested getting some beer, and I agreed. We picked up a few six-packs of Coors and downed them while we watched the movie. We headed out after the movie with me behind the wheel. I was cruising down Route 11 when two jerks in a Monte Carlo Super Sport pulled up alongside of us, wanting to race. Being young, stupid, and high on beer, I started to race them. Then out of nowhere came the flashing red lights and the siren. First, I hit the brakes. Then, I was skidding toward the guard rail at close to 80 mph. A broken nose, cracked ribs, whiplash, and the knowledge that I almost killed my friends taught me never to drink and drive again.

On a separate sheet, answer the following questions about "A Costly Lesson":

1. What is the topic sentence of "A Costly Lesson"? What is the writer's topic? The view?
2. Which of the who? what? when? where? why? how? questions are answered? What are the answers?
3. Are the supporting details adequate? Explain.
4. The writer chooses specific words. For example, instead of *beer*, he says *Coors*. Cite four other examples of specific words.
5. Are all the supporting details relevant to the topic sentence? Explain.
6. Cite three examples of transitions to signal chronological order.
7. Does the author bring the paragraph to a satisfying close? What approach does the author use for the closing sentence?

CHECKLIST FOR A NARRATIVE PARAGRAPH _____

Before submitting your narrative paragraph, be sure you can answer yes to all the questions in the following checklist:

1. Do you have a topic sentence that presents the event to be narrated and your view of the event?
2. Have you answered who? what? when? where? why? how? If one or more of these questions is unanswered, is it appropriate not to answer?
3. Have you used specific nouns, verbs, and modifiers?
4. Does every sentence advance the story?
5. If spoken words (conversation) are important to the story, have you included them and checked pp. 428–430 for correct punctuation?
6. Are your supporting details in chronological order?
7. Have you used transitions to signal chronological order?
8. Does your paragraph have a satisfying closing?

Writing Assignment

For your narrative paragraph, you have a choice of topics:

1. Tell a story about a first experience.
2. Narrate a childhood memory.
3. Narrate a school experience.
4. Tell a story about a time when you were angry.
5. Narrate an event that changed your thinking.
6. Tell a story about a time when you were disappointed.
7. Tell a story about a time when you were pleasantly surprised.
8. Tell the story of an embarrassing moment.
9. See p. 444 for narrative paragraph assignments based on the published essay "On Being 17, Bright, and Unable to Read." See p. 453 for an assignment based on "Living with My VCR."

If you choose one of the first seven topics, one of the topic sentences you drafted when you completed *Practice 4.2* may help. If you choose the eighth topic, the supporting details you developed when you completed *Practice 4.3* may help.

□   **TIPS FOR PLANNING YOUR**   □
        NARRATIVE PARAGRAPH

1. Brainstorm for ideas for your supporting details by answering the who? what? when? where? why? how? questions. See p. 2 for other idea-generation techniques.
2. Make a chronological list of everything that happened.

DESCRIPTION

Description gives the reader a clear mental picture of what is being described. Thus, writers of description choose words and details that will most clearly paint that mental picture.

Description can be a part of many kinds of writing encountered every day. For example, your college catalog may describe the beauty of your campus, your biology text may describe the appearance of a cell, and a mail order catalog may describe the features of the clothing it is selling. (For an example of description in a published essay, see "Expecting Friends" on p. 446.)

> A descriptive paragraph gives the reader a mental picture of what is being described.

A Sample Descriptive Paragraph

Here is a descriptive paragraph written by a student. As you read it, notice how carefully words and details were chosen to paint a clear mental picture.

The Plant

The plant I work in five days of every week is extremely depressing. Everywhere I look, there are strips of peeling green paint, revealing the dingy gray underneath. The gloom is highlighted by bright gold sparks welders throw as they fuse cold steel. To the right of my work area, three men (more like robots) hang parts like garments on moving clothesline conveyors. They don't smile, and they don't talk. They just work. Behind the robot-men, hoses swell like arteries as they pump the foul-smelling lacquer paint to sprayers that change dingy gray metal to various colors. To my left, gray metal desks roll down a conveyor toward more robot-men, who wrap them in plastic. As the desks roll by, air tools scream as they drive screws to fasten parts, and giant presses pound, pound, pound as they gobble up steel to transform into useful shapes. Each day I remind myself that I will one day earn my degree, so I do not have to work in this depressing factory.

The Topic Sentence

> The topic sentence for a descriptive paragraph mentions what you are describing and your dominant impression.

The topic sentence for a descriptive paragraph will include your topic and your view of the topic. The topic is what you describe; the view is your dominant impression of what you are describing. (A *dominant impression* is your main reaction to what you are describing.) Take another look at the topic sentence of "The Plant":

The plant I work in five days of every week is extremely depressing.

The writer's topic (what is described) is *the plant where the writer works.* The writer's dominant impression of (main reaction to) the plant is that it is *extremely depressing.*

> The topic should be narrow enough to be treated in one paragraph. The dominant impression should be expressed in specific language.

When you shape your topic sentence, keep your topic narrow enough for treatment in one paragraph. It would be difficult, for example, to describe your whole house in one paragraph, but you could describe your bedroom.

Also be sure to express your dominant impression in specific language. Avoid words like *nice, bad, great,* and *awful,* and use more specific alternatives like *peaceful, hectic, exciting,* and *run-down.*

Practice 4.6

Write a topic sentence for each of the subjects given. Include what you are describing and your dominant impression. Also, be sure your topic is narrow enough, and be sure your dominant impression is expressed in specific language. The first one is done as an example. (If you have trouble thinking of ideas, try listing or freewriting.)

1. a campus cafeteria at noon *At noon, the cafeteria in*

   Beeman Hall is a hectic place.

2. your bedroom _____

   _____

3. a particular outdoor area on campus _____

   _____

4. a kitchen after a five-year-old has made breakfast _____

_____

5. a favorite restaurant _____

_____

6. your writing classroom _____

_____

Supporting Details

The supporting details for a descriptive paragraph are sensory details. *Sensory details* appeal to one of the five senses (sight, sound, smell, taste, and touch). Most of the details in "The Plant" appeal to sight, but some details appeal to sound ("air tools scream" and "presses pound"), one detail appeals to smell ("foul-smelling lacquer"), and one appeals to touch ("cold steel").

In a descriptive paragraph, words must be specific. The writer of "The Plant" chose specific nouns, verbs, and modifiers like these:

> Descriptive details are sensory details.

> In a descriptive paragraph, nouns, verbs, and modifiers are specific.

strips of peeling green paint   air tools scream

hoses swell like arteries   gobble up steel

giant presses pound   dingy gray

Now is a good time to review the discussion of specific word choice on p. 63.

Practice 4.7: Working Together

With some classmates, write one description that could be used as supporting detail for each topic sentence. Be sure your words are specific. Also, try to appeal to a different sense in each sentence. The first one is done as an example.

1. Dan's old car is ready for the junk yard. *The tail pipe, eaten away by rust, hangs so low it almost scrapes the ground.*

_____

2. The children's playroom is a disaster area. _____

_____

_____

3. The mall on Christmas Eve was hectic. _____

_____

_____

4. Eleni's backyard is beautifully landscaped. _____

_____

_____

5. The atmosphere of the Paris Cafe is romantic. _____

_____

_____

6. My grandmother's attic is spooky. _____

_____

_____

Transitions That Signal Spatial Order

> Descriptive paragraphs often have transitions that signal spatial order.

A spatial arrangement often works well for descriptive details. With a spatial arrangement, you move from front to back, from top to bottom, from inside to outside, from left to right, or in some other ordered way across space. To help your reader identify the spatial arrangement, use transitions that signal spatial order. These appear in the chart on p. 25.

The writer of "The Plant" used transitions to signal spatial order. Some of these are listed here:

To the <u>right of</u> my work area
<u>Behind</u> the robot-men
<u>To my left</u>, gray metal desks

Practice 4.8

The following descriptive paragraph was written by a student. Notice the specific words and the details that appeal to the senses. Answer the questions after the paragraph to check your understanding.

Spring Is Here

The view from my bedroom window yesterday told me that spring is definitely here. Across the street, George was washing his Yamaha 750 as Billy Ocean's voice filled the air surrounding the portable tape deck on the driveway. Next door, Mr. Cardero's Chrysler sat with its top down, awaiting the first topless ride of the season. At the base of the large oak in my front yard, two squirrels picked at something in the grass. With the roar of a lawn mower starting up nearby, they scurried up the trunk and out of sight. Lovers walked slowly down the sidewalk hand in hand, talking and smiling the way lovers do. They passed a jogger resting against a lamppost, too tired to go on. A Day-lite Window Cleaning Company truck eased down the street looking for the house needing the streaks and smears removed from its windows. Directly below, Katie and Barbie whizzed by on their bikes. Before closing my window, I inhaled deeply the fresh smell of spring. It is here at last.

On a separate sheet, answer the following questions about "Spring Is Here":

1. What is the topic sentence? According to the topic sentence, what will be described, and what is the dominant impression?

2. What senses are appealed to? Give an example of a description that appeals to each of these senses.

3. Give five examples of specific word choice.

4. Give three examples of transitions to signal spatial order.

5. Are all the supporting details relevant? Explain.

6. Does the paragraph come to a satisfying finish? Explain.

CHECKLIST FOR A DESCRIPTIVE PARAGRAPH ＿＿＿

Before submitting your descriptive paragraph, be sure you can answer yes to the following questions:

1. Does your topic sentence mention what will be described and your dominant impression?
2. Is your topic narrow enough for one paragraph? Is your dominant impression expressed in specific language?
3. Have you used sensory details that appeal to as many senses as possible?
4. Have you used specific nouns, verbs, and modifiers?
5. Have you included enough descriptions to show why you formed your dominant impression?
6. Have you used transitions, especially spatial ones, where needed?
7. Are all your details relevant to both your topic and your dominant impression?

Writing Assignment

Pick one of the following topics for your descriptive paragraph:

1. Use one of the topic sentences from *Practice 4.6.*
2. Describe a place you go when you want to be alone.
3. Describe your favorite night spot.
4. Describe your study area or the library reference room.
5. See p. 449 for an assignment based on the published essay "Expecting Friends."

☐ TIPS FOR PLANNING YOUR ☐
DESCRIPTIVE PARAGRAPH

1. Write an early version of your topic sentence that includes what you are describing and your dominant impression.
2. If you have trouble deciding on your dominant impression, complete this sentence:

The place I am describing makes me feel ＿＿＿＿＿＿＿＿＿.

Fill in the blank with an emotion or mood (cheerful, depressed, nervous, excited, angry, scared, peaceful, etc.)

3. Make a list of the details you will include. Try to include some descriptive words, but don't worry about getting the descriptions down in perfect form. For example, your list might include something like "smelled bad." Later you can revise that to a more specific "smelled like stale cigar smoke."

4. Number the ideas in your list in the order in which they will appear in your draft.

5. See p. 2 for additional idea-generation techniques.

ILLUSTRATION

Writers and speakers use examples to make their points clear. Consider this conversation between Bob and Julio:

Bob: The food in this cafeteria stinks.

Julio: What do you mean?

Bob: The meat is always rubbery, the mashed potatoes are cold, and the Jell-O is hot.

To explain what he meant, Bob gave examples: rubbery meat, cold potatoes, and hot Jell-O. Another name for an example is an *illustration*. A paragraph with supporting details made up of examples is an *illustration paragraph*.

Because examples clarify points and make the general more specific, illustration is a frequent component of all writing, whether it is description, narration, exposition, or persuasion. (For examples of illustration in published essays, see "Expecting Friends" on p. 446 and "How Dictionaries Are Made" on p. 459.)

> An illustration paragraph has examples for supporting details.

A Sample Illustration Paragraph

The following illustration paragraph, written by a student, will be used to explain several points about illustration:

With My Head in the Clouds

As someone who is 6 feet 9 inches tall, I speak with authority when I say that the world is not set up for tall people. For example, everything that is supposed to be high is too low. Not long ago I was home for dinner with my parents. As I stood up from the table to go into the kitchen, I slammed my head into the chandelier, causing the lights to sway wildly and my head to throb annoyingly for hours. Each time I enter a room, I must duck to avoid hitting my head on a door frame. Beds are also not made with the very tall in mind. I do not fit in a standard size bed, so I have to sleep diagonally across a double bed to keep my feet from dangling off the end. Cars are an even bigger problem. I have to recline my seat and push it back to keep my head from scraping the ceiling. Because this is so uncomfortable and a little bit dangerous, I often drive with the sunroof open so I can keep the seat in a proper position. Of course, there is still the problem of getting into the car. I will smash my head if I forget to fold myself over like an envelope. Most people think that height has its advantages, but on most days, I do not see them.

Supporting Details

The supporting details for an illustration paragraph are examples that develop the topic sentence. Look again at "With My Head in the Clouds." The topic sentence presents this idea as the central point of the paragraph:

. . . the world is not set up for tall people.

To support this point, the author uses several examples:

Everything that is supposed to be high is too low. (the chandelier; door frames)

Beds are too small.

Cars are too small. (adjusting the seat; driving with the sunroof open; getting into the car)

> To have adequate detail, you must use enough examples. To have specific details, you must use specific words and follow general statements with specific ones.

To have adequate detail, you should have enough examples to support your topic sentence. In one paragraph, three examples is usually enough. If they are highly detailed, two examples may be enough. In addition, use specific nouns, verbs, and modifiers to make your examples specific and follow general statements with specific ones.

> Sometimes examples can be effectively arranged in an emphatic or chronological order.

It is often effective to place your examples in emphatic order, saving your strongest example for last. (See p. 20 on emphatic order.) The examples in "With My Head in the Clouds" are in emphatic order. The clue to this is that the last set of examples is introduced with the words "an even bigger problem." If your examples occurred in a particular time order, you can arrange them in chronological order (discussed on p. 19).

Practice 4.9: Working Together

Complete this practice with some classmates. Under each topic sentence, list three examples that can be used for supporting details. The first one is done as an example.

1. Ms. Lyons did more work than the average fifth-grade teacher.

   She took her class camping to collect leaf specimens.

   She visited a sick student at home to tutor her.

   She skips lunch to grade papers.

2. Tension is a part of a college student's life.

   _____

   _____

   _____

3. Cars can be more trouble than they are worth.

   _____

   _____

   _____

4. Television advertisements often mislead the public.

   _____

   _____

   _____

5. Parents sometimes take children where they do not belong.

   _____

   _____

   _____

6. Shopping malls are a source of entertainment.

   _____

   _____

   _____

Transitions That Signal Illustration, Addition, and Emphatic Order

In Chapter 1 you learned that *transitions* help the reader identify the order of ideas. When you write your illustration paragraph, three kinds of transitions may be helpful: transitions that signal illustration, transitions that signal addition, and transitions that signal emphatic order. These appear in the following chart:

Transition Chart

Transitions that Signal Addition	also, and, and then, in addition, too, furthermore, further, moreover, equally important, another, first, second, third . . .
	The children hid from the babysitter at bedtime. *Another example* of their bad behavior occurred when they hid her car keys.
Transitions that Signal Illustration	for example, for instance, an illustration of this, to illustrate
	Juan's math teacher is too easy. *For instance,* she has not assigned homework for at least a month.
Transitions that Signal Emphatic Order	more important, most important, most of all, best of all, of greatest importance, least of all, even better, the best (worst) case (example, instance, time)
	Louise is often thoughtless. *One of the worst cases* of her thoughtlessness occurred when she did not pick up her six-year-old sister at school because she wanted to finish watching her soap opera.

Practice 4.10

Reread "With My Head in the Clouds" on p. 93. Notice that most of the examples are introduced with a transition. On a separate sheet, list the transitions that introduce examples, and tell what each signals.

Practice 4.11

The illustration paragraph that follows is a revision of a piece written by a student. Read it and answer the questions to test your understanding.

One Step Forward and Two Steps Back

Americans are proud of their technological advancements, but technology often comes with a price. Consider the cordless phone, for example. Yes, it gives us freedom to move around. However, more often than not, these phones cross frequencies with other phones so that we hear other people's conversations, and they hear ours. What we gain in mobility we lose in privacy. We also lose clear conversations, for these phones snap, crackle, and pop more than most breakfast cereals. The information highway is another example. It offers computer users almost limitless access to a staggering amount of information. However, users are so glued to their computer screens day and night that they no longer have a life away from their pcs. Once on the information highway, people become so obsessed that they do not take the exit ramp. Another example, one that I read about, concerns the computer-designed magnesium wheels General Motors put on its cars not too long ago. Thanks to a computer error, the tire seals did not fit properly. As a result, thousands of car owners woke up to discover that their brand new cars had flat tires. Certainly, technological advances make life easier, but they are not without their problems.

On a separate sheet, answer the following questions:

1. What is the topic sentence of "One Step Forward and Two Steps Back"? What is the writer's topic? The view of the topic?
2. How many examples does the writer use?
3. Are the supporting details adequate? Explain.
4. Are all the supporting details relevant? Explain.
5. List the transitions the writer uses to introduce examples and tell what they signal.
6. Does the paragraph have a satisfying closing? Explain.

CHECKLIST FOR AN ILLUSTRATION PARAGRAPH

Before submitting your illustration paragraph, be sure you can answer yes to all the questions in this checklist:

1. Do you have a topic sentence that presents your topic and view?
2. Do you have enough examples to support your topic sentence?
3. Have you used specific nouns, verbs, and modifiers?
4. Have you followed general statements with specific ones?
5. Have you used transitions to move from example to example?
6. Does your paragraph have a satisfying finish?

Writing Assignment

You have a choice of topics for your illustration paragraph:

1. Write an illustration paragraph with one of the topic sentences from *Practice 4.9.* You may be able to use some or all of the examples you generated when you completed the exercise.
2. Write a paragraph illustrating *one* of the personality traits of someone you know. First, pick a person (your best friend, a boss, your cousin, a neighbor, a teacher, etc.). Then decide on a personality trait (greedy, generous, optimistic, lazy, ambitious, sloppy, neat, stubborn, fair, cooperative, loving, etc.). Your supporting details will be examples of the person showing the trait.
3. Use examples to illustrate the following:
    High school did (or did not) prepare me for college.
4. Use examples to illustrate the following:
    Things are not always what they seem.
5. See p. 449 for an assignment based on the published essay "Expecting Friends." See p. 453 for an assignment based on "Living With My VCR."

☐ TIPS FOR PLANNING YOUR ☐ ILLUSTRATION PARAGRAPH

1. If you need help discovering ideas, freewrite for 10–15 minutes (see p. 11).

2. Place each example at the top of a column. Under each example, list the details you will include to develop the example.

3. Write an early version of your topic sentence. Be sure it includes your topic and your view of the topic.

4. Number the examples in the order in which they will appear in your first draft. Consider whether a chronological or emphatic order is desirable.

5. See p. 2 for additional idea-generation techniques.

PROCESS ANALYSIS

> A process analysis explains how something is made or done.

A process analysis explains how something is made or done. We encounter process analyses often: a recipe tells how a particular dish is made; instructions packaged with a toy tell how that toy is put together; magazine articles tell us how to save money on home mortgages and how to improve our marriages. (For examples of process analysis in published essays, see "Green Frog Skin" on p. 455 and "How Dictionaries Are Made" on p. 459.)

A Sample Process Analysis

The following process analysis, a revision of a piece written by a student, will be used to illustrate several points.

Making Money with a Garage Sale

If you plan it right, you can make a great deal of money from a garage sale. First, you must gather all the saleable items collecting dust in your basement and attic. Do not include anything badly broken, but keep everything else. The items you think are the most worthless are likely to be the first to sell. Toys and tools are hot sellers, but clothes (unless they are children's) probably will not sell very well. Next—and this is very important—clean this junk up. Dirty items will not sell, but you will be surprised at the weird stuff that goes if it is clean. Once your items are clean, it is important to display them properly, so get lots of tables, even if you have to rent them. Arrange everything attractively, trying to keep housewares together, toys together, and so forth. Now for the most important part, pricing. I have just three words of advice: cheap! cheap! cheap! Remember, this trash has been in your basement collecting spider eggs for the past five years, so do not get greedy. Price it to move because the last thing you want to do is drag this stuff back in the house because it did not sell. If you really want a great sale, advertise. Put signs up and place an ad in the classifieds. Finally, pamper your customers by providing grocery bags for carrying those marvelous purchases home in, and by serving coffee—for twenty-five cents a cup, of course. Believe me, follow this advice, and you can turn your unwanted items into extra cash.

The Topic Sentence

The topic sentence for a process analysis includes the topic and view of the topic. The topic is the process. The view of the topic can explain why you think the reader should understand the process. Look again at the topic sentence of "Making Money with a Garage Sale":

> The topic sentence of a process analysis mentions the process that will be explained and why the reader should understand the process.

If you plan it right, you can make a great deal of money from a garage sale.

In this case the topic (process to be explained) is having a garage sale. The view of the topic (why the reader should understand the process) is that, with the right planning, there is money to be made.

Practice 4.12

For each topic sentence, tell the process to be explained and why the reader should understand the process. The first is done as an example.

1. If you want to keep your sanity, register the way I do.

   Process *registration (registering the way the author does)*

   Reason to understand process *to keep sanity*

2. To get the best value for your money, shop carefully for a used car.

   Process _____

   Reason to understand process _____

3. In order to survive, every baby-sitter should know how to handle children who act like monsters.

   Process _____

   Reason to understand process _____

4. To move up the corporate ladder, you must learn how to network.

   Process _____

   Reason to understand process _____

5. College students must learn how to relax so the pressures of studying do not overwhelm them.

   Process _____

   Reason to understand process _____

6. To have a successful garden, you must plan carefully.

   Process _____

   Reason to understand process _____

Supporting Details

The supporting details for a process analysis are the steps in the process. Look back at "Making Money with a Garage Sale," and you will see that the supporting details are all the things a person must do—all the steps that must be performed—in order to have a profitable garage sale. A brief description of items needed to perform the process is sometimes included as well.

Sometimes it is necessary to include something that should *not* be done, as a warning to the reader. For example, in "Making Money with a Garage Sale," the reader is cautioned not to include badly broken items.

If the proper way to perform a step is not clear, you should explain. Notice in "Making Money with a Garage Sale" that the writer explains how to display items properly—use lots of tables, arrange things attractively, and keep like things together.

Finally, the supporting details for a process analysis are most often arranged in a chronological (time) order. This means the steps are given in the order they are performed.

> Supporting details for a process analysis are the steps performed. Sometimes the writer must also explain what is *not* done or the way to perform a step.

> The supporting details are usually arranged in chronological order.

Practice 4.13: Working Together

With some classmates, pick three of the following processes. On a separate sheet, list the steps performed in each of these processes.

1. checking a book out of your campus library
2. picking an advisor
3. registering with a minimum of trouble
4. buying a used car
5. studying for an exam
6. failing an exam (be humorous)
7. Christmas shopping at the last minute
8. editing
9. interviewing for a job
10. dieting successfully

Transitions That Signal Chronological Order

If the supporting details in your process analysis are arranged in chronological order, you should signal that order with transitions (see p. 24). Notice that in "Making Money with a Garage Sale," the writer uses several transitions to signal chronological order:

First, you must gather . . .
Next—and this is very important . . .
Now for the most important part . . .
Finally, pamper your customers.

Practice 4.14

The following process analysis was written by a student. Study it and then answer the questions that follow.

How to Make a Foul Shot

Because a basketball game can be won or lost at the foul line, a player must learn how to make a foul shot. First, the player should stand at the center of the foul line with feet apart and weight evenly distributed. The stance should feel comfortable and balanced. The basketball should be held with the shooting hand at the back of the ball with the fingers spread. The nonshooting hand should be at the side of the ball to help guide the shot. Next, the shooter must focus hard on the front of the basketball rim. With knees bent, the elbow of the shooting arm held in, and the shooting wrist slightly bent backward, the player pushes the ball from in front of the face up toward the basket. To do this, the player should extend the shooting arm rapidly but smoothly while snapping the wrist forward. The shooter must be careful not to stop too soon but instead follow through with the movement of the shooting arm and wrist until the ball is completely released and headed for the basket for that all-important point.

On a separate sheet, answer the following questions about "How to Make a Foul Shot":

1. What is the topic sentence of "How to Make a Foul Shot"? What process will be analyzed? Why is it important to understand the process?

2. Where does the writer explain how to perform a step?

3. Where does the writer say what *not* to do?

4. In what order are the supporting details arranged?

5. The writer uses two transitions to signal chronological order. What are they?

6. Are all the steps in the process clearly explained?

7. Are all the supporting details relevant to the topic sentence?

8. Does the essay come to a satisfying close? Explain.

CHECKLIST FOR A PROCESS ANALYSIS _____

Before submitting your process analysis, be sure you can answer yes to the following questions:

1. Do you have a topic sentence that mentions the process and why the reader should understand the process?

2. Have you included every step in the process?

3. Where necessary, have you explained how steps are performed?

4. If it is important, have you explained what *not* to do?

5. Have you used specific nouns, verbs, and modifiers?

6. Are supporting details in a chronological or other suitable order? Have you signaled the order with transitions?

7. Are all of your details clearly relevant to the topic sentence?

8. Does your paragraph have a satisfying closing?

Writing Assignment

For your process analysis paragraph, you have your choice of topics:

1. Use one of the processes in *Practice 4.13*. For three of these, you have already listed the steps performed.

2. Use one of the topic sentences in *Practice 4.12*.

3. Pick something you do better than many people and describe that process.

4. Explain how to impress someone on the first date.

5. See p. 461 for an assignment based on "How Dictionaries Are Made."

☐ TIPS FOR PLANNING YOUR ☐ PROCESS ANALYSIS

1. Write an early version of your topic sentence that mentions the process and why the reader should understand the process.

2. List every step performed in the process—do not leave anything out.

3. Is there anything the reader should be careful not to do? If so, add that to your list.

4. Number the steps in your list in the order they are performed.

DEFINITION

A *definition* explains the meaning of something. Many times, it explains the meaning of a complex term or idea. For example to help explain the United States's political system, a political science text can define *electoral college* in one or more paragraphs. Sometimes a writer wants to express his or her personal meaning for a term. For example, stress can mean different things to different people. To express *your* meaning, you can define stress from a college student's point of view.

For an example of definition in a published essay, see "On Being 17, Bright, and Unable to Read" on p. 441.

A Sample Definition Paragraph

The following definition, written by a student, will be used to illustrate several points about writing definition. As you read, notice that the paragraph presents the writer's personal meaning.

> A definition paragraph explains a complex term or the writer's personal meaning of a word.

The Crazed Coupon Clipper

The crazed coupon clipper is a fanatic. Fired up at the prospect of saving a few quarters, this species accumulates hundreds, even thousands, of cents-off coupons. Strangely though, it does not even matter if the clipper can use the products the coupons are good for. My father has been a crazed clipper for years. His coupon envelope marked "pets" is so fat with coupons for dog biscuits, cat food, and flea collars you would think we had dozens of cats and dogs running around. The funny thing is, we have not owned a dog, cat, or any other four-legged animal since I was born. While the clipper may appear to be organized (having coupons arranged alphabetically in labeled envelopes), do not be fooled—every crazed clipper has grocery bags, shoe boxes, and crates hidden at the back of the closet with unfiled, largely expired coupons jammed in. The clipper is harmless for the most part; however, the species can be dangerous when turned loose in a market that offers double-coupon savings. Stay out of these places, for dozens of crazed clippers will be there with glazed eyes and fistsful of coupons. So ecstatic are they at the prospect of doubling their savings that they race their carts frantically about, snatching products in a savings frenzy. More than once, normal shoppers have been run over by clippers crazed by the thought of saving twice as much. So beware! If ever you open your newspaper only to find rectangular holes where the news used to be, you no doubt have a crazed coupon clipper under your roof.

The Topic Sentence

The topic sentence for a definition paragraph includes the term being defined (this is your topic) and a main characteristic of what is being defined (this is your view of the topic). Take another look at the topic sentence of "The Crazed Coupon Clipper":

> The crazed coupon clipper is a fanatic.

The writer's topic is the *coupon clipper;* this is the term to be defined. The main characteristic of the coupon clipper is that he or she is a *fanatic;* this is the writer's view of the topic.

> The topic sentence of a definition paragraph includes the term being defined and a main characteristic of the term.

Practice 4.15

Write topic sentences for paragraphs defining each of the terms given. Be sure to mention a main characteristic of what you are defining. The first one is done as an example.

1. optimism *Optimism is the ability to think positively even when things look the worst.*

2. the health nut _____

3. exam anxiety _____

4. courage _____

5. an intellectual _____

6. the Monday blues _____

Supporting Details

The supporting details for a definition paragraph show that the main characteristic of the term is what you say it is. One way to show this is to use description. "The Crazed Coupon Clipper" relies on description to show what the clipper is like in a store that offers double-coupon savings.

Examples can also be part of your supporting details. In "The Crazed Coupon Clipper," the writer's father is an example that shows the clipper clips coupons for products that are not used.

If your audience has a misconception about what you are defining, you may explain what something is *not.* For example, when defining *patriotism,* you may explain that patriotism is *not* a blind love of every aspect of a country. After this explanation, you can go on to explain what patriotism *is:* loving a country while disliking its faults and trying to correct them. In "The Crazed Coupon Clipper," the writer explains that the clipper is not really as organized as he or she appears.

In addition, try not to write a definition that sounds as if it really came from a dictionary. The definition should be in your personal writing style. Also, avoid stating the obvious. For example, if you are defining *situation comedy,* do not say that it is a kind of television program. Finally, do not use a term in its own definition. If you are defining a *floppy disk,* do not say, "A floppy disk is a disk that. . . ."

> The supporting details for a definition paragraph show that the main characteristic is what you say it is.

> The supporting details may include description and examples.

> The supporting details may mention what something is *not.*

> Do not write a definition that sounds like it came from a dictionary, and do not state the obvious or use a term in its own definition.

Practice 4.16: Working Together

Complete this practice with some classmates. Assume you are writing a definition paragraph with this topic sentence:

Writer's block is the curse of the writing student.

1. List three ideas that could be used for supporting details. (If you are stuck for ideas to complete numbers 1–4, try one or more of the idea-generation techniques.)

   _____

   _____

   _____

2. List an example that could be used to develop one of the ideas you wrote for number 1. _____

   _____

3. List three details that could be included in a description of a student with writer's block. _____

   _____

   _____

4. Mention one thing that writer's block is *not*. _____

_____

Practice 4.17

The following definition paragraph was written by a student. Read it and answer the questions that follow.

Christmas Spirit

Christmas spirit is a joyous feeling that results from the anticipation of a wondrous celebration. It is a feeling of excitement as you walk through the mall and realize Christmas carols are filtering through the speaker system. It is the tingle you get when your eyes catch the snow and tinsel shimmering in store windows draped in red and green. When you step outside and feel the brisk, cold wind brush your face, Christmas spirit is the hope for a white December 25, the hope for the beauty of quarter-sized snowflakes floating down to blanket a frozen earth. Christmas spirit is the joy of helping people. It is Mr. Jones shoveling the walk of an elderly neighbor or Mrs. Smith distributing loaves of her Christmas bread to shelters and halfway houses or children collecting toys for the poor. No, Christmas spirit has not been commercialized as some say. It is the special excitement people feel as they look forward to the one day of the year devoted exclusively to peace and love.

On a separate sheet, answer the following questions about "Christmas Spirit":

1. What is the topic sentence of "Christmas Spirit"? According to the topic sentence, what term will be defined, and what is the main characteristic of the term?
2. Which two sentences provide description?
3. Which sentence provides examples?
4. Give three examples of specific word choice.
5. Where does the writer explain what Christmas spirit is *not?*

6. Has the writer avoided obvious statements? Has the writer avoided a dictionary style?

7. Are the supporting details adequate? Explain.

8. Are all the details relevant? Explain.

9. Does the paragraph come to a satisfying close? Explain.

CHECKLIST FOR A DEFINITION PARAGRAPH _____

Before submitting your definition, be sure you can answer yes to every question on the following list:

1. Do you have a topic sentence that mentions the term to be defined and a main characteristic of the term?

2. Have you provided enough supporting details to convince your reader that the main characteristic is what you say it is?

3. Have you used description and examples where these would be helpful?

4. If necessary, have you explained what the term is *not?*

5. Have you avoided stating the obvious? Have you avoided a dictionary style?

6. Have you used specific nouns, verbs, and modifiers?

7. Are all your details relevant to your term and its main characteristic?

8. Does your paragraph have a satisfying closing?

Writing Assignment

Here is a choice of topics for your definition paragraph:

1. Define one of the terms in *Practice 4.15.* If you choose one of these, you already have a draft of a topic sentence.

2. Define writer's block. If you choose this, you may be able to use some of the ideas you developed for *Practice 4.16.*

3. Define a college student.   7. Define jock.

4. Define pressure.   8. Define freshman.

5. Define blind date.   9. Define friendship.

6. Define working mother.   10. Define tacky.

☐   **TIPS FOR PLANNING YOUR**   ☐
DEFINITION PARAGRAPH

1. Brainstorming may help you come up with ideas. In particular, the following questions may be helpful:

    A. What are three characteristics of what I am defining?

    B. What, if anything, can I describe?

    C. What examples can I provide?

    D. What is my topic *not?*

    E. What is my topic similar to?

    F. What is my topic different from?

    G. What does it look like? Sound like? Feel like?

    H. Why is it valuable?

    I. What can it be used for?

2. Write an early version of your topic sentence. Be sure it mentions what will be defined and a main characteristic.

3. Make a list of ideas you will include and number them in the order they will appear in your draft.

4. See p. 2 for additional idea-generation techniques.

COMPARISON AND CONTRAST

> A comparison shows similarities; a contrast shows differences; a comparison and contrast shows both similarities and differences.

A paragraph that *compares* shows how two things are similar, a paragraph that *contrasts* shows how two things are different, and a paragraph that *compares and contrasts* shows both similarities and differences.

Comparison and contrast are important because they often help us decide which of two people or things is better. For example, by comparing and contrasting two political candidates, we can decide who to vote for. By comparing and contrasting two cars, we can decide which to buy. Comparison and contrast also help us better understand the items compared and contrasted. For example, by comparing and contrasting the workings of the human brain and a computer (as author Robert Jastrow has done), we can better understand the operation of both.

For examples of comparison and contrast in published essays, see "If You Had to Kill Your Own Hog" on p. 471, "How Dictionaries Are Made" on p. 459, and "Abortion, Right and Wrong," on p. 478.

Sample Comparison and Contrast Paragraphs

The following paragraphs were written by students. They will be used to illustrate several points about comparison and contrast.

Shake the Image of the Sheik

The Arab sheik is nothing like his media image. As a result of media portrayal, the sheik is commonly considered to have a protruding paunch, bulging eyes, and a hawk-like nose. He sports a bushy mustache and headdress. The sheik is typically thought to be self-indulgent and cruel to others. He is thought to live a life of luxury and lust amid oil wells and harems of beautiful women. His days are said to be spent in idleness and his nights in reckless passion. In reality, the sheik is very different. Physically, his looks and dress vary. He can be dressed in western clothes. He can be thin, with small eyes and flat stomach. He is a dedicated man, who often sacrifices much to his people. He is a Muslim religious leader, scholar, or head of an Arab family, clan, tribe, or village, respected for his leadership abilities and wisdom. In the ancient Middle East, the sheik was the one that people went to for advice. He was the head of the institutions that controlled law, religion, and education. He was not and is not the arrogant womanizer who struts around the desert, leading a life of leisure and comfort. That image was created by Hollywood directors. It is unfair and untrue.

College and Professional Football Coaches

In some ways college and professional football coaches are alike, but in other ways they are different. Both kinds of coaches are under a great deal of pressure to win, and both can lose their jobs if they do not. Similarly, both kinds of coaches must be experienced. There are very few young head coaches. Usually both college and professional coaches spend years as assistant coaches learning from other coaches. Of the many differences between college and professional coaches, none is greater than coaching style. The college coach is conservative. He will continually run his fullback up the middle rather than engage in any razzle-dazzle. On the other hand, the pro coach is on a never-ending mission to surprise and confuse the opposing team. College coaching can be more of a struggle than pro coaching.

The college coach will not always have outstanding material, which makes it harder to put together a winning team. The pro coach, however, knows that his players are among the best. Finally, a big difference between the college and pro coach is the job itself. The pro coach coaches, and that is pretty much it. In contrast, the college coach must coach and recruit promising high school players, convince alumni to make contributions, and maintain good relationships with classroom teachers. Although there are similarities, the differences make the college coach's job harder than the professional coach's.

The Topic Sentence

The topic sentence for comparison and contrast includes the writer's topic and view. It can also indicate whether the paragraph will compare, contrast, or both.

The topic sentence for comparison and contrast includes the writer's topic and view of the topic. The topic is the items to be compared and/or contrasted. The view can be how the writer feels about the items. Take another look at the topic sentence of "Shake the Image of the Sheik":

The Arab sheik is nothing like his media image.

The writer's topic is the Arab sheik. The writer's view is that there is a difference between the media image of the sheik and the real sheik.

Now look at the topic sentence of "College and Professional Football Coaches":

In some ways college and professional football coaches are alike, but in other ways they are different.

The topic is college and professional football coaches. The writer's view is that they are alike in some ways and different in others.

Notice that both topic sentences indicate whether the paragraph will compare, contrast, or both. The first topic sentence makes clear that the writer will contrast, and the second topic sentence makes clear that the writer will compare and contrast.

Practice 4.18: Working Together

With some classmates, write a topic sentence for each subject that presents both topic and view. Try to indicate whether the paragraph will compare, contrast, or both. The first one is done as an example.

1. two friends *My friend Jeremy is always optimistic, but Phyllis constantly expects the worst.*

2. two teachers _____

   _____

3. two situation comedies _____

   _____

4. two ways of studying _____

   _____

5. two birthday celebrations you have had _____

   _____

6. high school and college _____

   _____

Supporting Details

When you compare, your supporting details explain the ways the items are alike; when you contrast, your supporting details explain the ways the items are different; when you compare and contrast, your supporting details explain the points of similarity and the points of difference.

Be careful, however, to avoid statements of the obvious. For example, if you contrast your history and science teachers, it would be silly to note that they teach different subjects.

> Avoid statements of the obvious.

Ordering Supporting Details

Your supporting details can be ordered two ways: subject-by-subject or point-by-point. In a *subject-by-subject pattern,* you say everything about your first subject and then you go on to say everything about your second subject. "Shake the Image of the Sheik" follows this pattern. First the writer explains the popular image, and then she explains what the Sheik actually *is* like. An outline of this paragraph using the subject-by-subject pattern looks like this:

A subject-by-subject pattern discusses first one subject and then the other. The same points should be discussed for both subjects.

I. Popular image
   A. Appearance
   B. Personality
   C. Life style
II. Reality
   A. Appearance
   B. Personality
   C. Life style

Notice that the writer discusses the same points (appearance, personality, life style) for both subjects. You too should discuss the same points for both subjects.

The ideas in the contrast part of "College and Professional Football Coaches" are ordered in a *point-by-point pattern.* A point is made about one subject and then it is made about the second subject. Another point is made about the first subject and then it is made about the second, and so on. Here is an outline of the contrast portion of "College and Professional Football Coaches":

The point-by-point pattern alternates between subjects. The points discussed for one subject should also be discussed for the other.

I. Coaching style
   A. The college coach
   B. The professional coach
II. Amount of struggle
   A. The college coach
   B. The professional coach
III. The job itself
   A. The professional coach
   B. The college coach

To compare and contrast, first mention the similarities and then explain the differences using a point-by-point pattern.

Notice that with the point-by-point pattern, too, the writer must treat the same points about both subjects.

If you want to discuss both similarities and differences, you can do what the writer of "College and Professional Football Coaches" does. You can briefly mention the similarities and then go on to explain the differences using a point-by-point pattern.

Practice 4.19

1. Read "Let's Hear It for Tradition" on p. 117. The supporting details are arranged in a point-by-point pattern. To understand this pattern better, complete the following outline of the paragraph.

   I. Number of people

      A. In the past

      B. Now

   II. Food preparation

      A.

      B.

   III. Opening gifts

      A.

      B.

   IV.

      A.

      B.

2. Read "College Is Not What I Expected" on p. 116. The supporting details are arranged in a subject-by-subject pattern. To understand this pattern better, complete the following outline.

   I. What college was expected to be

      A. Fun

      B. Meeting people

      C.

   II. What college really is

      A.

      B.

      C.

Transitions That Signal Comparison and Contrast

When you write a comparison and contrast paragraph, you may need to draw on transitions that signal comparison and contrast. These appear in the following chart:

Transition Chart

Transitions that Signal Comparison	similarly, in like manner, likewise, in the same way

The college football coach must have years of experience before he becomes a head coach. *Similarly,* a professional football coach is an assistant coach for a long time before taking on the top spot.

Transitions that Signal Contrast	in contrast, however, on the other hand, on the contrary, conversely, but

I thought motherhood would be nothing but bliss. *However,* I soon learned it is a trying time.

Practice 4.20

There are three transitions of contrast and one transition of comparison in "College and Professional Football Coaches" (p. 111). On a separate sheet, write the sentences that contain these transitions; underline each transition.

Practice 4.21

The following paragraphs were written by students. Read them and answer the questions that follow.

College Is Not What I Expected

Now that I have been a college student for half a year, I can say that college is not what I thought it would be. After being accepted at YSU, I thought about all the fun I would have living away from home. I figured I would meet a lot of new people and do a lot of new things. I never had much trouble with my high school classes, so I did not think college work would be too tough. After being here a short time, I know I was wrong. I have not had much fun yet. Most of the night life centers around bars, and I am not much of a drinker. I have been to a few parties, but everyone seems to know everyone else, and no one knows me. I usually stand around with my roommate, and usually we go home early without meeting anyone. Most of the time I cannot go out anyway because I have to study so much. The homework keeps me up late at night, and still it is a struggle to get C's. Everyone tells me I need more time to adjust to college life, so maybe things will look up for me soon, and college will be more like I expected it to be.

Let's Hear It for Tradition

The Christmas gatherings we used to have at my grandparents' house were much better than the celebrations I now have at my house. It used to be that all the aunts, uncles, and cousins gathered for a festive reunion. Now the gathering is just my husband, my children, and me. In the past, every family brought a tasty dish, so no one had too much work to do. Now I spend days knocking myself out making turkey with all the trimmings. My aunts used to bake scrumptious cobblers and pies to go with all the traditional holiday cookies. Somehow my children's iced trees and stars do not compare, although they are special in their own right. At my grandparents' there was a ritual for opening gifts that took the whole afternoon. Everyone took turns opening one gift at a time. This stretched out the excitement and allowed everyone a chance to ooh and aah. In contrast, my children rip into their gifts in record time without savoring anything. There was conversation and laughter at my grandparents'. Everyone tried to catch up on what had happened since the last gathering. Now, however, we talk about what we talk about any other day. I miss the old gatherings. However, Grandma and Grandpa and most of the aunts and uncles are gone, and the rest of us are too scattered around the country to have many gatherings.

1. What is the topic sentence for each paragraph? What does each topic sentence mention as the topic and the view of the topic? Do the topic sentences indicate the writer will compare, contrast, or do both?

2. For each paragraph indicate whether the detail is arranged in a subject-by-subject pattern or point-by-point pattern.

3. In each paragraph, are the points discussed for one subject also discussed for the other?

4. Does either paragraph include statements of the obvious?

5. In "Let's Hear It for Tradition," what transitions signal contrast?

6. Does either paragraph have a problem with adequate or relevant detail? Explain.

7. Do the paragraphs come to a satisfying close? Explain.

CHECKLIST FOR COMPARISON AND CONTRAST

Before submitting your paragraph, be sure you can answer yes to every question on the following list:

1. Do you have a topic sentence that mentions your topic (what will be compared and/or contrasted) and your view of your topic?

2. Have you avoided obvious comparisons and contrasts?

3. Have you ordered your details with either a point-by-point or subject-by-subject pattern?

4. Have you discussed the same points for both subjects?

5. Have you used transitions, especially of comparison and contrast, where these are needed?

6. Have you used specific nouns, verbs, and modifiers?

7. Are all supporting details relevant to the topic sentence?

8. Does your paragraph have a satisfying closing?

Writing Assignment

To keep your paragraph manageable, explain just the differences between two subjects. If you want to treat similarities or both similarities and differences, speak to your instructor first. Also, be sure to keep your focus narrow. You probably cannot discuss all the differences in a single paragraph, so limit yourself to a few key ones.

Here is a choice of topics:

1. Use one of the topic sentences you wrote for *Practice 4.18.*

2. Contrast any of the following:

    two ways of dieting

    two ways to ask for a date

two ways to study

two automobiles

two situation comedy characters

two soap opera characters

the techniques of two athletes who play the same sport

3. Contrast the way something is (or was) with the way you thought it would be.

□ TIPS FOR PLANNING YOUR   □
COMPARISON AND CONTRAST

1. List every comparison and/or contrast you can think of without evaluating the worth of your ideas. Then go back and circle the ones you want to use. Remember, you cannot mention everything, so stick with the key points. (If you have trouble thinking of ideas, try some of the idea-generation techniques.)

2. Write an early version of your topic sentence that mentions what will be compared and/or contrasted and your view.

3. Outline your ideas. Using the point-by-point pattern, or the subject-by-subject pattern, modeled on p. 114. If you are mentioning many points, a point-by-point pattern may be easier for your reader to follow.

4. Rather than outlining your ideas, place each of your points on a separate index card. Arrange the cards in either a point-by-point or a subject-by-subject pattern and write your draft from the cards.

CAUSE-AND-EFFECT ANALYSIS

A *cause-and-effect analysis,* explains why something happens (causes) or the results of an event (effects). Because people need to understand why events occur and the effects of those events, cause and effect analysis occurs frequently. For example, a biology textbook may explain why leaves change color in the fall, and a magazine article may explain why women live longer than men. Similarly, a newspaper editorial may predict the effects of passing a tax bill, or an advertisement may explain the effects of using a particular medication.

> A cause-and-effect analysis explains the causes of something or the effects of something.

For examples of cause-and-effect analysis in published essays, see "On Being 17, Bright, and Unable to Read" on p. 441, "Black Men and

Public Space" on p. 481, and "What Mothers Teach Their Daughters" on p. 476.

Sample Cause-and-Effect Analyses

Each of the following cause-and-effect analyses was written by a student. The first paragraph explains causes, and the second explains effects. These paragraphs will be used to illustrate points about cause-and-effect analysis.

Fitness and the Media

The media are causing people to feel dissatisfied with their bodies. At any time of the day or night, a half dozen aerobics or weight training programs are on television. The people on these shows do not have normal bodies—they have super bodies. Normal channel surfing folks see these people and instantly feel inadequate. Commercials are no better. They are loaded with bodies beautiful selling Nordic Tracks, exercise videos, and health spa memberships. One look at these people and a perfectly healthy, reasonably fit person feels hopelessly out of shape. Leafing through a magazine does not bring any relief, either. The pages are filled with ads for Slimfast and articles about how to cut fat. Of course, all are illustrated by bodies with 0% body fat, so the reader, no matter how fit and trim, feels like a whale. It is time the media bombardment stopped because it is causing people with perfectly fine bodies to feel dissatisfied with themselves.

What Happened When I Quit Smoking

When I quit smoking two years ago, I was miserable. First of all, I gained fifteen pounds. As a result, I looked terrible, and I was like a sausage in a casing when I wore my clothes. Even worse, I was so irritable no one could stand to be near me. I snapped at people and picked fights with my best friend. Once I screamed at my girlfriend and called her a nag when she reminded me to go buy my mother a birthday present. I did not mean it, but she spent the rest of the night in tears. For the first month, I was actually hallucinating. I would turn suddenly, thinking I heard a sound, or jump up startled, feeling like something clammy had touched me. At night I would wake up in a cold sweat after dreaming about smoking a Winston. It has been two years since I have had a cigarette, and I am in much better shape now, but I still have some weight to lose and in social situations I still get a little jumpy.

The Topic Sentence

The topic sentence for a cause-and-effect analysis can mention your topic and whether you are treating causes or effects. For example, look again at the topic sentence of "Fitness and the Media":

The media are causing people to feel dissatisfied with their bodies.

The writer's topic is the media. The topic sentence indicates that causes will be explained since it is stated that the media are *causing* people to feel dissatisfied with their bodies.

> The topic sentence mentions the topic and suggests whether causes or effects will be explained.

Now look at the topic sentence of "What Happened When I Quit Smoking":

When I quit smoking two years ago, I was miserable.

Here the topic is the time the writer quit smoking. The words *I was miserable* present an effect that will be explained.

Practice 4.22

For each of the following subjects, write a topic sentence for a cause-and-effect analysis. Then indicate whether the paragraph will explain *causes* or *effects*. The first one is done as an example. (If you cannot think of ideas, try one or more of the idea-generation techniques.)

1. homelessness *Both economic and social factors can lead to homelessness.*

2. losing a job _____

   _____

3. math anxiety _____

   _____

4. moving to a new city _____

   _____

5. working while attending school _____

_____

6. teenage pregnancy _____

_____

Supporting Details

> The statement of cause or effect is a general statement that should be followed by one or more specific statements. The specific statements can be explanation, examples, description, or narration.

Each time you mention a cause or an effect, think of that sentence as a general statement that must be followed by one or more specific statements (see p. 68 for a discussion of following general statements with specific ones). The specific statements can be explanation, illustration, description, or narration. For example, look again at "Fitness and the Media." The first cause is given in the general statement, "At any time of the day or night, a half dozen aerobics or weight training programs are on television." This is followed by specific explanation that the people on these shows make others feel inadequate.

Now look again at "What Happened When I Quit Smoking." The general statement of the first effect is gaining fifteen pounds. This is followed by the specific description of looking like a sausage in a casing. Sometimes a general statement of cause or effect is followed by a brief narration. This is the case when the writer follows the general statement of being irritable with the story of making his girlfriend cry. Examples, too, can follow a general statement of cause or effect. Notice that after the general statement of hallucinations as an effect, the writer gives a specific example of a hallucination.

Practice 4.23: Working Together

Complete this practice with some classmates. After each topic sentence, write one cause or one effect (whichever is appropriate) in a general statement. Then note a specific point that could be made after the general statement. The first one is done as an example. (If you need help discovering ideas, try the idea-generation techniques.)

1. Our football team is doing poorly for three reasons.

general statement: *Many of our starters are inexperienced freshmen.*

specific point: *Nichols, the quarterback; Sanders, the end; Zanders and Michaelson in the backfield are all first-year players.*

2. Jan is failing history, and no one is surprised.

   general statement: _____

   _____

   specific point: _____

   _____

3. The rate of teenage drinking has increased for a number of reasons.

   general statement: _____

   _____

   specific point: _____

   _____

4. Owning a pet can be beneficial.

   general statement: _____

   _____

   specific point: _____

   _____

5. Several benefits will come from raising teacher salaries.

   general statement: _____

   _____

   specific point: _____

   _____

6. If the school levy is not passed, the result will be disastrous.

   general statement: _____

   _____

specific point:_____

_____

Transitions That Signal Effect

These transitions signal that one thing is the result of another:

as a result	hence	because
consequently	therefore	then
thus	for this reason	

Let's look again at these sentences from "What Happened When I Quit Smoking": "First of all, I gained fifteen pounds. *As a result,* I looked terrible. . . ." The italicized transition signals that what comes after it is a result of what comes before it. If your paragraph explains effects, you will probably use some of the transitions in the preceding list.

Practice 4.24

Here are two cause-and-effect analyses written by students. Read them and answer the questions that follow.

Why Children Grow Up Too Fast

The reasons children become sexually active at an early age are clear. For one thing, there is a great deal of peer pressure for sexual experimentation. I know one fourteen-year-old who ran around with sixteen- and seventeen-year-olds. The older kids made it clear that to be accepted, the fourteen-year-old would have to demonstrate her maturity by sleeping with a particular seventeen-year-old. Parents are also a contributing factor. Parents are now more open with their sexual displays and speech. They tell dirty jokes in front of children and tease about sex in front of them. Parents are also more lenient. They are letting their children wear makeup, date, and wear mature fashions at a younger age, all of which contribute to a child's growing up faster. Finally, the greater sexual explicitness of rock lyrics has caused children to mature faster. These lyrics teach kids that sex is expected and virginity is outdated. Thus, it is no surprise that today's youth are engaging in sex at an early age.

Raising the Driving Age

Recently, there has been some discussion about raising the driving age from sixteen to seventeen, and perhaps even eighteen; however, I believe that raising the driving age would have negative consequences. First of all, many teenagers hold jobs that require them to drive distances to get to work. If sixteen-year-olds cannot drive, they cannot work, and if they cannot work, then they cannot bring extra income into the family. This could create a financial hardship in some cases. Furthermore, teens who do not work are more likely to get into trouble because they have too much time on their hands. You might think that parents, particularly mothers, could drive their teenagers to work, but both mothers and fathers are working these days and unavailable to drive their children around. Also, because both parents work now, teenage drivers are a real help. The working mother, in particular, appreciates having a sixteen-year-old around to help with errands. Take away the sixteen-year-old's license and the already overworked working mother has an even harder time. Finally, if the sixteen-year-old cannot drive, then dating becomes difficult. Teenagers are supposed to date. It is a part of the maturation process. Yet modern dating requires a car to get to malls, theatres, restaurants, and parties. Without a license, the sixteen-year-old would be denied this important part of growing up. Yes, teenage drivers have accidents, but they are often because of lack of experience, not age. A new seventeen-year-old driver is just as likely to have an accident as a sixteen-year-old. So, let's not take away the sixteen-year-old's ability to drive. Both the sixteen-year-old and the family would suffer.

On a separate sheet, answer the following questions about "Why Children Grow Up Too Fast" and "Raising the Driving Age":

1. Which paragraph explains causes and which explains effects?

2. What is the topic sentence for each paragraph? Which words mention the topic? Which words mention whether causes or effects will be explained?

3. In "Why Children Grow Up Too Fast," which sentences present general statements of cause? In "Raising the Driving Age," which sentences present general statements of effect?

4. Are the general statements followed by specific ones?

5. In "Why Children Grow Up Too Fast," one general statement is followed by an example. What is that example?

6. Cite two examples of transitions that signal effect.

7. Are there any problems with adequate or relevant detail? Explain.

8. Do the paragraphs come to a satisfying close? Explain.

CHECKLIST FOR CAUSE-AND-EFFECT ANALYSIS

Before submitting your cause-and-effect analysis, be sure you can answer yes to every question on the following list:

1. Do you have a topic sentence that mentions your topic and whether you will explain causes or effects?

2. Are all your general statements of cause or effect followed by specific explanation, example, narration, or description?

3. Where needed, have you used transitions to signal effect and transitions to signal addition?

4. Have you used specific nouns, verbs, and modifiers?

5. Are all your supporting details relevant to your topic sentence?

6. Does your paragraph have a satisfying closing?

Writing Assignment

Here are possible topics for your cause-and-effect analysis. Remember to settle on causes or effects; do not try to explain both.

1. Use one of the topic sentences you wrote for *Practice 4.22.*

2. Explain what would happen if (you fill in the blank). For example, you can explain what would happen if tuition were lowered, if there were no required courses, if smoking were illegal, if public schools were in session eleven months, and so forth.

3. Explain how attending college has affected you.

4. Explain what causes people to drop out of high school.

5. See p. 444 for an assignment based on "On Being 17, Bright, and Unable to Read."

CLASSIFICATION

A *classification* places items in groups according to some principle. For example, colleges can be classified or grouped according to their location, according to their size, according to their course offerings, or according to how expensive they are. To classify cars, you might identify these groups: high-performance cars, luxury cars, and family cars. Items are placed in a group because they share characteristics. Thus, all cars in the high-performance group have similar features (such as engine size and the ability to travel fast); all cars in the luxury group have similar features (such as leather seats and electronic dashboards); and all cars in the family car group have similar features (such as seating for six or more and good gas mileage). Classification is important because it helps us sort and group things. To appreciate its importance, think of how hard it would be to find a book in the library without a classification system.

> A classification paragraph places items in groups according to some principle.

For an example of classification in a published essay, see "Cinematypes" on p. 463.

A Sample Classification Paragraph

The following classification paragraph, written by a student, will be used to illustrate several points about classification.

Different Kinds of Shoppers

After working at K-Mart for over a year, I have come to know well the four different kinds of shoppers. The first shopper is the browser. Browsers have endless amounts of time to waste. Nonchalantly, they wander around my department picking up every item that catches the eye. Unfortunately, browsers never put things back in the right place, so I have to straighten stock when they leave. The browsers are also a pain because they want to look at every item locked in the showcase. Of course, after all this, the browsers leave without buying a thing. The dependent shoppers are also annoying. They have to be shown where everything is, including the items in front of their noses. Dependent shoppers never bother to look for anything. They walk through the front door, find a clerk, and ask him or her to get a dozen items. The hit-and-run shoppers are much easier to deal with. They are always frantic and rushed. They will buy anything, regardless of price, if they can get it fast. Price does not matter. One recent hit-and-runner raced in, asked breathlessly if he could pay for a stereo by check, picked out the first one he saw, and bought two of them. He wrote a check for over four hundred dollars as if it were $1.98 and raced out. Independent shoppers are the easiest to deal with. They want no part of sales clerks except for ringing up the sales. Independent shoppers find what they want on their own, put things back in the right places, and never ask questions. As far as I am concerned, this world needs more independent shoppers.

The Topic Sentence

> The topic sentence mentions the topic and indicates that things will be placed in groups.

The topic sentence for a classification paragraph presents the topic and includes words that let the reader know the paragraph will place things in groups. Look again at the topic sentence of "Different Kinds of Shoppers":

> After working at K-Mart for over a year, I have come to know well the four different kinds of shoppers.

This topic sentence indicates that the writer's topic is shoppers. The words "the four different kinds of shoppers" indicate that the paragraph will place things into groups (classify them).

Practice 4.25

The sentences below could be topic sentences for classification paragraphs. Underline the topic once and underline twice the words that indicate items will be placed in groups. The first one is done as an example.

1. <u>Three chief types</u> of <u>baby-sitters</u> can be identified by most mothers of small children.

2. All automobiles fall into one of three groups.

3. An athlete soon learns of the several kinds of coaches.

4. Four categories of employers exist in the workplace.

5. Most horror movies are one of three types.

6. Four ways to study for an exam are practiced by college students.

Supporting Details

Place things in groups according to *only one* principle. For example, you may group shoppers according to how hard they are to deal with (this is what the writer of "Different Kinds of Shoppers" has done), or you can group shoppers according to age, or you can group shoppers according to how carefully they shop. However, you cannot mix the groupings. You cannot discuss the careful shopper, the careless shopper, and the teenage shopper, for you would be using two different principles of classification.

When you develop your supporting details, think of each sentence that presents a particular group as a general statement that must be followed by specific statements. For example, look again at "Different Kinds of Shoppers." Each of the following sentences presents a group:

> Place items in groups according to a single principle of classification.

The first shopper is the browser.

The dependent shoppers are also annoying.

The hit-and-run shoppers are much easier to deal with.

Independent shoppers are the easiest to deal with.

> The sentence that mentions a particular group is a general statement that must be followed by specific statements that describe the group.

After each general statement that presents a group, specific statements explain what the members of the group are like.

Practice 4.26: Working Together

This exercise, which you can complete with classmates, will let you practice grouping according to a principle of classification. On a separate sheet, list things included in the broad category given. Then study your list and write down one principle of classification. Next state the groups that fit in the classification, and give items in the groups. More than one principle of classification will be possible, and you may not use every point in your list when you give the groups and items in the groups. The first one is done as an example.

1. kinds of examinations (list)

open book	*multiple choice*	*midterms*
take home	*true/false*	*finals*
in-class	*fill-in-the-blanks*	*fair*
essay	*hard*	*unfair*
objective	*opinion*	*evaluation*
definition	*easy*	*matching*

principle of classification *degree of difficulty*

group 1 *easy*

group 2 *moderately hard*

group 3 *hard*

items in group 1 *true/false, matching*

items in group 2 *multiple choice*

items in group 3 *essay, fill-in-the-blanks*

2. kinds of teachers (list on separate sheet)

principle of classification _____

group 1 _____

group 2 _____

group 3 _____

people in group 1_____

people in group 2_____

people in group 3_____

3. kinds of restaurants (list on separate sheet)

principle of classification _____

group 1 _____

group 2 _____

group 3 _____

items in group 1 _____

items in group 2 _____

items in group 3 _____

4. kinds of friends (list on separate sheet)

principle of classification _____

group 1 _____

group 2 _____

group 3 _____

people in group 1_____

people in group 2_____

people in group 3_____

Practice 4.27

After each topic sentence, list three classification groups. Then state the principle of classification. The first one is done as an example.

1. There are three kinds of dinner parties.

group 1 *formal* _____

group 2 *semiformal* _____

group 3 *casual*

principle of classification *degree of formality*

2. Bosses fall into one of three groups.

   group 1 _____

   group 2 _____

   group 3 _____

   principle of classification _____

3. It is possible to identify three kinds of birthday celebrations.

   group 1 _____

   group 2 _____

   group 3 _____

   principle of classification _____

4. A salesclerk is usually one of three types.

   group 1 _____

   group 2 _____

   group 3 _____

   principle of classification _____

5. Radio stations can be classified according to the audience they appeal to.

   group 1 _____

   group 2 _____

   group 3 _____

   principle of classification _____

6. A person can have one of three kinds of neighbors.

   group 1 _____

group 2 _____

group 3 _____

principle of classification _____

Practice 4.28

Study this classification paragraph written by a student and answer the questions that follow.

Three Kinds of Students

College students fall into three categories: the grinds, the goof-offs, and the well-adjusted. The grinds are easily recognized. They live for school, so they spend all their waking hours in pursuit of an education. You know them: they answer every question, they do every assignment, and they linger after class to discuss the lecture with the teacher. When not in class, they are in the library, and when not in the library, they are in the bookstore buying a 300-page book for extra-credit reading. The grinds always throw off the curve because they study so hard. The next group is the goof-offs. They are the ones in school to party hearty. You won't see them in class or in the library—they're too busy shooting pool in the student union or drinking suds in a local bar. As for the bookstore, well, the good-offs haven't found it yet because they haven't bought their books. The goof-offs are important to academic life because they help balance out the curve the grinds keep throwing off. Between the grinds and the goof-offs are the well-adjusted. They study and pull passing grades, but they know how to party, too. They might skip a good time to cram for finals, but they are known to party instead of study for a test that only counts 25 percent. The well-adjusted know life is short, so they take college seriously but know the importance of fun as well. Fortunately, on our campus the well-adjusted outnumber the grinds and goof-offs.

On a separate sheet, answer the following questions about "Three Kinds of Students":

1. What is the topic sentence? What is the topic? Which words mention that items will be placed in groups?
2. What is the principle of classification?
3. What general statements mention the particular groups?
4. Are there enough specific statements after the general statements?
5. Does the paragraph come to a satisfying close? Explain.

CHECKLIST FOR A CLASSIFICATION PARAGRAPH

Before submitting your classification, be sure you can answer yes to all the following questions:

1. Do you have a topic sentence that presents the topic and mentions that items will be placed in groups?
2. Have you classified according to a single principle?
3. Do you have general statements that mention each group?
4. Are your general statements followed by specific details?
5. Does your paragraph have a satisfying closing?

Writing Assignment

For your classification paragraph, you have a choice of topics:

1. Use one of the principles of classification in *Practice 4.26.*
2. Use one of the topic sentences in *Practice 4.27.* You may want to use the groups and principle of classification you developed when you completed this exercise.
3. Classify types of scary movies.
4. Classify types of sports fans.
5. Classify methods of studying.

□   TIPS FOR PLANNING YOUR   □
CLASSIFICATION PARAGRAPH

1. To decide on a principle of classification, list every way you can classify your subject. For example, if your subject is restaurants, you could list these ways to classify:

food   decor and atmosphere

service   price

patrons   location

Study your list and decide on your principle of classification.

2. Make columns on a sheet for each of the groups in your classification. For example, if you were classifying restaurants according to their food, you might have one column for fast food,
one for homestyle cooking, and one for gourmet food. In each
column list every characteristic you can think of, without paus-
ing to decide if your ideas are good or not.

3. Study your columns and cross out the ideas you do not want
to include. Decide which group you want to handle first, second, and third, and number the columns accordingly.

4. Write an early version of your topic sentence that includes your
topic and words that mention what you will classify.

PERSUASION

Persuasion, which aims to convince a reader to think or act a particular way, is a big part of our lives. Advertisements try to persuade
us to buy certain products, classmates try to persuade us to lend them
our biology notes, friends try to persuade us to vote for their favorite
candidates. Similarly, we try to persuade teachers to postpone exams,
friends to lend us their cars, and parents to send us more money.

> A persuasive para-
> graph aims to con-
> vince a reader to
> think or act a certain
> way.

For examples of persuasion in published essays, see "Green Frog
Skin" on p. 455, "If You Had to Kill Your Own Hog" on p. 471, and
"What Mothers Teach Their Daughters" on p. 476.

A Sample Persuasive Paragraph

The following persuasive paragraph, written by a student, will be
used to illustrate several points about persuasion.

Wear a Helmet

Every state should pass a law requiring motorcyclists to
wear helmets. First of all, helmets provide increased visibility. Motorcycles are sometimes hard to see, but the glare
from a helmet can help solve this problem. Many times I

have seen the flash of a helmet before I have seen the motorcycle itself. Because automobile drivers are not conditioned to look for motorcyclists, anything that increases the cyclist's visibility will improve safety. The main reason for requiring helmets is decreasing the number of deaths. As proof of this, I offer a friend of mine who swerved to miss a car that pulled out in front of him. As a result, my friend hit a ditch at sixty miles per hour. He had several broken bones and some horrendous bruises, but because he was wearing a helmet, he did not sustain a head injury that could have killed him. Another friend of mine was married only three months when a car pulled out in front of his '58 Harley. Wearing no helmet, he hit the car at thirty miles per hour. He flew off the bike and hit his head on the curb. After a week in a coma, he died. If he had worn a helmet, he might have lived. Because helmets increase visibility and provide protection, all motorcyclists should be required by law to wear them.

The Topic Sentence

The topic sentence for a persuasive paragraph includes the writer's topic and the writer's stand on the topic. Look again at the topic sentence of "Wear a Helmet":

> The topic sentence should include the writer's topic and the writer's stand on the topic.

Every state should pass a law requiring motorcyclists to wear helmets.

The writer's topic is helmets for motorcyclists. The writer's stand on the topic is that all states should require them.

Practice 4.29

1. For each of the following topic sentences, underline once the writer's topic and underline twice the writer's stand on the topic. The first one is done as an example.

   A. O'Cleary is without a doubt the best candidate for governor.

   B. Our elderly are not treated well.

   C. Students should have a say in the hiring and firing of teachers.

   D. Drug testing should be required of all professional athletes.

   E. Mandatory seat belt laws should be passed in all states.

   F. Everyone should take a year off after high school before starting college.

2. For each of the following subjects, write a topic sentence for a persuasive paragraph. The first one is done as an example.

   A. placing warnings on record albums with sexually explicit lyrics.

   It serves no useful purpose to put warnings on records with

   sexually explicit lyrics.

   B. mandatory recycling _____

   _____

   C. having to pass an exam to get a high school diploma

   _____

   _____

   D. sending women into combat _____

   _____

   E. the sale of handguns _____

   _____

   F. required courses in college_____

   _____

Supporting Details

The supporting details are the reasons for your stand. Since your goal is to persuade, you will include the reasons most likely to convince your reader to think or act the way you want.

Each time you present a reason, you are providing a general statement that must be followed by specific statements. In "Wear a Helmet," the reasons for the writer's view are presented in these general statements:

First of all, helmets provide increased visibility.

The main reason for requiring helmets is decreasing the number of deaths.

Each of the general statements is followed by specific statements. The first general statement is followed by the explanation that the helmets produce glare and by an example of the writer seeing this glare.

> The supporting details are the reasons for the writer's stand.

> Each reason is presented in a general statement that must be followed by specific statements.

> Details are often arranged in an emphatic order.

> Transitions that signal emphatic order are often used.

The second general statement is followed by two examples of what happened to the writer's friends.

Typically the supporting details are arranged in an emphatic order (see p. 20). That is, they gradually build up to the most convincing reason, which appears last. Writers often use transitions that signal this emphatic order. These transitions are discussed in Chapter 1, and now is a good time to review that material (see p. 24).

Practice 4.30: Working Together

With some classmates, list three reasons to support each topic sentence. The first one is done as an example. If you have trouble thinking of reasons, try listing, brainstorming, or freewriting.

1. Little League baseball places too much pressure on young children.

    A. *pressure to win*

    B. *pressure not to let teammates down*

    C. *pressure not to let parents down*

2. Beer and wine commercials should (or should not) be banned.

    A. _____

    B. _____

    C. _____

3. Places with over seventy-five employees should (or should not) have a day-care center.

    A. _____

    B. _____

    C. _____

4. Parents should (or should not) help select the textbooks used in public schools.

    A. _____

    B. _____

    C. _____

5. Alcohol should (or should not) be banned on college campuses.

A. _____

B. _____

C. _____

6. An eleven-month school year is (or is not) a good idea.

A. _____

B. _____

C. _____

Practice 4.31

Here is a persuasive paragraph written by a student. Read it and answer the questions that follow.

Nine Is Too Young

Where I live, nine-year-olds play organized football, but I think nine is too young. First, football consumes too much of a youngster's time. In August, when most kids are swimming, riding their bikes, or away at camp, the boys who play football are practicing three hours a day. It gets worse when school starts because the players have no time for homework. A more serious problem is that these children are not playing with kids their own age. The teams are decided according to weight. Thus, a boy who is a little chubby does not participate with kids his own age but older ones, who may not take kindly to having a younger kid around. I know my brother had this problem. He played with older guys, and all they did was tease him and call him "baby." The worst problem of all is that nine-year-old bodies cannot withstand the punishment the rough game of football subjects them to. Yes, the players wear equipment, but this does not fully protect, especially when the coaches are screaming, "Hit 'em hard and hit 'em low." This explains why my brother broke his leg in a preseason scrimmage game. If I were a parent, I would not allow my nine-year-old to play organized football.

On a separate sheet, answer the following questions:

1. What is the topic sentence of "Nine Is Too Young"? What is the writer's topic? The writer's stand on the topic?

2. Write the general statements that present the reasons for the writer's stand.

3. The first general statement that presents a reason is followed by: (pick one)

    A. explanation

    B. example

    C. explanation and example

4. The second general statement that presents a reason is followed by: (pick one)

    A. explanation

    B. example

    C. explanation and example

5. The third general statement that presents a reason is followed by: (pick one)

    A. explanation

    B. example

    C. explanation and example

6. Are the supporting details adequate? Explain.

7. In what order are the supporting details arranged? What words signal that order?

8. Does the paragraph have a satisfying closing? Explain.

CHECKLIST FOR A PERSUASIVE PARAGRAPH _____

Before submitting your persuasive paragraph, be sure you can answer yes to the following questions:

1. Do you have a topic sentence that presents your topic and your stand on the topic?

2. Have you presented each reason for your stand in its own general statement?

3. Have you followed each general statement with specific statements?

4. Are your supporting details arranged in an emphatic or other logical order?

5. If needed, have you used transitions to signal emphatic order?

6. Does your paragraph have a satisfying closing?

Writing Assignment

Here is a choice of topics for your persuasive paragraph:

1. Use topic sentence B, C, D, E, or F in number 1 of *Practice 4.29.*

2. Use one of the topic sentences you developed in response to number 2 of *Practice 4.29.*

3. Use one of the topic sentences from *Practice 4.30.* You may also use some or all of the reasons you developed when you completed this exercise.

4. Write a paragraph to persuade someone who graduated from your high school to attend your college.

5. Complete this sentence: _____
   is (or was) the best television show on the air. Try to persuade your reader of the truth of this statement.

6. Write a paragraph to convince your reader that a specific change is needed at your college (a change in registration, course requirements, dorm rules, parking facilities, etc.).

7. Write a paragraph to convince your reader that giving final examinations is a good (or bad) practice.

□ TIPS FOR PLANNING YOUR □ PERSUASIVE PARAGRAPH

1. Write an early version of your topic sentence that includes your topic and your stand on the topic.

2. List every reason you can think of to support your stand. Do not evaluate how good your ideas are; just write everything that occurs to you.

3. Study your list and cross out the reasons that are not very persuasive. Try to discover three good reasons for your view (or two reasons that you can develop well).

4. If possible, number your ideas in an emphatic order, saving your most persuasive reason for last.

5. After each general statement that presents a reason for your stand, ask yourself whether you can explain the reason, give an example, or tell a story.

THREE

THE ESSAY

CHAPTER

5

Writing an Essay

In college, you will often write compositions made of several paragraphs. These compositions are called *essays*. Because the essay has several paragraphs, it allows you to develop a topic in more detail than is possible in a single paragraph. When you write research papers, book reviews, reports, summaries, and other papers in your classes, you will use the essay form so you can treat your topic in the appropriate depth. To help you write essays, in this chapter you will learn:

An essay is a composition made of several paragraphs.

1. how to structure an essay
2. how to plan an essay
3. how other students have developed essays with narration, description, each of the kinds of exposition, and persuasion

143

THE PARTS OF AN ESSAY

An essay has three parts:

introduction

supporting paragraphs

conclusion

The parts of an essay are the introduction, supporting paragraphs, and conclusion.

Each part serves an important purpose. The *introduction* presents the writer's central point and stimulates the reader's interest in that point. The *supporting paragraphs* provide the details that support or develop the central point. The *conclusion* brings the essay to a satisfying finish.

THE PARTS OF AN ESSAY

Essay Part	*Function*
introduction	presents the writer's central point and stimulates interest in that point
supporting paragraphs (at least 2)	provide details to develop the central point
conclusion	brings essay to a satisfying close

You may have noticed the similarities between essay and paragraph parts. These similarities are shown in this chart.

Paragraph Part		*Function*		*Essay Part*
topic sentence	→	presents writer's central point	←	introduction
supporting details	→	develop writer's central point	←	supporting paragraphs
closing	→	brings writing to satisfying close	←	conclusion

A Sample Essay

The following essay, written by a student, illustrates the three essay parts. As a study aid, these parts are labeled in the margin.

Let's Pay College Athletes

College athletics is big business. A great deal of money is at stake, so colleges are under pressure to recruit the best players. To do so, they offer full and partial scholarships, hoping to lure players to their schools. However, rather than offer scholarships, colleges should pay the players a salary.

Introduction: The first three sentences create interest and the last presents the central point, which is that colleges should pay their athletes.

Athletes attending school on scholarships have a difficult time. To keep their scholarships, they must carry full-time loads. Because their sport demands so much of their time, they often find that they do not have enough time to study. As a result, their grades suffer. However, if athletes were paid, they could attend part-time and perform better academically because they were not stretched so thin.

Supporting paragraph: Sentence 1 presents the first point to support the central point (athletes on scholarships have a difficult time). The rest of the paragraph develops the point.

Some people say that without athletic scholarships many students could not afford to attend school, but this is not true. Paid athletes would simply use their salary to pay for tuition and books. Some athletes may even decide to save their salary and wait to attend school until they are finished playing ball. They could thus attend during the off-season or when their athletic careers are over, when they can really focus on their studies.

Supporting paragraph: Sentence 1 presents the second point to support the central point (without athletic scholarships, people could still afford to attend school). The rest of the paragraph develops the point.

Paying college athletes would also eliminate the people who are in college but who will never graduate. Some scholarship athletes were recruited to play ball, but they really are not college material. Paid athletes would not have to take classes, and we would be left with qualified students in the classroom, not athletes who are marking time for four years or trying to get a shot at the pros. Furthermore, the seats these athletes now occupy could go to academically qualified students who <u>do</u> want to graduate.

Supporting paragraph: Sentence 1 presents the third point to support the central point (eliminating athletes who will never graduate). The rest of the paragraph develops this point.

If we paid athletes, colleges would benefit financially. Attendance would be up at games because the level of play would be high. Also, tuition could be collected from the students who take the athletes' places in classrooms.

Supporting paragraph: Sentence 1 presents the fourth point to support the central point (colleges would benefit financially). The rest of the paragraph develops this point.

Awarding athletic scholarships is an old tradition. However, not all traditions stand the test of time. Now we should reconsider how we recruit athletes. Why not just pay them and let them decide if they want to use the money to attend college? Everyone would benefit.

Conclusion: This paragraph brings the essay to a satisfying finish.

The Introduction

> The lead-in creates interest in the essay, and the thesis indicates what the central point is.

The introduction has two purposes: it stimulates interest in the essay and it mentions what the central point will be. The portion of the introduction that stimulates interest is the *lead-in.* The portion that presents the central point is the *thesis.*

The Lead-in   To stimulate interest in the essay, a writer can approach a lead-in in several ways.

1. Give Background Information.   Tell your reader something he or she should know to understand the importance of your thesis or some of the detail in your essay.

On the first day of classes, students who applied for guaranteed student loans were inconvenienced by a lack of funds. It was clear that the loans should be distributed in advance.

The writer's central point is that guaranteed student loan funds should be distributed in advance. The first sentence is the lead-in, which provides the background fact that students did not have their loans on the first day of school.

2. Tell a Story.   A brief story can create interest in your essay and help prove the truth of the thesis.

When I was nine, I woke up in the middle of the night to the sounds of yelling. Terrified, I went to the top of the stairs and discovered my parents were screaming at each other. I sat there, confused and shaken, and unable to move. Then the horrible thing happened. I watched my father throw a vase at my mother. It missed her and shattered against the wall. However, from that moment on, I knew that married people should not stay married "for the sake of the children."

The thesis is that people should not stay married because they think divorce will hurt the children. To create interest in this point and help prove its truth, the writer tells a story from her childhood.

3. Ask a Question That Relates to Your Thesis.

Do you change from a nice, polite, helpful, caring individual into a monster when you park in one of the campus parking decks? If so, you are not alone, because parking in these structures brings out the worst in everybody.

The question in the lead-in relates to the writer's thesis: parking in the campus decks brings out the worst in people.

4. Describe a Person or a Scene.

My legs were shaky and weak. My whole body trembled, and my heart pounded violently in my throat. My palms were wet. The smell of chlorine sickened my stomach as the screams of children having fun and the hum of gossiping adults surrounded me. I knew I had to jump if I was ever going to overcome my fear of water.

The writer's thesis is his effort to overcome his fear of water by jumping in. The lead-in creates interest by describing how the writer felt just before the jump.

5. Use an Interesting Quotation.   However, be sure that the quotation is not an overused expression such as "Don't count your chickens before they hatch."

In "School Is Bad for Children," John Holt says that "any kid in class who, for whatever reason, would rather not be there not only doesn't learn anything himself but makes it a great deal tougher for anyone else." Because Holt is right, I believe we should abolish compulsory school attendance.

The writer's thesis is that we should abolish compulsory attendance. The quotation in the lead-in is not an overused saying likely to bore a reader.

The Thesis   The thesis is the sentence in the introduction that indicates what the central point of the essay is. The thesis should indicate the writer's topic and the writer's view of the topic. Look again at the thesis of "Let's Pay College Athletes":

However, rather than offer scholarships, colleges should pay the players a salary.

In this case, the writer's topic is paying players. The view of the topic is that colleges should do so.

Sometimes you can shape an effective thesis by mentioning your topic, view, and the main points you will make in your supporting paragraphs. Here is such a thesis:

> The thesis includes the writer's topic and the writer's view of the topic.

> To be effective, the thesis should have all the qualities of a topic sentence of a one-paragraph composition.

I love my brothers, but living with them is difficult because they eat all the food, they expect me to be their maid, and they treat me like a child.

This thesis lets the reader know the topic (living with the writer's brothers), the writer's view (it is difficult), and the ideas that will be developed in the supporting paragraphs (the brothers eat all the food, they want the writer to be their maid, and they treat the writer like a child).

In addition to noting the topic and view, an effective thesis is like the topic sentence of a one-paragraph composition in other ways. These are listed for you here:

1. The thesis should not be a statement of fact.
2. The thesis should not be too broad.
3. The thesis should not include vague words.
4. The thesis should not be a formal announcement.
5. The thesis should not mention the title.

Turn now to pages 55–56 and review these qualities.

Practice 5.1

On a separate sheet, write the thesis for each of the sample introductions on pages 146–147. For each thesis, underline the topic once, and underline the view of the topic twice.

Practice 5.2: Working Together

For each topic given, work with some classmates to write a thesis for an essay. Include a topic and your view of the topic. Also, be sure to meet the five requirements for an effective thesis. The first one is done as an example.

1. a favorite relative *My cousin Lee is very stubborn.* _____

2. the best way to relax (Mention two or three points that will be developed in supporting paragraphs.) _____

3. the joys of college life _____

_____

4. the frustrations of college life _____

_____

5. television advertisements _____

_____

6. exam anxiety _____

_____

Supporting Paragraphs

Supporting paragraphs provide detail to prove the truth of the idea in the thesis. Thus, in "Let's Pay College Athletes," the supporting paragraphs (paragraphs 2, 3, 4, and 5) provide details to prove that paying college athletes is a good idea.

Supporting paragraphs have two parts: the topic sentence and the supporting details. The topic sentence presents the focus of the supporting paragraph, and the supporting details develop that focus.

The Topic Sentence   The topic sentence presents the focus of the supporting paragraph. Here are the topic sentences for the supporting paragraphs of "Let's Pay College Athletes":

Athletes attending school on scholarships have a difficult time.

Some people say that without athletic scholarships many students could not afford to attend school, but this is not true.

Paying college athletes would also eliminate the people who are in college but who will never graduate.

If we paid athletes, colleges would benefit financially.

Notice that each topic sentence presents some aspect of the thesis. That is what a topic sentence does: it indicates which aspect of the thesis will be discussed in the supporting paragraph. Also notice that each topic sentence is relevant to the thesis. This is an important point to remember: all your topic sentences must be related to the thesis.

Supporting Details   Supporting details develop the point in the topic sentence. Look back at the supporting paragraphs of "Let's Pay

> Supporting paragraphs prove that the thesis idea is true. They develop the thesis.

> A supporting paragraph has a topic sentence and supporting details.

> The topic sentence presents the focus of the supporting paragraph; this will be the aspect of the thesis to be discussed. The topic sentence must be relevant to the thesis.

> Supporting details develop or support the idea in the topic sentence.

College Athletes" to see how the supporting details develop the topic sentences.

When you studied the one-paragraph composition, you learned the characteristics of effective supporting details. These characteristics also apply to the essay. They are listed for you here:

1. Supporting details must be adequate.
2. Supporting details must be relevant.
3. Supporting details must be specific.
4. Specific words should be used where appropriate.
5. General statements should be followed by specific ones.
6. Supporting details may be arranged in spatial, chronological, or emphatic order.

Review pages 59–74 on the characteristics of effective supporting details.

Practice 5.3

Pick two thesis statements you wrote when you completed *Practice 5.2*. For each of these thesis statements, write two topic sentences that could be in supporting paragraphs. Be sure the topic sentences are relevant to the thesis. (If you need help thinking of ideas, try listing, clustering, brainstorming, or freewriting.)

Example

Thesis: *My cousin Lee is very stubborn.*

Topic sentence: *Once Lee refused to go to the prom because he wasn't chosen for the prom committee.*

Topic sentence: *Lee will never apologize to anyone for anything, even when he knows he is wrong.*

1. Thesis: _____

_____

Topic sentence: _____

_____

Topic sentence: _____

_____

2. Thesis: _____

_____

Topic sentence: _____

_____

Topic sentence: _____

_____

Practice 5.4: Working Together

The following are thesis statements and topic sentences for three essays. With some classmates, write relevant supporting details to develop the topic sentences. The first one is done as an example. (If you need help with ideas, try the idea-generation techniques.)

1. Thesis: Baby-sitting is not an easy way to make money.

Topic sentence: The children can be difficult to care for.

Supporting detail: *Charlie refused to eat supper.*

Supporting detail: *Carlotta wasn't toilet-trained.*

Supporting detail: *Ed hit his brother.*

Topic sentence: The parents can be just as hard to deal with.

Supporting detail: *The Calloways returned at 3 a.m.*

Supporting detail: *The Drakes did not pay.*

Supporting detail: *The Kellys didn't tell me where they were going.*

2. Thesis: Being a college student has changed Leonid.

Topic sentence: First, Leonid is more responsible.

Supporting detail:_____

Supporting detail:_____

Supporting detail:_____

Topic sentence: Also, Leonid is more ambitious.

Supporting detail:_____

Supporting detail:_____

Supporting detail:_____

3. Thesis: Two kinds of salesclerks work in the mall.

Topic sentence: The first kind of clerk ignores me.

Supporting detail:_____

Supporting detail:_____

Supporting detail:_____

Topic sentence: The second kind of clerk smothers me with attention.

Supporting detail:_____

Supporting detail:_____

Supporting detail:_____

4. Thesis: In my study skills class I learned an excellent way to study.

Topic sentence: Preparations before sitting down to study are important.

Supporting detail:_____

Supporting detail:_____

Supporting detail:_____

Topic sentence: Students should follow a specific procedure once they sit down to study.

Supporting detail:_____

Supporting detail:_____

Supporting detail:_____

The Conclusion

The conclusion brings the essay to a satisfying finish. Some approaches to the conclusion are illustrated here.

> The conclusion brings the essay to a satisfying finish.

1. Refer to the Topic or View Presented in the Thesis.   Here is an example for an essay with this thesis: Student loans should be distributed before the term begins.

Students count on their loan money to pay for tuition, books, and other college related expenses. Therefore, to avoid problems for students, the loans should be given out before classes begin.

2. Summarize the Main Points of the Essay.   Here is an example for an essay with this thesis: We should abolish compulsory school attendance.

Compulsory attendance serves no purpose because when students are required to attend against their will, they disrupt the classroom and distract the teacher's attention. Students who do not want to be in school will not learn anyway, so we should let them leave and enter the workforce or the military, where they can contribute to society and earn their way in the world.

3. Introduce an Idea Closely Related to the Thesis or Main Points of the Essay.   Here is an example for an essay with this thesis: I knew I had to jump in the pool if I was ever going to overcome my fear of water.

Now that I have overcome my fear of water, I feel better about myself. I realize that I can face whatever obstacles are in my path by using the same courage I used to jump in the pool.

4. Combine Approaches.   Here is an example for an essay with this thesis: People should not stay married "for the sake of the children." The conclusion combines a restatement of the thesis and a summary of main points.

> More often than not, staying married for the sake of the children is a mistake. The spouses' resentment and anger grow until the children are affected by the tension. Ultimately, the children are better off living with one parent in an atmosphere of harmony than with two parents in an atmosphere of discord.

Practice 5.5

The following student essay lacks a conclusion. On a separate sheet, write a suitable conclusion and indicate the approach or combination of approaches you used.

Braces at Twenty

I was seventeen and without a care in the world when my mother woke me at 9:00 a.m. for my dental appointment. After the dentist finished checking my teeth, he informed me that I had no cavities, but I needed braces. The news came as a total shock because I thought only children got braces. I have had them for three years now, and I can truly say that having braces at the age of twenty creates serious problems.

Because the braces make me look younger than I really am, people never believe I am twenty and in college. Once when I met a friend's father, he wanted to know what high school I went to. When I go to the local bars, the person carding twists my ID every possible way, sure that it is a fake and I am too young to drink. When I am out with friends, people always think I am the kid brother who is tagging along. All of this makes me feel very self-conscious.

The braces also affect my social life. I am afraid girls don't want to go out with someone who wears braces, so I hesitate to ask for dates. If I do manage to get a date, I am in the embarrassing situation of excusing myself after I eat so I can go get the food out of my braces. Kissing isn't the fun it should be, either, because when my lips are pressed against the metal, they get sore.

Worst of all, the braces are painful. By the age of seventeen, a person has adult teeth that are pretty well set. When the dentist tightens my braces, all the teeth in my mouth hurt because they are difficult to move. I am unable to eat anything harder than Jell-O for a week. The tightening of my braces also gives me headaches from my upper jaw to the top of my skull. The insides of my lips become raw, and it is difficult to talk. It seems that as soon as the pain passes, it is time to go back to the dentist to get my braces tightened again.

PLANNING THE ESSAY WITH AN OUTLINE MAP

Many writers find that outlining an essay before writing the first draft helps ensure solid organization, adequate detail, and relevance. After generating ideas and before drafting, try writing an outline map. To do this, fill in a mapping form like the one that follows:

Approach to lead-in: _____		
Early version of thesis: _____		
Paragraph 2 Topic Sentence Idea	Paragraph 3 Topic Sentence Idea	Paragraph 4 Topic Sentence Idea
Supporting Detail Supporting Detail Supporting Detail	Supporting Detail Supporting Detail Supporting Detail	Supporting Detail Supporting Detail Supporting Detail
Approach to conclusion: _____		

To illustrate how the outline map can help you plan an essay, here is a completed map for the essay "Let's Pay College Athletes" on p. 145:

Approach to lead-in:	*Reasons for scholarships—to get good players.*		
Early version of thesis:	*Instead of getting scholarships, college ball players should be paid a salary.*		
Paragraph 2 Topic Sentence Idea	*Paragraph 3 Topic Sentence Idea*	*Paragraph 4 Topic Sentence Idea*	*Paragraph 5 Topic Sentence Idea*
Being a scholarship athlete is hard.	*Athletes without money could still go to school*	*Would eliminate students who do not want to be in school.*	*Would make more money*
Must be full-time student. *Sport is time-consuming.* *Without scholarship, could attend part-time.*	*Use salary for expenses.* *Attend while playing or later*	*Fewer unqualified students in classes.* *Places available for more qualified students.*	*Better games— bigger attendance.* *More tuition from students who take athlete's places.*
Approach to conclusion:	*The fact that we've always had athletic scholarships doesn't mean we should continue to have them.*		

The outline map allows you to check the relevance of your topic sentences and supporting details. You can compare each topic sentence idea against the early version of your thesis to be sure each one is relevant to the thesis. Similarly, you can check the details in each column against the topic sentence idea at the top of the column to be sure each is relevant to the topic sentence.

The outline map can also help you decide if your detail is adequate. If you have few details in a column, you may need to generate additional ideas.

The number of columns (supporting paragraphs) in a map will vary from essay to essay. However, you should have at least two.

If you do not have enough ideas to fill in the map, return to idea generation and then finish the map.

Practice 5.6

The following essays were written by students. Read them and answer the questions that follow to test your understanding.

Herbie's Hazards

It was absolutely perfect in my eyes, and everyone agreed that I was lucky to get such a dandy little car. What I did not know was that it had a mind of its own. I never thought my Volkswagen bug would have so many problems.

One chilly November evening I jumped into "Herbie" ready to cruise. I flipped on both the radio and the heat— I got sound but no warmth. All winter I gave him countless chances to impress me with heat, but by February I became used to the cold air and made my peace with the fact that Herbie was not perfect.

In July I realized Herbie was mixed up. He had his seasons switched. All summer, with the windows down, I felt suffocating heat. I later learned that when the engine heated up, the car did too. The hot air pushed its way through the back of the car and settled directly under my seat. Through June, July, and August I drove with sweat rolling down my forehead.

Herbie came to me equipped with no parking gear. The lack of a parking gear was not a problem at first. However, once at a friend's house I began to get out of the car when it started to roll backwards. After that, I carried a brick to wedge under the back wheel, and I avoided parking on even the smallest hills.

For awhile, Herbie had a unique way of expressing himself. He communicated through his horn. One day out of nowhere the horn tooted. It was not stuck. It just beeped once and stopped. Then, every time I made a turn, the horn tooted. Repairing a short in the wiring took care of that, however. Unfortunately, now Herbie only toots half of the time that I press the middle of the steering wheel.

Poor Herbie is getting worse. The hole in the floor of my backseat is growing, and the street is now visible. No matter how much it hurts, Herbie needs to be put to rest.

On a separate sheet, answer the following questions about "Herbie's Hazards":

1. What is the thesis of "Herbie's Hazards"? What is the topic? What is the writer's view of the topic?

2. What approach is used for the lead-in?

3. What are the topic sentences of the last two supporting paragraphs? What paragraph focus does each topic sentence present?

4. Is each topic sentence relevant to the thesis? Explain.

5. Are the supporting details adequate? Explain.

6. Are the supporting details relevant? Explain.

7. For the most part, the supporting details are arranged in what kind of order?

8. What approach is used for the conclusion?

A Girl and Her Dog

Adolph is a three-year-old, ninety-five pound, red-haired Doberman pinscher with long, floppy ears. As an adult, Adolph is easy to get along with. However, throughout his puppyhood Adolph was a real problem.

When I brought Adolph home, I was enchanted with him. A somewhat rude awakening followed, when the adorable canine proceeded to leave puddles and other, unmentionable matter in any place that suited him. Of course, that was to be expected at first, and I promptly began instruction in the proper use of old newspapers. The lessons produced rather good results at first. But then I got a summer job and was gone most of the day. Progress was delayed, and Adolph began to assume that the newspapers were placed on the floor for his reading pleasure. Even worse, when he was through reading, Adolph used his nails and teeth to shred the papers. It took hours to find the bits of torn paper that ended up scattered through the house. It was months before I got him straightened out.

As soon as that problem was solved, a worse one began. I discovered teeth marks that penetrated the walnut finish of Grandmother's antique coffee table. Shortly after, I stumbled on two pairs of the most expensive shoes I will ever own, lying in a chewed heap outside of the closet. Next, I found my virgin wool sweater ruined from snags made by dog claws. Then, the only lamp in the living room was knocked over and shattered by a four-legged marauder. The ungrateful mutt had the opportunity to chew on the best rawhide bones money could buy, but he would rather gnaw, scratch, and destroy my most prized possessions.

I thought Adolph's puppyhood would never end. I was so frustrated I even thought about giving him away. However, I am glad now that I did not because Adolph is my most loyal friend.

On a separate sheet, answer the following questions:

1. What is the thesis of "A Girl and Her Dog"? What is the writer's topic? What is the writer's view of the topic?

2. What approach is used for the lead-in?

3. What is the topic sentence for each supporting paragraph? (One topic sentence is not the first sentence of the paragraph.) What does each topic sentence present as the focus?

4. Is each topic sentence relevant to the thesis?

5. Are the supporting details adequate? Explain.

6. Are the supporting details relevant? Explain.

7. In what two orders are the details arranged?

8. What approach is used for the conclusion?

STUDENT ESSAYS TO STUDY

The student essays that follow illustrate the types of writing explained in Chapter 4: narration, description, exposition (illustration, process analysis, cause and effect analysis, definition, comparison and contrast, and classification), and persuasion.

The first essay is a narration; it is an expansion of the paragraph on p. 85. Before studying this essay, review the discussion of narration beginning on p. 81. (For an example of narration in a published essay, see "On Being 17, Bright, and Unable to Read" on p. 441.)

A Costly Lesson

Most teenagers think nothing bad can happen to them and that warnings are really meant for the other person. Sure, I had heard many warnings about the dangers of drinking and driving, but I never paid them much attention. I guess I thought I was indestructible. However, a car accident two years ago taught me firsthand that drinking and driving can be a deadly combination.

It was the night before Easter, and Kevin, Mickey, David, and I were bumming around. I had my dad's car until 1:00, so we decided to catch Nightmare on Elm Street (I don't remember which part) at the drive-in. Kevin said scary movies were more fun with beer, and I agreed. We picked up a few six-packs of Coors and downed them while we watched the blood and gore.

We headed out after the movie with me behind the wheel, Kevin next to me, and Mickey and David in the back. It was only 11:30, so we decided to cruise around until I had to have the car home. I felt a little light-headed, but I was sure I was in control. Coming out of the drive-in, I ran up over the curb. Kevin suggested that he drive, but I said I could handle it.

The next thing I remember, I was cruising down Route 11 at a pretty good clip. Two jerks in a Monte Carlo Super Sport pulled up alongside of us wanting to race. Mickey and David said, "Forget it, man," but being young, stupid, and high on beer, I started to race them.

We had gone about half a mile with me clearly in the lead when out of nowhere came the flashing red lights and siren. I checked my rearview mirror, and sure enough, it was the Highway Patrol. First, I hit the brakes. Then, I was skidding toward the guardrail at close to 80 mph. It was only seconds before we hit, but in that time I learned the meaning of pure terror. I was sure I would die and take my best buddies with me.

When I woke up in the hospital, I learned that I was lucky. I only had a broken nose, cracked ribs, and whiplash. Mickey and David had concussions and assorted cuts and bruises—they were lucky too. However, Kevin had not been wearing a seat belt. He was in a coma. He remained in a coma for two days. He is better now, but he has no memory of that night.

Needless to say, I had to go to court and answer to my parents and my friends' parents. However, the knowledge that I almost killed my friends taught me to listen to warnings and to never drink and drive again.

The next essay is a description. Before studying it, review the discussion of description beginning on p. 87. (For an example of description in a published essay, see "Expecting Friends" on p. 446.)

My Place of Solitude

Whenever I need to be alone, I go to Cherry Flat, a little-known area in the mountains of Sequoia National Forest. It is a peaceful, isolated, rustic place.

To get to Cherry Flat, I have to ascend Sugarloaf Mountain. The road resembles a snake. The turns are so sharp I cannot resist the temptation to take a quick peek back to make sure the rear end of my car made it around with me. A little-used turnoff at the summit leads down a deeply rutted, muddy lane to Cherry Flat.

Cherry Flat is a primitive campground. There is only a small, unpainted, rough wood hut with a half moon cut into the door. The only place to pitch a tent is on one of the four flat spots carved out of the sloping hillside.

Any hardship I encounter because of the lack of conveniences is made up by the spectacular scenery. Majestic mountains surround the camp. Redwood Mountain stands to the north; Burnt Point is to the east, and Big Baldy, its granite dome glistening, to the west. The Kaweak River at the bottom of the gorge resembles a silvery ribbon. My eyes are slowly pulled upward following the march of tall pines to the crest of Redwood Mountain where the azure sky begins.

After setting up camp, I hike down the mountain and explore along the river. The trail is a mile long and drops one thousand feet in elevation on its way to the bottom. Halfway, I stop for a sip of clear, cool spring water that is trickling down the face of a rock ledge. Down a steep section and around a bend, the path leads past Disappearing Creek. In a small pool are brilliantly colored rainbow trout. The fish, when they sense my presence, dart away to hide. Lying on a smooth, warm boulder beside the swift running river, I like to watch the billowy clouds float by. The trail ends by a small waterfall. Water spills over the edge and falls twenty feet into a deep pool below. Ripples radiate outward and lap gently on the shore.

As the light grows dim and the clouds glow orange and

pink, the sun inches its way behind a mountain top. I relax and enjoy a cold drink back at camp—a fitting end to a peaceful day.

The next essay is an example of illustration; it is an expansion of the paragraph on p. 97. Before studying the essay, review the discussion of illustration beginning on p. 93. (For an example of illustration in a published essay, see "Expecting Friends" on p. 446.)

One Step Forward and Two Steps Back

Americans love technology. Every time some new time-saving or labor-saving device hits the market, we rush out to buy it. Price is no object. If it is new and more advanced, we want it. Americans are proud of our technological advancements, but technology often comes with a price.

Consider the cordless phone, for example. Yes, it gives us freedom to move around. However, more often than not, these phones cross frequencies with other phones so that we hear other people's conversations, and they hear ours. What we gain in mobility, we lose in privacy. We also lose clear conversations, for these phones snap, crackle, and pop more than most breakfast cereals. If you use your phone for business, that can be a real problem. Then, there is the matter of finding the phone in the first place. Since the user tends to leave the phone wherever the last conversation ended, hunting the phone up for the next call can be a frustrating challenge. If you were the last user, chances are good that you will find it after painstakingly recalling the events of the previous five hours, but if someone else in your household has used it—forget finding the thing. It can be anywhere from the tool chest in the basement to the potted plant on the back porch. Of course, since no one replaces the phone in its cradle for recharging, the chances are good that your conversation will be cut off mid-sentence as your batteries sputter to the end of their lives.

The information highway is another example. It offers computer users almost limitless access to a staggering amount of information. However, users are so glued to their computer screens day and night that they no longer have a life away from their pcs. Almost weekly, some new service, bulletin board, or information source is added to the highway, so users can never feel on top of things. They must spend ever increasing amounts of time "staying informed." Thus, once on the information highway, people become so obsessed that they do not take the exit ramp.

Another example that I read about concerns the computer-designed magnesium wheels General Motors put on its cars not too long ago. Thanks to a computer error, the tire seals did not fit properly. As a result, thousands of car owners woke up to discover that their brand new cars had flat tires. By the time GM figured out what went wrong, recalled the cars, and fixed them, it had lost a tremendous amount of money. The people who bought the cars were frustrated and unhappy, so it is unlikely they will buy GM products again soon.

It is commonly believed that everything has its price, and technological devices are no different. They may make life easier, but they are not without their problems.

The next essay, an example of process analysis, is an expansion of the paragraph on p. 99. Before studying the essay, review the discussion of process analysis beginning on p. 99. (For examples of process analysis in published essays, see "How Dictionaries Are Made" on p. 459 and "Green Frog Skin" on p. 455.)

Making Money with a Garage Sale

Have you noticed how many garage sales there are every spring, summer, and fall? Do you assume people must be crazy to flock to these things just to buy other people's junk? Maybe they are crazy, but people do love to buy other people's used stuff, and if you plan it right, you too can make a great deal of money from a garage sale.

First, you must gather all the saleable items collecting dust in your basement and attic. Do not include anything badly broken, but keep everything else. The items you think are the most worthless are likely to be the first to sell. Remember that Buddha statue with the clock in the belly that you would not be caught dead having in your living room? That will sell. So will the velvet painting of Elvis, the pink lawn flamingoes, and all those trashy trip souvenirs. Toys and tools are hot sellers, but clothes (unless they are children's) probably will not sell very well.

Next—and this is very important—clean this junk up. Dirty items will not sell, but you will be surprised at the weird stuff that goes if it is clean. Two days before the sale, take an afternoon, a bottle of Fantastik spray cleaner, and some paper towels and get the years of dust and grime wiped away. Be careful, though. Once this stuff is clean, you may be tempted to keep it. This would be a big mistake. Not only will you not make a profit, but you will be stuck with your own junk again.

Once your items are clean, display them properly. Get lots of tables, even if you have to rent them. Arrange everything attractively, trying to keep housewares together, toys together, and so forth. Do not crowd the items, and put large objects to the rear of the table so you do not hide the smaller things from the discriminating eyes of eager bargain hunters.

The most important part is pricing. I have just three words of advice: cheap! cheap! cheap! Also, be prepared to bargain. Shoppers will often ask if you will take less than you are asking, and your answer should always be yes. Remember, this trash has been in your basement collecting spider eggs for the past five years, so do not get greedy. Price it to move because the last thing you want to do is drag this stuff back in the house because it did not sell. Also, write the price of each item on a white sticker placed on the object.

If you really want a great sale, advertise. Put signs up on telephone poles and trees, directing people to the sale, and place an ad in the classifieds.

Finally, pamper your customers. Provide grocery bags for carrying those marvelous purchases home in, and serve coffee—for twenty-five cents a cup of course. If the day is hot, lemonade or iced tea at a reasonable price is always a hit.

Follow these steps, and you can pocket a significant amount of money. I once made two hundred dollars with a garage sale and got my basement cleaned out for good measure.

The next essay is an example of definition. Before studying it, review the characteristics of definition on p. 104. (For an example of definition in a published essay, see "On Being 17, Bright, and Unable to Read" on p. 441.)

Runner's High

Some people run religiously (usually five or six times a week); some run periodically (usually five or six times a month); and some run whenever they feel an urge to be physically fit (usually once a year). What makes these people run? What inner drive makes them go out onto the lonely road, with their Walkmans by their sides and their large sticks to beat off attacking dogs? Do they like the feel of Ben Gay rubbed all over their tired, aching bodies? No, these people run to experience that special feeling known as runner's high.

Some runners feel this high when they begin running, while others feel the rush as soon as they are finished. The most common time to feel the high, though, is about halfway into the run when the adrenalin is pumping.

The high is difficult to explain to nonrunners, but put simply it feels like getting an A on a final exam that you were <u>sure</u> you failed. The high takes you by surprise. Just when you feel as if you are about to see your dinner come out through your nose, the high picks you up and gives you incentive to keep going. The high is similar to a painkiller in the way it suppresses the pain in your joints. It also relaxes your tense muscles. In some instances, it even replenishes your energy, which makes you go farther and faster.

The high can even be the deciding factor in a race. If a runner peaks too early and experiences the high, then the runner will more than likely "hit the invisible wall" sooner and therefore lose the race.

If the high lasted longer than its normal few seconds (or even minutes in distance races), then the track world would have an incredible number of outstanding runners. However, all good things end, and a runner's high disappears just as suddenly as it comes.

Many people wonder why runners make themselves suffer so much just to achieve a few moments of bliss. Unfortunately, there is no way to explain this to someone who has never experienced runner's high.

The next essay is an example of contrast. Before studying it, review the characteristics of comparison and contrast on p. 110. (For examples of comparison and contrast in published essays, see "If You Had to Kill Your Own Hog" on p. 471, "How Dictionaries Are Made" on p. 459, and "Abortion, Right and Wrong" on p. 478.)

My Two Homes

When I was young, my parents got divorced. I ended up living with my mom, and she did not have a job. We were living on welfare. When I was in the third grade, I moved in with my dad. He had a good job, which put him in the upper middle class. The differences between living with my two parents were dramatic.

When I lived with my mom, we lived in a low-income housing project. The neighborhood was rundown, and the crime rate was high. The only people who went out after dark were looking for trouble, and they usually found it. Even during the day, we had to be careful.

We did not own a car. We spent countless days waiting in the rain, sleet, and snow for a bus, which was almost always late. One cold day, my mom, brother, and I all got done grocery shopping at the Millcreek Mall Loblaws. Mom and I each had two full bags of groceries. As we were walking out of the store, we saw the last downtown bus about to leave. We sent my little brother chasing after it, so it would wait for us. We made the bus, but by the time we got downtown, we missed the last bus that took us home. Since we did not have enough money for a taxicab, we walked home from Ninth and State Street to Thirty-Eighth and Garden. That is twenty-six streets uphill and about twenty streets over. That is an awfully long walk with a little brother and four heavy grocery bags.

I also did not have many clothes. Sometimes I would be made fun of because of my clothes. They did not always fit well, and sometimes you could tell they were from the Salvation Army. I remember one day I got a brand new pair of shoes. I was so proud of my new shoes. I went to school, and a girl named Janet said to me, "Those are nice shoes. Now all you need are new pants, new shirts, and a new haircut." I was crushed.

When I was in the third grade, I moved in with my dad. He lived in the suburbs in his own house. The neighborhood was beautiful, with trees, flowers, and lots of beautiful homes. Walking was safe, day or night. No one worried about what other people were up to.

My dad had two cars, one for him and one for his new wife. Everywhere we went, we had a ride. We never had to wait for the bus, take a taxi, or walk for miles at a time.

My dad took me shopping and bought me clothes. Everything was brand new and stylish. None of the clothes had holes in them, and they all fit me perfectly.

As nice as it was at my dad's, I could not really enjoy it. I just kept wishing my mom had some of the things I was getting. My biggest wish was to win the lottery and buy my mom a house and give her everything I had. When I am through college and making money, I plan to buy Mom every luxury I can. She deserves it.

The following essay is an example of cause-and-effect analysis; it is an expansion of the paragraph on p. 120. Before studying the essay, review the characteristics of cause-and-effect analysis on p. 119. (For examples of cause-and-effect analysis in published essays, see "On Being 17, Bright, and Unable to Read" on p. 441, "Black Men and Public Space" on p. 481, and "What Mothers Teach Their Daughters" on p. 476.)

What Happened When I Quit Smoking

People who have never smoked do not understand how difficult it is to kick the habit. They think quitting is a relatively simple matter of throwing the cigarettes away and never lighting up again. However, these people are wrong. When I quit smoking two years ago, I was miserable.

First of all, I gained fifteen pounds. As a result, I looked terrible, and I was like a sausage in a casing when I wore my clothes. Every morning it was a struggle to find something to put on that did not cut off my circulation. When I looked in the mirror, I was depressed by my appearance and self-conscious about how terrible I looked. I tried not to eat, but I had to do something if I was not going to smoke, and eating was the only alternative because it kept my hands and mouth busy.

Even worse, I was so irritable no one could stand to be near me. I snapped at people and picked fights with my best friend. I knew I was being unreasonable, but I could not help myself. Once I screamed at my girlfriend and called her a nag when she reminded me to go buy my mother a birthday present. I did not mean it, but she spent the rest of the night in tears.

For the first month, I was actually hallucinating. I would turn suddenly, thinking I heard a sound, or jump up startled, feeling like something clammy had touched me. Once in a movie theatre, I jumped a foot out of my seat because I thought I felt someone put a hand on my shoulder.

Even in my sleep there was no relief. I would wake up in a cold sweat several times a night after dreaming about smoking a Winston. Then I would lie in bed and shake, unable to get back to sleep because the craving was so bad. I would feel depressed because the pleasure I felt from smoking in my dream was not real.

It has been two years since I have had a cigarette, and I am in much better shape now, but I still have some weight to lose and in social situations I still get a little jumpy. Believe me, people who think it is easy to quit smoking have never been through what I have gone through.

The following essay is an example of classification. It is an expansion of the paragraph on p. 127. Before studying the essay, review the characteristics of classification on p. 127. (For an example of classification in a published essay, see "Cinematypes" on p. 463.)

Different Kinds of Shoppers

Anyone who has been a salesclerk knows that shoppers fall into different categories. After working at K-Mart for over a year, I have come to know well the four different kinds of shoppers.

The first shopper is the browser. Browsers do not have much to do with their lives, so they have endless amounts of time to waste. Nonchalantly, they wander around my department picking up every item that catches the eye. Unfortunately, browsers never put things back in the right place, so I have to straighten stock when they leave. I guess browsers think that salesclerks have as much time on their hands as they do. The browsers are also a pain because they want to look at every item locked in the showcase. Of course, after all this, the browsers leave without buying a thing.

The dependent shoppers are also annoying. They have to be shown where everything is, including the items in front of their noses. Dependent shoppers never bother to look for anything. They walk through the front door, find a clerk, and ask him or her to get a dozen items. Dependent shoppers can never make decisions for themselves. "Which color do you think is best?" they ask, and "Which watch do you think my niece will like better?" Half the time they just walk away without buying anything because they cannot decide what to get. Of course, they never leave empty-handed unless the salesclerk has spent at least fifteen minutes with them.

The hit-and-run shoppers are much easier to deal with. They are always frantic and rushed. They will buy anything, regardless of price, if they can get it fast. Price does not matter. One recent hit-and-runner raced in, asked breathlessly if he could pay for a stereo by check, picked out the first one he saw, and bought two of them. He wrote a check for over four hundred dollars as if it were $1.98 and raced out.

Independent shoppers are the easiest to deal with. They want no part of salesclerks except for ringing up the sales. They are the shoppers who have done their homework. They know what they want, the particular brand, and the amount they are willing to pay. They find what they want on their own, put things back in the right places, and never ask questions. An independent shopper can walk into a store and five minutes later walk out again with the desired item.

Any salesclerk will tell you that dealing with the public is not easy. As far as I am concerned, this world needs more independent shoppers.

The next essay is an example of persuasion. It is an expansion of the paragraph on p. 139. Before studying the essay, review the characteristics of persuasion on p. 140. (For examples of persuasion in published essays, see "Green Frog Skin" on p. 455, "If You Had to Kill Your Own Hog" on p. 471, and "What Mothers Teach Their Daughters" on p. 476.)

Nine Is Too Young

Where I live, nine-year-olds are eligible to play in an organized football league. However, after watching my nine-year-old brother play in the league, I am convinced that nine is too young for a child to play organized football.

First, football consumes too much of a youngster's time. The season begins early in August and continues to the end of October. In August, when most kids are swimming, riding their bikes, or away at camp, the boys who play football are practicing three hours a day. Nine-year-olds should be running around the neighborhood having fun; they should not have to spend three hours a day in intensive training for a sport. The practices are so tiring that afterwards the kids do not have any energy left to play with their friends, so they miss out on the fun of summer.

A more serious problem is that these children are not playing with kids their own age. The teams are decided according to weight. Thus, a boy who is a little chubby does not participate with kids his own age but older ones, who may not take kindly to having a younger kid around. I know my brother had this problem. He played with older guys, and all they did was tease him and call him "baby." As a result, he lost his self-confidence and had a miserable time. Unfortunately, the coaches do not intervene to stop the teasing. They believe the boys should "be tough" and fight their own battles.

The worst problem of all is that nine-year-old bodies cannot withstand the punishment the rough game of football subjects them to. Yes, the players wear equipment, but this does not fully protect, especially when the coaches are screaming, "Hit 'em hard and hit 'em low." This explains why my brother broke his leg in a preseason scrimmage game. Also, some nine-year-olds try too hard to bulk up for the game. They start lifting weights, which can permanently damage a young body.

If I were a parent, I would not allow my nine-year-old to play organized football. In fact, I would fight to get the minimum age raised to at least eleven.

CHECKLIST FOR AN ESSAY

Before submitting your essay, be sure you can answer yes to these questions:

1. Does your introduction have a lead-in designed to create interest in your essay?
2. Does your introduction have a thesis that presents your topic and your view of the topic?
3. Is the thesis narrow enough? Did you avoid a statement of fact?
4. Does the thesis avoid a formal announcement?
5. Did you avoid inappropriate vague words in the thesis?
6. Does each supporting paragraph have a relevant topic sentence that presents the focus of the paragraph?
7. Are all the details in each supporting paragraph relevant to the topic sentence?
8. Are the details adequate and specific?
9. Are your details arranged in a logical order?
10. Have you used transitions where they are needed?
11. Does your conclusion bring the essay to a satisfying finish?

12. Have you edited carefully, more than once?

13. Did you proofread slowly and carefully, one word and punctuation mark at a time?

Writing Assignment

For your essay, you have a choice of topics.

1. Use one of the thesis sentences you developed for *Practice 5.2.* If you use one of these, check your responses to *Practice 5.3* for possible topic sentences.

2. In "Herbie's Hazards" on p. 157, the writer tells of the disadvantages of the car she bought. In "A Girl and Her Dog," on p. 158, the writer tells of the problems she faced when her dog was a puppy. Like these writers, write an essay that tells about the disadvantages or problems you have experienced with something.

3. Write an essay to the seniors at a local high school explaining what they can expect if they attend your college.

4. Like the writer of "A Costly Lesson" on p. 160, tell the story of a time when you learned something important.

5. Use examples to illustrate the best or worst job you have had.

6. Like the writer of "My Place of Solitude" on p. 161, describe a place where you like to be alone.

7. Like the writer of "Making Money with a Garage Sale" on p. 163, describe how to do or make something that can earn a person some money.

8. Like the writer of "Runner's High" on p. 164, define a feeling or emotion.

9. Contrast the way something was and the way you expected it to be.

10. Like the writer of "What Happened When I Quit Smoking," p. 167, explain the causes or effects of something you did.

11. Read "Different Kinds of Shoppers" on p. 168 and then classify the different kinds of salesclerks.

12. Read "Nine Is Too Young" on p. 169 and write an essay arguing that nine is not too young to play football.

13. For additional essay assignments, see pp. 444-445, p. 449, pp. 453-454, pp. 457-458, p. 461, and p. 466.

☐ TIPS FOR WRITING AN ESSAY ☐

Planning

1. Try one or more of the idea-generation techniques to find ideas for your essay. (See p. 2.)

2. Fill in an outline map like the one on p. 155.

Writing

1. Using your outline map as a guide, write your draft in one sitting, without worrying about grammar, usage, and such. Skip troublesome parts and push on to the finish.

2. To be more objective when you revise, leave your draft for a day.

Rewriting

1. To check your thesis, put one line under the topic and two lines under the view of the topic.

2. Give your introduction to two people to read. Ask them if this paragraph arouses their interest.

3. Put a wavy line under the topic sentence of each supporting paragraph. Check these topic sentences against the thesis to be sure they are relevant.

4. Check every sentence in each supporting paragraph for relevance to the topic sentence.

5. Circle each general noun, verb, and modifier. If some of these are too vague, find more specific alternatives.

6. Read your draft aloud. If you hear any abrupt shifts in direction, transitions may be needed.

7. Give your draft to someone whose judgment you trust. Ask that person to tell you if anything is unclear and if any point needs additional development. Also ask that person if your conclusion brings the essay to a satisfying finish.

8. Check p. 33 for editing procedures.

9. Copy or type your draft into final form and consult p. 35 for proofreading procedures.

CHAPTER

6

Identifying Subjects and Verbs

In order to write effective sentences, writers must be able to identify subjects and verbs. To help you do so, this chapter will explain how to:

1. identify subjects in a variety of sentences
2. identify different kinds of verbs

SUBJECTS AND VERBS

A sentence has both a subject and a verb. A *subject* is one or more words telling who or what the sentence is about. A *verb* is one or more words telling what the subject does or how the subject exists.

s.   v.
Babies cry.

Babies: tells who the sentence is about, so this word is the subject.

cry: tells what the subject does, so this word is the verb.

Pretest

To see how well you currently find subjects and verbs, underline each subject once and each verb twice. If you are unsure, do not guess; just move on. Check your answers in Appendix III.

1. Before work, Jeffrey's mother packed Jeffrey's school lunch.

2. Tuition at this school is the second lowest in the state.

3. Marcos has eaten peanut butter sandwiches for lunch every day this week.

4. Mother returned to school and studied business administration.

5. Many people in this city do not know about the proposed industrial park.

6. Joan and her brothers bought their parents a VCR for their anniversary.

7. The carton of Grandmother's clothes is in the attic.

8. Jacques has been studying for his law school entrance examination.

9. Are the keys still in the car?

10. There will be no excuse for tardiness.

11. Please answer me.

12. At last the holidays are over, and all of us can relax and recover.

13. The students in the reference room of the library are making too much noise.

14. There can be no accidents this time.

15. At the end of the summer, my parents and I will move to Texas and buy a small horse ranch.

IDENTIFYING VERBS

You may find the subject and verb of a sentence more easily if you first find the verb and then go on to find the subject. The verb will be the word or words that change form to show present, past, and future times (known as *tenses*).

I walk five miles every day.

In this sentence, the verb is *walk.* We know this because *walk* is the word that changes form to show present, past, and future time.

present tense:	Today I *walk.*
past tense:	Yesterday I *walked.*
future tense:	Tomorrow I *will walk.*

Because verbs indicate time, you can locate them with a simple test. Speak the words *today I, yesterday I,* and *tomorrow I* before a word or word group. If the result is sensible and if that word or word group changes form, it is a verb. Try the test with this sentence:

The wide receiver fumbled the football.

Can we say, "Today I *the*"? "Yesterday I *the*"? "Tomorrow I *the*"? No, we cannot, so *the* is not a verb. Can we say "Today I *wide*"? Can we say "Today I *receiver*"? "Today I *football*"? No, of course not, so *wide, receiver,* and *football* are not verbs.

Notice, however, what happens if we apply the test to *fumbled:*

Today I *fumble.*

Yesterday I *fumbled.*

Tomorrow I *will fumble.*

Fumble changes form to indicate different tenses (times), so it is a verb.

CAUTION: Some words can be verbs in some sentences and subjects in others. *Run* is such a word.

run as subject:	My morning *run* was refreshing.
run as verb:	I *run* five miles before breakfast every day

A word that tells who or what a sentence is about is the subject of a sentence, even if it changes form to show time. (Subjects are discussed on p. 181.)

Practice 6.1

Circle the verb in each of the following sentences. If you are unsure, use the test you just learned. The first one is done as an example.

1. Jennifer (studies) at least three hours each day.
2. The early morning fog creates hazardous driving conditions.
3. The customer demanded a refund for the faulty product.
4. Joey, a 6'7" basketball player, earned a partial athletic scholarship to Stanford University.
5. During the late afternoon rush hour, traffic slowed to 20 miles an hour on Interstate 680.
6. The ending of the lengthy mystery proves a disappointment to most readers.

Practice 6.2

Circle the verb in each of the following sentences. If you are unsure which word is the verb, use the test you learned. In two sentences, the verb is two words. The first one is done as an example.

1. Jan's band (performed) at the New Year's Eve dance.
2. Fearful of new situations, Chris refused to go away to college.
3. My father will begin physical therapy two weeks after his surgery.
4. At the little gallery on Seventh Avenue, Carlo will display his latest oil paintings.
5. Colorful and attractive, the Builders' Association Dream House reflects the best in modern design and craftsmanship.
6. More women major in science now than ever before.

Action Verbs, Linking Verbs, and Helping Verbs

To be a sentence, a word group must have a *verb.* The most common kind of verb is the *action verb,* which shows activity, movement, thought, or process. Here are some examples:

Action verbs showing activity or movement: hit, yell, dance, kick, walk, run, eat, play

Action verbs showing thought: think, consider, wonder, remember, want, ponder

Action verbs showing process: learn, try, read, enjoy

Another kind of verb is the *linking verb,* which links the subject to something that renames or describes that subject. Here are two examples:

Roberto *is* the best skier in the group. [The verb *is* does not show action. Instead it links the subject *Roberto* with words that describe the subject—"the best skier in the group."]

Yolanda *was* my best friend. [The verb *was* does not show action. Instead it links the subject *Yolanda* with words that rename the subject—"my best friend."]

Review the following list of linking verbs so you will recognize them in your own sentences:

am	was	appear	taste
be	were	feel	smell
is	been	seem	look
are	being	sound	become

An action verb or linking verb can appear with another verb, called a *helping verb.* Here are some examples:

Grandma Ramirez *can speak* three languages. [The action verb is *speak;* the helping verb is *can.*]

The train *will be* late. [The linking verb is *be;* the helping verb is *will.*]

Review the following list of helping verbs so you will recognize them in your own sentences:

am	been	could	have
be	being	will	has
is	may	should	had
are	must	do	shall
was	might	did	
were	can	does	

NOTES:
  1. Some verbs are on both the linking and helping verb lists (*am, is, are, was, were,* for example). When these verbs appear alone, they are linking verbs. When they appear with other verbs, they are helping verbs.

linking verb: The food *is* too spicy.

helping verb: The tree *is* dropping its leaves.

---

2. A sentence can have more than one helping verb.

two helping verbs: The plane *has been* delayed.

three helping verbs: I *will have been* gone by then.

3. *Have, has, had* are usually helping verbs. However, the following examples show two times when they are action verbs:

A cat *has* kittens. (*Has* means "gives birth to.")

We *have* lunch at noon. (*Have* means "eat.")

Practice 6.3

Indicate whether each underlined verb is an action verb, linking verb, or helping verb. The first one is done as an example.

1. The excited child <u>was</u> <u>waving</u> at his mother.

   was — helping   *waving — action*

2. For almost an hour no one <u>said</u> a word.

3. Emilio and Rose <u>were</u> childhood sweethearts.

4. My family <u>has</u> <u>been</u> <u>living</u> in Ohio for three generations.

5. Lucille <u>feels</u> sorry for every stray animal she <u>sees</u>.

6. Gregory <u>will</u> <u>be</u> delighted with the new microscope he <u>is</u> <u>getting</u> for his tenth birthday.

Practice 6.4

Circle every verb. If you have trouble identifying the verb, use the test. The first one is done as an example.

1. I (remember) very little about the early years of my childhood in Atlanta.

2. Far from home, the soldier eagerly read the letter from his mother.

3. The city will begin demolishing the old housing development next month.

4. With a few more years of training, Kim could have been a concert violinist.

5. Grandfather seems more tired than usual today.

6. During each press conference, reporters have questioned the president carefully about his foreign policy.

7. Jana was with us last night until 10:00.

8. After her lecture, Professor McKenna will answer your questions.

9. Because of the heavy winds and flash floods, the residents of the coastal town should have been evacuated by nightfall.

10. I am the person responsible for advance ticket sales for the charity art auction.

Sentences with More Than One Verb

A single sentence can have more than one verb, and each of these verbs can be composed of one or more words. Here is an example:

Paul *sat* at the window and *waited* for Maria.

This sentence has two one-word verbs: *sat* and *waited*. Now study this sentence:

My sister *arrived* at noon, but I *had gone*.

This sentence also has two verbs, but this time one is composed of one word, and the other is composed of two.

A sentence can contain any number of verbs, and each of these verbs may be composed of a different number of words. The next sentence illustrates this point. The verbs are underlined as a study aid.

As the storm pounded the small, coastal town, volunteers evacuated residents who had ignored earlier warnings that winds could damage property and threaten life.

NOTE: Be careful of descriptive words such as *not, just, never, only, already,* and *always.* These words are not verbs, although they often appear with verbs.

Earl will not agree to such a scheme. (The verb is *will agree.*)

> NOTE: A verb that follows *to* is known as an *infinitive.* The infinitive form will never be part of the complete verb functioning with the subject.
>
> I hesitated to answer the question. (The complete verb is *hesitated,* not *answer,* which follows *to*).

Practice 6.5

Underline each complete verb. Remember, a verb that follows *to* is not part of the complete verb, and descriptive words are not part of the verb. The first one is done as an example.

1. The tornado <u>had struck</u> before the warning siren <u>sounded.</u>
2. The class asked the instructor when the final examination would be given.
3. The fire alarm sounded, but many people ignored it because there had been so many false alarms in the past.
4. If I were you, I would take Professor Goldstein for history.
5. It will be years before we know the full effects of the new tax law.
6. If interest rates rise again, many people will not purchase new homes.

Practice 6.6

Underline each complete verb. Remember, verbs that follow *to* are not part of the complete verb, and descriptive words are not verbs. The first one is done as an example.

1. The versatile entertainer <u>sang,</u> <u>danced,</u> and <u>told</u> jokes.
2. Julio always asks the most perceptive questions in class.
3. Michael visited several car lots before he decided which used car to buy.
4. In his younger days, Sammy Davis, Jr., sang, danced, and played the drums in his Las Vegas act.
5. In my son's third-grade math class, students will learn how to multiply.
6. Jane has already left because she wants to arrive early.

IDENTIFYING SUBJECTS

The *subject* of a sentence is who or what the sentence is about. You can locate the subject by asking "who or what?" before the verb. The answer will be the subject of the sentence. Consider this sentence:

Lee earned the highest grade on the history midterm.

The verb in this sentence is *earned.* To find the subject, ask, "who or what earned?" The answer is "*Lee* earned." Therefore, *Lee* is the subject. Now look at this sentence.

Before Easter my cat was ill.

The verb is *was.* Ask "who or what was?" and the answer is *cat. Cat,* then, is the subject of the sentence.

Practice 6.7

Underline the subject once and the verb twice. If you have trouble locating the verb, look for the word or words that change form to show time; if you have trouble finding the subject, ask "who or what?" before the verb. The first one is done as an example.

1. The workers carefully unloaded their supplies.
2. The tenants complained about the loud music in Apartment 4.
3. The schoolchildren have accumulated stacks of old newspapers for the paper drive.
4. The proud parents snapped dozens of pictures of their children in the school play.
5. Carl Sagan's lecture will be postponed until the first of the year.
6. Lizette could not finish her fourth piece of pizza.

Practice 6.8

Underline the subject once and the verb twice. If you have trouble locating the verb, look for the word or words that change form to show time; if you have trouble locating the subject, ask "who or what?" before the verb. The first one is done as an example.

1. The mail carrier could not fit the bulky package in the mailbox.

2. Beside the garage, daffodils are pushing through the partially frozen earth.

3. Henry's oldest friend is arriving on the ten o'clock bus.

4. A new personal computer will cost two thousand dollars.

5. The new father smiled warmly at his infant son.

6. The faded blue suit is no longer wearable.

Sentences with Prepositional Phrases

A *preposition* shows how two things are positioned in time or space. Here are two examples.

The wallet was *behind* the couch. [*Behind* is a preposition; it shows how the wallet and couch are positioned in space: one is behind the other.]

We had dinner *before* the concert. [*Before* is a preposition; it shows how dinner and the concert are positioned in time: one was before the other.]

You can identify most (but not all) prepositions if you think of a box and a baseball. Any word that can describe the relationship of the baseball to the box is a preposition. The baseball can be *in* the box, *on* the box, *near* the box, and *under* the box; so *in, on, near,* and *under* are prepositions. Here is a list of some common prepositions:

about	before	in	through
above	between	into	to
across	by	like	towards
after	during	of	under
among	for	on	up
at	from	over	with

A *prepositional phrase* is a word group that begins with a preposition. Here are some examples of prepositional phrases. The prepositions are underlined as a study aid.

about this time	among my best friends	at noon
by tomorrow	into the lake	to me
in the back	over the rainbow	on the dog

The subject of a sentence will never be part of a prepositional phrase. Therefore, to find the subject of a sentence, cross out all prepositional phrases first. The subject will be among the remaining words, as the following sentence illustrates:

The leader ~~of the scouts~~ is a wilderness expert. (The subject is leader.)

Now consider this sentence:

A box of old clothes is on the kitchen table. (The subject is box.)

If you do not eliminate the first prepositional phrase in the preceding sentence, you might be fooled into thinking the subject is *clothes.* This sentence demonstrates the importance of crossing out prepositional phrases before identifying subjects.

Practice 6.9

Cross out the prepositional phrases and then underline the subject. The first one is done as an example.

1. ~~In the middle of the night~~ heavy winds damaged the orchard.
2. The top of the dresser is covered with dust.
3. The flock of geese flew in formation across the horizon.
4. At the back of the lecture hall, one student slept with his head resting on a pile of books.
5. The last twenty minutes of the movie were fast-paced and cleverly directed.
6. With a little practice anyone can learn word-processing skills.

Practice 6.10

Cross out the prepositional phrases and then underline the subject. The first one is done as an example.

1. The pile ~~of leaves~~ must be raked ~~into the street~~.
2. Six of us plan to visit New York during winter break.
3. The entire defensive line of the football team earned high grades last semester.

4. Some people with allergies find it difficult to live in this part of the country.

5. This stack of old encyclopedias can be taken to the used book sale.

6. In the corner, the mother cat stretched out for her nap.

Sentences with Inverted Order

The subject usually comes before the verb, as in this example:

     s.   v.

The children romped with the playful dog.

Sometimes the subject comes *after* the verb. Then the sentence has *inverted order.* A sentence that asks a question has inverted order:

  v.   s.

Is the soup hot enough?

In this sentence the verb *is* comes first. When we ask "who or what is?" we get the answer *soup,* so *soup* is the subject. In this case, the subject comes after the verb.

A sentence that begins with *there is, there are, there was, there were, here is, here are, here was, here were* will also have inverted order.

     v.   s.

There were twenty people on a waiting list for that apartment.

The verb is *were,* and the subject is *people.* (*Were* is the verb because it changes form to indicate different tenses, and *people* is the subject because it answers the question "who or what were?")

Practice 6.11

The following sentences have inverted order. For each sentence, underline the subject once and the verb twice. Remember, find the verb first and then find the subject by asking "who or what?" before the verb. The first one is done as an example.

1. Here <u>are</u> the <u>folders</u>.
2. Is the storm over yet?
3. There are twelve people in this elevator.

4. Was your week in Ft. Lauderdale relaxing?

5. In the kitchen drawer were three dirty knives.

6. Here are the missing files.

Practice 6.12

The following sentences have inverted order. For each sentence, underline the subject once and the verb twice. Remember, find the verb and then find the subject by asking "who or what?" before the verb. The first one is done as an example.

1. There are only three people here.

2. Is the exam next Tuesday or next Wednesday?

3. On the window sill sat the fat calico cat.

4. There is some confusion about the new graduation requirements.

5. Are you free for dinner Thursday night?

6. Beside the peaceful brook sat Rusty and his dog.

Sentences with Understood Subjects

When a sentence gives a command or makes a request, the subject may not be written out. If the subject is not written out, it is understood to be *you*. Here is an example:

Get out of here right now!

The verb in this command is *get*. The subject is understood to be the unwritten *you* (*You* get out of here right now!).

Now consider this sentence:

Please bring me the newspaper.

The verb in this request is *bring*. The subject is understood to be the unwritten *you* (*You* please bring me the newspaper.).

Practice 6.13

Rewrite each sentence so that the understood subject is stated. The first one is done as an example.

1. Leave me alone.

   You leave me alone.

2. Ask Andy for the answer to that question.

   _____

3. Don't ever do that again.

   _____

4. Give Jacob the notes from this morning's biology class.

   _____

5. Take the money and run.

   _____

6. Do that and you will be sorry.

   _____

Sentences with More Than One Subject

A sentence can have more than one subject:

The *money* and the *credit cards* were stolen from my wallet.

The verb in this sentence is *were stolen.* When we ask "who or what were stolen?" we get the answer *money* and *credit cards.* Thus, *money* and *credit cards* are both subjects.

Now study this sentence:

Greg slid into home plate as the shortstop made a play at second base.

This sentence has two verbs: *slid* and *made.* When we ask "who or what slid?" we get *Greg* for an answer; when we ask "who or what made?" we get *shortstop* for an answer. Therefore, this sentence has two subjects: *Greg* and *shortstop.*

Practice 6.14

Each sentence has more than one subject. Circle each of these subjects. If you have any trouble, begin by finding the verb or verbs (the word or words that change form to show tense) and then ask "who or what?" The first one is done as an example.

1. Both (Senator Polanski) and (Governor Perry) favor the proposed jobs bill.

2. The school board and the leaders of the teachers' union met behind closed doors for most of the afternoon.

3. Police work is rewarding, but police officers do not make much money.

4. Too many accidents have occurred at the junction of Routes 11 and 45, so a traffic light will be installed.

5. The singer and her accompanist performed an encore in response to the standing ovation.

6. The rain fell for hours, and soon the small streams began to flood low-lying areas.

Practice 6.15

Each sentence has more than one subject. Circle each of these subjects. If you have trouble, find the verbs and then ask "who or what?" The first one is done as an example.

1. Your (time) and your (energy) are needed on this project.

2. The rabbit and her young fled in panic when the lawn mower ran over their burrow.

3. Both the manager and the assistant manager apologized for the poor service.

4. The fire alarm sounded, so the students filed out of the room in an orderly fashion.

5. I planted a garden in my backyard, but the rabbits ate most of my crops.

6. Two robins and three sparrows fed contentedly at the bird feeder outside the kitchen window.

Post Test

Underline the subjects once and the verbs twice. If the subject is understood, write it in and underline it. You will have to draw on everything you have learned so far about subjects and verbs.

1. Six of us had decided to travel to Bowling Green for the big game.

2. For the past year, Scott, Lisa, and Maria have volunteered to work in the children's hospital for three hours every week.

3. The first American to orbit the earth was John Glenn.

4. Luis will never agree to your plan, but you may convince Margo.

5. As the price of cigarettes rises, more people will quit smoking.

6. The trees in Vermont have already changed color.

7. The quarterback faked a pass and then ran up the middle for a five-yard gain.

8. Why are you going alone on your vacation?

9. Behind the old barn there is a beautiful patch of clover in bloom.

10. Take this book with you and return it to the library.

11. Here is the report, but I must have it back in a week.

12. On the top shelf of my closet are the clothes for the rummage sale.

13. More people must be told about organ donation programs, for such programs save lives.

14. Since Mario quit smoking, he has become irritable and generally unpleasant.

15. As more people become comfortable with computers, information will be processed faster than ever.

16. To me, cigarette smoking is offensive.

17. The pile of dirty clothes in the closet is beginning to smell.

18. Add the eggs before you add the flour and salt.

19. Peter, Helen, and David decided that they would never campaign for Jeffrey in the student council election.

20. The question of fair play must be considered in this case.

CHAPTER
7

Writing Effective Sentences

This chapter will help you learn to shape sentences to communicate your ideas clearly, effectively, and with a level of sophistication appropriate for a college student. You will learn how to

1. use coordination to show the relationship between ideas
2. use subordination to show the relationship between ideas
3. achieve sentence variety for a pleasing rhythm
4. use transitions to show the relationship between ideas and achieve a pleasing rhythm
5. achieve parallelism for balanced sentences

IDENTIFYING CLAUSES

A *clause* is a group of words with both a subject and a verb (see Chapter 6 on how to identify subjects and verbs). The following word groups are clauses (the subjects are underlined once, and the verbs are underlined twice).

the snow fell softly

after the marathon runner crossed the finish line

Helen was not invited to the reception

before the storm warnings were issued

The following word groups are *not* clauses because they do not have both a subject *and* a verb. (Word groups that do not have both a subject *and* a verb are *phrases.*)

seeing the log in his path

in the pantry

behind the sofa in the den

frightened by the snarling dog

Practice 7.1

Place an *X* next to each clause. Remember, a clause has both a subject and a verb. If you are unsure how to identify subjects and verbs, see Chapter 6.

A. _____ before Lorenzo could finish his sentence

B. _____ around the corner from my house

C. _____ against the wishes of her parents and friends

D. _____ she means well

E. _____ wishing I could help you more

F. _____ the lead singer was the best performer in the show

G. _____ federal funds were requested to repair the dam

H. _____ not wanting to intrude on Martha's privacy

I. _____ the construction foreman took full responsibility for the damage

J. _____ a hawk soared in the distance

Two Kinds of Clauses

There are two kinds of clauses: a clause that can stand as a sentence is a *main clause;* a clause that cannot stand as a sentence is a *subordinate clause.*

The following clauses are main clauses because they can be sentences. In fact, if you add capital letters and periods, you *do* have sentences.

main clause: the movie ended very late

sentence: The movie ended very late.

main clause:	freedom of speech is our most valuable liberty
sentence:	Freedom of speech is our most valuable liberty.
main clause:	her advice was not very helpful
sentence:	Her advice was not very helpful.

The following are subordinate clauses. They have subjects and verbs (all clauses do), but they cannot be sentences. To realize this, read the clauses out loud to hear that something more is needed.

subordinate clause:	because the union went on strike
subordinate clause:	as the doctor examined the patient's throat
subordinate clause:	when the pitcher threw his best curve ball

Subordinate clauses begin with words like those in the following list. Learning this list will help you recognize subordinate clauses more easily.

after	as soon as	if	until	whether
although	as though	in order to	when	while
as	because	since	whenever	
as if	before	so that	where	
as long as	even though	unless	wherever	

☐ TIP FOR IDENTIFYING CLAUSES ☐

To decide whether a clause is main or subordinate, imagine your-self speaking the words to someone. If the listener would be left hanging on waiting for more, the clause is a subordinate clause. If the words would leave the listener with a sense of completeness, the clause is a main clause.

when the sun set behind the ridge

(Speak these words, and the listener is left hanging on, waiting for more. The clause is subordinate.)

the sun set behind the ridge

(Speak these words, and the listener is not left waiting for more. The clause is a main clause.)

Practice 7.2

Write *SC* next to each subordinate clause and *MC* next to each main clause.

A. _____ after Tony checked the locks on the doors

B. _____ when he tried desperately not to show fear

C. _____ we asked the committee to reconsider its report

D. _____ the board of trustees raised tuition

E. _____ when the last vote was counted

F. _____ because the summer drought created a food shortage

G. _____ I left for the appointment ten minutes late

H. _____ before the movers lifted the chest of drawers in the attic

I. _____ the consumer price index points to a recession

J. _____ since Jan was awarded two scholarships

COORDINATION: METHOD I

Coordination is the proper joining of two main clauses in one sentence. (Remember, main clauses can stand as sentences.)

One way to join two main clauses in one sentence is to connect the main clauses with one of the following:

| , and | , or | , so |
| , but | , for | , yet |

Here are two main clauses:

The traffic light at Fifth and Elm is not working.

No major accidents have been reported.

Here are the main clauses properly joined in one sentence with a comma and the word *but:*

The traffic light at Fifth and Elm is not working, but no major accidents have been reported.

Here are two other main clauses:

Jake's frustration was building quickly.

He decided to get away for the weekend and relax.

These main clauses can be properly joined with a comma and the word *so:*

Jake's frustration was building quickly, so he decided to get away for the weekend and relax.

The words that can be used with a comma to join main clauses are called *coordinating conjunctions.* They appear in the chart that follows.

COORDINATING CONJUNCTIONS

1. , and (to show addition)

    Three of us wanted to visit the museum, and two of us wanted to see a play.

2. , but (to show contrast)

    , yet (to show contrast)

    Your plan is a good one, but we do not have the money to implement it.

    Your plan is a good one, yet we do not have the money to implement it.

3. , or (to show an alternative or choice)

    Professor Jennings explained that we could write a ten-page research paper, or we could take a final examination.

4. , for (means "because")

    The linoleum floor in the basement was buckling, for water had seeped in during the spring rains.

5. , so (means "as a result")

    The new model cars are in the showrooms, so now is the time to get a good deal on last year's models.

Coordination Rule: Method 1

Two main clauses can be joined as a single sentence with a comma and a coordinating conjunction.

Keep in mind that too much coordination in the same sentence creates an undesirable effect because the clauses seem carelessly strung together:

I got in the car, and I started to back out of the garage, but I forgot that the garage door was closed, so I hit the door at about 20 mph, and I caused over a thousand dollars of damage to both the car and the garage.

To solve the problem of excessive coordination, reduce the number of main clauses in the same sentence.

When I got in the car and started to back out of the garage, I forgot that the garage door was closed. I hit the door at about 20 mph and caused over a thousand dollars of damage to both the car and garage.

The discussion of subordination beginning on p. 204 will show you how to use subordinate clauses to avoid excessive coordination.

Practice 7.3

The following sentences are made up of two main clauses. To join the clauses properly, place a comma and write an appropriate coordinating conjunction on the blank.

1. Harry's throat was sore and raspy _____ his temperature was well above normal.

2. Scattered afternoon thunder showers are predicted _____ Enrico decided to begin painting the house anyway.

3. Mother enrolled in college _____ she has always regretted marrying before she earned her business degree.

4. The Bears were behind by five runs in the fourth inning _____ Coach Hernandez was forced to change pitchers.

5. Nicotine-flavored gum can help a person quit smoking _____ it is no substitute for will power.

6. We could travel the turnpike and arrive quickly _____ we could take the back roads and enjoy the countryside.

7. In the lake behind the house, Gregory caught a three-foot catfish _____ Elliot caught a four-foot bass.

8. This afternoon while we are in Charleston, we can visit Ft. Sumter _____ we can go to an authentic plantation.

9. The highway department received a 30 percent increase in revenue _____ two-thirds of the roads remain in disrepair.

10. The board of education decided to cancel night football games _____ too much vandalism was occurring when the games were over.

Practice 7.4

Join the main clauses in one sentence, using a comma and coordinating conjunction. The first one is done as an example.

1. To earn tuition money, Helen dropped out of school for a semester.

   She took a job as a nurse's aid.

   To earn tuition money, Helen dropped out of school for a semester,

   and she took a job as a nurse's aid.

2. Maria and John are poor choices to head the committee.

   They are disorganized and unreliable.

   _____

   _____

3. The plot of the movie was boring and predictable.

   The actors were fresh and engaging.

   _____

   _____

4. You can borrow my typewriter to type your term paper.

   You can pay a typist to do it for you.

   _____

   _____

5. The National Weather Service issued a thunderstorm warning.

   The umpire postponed the Little League championship game.

   _____

   _____

6. Michael passed the ball to Jeff.

   Jeff kicked it into the net to score the winning goal.

   _____

   _____

7. Many people thought videocassette recorders would seriously hurt the movie industry.

The opposite has proved to be true.

_____

_____

8. Currently, no cure exists for myasthenia gravis.

Researchers are working hard to help those afflicted with this neurological disorder.

_____

_____

9. Those in need of extra help can visit the Tutoring Center.

They can go to the Student Services Office.

_____

_____

10. Self-hypnosis can help people suffering from stress.

It is an effective relaxation technique.

_____

_____

11. Lorenzo began a rigorous exercise program.

He had to lose ten pounds before winter practice drills began.

_____

_____

12. With the new state funds, the school board hired three teachers.

They decided to remodel the high school library.

_____

_____

13. Thirty students were accepted into the medical program.
    Only two-thirds of them will eventually graduate.

    _____

    _____

14. Not everyone enjoyed the theatre department's production.
    Those who did raved about it.

    _____

    _____

15. Be sure to determine what you need before buying a computer.
    You could end up with a system that does not fill your needs.

    _____

    _____

16. Fifty percent of the student body was absent with the flu.
    The principal still did not cancel classes.

    _____

    _____

17. The luxury hotel boasts the ultimate in service.
    It claims to serve the best food in the state.

    _____

    _____

18. Wear brightly colored clothing when jogging in the street.
    Drivers might not see you until it is too late.

    _____

    _____

19. Colleges should begin offering more classes at night.
Many potential students work during the day.

_____

_____

20. For this apartment to be livable, we must scrub all the walls.
We must have the carpets cleaned.

_____

_____

Practice 7.5

On a separate sheet, write eight sentences. Each sentence should have two main clauses joined with a comma and a coordinating conjunction. Use each coordinating conjunction at least once.

COORDINATION: METHOD II

A second way to join main clauses in one sentence is to connect the clauses with one of the following:

; however,	; furthermore,	; consequently,
; nevertheless,	; therefore,	; moreover,
; nonetheless,	; thus,	

Here are two main clauses (word groups that can be sentences):

The editorial in Sunday's paper made a good point.
It will not change many people's minds.

Here are the main clauses properly joined in one sentence with a semicolon and the word *however* and a comma:

The editorial in Sunday's paper made a good point; however, it will not change many people's minds.

Here are two other main clauses:

Next fall, tuition will increase by 10 percent.
The cost of living in a dorm will rise by 5 percent.

These main clauses can be properly joined with a semicolon and the word *furthermore* and a comma:

Next fall, tuition will increase by 10 percent; furthermore, the cost of living in a dorm will rise by 5 percent.

The words that can be used with a semicolon and a comma to join main clauses are *conjunctive adverbs.* A chart of the conjunctive adverbs follows.

CONJUNCTIVE ADVERBS

1. ; however, (means "but")

    ; nevertheless, (means "but")

    ; nonetheless, (means "but")

    The snow plows worked through the night to clear the roads; however, many streets were still impassable.

    The snow plows worked through the night to clear the roads; nevertheless, many streets were still impassable.

    The snow plows worked through the night to clear the roads; nonetheless, many streets were still impassable.

2. ; furthermore, (means "in addition")

    ; moreover, (means "in addition")

    To save money, the transit system must raise fares; furthermore, it plans to reduce the number of buses in operation.

    To save money, the transit system must raise fares; moreover, it plans to reduce the number of buses in operation.

3. ; therefore, (means "as a result")

    ; thus, (means "as a result")

    ; consequently, (means "as a result")

    I am hoping to earn a scholarship my sophomore year; therefore, I must maintain a B average.

    I am hoping to earn a scholarship my sophomore year; thus, I must maintain a B average.

    I am hoping to earn a scholarship my sophomore year; consequently, I must maintain a B average.

Coordination Rule: Method II

Two main clauses can be joined in a single sentence with a semicolon, a conjunctive adverb, and a comma.

Practice 7.6

The following sentences are made up of two main clauses. Join the clauses properly with a semicolon, an appropriate conjunctive adverb, and a comma. (The chart on p. 199 will help you.)

1. The temperature only went up to 65 degrees *; however,* most of us decided to go swimming anyway.

2. The mayor spoke to city council members for over an hour _____ he was unable to persuade them to pass the new budget bill.

3. The examination has five essay questions and thirty true and false questions _____ I was able to complete it in less than the time allowed.

4. Julian is the top rebounder on the basketball team _____ he is a star defensive lineman on the football team.

5. Many researchers claim that children who watch violence on television become desensitized to violence in real life _____ too few parents control the amount of violence their children watch on the small screen.

6. Federal funding for public television has been drastically cut _____ contributions from private businesses are being sought.

7. After the storm, power was not restored for twenty hours _____ much of the food in my refrigerator had to be thrown out.

8. Dr. Juarez explained that caffeine interferes with the body's absorption of iron _____ caffeine can contribute to the formation of cysts.

9. To write an effective persuasive essay, avoid personal attacks _____ acknowledge the point of view of those who disagree with you.

10. Some parents believe schools should pile on the homework _____ recent studies reveal that excessive amounts of homework are counterproductive.

Practice 7.7

Join the main clauses in one sentence with a semicolon, a conjunctive adverb, and a comma. The first one is done as an example.

1. Jeremy is a most charming child.
   He is a loyal, caring friend.

   Jeremy is a most charming child; furthermore, he is a loyal,

   caring friend.

2. For years there were more teachers than teaching jobs.
   Now this trend is beginning to reverse itself.

   _____

   _____

3. To locate the escaped convict, the police set up roadblocks.
   They conducted a house-to-house search.

   _____

   _____

4. The library's card catalog is now fully computerized.
   It is easier to determine if a particular title is on the shelf.

   _____

   _____

5. Good writing skills are important for success in college.
   They are just as important on the job.

   _____

   _____

6. The school tax levy was defeated by voters.
   No new school texts can be purchased this year.

   _____

   _____

7. The new automobile assembly plant will be open by November.
   The unemployment rate in this area should drop.

   _____

   _____

8. Carlo was accepted into graduate school to study chemistry.
   He was awarded a scholarship for academic excellence.

   _____

   _____

9. Louise has been a hospital volunteer for three years.
   Now she has decided to apply for a paid position.

   _____

   _____

10. Writers who wait for inspiration may never get much done.
    Writers who freewrite for ideas will make more progress.

    _____

    _____

11. Gary was in top condition for the marathon.
    He still did not expect to place in the top ten.

    _____

    _____

12. Susan pretended she was not bothered by losing her job.
    Those close to her knew she was depressed.

    _____

    _____

13. The assembly-line workers ended their two-week strike.
    The plant would be back in operation by mid-afternoon.

    _____

    _____

14. Ivana earned a scholarship for her high math grades.
    She won a scholarship to play on the women's basketball team.

    _____

    _____

15. Some students become overly nervous when they take exams.
    They are too tense to perform well.

    _____

    _____

16. The firefighters were granted a 5-percent pay raise.
    They still make less than they deserve.

    _____

    _____

17. Phillip and Ricardo fought constantly.
    They remained close friends.

    _____

    _____

18. Most people avoid Sue Ellen because she is so stuck-up.
    She constantly brags about herself.

    _____

    _____

19. Route 11 is heavily congested at 5:00.
    I recommend taking the bypass.

    _____

    _____

20. Air fares have gone up dramatically in the past six months.
    Fewer people are booking flights.

    _____

    _____

Practice 7.8

On a separate sheet, rewrite the following paragraph by joining some
sentences with the coordination methods described earlier. Then read

your revised version out loud to notice how much more smoothly it reads than the original. (More than one satisfactory revision is possible.)

A new amusement park ride is currently in the planning stages. Passengers will bounce off walls and posts. They will control giant flippers that knock their car back up a hill. The ride is called Mega Ball. It will make passengers feel like the silver ball in a pinball machine. They will be able to control their ride as they can in bumper cars. They will get the thrill of a scary ride. If they hit the flipper at the right time, they can have a longer ride. They do not even have to put in another quarter.

SUBORDINATION: METHOD I

You have already learned that a *main clause* has a subject and a verb and can stand as a sentence. You have also learned that a *subordinate clause* has a subject and a verb, but it cannot stand as a sentence. Here are examples of a main clause and a subordinate clause:

main clause:	the doctor explained the symptoms of chicken pox
subordinate clause:	when the doctor explained the symptoms of chicken pox

In addition, you have learned that a subordinate clause is introduced by one of the *subordinating conjunctions,* words like the following:

after	as soon as	if	until	whether
although	as though	in order to	when	while
as	because	since	whenever	
as if	before	so that	where	
as long as	even though	unless	wherever	

A subordinate clause and a main clause can be joined in the same sentence. This joining is called *subordination.* Here are a subordinate clause and a main clause:

subordinate clause:	since the polls do not close for another hour
main clause:	we do not know the election results

Now here are the subordinate clause and the main clause joined in one sentence:

> Since the polls do not close for another hour, we do not know the election results.

In the preceding example, the subordinate clause comes before the main clause. You can also place the main clause first:

> We do not know the election results since the polls do not close for another hour.

Here are another subordinate clause and main clause:

subordinate clause: when I graduated from high school

main clause: I expected to join the army.

Now here are the subordinate clause and the main clause joined in one sentence:

> When I graduated from high school, I expected to join the army.

or

> I expected to join the army when I graduated from high school.

PUNCTUATION NOTE: When the subordinate clause comes before the main clause, place a comma after the subordinate clause.

Practice 7.9

Each sentence has a main clause and a subordinate clause. Underline the subordinate clause once and the main clause twice. Draw a circle around the subordinating conjunction that introduces the subordinate clause. The first one is done as an example. (Notice the commas after the subordinate clauses at the beginning of sentences.)

1. (When) Paul saw the stranded motorist, he quickly pulled to the side of the road to help.
2. If it does not rain in the next day or two, most of the corn crop will be lost.

3. Because Scarsella's serves the best food in town, the restaurant is always crowded.

4. The woman was clearly embarrassed when a cake with candles was brought to her table in the center of the crowded restaurant.

5. Diane decided to end her relationship with Howard since he had such a bad temper.

6. After the orchestra sounded its last note, the audience jumped to its feet.

7. Janice will leave for Florida when final exams are over.

8. Since I am working thirty hours a week in the record store, I can only attend school part-time.

9. The first-grade teacher was concerned about Tad because he seemed tired all the time.

10. While the insurance agent explained the difference between the two policies, I decided what to buy.

Practice 7.10

Join the main clause and subordinate clause into a single sentence. Place the subordinate clause first or last according to the directions given. (Be sure to place a comma after a subordinate clause that comes before the main clause.) The first one is done as an example.

1. (Place the subordinate clause first.)

   while the teacher explained cell division
   the class took notes furiously

   While the teacher explained cell division, the class took notes

   furiously

2. (Place the subordinate clause last.)

   because she had a frightening dream
   the child woke up crying

   _____

   _____

3. (Place the subordinate clause first.)

   until you exercise regularly and quit smoking
   you will be short of breath

4. (Place the subordinate clause last.)

   since she was not sure what she wanted to do after high school
   Gloria decided to enlist in the Navy

5. (Place the subordinate clause first.)

   although I loved the book
   I hated the movie version of *Catch 22*

6. (Place the subordinate clause last.)

   before he auditioned for the lead in *West Side Story*
   Juan took six weeks of voice lessons

Practice 7.11

Change one of the main clauses to a subordinate clause by placing an appropriate subordinating conjunction in front of it (see the list on p. 204). Then join the new subordinate clause and the remaining main clause into a single sentence. Place some of the subordinate clauses first and some of them last. Also, place a comma after a subordinate clause that comes first. The first one is done as an example.

1. Diane and Andy moved to Virginia.

   Seth and Janet were afraid they would not see them again.

   Because Diane and Andy moved to Virginia, Seth and Janet were

   afraid they would not see them again.

2. Cass was unsure of what courses she should take next semester.
She made an appointment with her academic advisor.

_____

_____

3. Kevin apologized for being inconsiderate.
Miguel still could not forgive him.

_____

_____

4. The senator has no money to finance a reelection campaign.
He decided not to seek a second term in office.

_____

_____

5. The employer improves working conditions.
The union has vowed to remain on strike.

_____

_____

6. Many people believe anger is a destructive emotion.
I find it to be a healthy, adaptive one.

_____

_____

Practice 7.12

On a separate sheet, write five sentences that join one main clause and one subordinate clause. Three of the sentences should begin with the subordinate clause (remember to place a comma after the subordinate clause that comes at the beginning).

SUBORDINATION: METHOD II

One kind of subordinate clause begins with one of these words:

who, whose (to refer to people)

which (to refer to things and animals)

that (to refer to people or things)

These words are called *relative pronouns,* and the subordinate clauses they introduce are called *relative clauses.*

The second method of subordination involves joining a main clause and a relative clause, like this:

sentence:	The boy who won the award is my son.
main clause:	the boy is my son
relative clause:	who won the award.

Here are other examples:

sentence:	The class that I am taking is time-consuming.
main clause:	the class is time-consuming
relative clause:	that I am taking
sentence:	Jocelyn, whose art is displayed in the student gallery, will paint your portrait.
main clause:	Jocelyn will paint your portrait
relative clause:	whose art is displayed
sentence:	You may use my car, which needs gas.
main clause:	you may use my car
relative clause:	which needs gas

If a relative clause is needed to identify who or what is referred to, it is *restrictive.* If the relative clause is not needed to identify who or what is referred to, it is *nonrestrictive.*

restrictive:

The police officer *who saved the child from drowning* is my neighbor.

["Who saved the child from drowning" is needed for identifying the police officer.]

nonrestrictive:

Officer Manuel, *who saved the child from drowning,* is my neighbor.

["Who saved the child from drowning" is not needed for identifying who saved the child because the person's name is given.]

> PUNCTUATION NOTE: Set off nonrestrictive relative clauses
> with commas:
>
> Bridgett, *who scored fifteen points,* was the most valuable player.
>
> Do not set off restrictive clauses:
>
> The watch *that I found* looks valuable.

Now here are sentences with relative clauses that begin with *whose*
and *which:*

That man, whose name I forget, is suspicious looking.

That movie, which appeals to me, is playing at the Strand.

Practice 7.13

Combine the sentences by turning the second sentence into a relative clause that begins with *who, whose, which,* or *that.* Place the relative clause after the subject of the first sentence. The first two are
done as examples. Remember to use commas if the relative clause is
not needed for identification.

1. The mayor does not plan to run for reelection.

The mayor does not get along with the city council.

The mayor, who does not get along with the city council, does not

plan to run for reelection.

2. The kitten is now a member of my family.

I found the kitten last week.

The kitten that I found last week is now a member of my family.

3. The large oak tree must be cut down.

The tree was struck by lightning.

_____

_____

4. The book of Longfellow's poems is very old and valuable.
   I found the book in Grandfather's attic.

   _____

   _____

5. Frank Mussillo has decided to retire at the end of the summer.
   Frank Mussillo has been fire chief of our town for thirty years.

   _____

   _____

6. The Theatre Guild's production of *Porgy and Bess* has been held over for another week.
   The production is playing to packed houses every night.

   _____

   _____

7. The house needed more repairs than they realized.
   Katherine and David bought the house.

   _____

   _____

8. The woman offered to give me directions.
   The woman noticed my confusion.

   _____

   _____

9. Marty finally sold a short story to a literary magazine.
   Marty has been writing in his spare time for ten years.

   _____

   _____

10. Aunt Maria's arrival was a pleasant surprise to all of us.
    The arrival was unexpected.

    _____

    _____

11. The police officer questioned the witnesses.
The police officer was off duty.

_____

_____

12. The man offered to draw us a map.
The man noticed we were lost.

_____

_____

Practice 7.14

On a separate sheet, write five sentences of your own with relative clauses. Remember to use commas with clauses that are not needed for identification.

Practice 7.15: Practice with Coordination and Subordination

The following paragraph can be improved with coordination and subordination. On a separate sheet, rewrite the paragraph according to the directions given at the end.

[1]A hotel in Florida, called Jules' Undersea Lodge, is located under the ocean. [2]The hotel is the size of a small house. [3]The hotel can accommodate six people. [4]You are ready to depart for the hotel. [5]A guide puts your belongings in a waterproof suitcase and secures it with screws to keep out water. [6]Then the guide takes you by boat to a platform from which you dive into the water. [7]Breathing fresh air pumped through a hose held in your mouth, you swim underwater to the lodge. [8]A guide carries your suitcase. [9]The guide swims with you. [10]The hotel itself has two bedrooms, a kitchen, and a living room. [11]The kitchen has a microwave and a fully-stocked refrigerator. [12]The living room has a VCR, stereo, and television. [13]You can relax in the lodge. [14]You can go diving outside. [15]You are ready to leave. [16]A guide swims with you back to the platform.

A. Join sentences 2 and 1 by making sentence 2 a relative clause.

B. Join sentences 4 and 5 by adding a subordinating conjunction to sentence 4 and making it a subordinate clause.

C. Join sentences 9 and 8 by making sentence 9 a relative clause.

D. Join sentences 11 and 12 by adding a comma and coordinating conjunction.

E. Join sentences 13 and 14 by adding a comma and coordinating conjunction.

F. Join sentences 15 and 16 by adding a subordinating conjunction to sentence 15 and making it a subordinate clause.

Practice 7.16: Practice with Coordination and Subordination

On a separate sheet, rewrite the following paragraphs so that they include coordination and subordination. Then read both the original and revision aloud to notice how much better the coordination and subordination make the revision sound. (Many different revisions are possible.)

Meredith West and Andrew King studied cowbirds for many years. West and King are scientists in North Carolina. A male cowbird sings. The female cowbird lets him know what songs she likes without making a sound. She likes a song. She lifts her wing.

Cowbirds in different parts of the country sing different tunes. West and King put male cowbirds from North Carolina with female cowbirds from Texas. The males learned to sing Texas cowbird songs. The scientists were puzzled. The males learned these songs. The females did not make a peep. They videotaped the birds. They saw that the females would flash a wing when they liked a song. The males would repeat the song. The females liked it. Now, if the birds could just learn some Billy Joel tunes.

SENTENCE VARIETY

To improve the flow of your writing and to achieve a mature style, use a variety of sentence structures. This mix of sentences structures is known as *sentence variety*. You have already learned about subordination and coordination. When you use these, you are contributing to sentence variety. In addition, you can achieve sentence variety by using the sentence structures described on the following pages.

Begin with One or Two *-ly* Words

Words that end in *-ly* are descriptive words called *adverbs*. Consider this sentence:

Mother carefully eased the heavy cake pans out of the oven.

Carefully is a descriptive word; it describes how Mother eased the pans out of the oven.

An *-ly* word can be an excellent way to open a sentence:

Carefully, Mother eased the heavy cake pans out of the oven.

Hoarsely, the cheerleaders shouted for a touchdown.

Patiently, Dr. Vardova explained differential equations.

> PUNCTUATION NOTE: When you open a sentence with an *-ly* word (adverb), place a comma after the word.

It is also possible to begin a sentence with two *-ly* words:

Slowly and steadily, the workers slid the refrigerator into the narrow space next to the stove.

Quickly yet cautiously, Frank crossed the narrow bridge.

Loudly but politely, she explained her complaint to the manager.

Softly, sweetly, the nurse sang a lullaby to the infant.

As you can tell from the preceding examples, two *-ly* words can be separated with *and, but, yet,* or a comma.

> PUNCTUATION NOTE: Two *-ly* words (adverbs) are separated with a comma when there is no word between them. Also, when a pair of *-ly* words opens a sentence, place a comma after the second *-ly* word.

Practice 7.17

Rewrite the following sentences so the *-ly* word or pair of *-ly* words opens the sentences. Remember to place commas correctly. The first one is done as an example.

1. Ronnie stubbornly refused to sell his car for even fifty dollars less than his asking price.

   Stubbornly, Ronnie refused to sell his car for even fifty dollars less

   than his asking price.

2. Dr. Chun performed his duties as head of the art institute efficiently and effortlessly.

   _____

   _____

3. Jan quietly entered the classroom ten minutes after the lecture had begun.

   _____

   _____

4. I shouted angrily at the truck driver who changed lanes and cut me off.

   _____

   _____

5. The baby-sitter gently yet firmly guided five-year-old Tommy upstairs for a nap.

   _____

   _____

6. Grandmother painstakingly worked on the needlepoint purse she was making for Aunt Tanya.

   _____

   _____

Practice 7.18

Open the following sentences with *-ly* words (adverbs) of your choice. At least two sentences should begin with a pair of *-ly* words. The first one is done as an example.

1. The frustrated salesclerk explained for the third time why she could not give the customer a refund.

   Loudly, the frustrated salesclerk explained for the third time why she could not give the customer a refund.

2. Valerie arranged the roses and mums in the antique vase.

   _____

   _____

3. Ted maneuvered the car around the fallen rocks.

   _____

   _____

4. Dominic cradled his newborn daughter in his arms.

   _____

   _____

5. Jeffrey ran around the bases after hitting his third home run of the season.

   _____

   _____

6. The first-grade teacher showed the class how to write cursive letters.

   _____

   _____

Practice 7.19

On a separate sheet, write two sentences of your own that begin with an *-ly* word (adverb) and two sentences that begin with a pair of *-ly* words. Remember to use commas correctly.

Begin with an *-ing* Verb or Phrase

The *-ing* form of a verb is the *present participle.* The present participle can be used as a descriptive word and an effective sentence opening. Consider this sentence:

Whistling, John walked past the cemetery.

Whistling is the *-ing* form of the verb *whistle*. In the preceding sentence, it describes John. Opening some of your sentences with present participles contributes to sentence variety. Here are more examples:

Crying, the child said that he fell off his bicycle.

Coughing, Maria left the classroom to get a drink of water.

Limping, Jody crossed the street.

You can also begin a sentence with an *-ing* verb phrase *(present participle phrase)*. An *-ing* verb phrase is the present participle (*-ing* verb form) and one or more words that work with it. Here is a sentence that opens with a present participle phrase:

Whistling softly, John walked past the cemetery.

In this case, the present participle phrase is *whistling softly,* which describes John.

By opening some of your sentences with present participle phrases, you can achieve sentence variety. Here are more examples:

Crying pitifully, the child said that he fell off his bicycle.

Coughing into her handkerchief, Maria left the classroom to get a drink of water.

Limping more than usual, Jody crossed the street.

CAUTION: Place the word the *-ing* word or phrase describes immediately after the *-ing* word or phrase, or the result will be rather silly. Here is an example:

Dancing in the moonlight, the band played a romantic song.

Dancing in the moonlight is a present participle phrase that is not followed by a word it can describe. As a result, the sentence says that the band was dancing in the moonlight. (For more on this point, see dangling modifiers on pp. 387–388.)

PUNCTUATION NOTE: When you begin a sentence with a present participle or a present participle phrase, follow the participle or phrase with a comma.

Practice 7.20

Rewrite the following sentences to open with the *-ing* verb or verb phrase. Remember to place commas correctly. The first one is done as an example.

1. Ron, studying for his midterms, fell asleep in the library.

   Studying for his midterms, Ron fell asleep in the library.

2. The collie ran across the yard, holding Amy's chemistry homework in his teeth.

   _____

   _____

3. Dr. Dominic, grinning, announced that everyone passed the exam.

   _____

   _____

4. The ten-year-old, fidgeting in his seat, was bored by the pastor's sermon.

   _____

   _____

5. Joyce and Mario drove across the desert Southwest singing Broadway show tunes all the way.

   _____

   _____

6. Dad, snoring, slept through the biggest upset in college football history.

   _____

   _____

Practice 7.21

Open the following sentences with the *-ing* words (present participles) of your choice. At least two sentences should begin with *-ing* verb phrases. Remember to place commas correctly. The first one is done as an example.

1. Mother prepared Thanksgiving dinner for fourteen people.

Working feverishly, Mother prepared Thanksgiving dinner for

fourteen people.

2. Donna explained why tax reform would hurt the middle class.

_____

_____

3. Juanita accepted her award for scholastic achievement in mathematics.

_____

_____

4. Pete and Lorenzo tried to tell us what was so funny.

_____

_____

5. Jerry bench pressed 250 pounds.

_____

_____

6. Diana planted tulip and daffodil bulbs in her spring garden.

_____

_____

Practice 7.22

On a separate sheet, write two sentences of your own that begin with an *-ing* verb (present participle) and two sentences that begin with an *-ing* verb phrase (present participle phrase). Be sure to follow the *-ing* verb or verb phrase with a word the participle can describe. Also, remember to use commas correctly.

Begin with an *-ed* Verb or Phrase

The *-ed* form of a verb is the *past participle.* The past participle can be used as a descriptive word and an effective sentence opening. Consider this sentence:

Frightened, the child crawled in bed with his parents.

Frightened is the *-ed* form of the verb *frighten.* In the preceding sentence, it describes the child. By opening some of your sentences with past participles, you can contribute to sentence variety in your writing. Here are more examples:

Tired, Dad fell asleep while watching the Raiders game.

Irritated, Mandy threw her books on the floor.

Excited, Leonard told his friends about his good fortune.

You can also begin a sentence with an *-ed* verb phrase *(past participle phrase).* An *-ed* verb phrase is the past participle (*-ed* verb form) and one or more words that work with it. Here is a sentence that opens with a past participle phrase:

Frightened by the dark, the child crawled in bed with his parents.

In this case, the past participle phrase is *frightened by the dark,* which describes the child.

Opening some of your sentences with past participle phrases will help you achieve sentence variety. Here are more examples:

Tired after raking the leaves, Dad fell asleep watching the Raiders game.

Irritated by her low exam grade, Mandy threw her books on the floor.

Excited about being promoted to manager, Leonard told his friends about his good fortune.

CAUTION: Place the word the *-ed* verb or phrase describes immediately after the *-ed* verb or phrase, or the result will be a silly sentence. Here's an example:

Delighted by the victory, a celebration was in order.

Delighted by the victory is a past participle phrase that is not followed by a word it can describe. As a result, the sentence says that a celebration was delighted by the victory. (For more on this point, see dangling modifiers on pp. 387–388.)

PUNCTUATION NOTE: When you begin a sentence with an *-ed* verb (past participle) or an *-ed* verb phrase (past participle phrase), follow the *-ed* verb or verb phrase with a comma.

Practice 7.23

Rewrite the following sentences so the *-ed* verb or verb phrase opens the sentence. Remember to place commas correctly. The first one is done as an example.

1. Dave, confused by Nora's moodiness, decided to postpone the marriage.

    Confused by Nora's moodiness, Dave decided to postpone the

    marriage.

2. The football team rode home in despair, defeated by the worst team in the league.

    _____

    _____

3. Barbara, refreshed after her aerobics class, was ready to study for her biology final.

    _____

    _____

4. The steak, cooked to perfection, was worth the twelve dollars I paid for it.

_____

_____

5. The police officer, angered, told Jeremy he was lucky to get off with just a warning.

_____

_____

6. The cookies, baked about three minutes too long, were too brown to sell at the charity bazaar.

_____

_____

Practice 7.24

Open the sentences with *-ed* verbs (past participles) of your choice. Begin at least two sentences with *-ed* verb phrases. Remember to place commas correctly. The first is done as an example.

1. The referee threw the coach out of the game.

Angered, the referee threw the coach out of the game.

2. The kitten curled into a furry ball and fell asleep.

_____

_____

3. Three-year-old Bobby ran crying to his nursery school teacher.

_____

_____

4. Maria ran frantically after the man who stole her purse.

_____

_____

Writing Effective Sentences   223

5. The tenants voiced their complaints to the apartment manager.

_____

_____

6. Lorenzo reached over and turned off the blaring alarm.

_____

_____

Practice 7.25

On a separate sheet, write two sentences of your own that begin with *-ed* verbs (past participles) and two sentences that begin with *-ed* verb phrases (past participle phrases). Be sure to follow the *-ed* verb or verb phrase with a word the participle can describe. Also, remember to use commas correctly.

Begin with a Prepositional Phrase

A *preposition* shows how two things relate to each other in time or space. (See p. 182 for a more detailed explanation of prepositions.) Here is a list of common prepositions:

about	behind	inside	through
above	between	into	to
across	by	of	toward
along	during	off	under
among	for	on	with
around	from	out	within
before	in	over	without

A *prepositional phrase* is a preposition and the words that work with it. Here are examples of prepositional phrases:

in May	across the street	toward the end of the book
behind me	during the concert	inside the oven
on top	out of bounds	without a doubt

Beginning some of your sentences with prepositional phrases will help you achieve sentence variety. Here are examples of sentences that begin with prepositional phrases:

Under the kitchen table, Rags sat contentedly chewing on his bone.

In the spring, the senior class will travel to Washington.

From now on, everyone in this state must wear a seat belt.

PUNCTUATION NOTE: A prepositional phrase that begins a sentence is usually followed by a comma. However, you may omit the comma after a prepositional phrase made up of two words:

Between the oak trees, two squirrels were chasing each other.

By noon, all the sale items were sold.

or

By noon all the sale items were sold.

Practice 7.26

Underline the prepositional phrases in the following sentences. (Several of the sentences contain more than one prepositional phrase.) The first one is done as an example.

1. The infant began crying in the middle of the night.
2. At ten o'clock, the church bells chimed in unison.
3. Charlie announced that there was a thief among us.
4. The truth of the matter is that no one cares.
5. With the help of everyone, the fund-raiser can be a huge success.
6. By daybreak, a foot of snow had fallen in our city.

Practice 7.27

Combine the two sentences into one sentence that begins with the prepositional phrase or phrases in the second sentence. Remember to use commas correctly. The first one is done as an example.

1. The children woke up.
   They woke up in the middle of the night.

   In the middle of the night, the children woke up.

2. The fire alarm sounded.
   It sounded during our history examination.

   _____

   _____

3. The members of the committee decided to change the bylaws.
   They decided at their spring meeting.

   _____

   _____

4. The orchestra played a Gershwin medley.
   They played the medley after a fifteen-minute intermission.

   _____

   _____

5. A more efficient registration process will be tested.
   It will be tested at the beginning of the fall semester.

   _____

   _____

6. The flowering crab was severely damaged.
   It was damaged after the unexpected spring frost.

   _____

   _____

Practice 7.28

On a separate sheet, write four sentences that begin with prepositional phrases. Remember to place a comma after each phrase, unless it is only two words; then, the comma is optional.

Practice 7.29 Practice with Sentence Variety

On a separate sheet, rewrite the paragraph to add more sentence variety. Use a combination of the techniques you have learned: coordination, subordination, *-ly* openers, *-ed* verb openers, *-ing* verb openers, and prepositional phrase openers. You may add words and change word order.

Amelia Earhart and her navigator tried to fly around the world during the summer of 1937. They were supposed to stop at Howland Island to refuel. They never arrived. The pilot radioed compass readings hoping to be guided in. These, sadly, were the last words heard from Earhart. The plane was declared lost at sea after a long naval search. A number of theories have been advanced to explain Earhart's disappearance. Some say Earhart was spying for the United States. They say she was shot down over the Marshall Islands. The Marshall Islands were held by Japan. Others say a navigational error caused Earhart to miss Howland Island and crash at sea. Still others say the plane ran out of gas and crash-landed. The real cause of Earhart's disappearance will probably never be learned, although people will always admire the courage of the person who was the first woman to fly across the Atlantic Ocean.

PARALLELISM: WORDS IN SERIES AND PAIRS

Parallelism refers to balance. For your sentences to have the necessary parallelism or balance, words that form pairs or series should all have the same form. Here is an example:

Pat enjoys skating and reading.

In this example, two words form a pair: *skating* and *reading*. Since both words take the same form (*-ing* verb forms), the sentence has the necessary parallelism or balance.

Here is another example of a sentence with parallelism. This time, there is balance among words that form a series:

Janet and Rico found the movie fresh, funny, and surprising.

In this example, three words form a series: *fresh, funny,* and *surprising.* Since each of these words takes the same form (each is an adjective that describes *movie*), the sentence has the necessary parallelism.
Now here is a sentence that lacks parallelism:

> The doctor told the heart patient to avoid salt and that he should get more exercise.

In this example, two elements form a pair: *to avoid salt* and *that he should get more exercise.* The first element is a verb phrase, while the second is a clause. Because the elements in the pair take different forms, the sentence lacks parallelism. To achieve the necessary balance, the sentence needs two verb phrases or two clauses:

> The doctor told the heart patient to avoid salt and to get more exercise. (two verb phrases)

or

> The doctor told the heart patient that he should avoid salt and that he should get more exercise. (two clauses)

Here is another sentence that lacks parallelism:

> This course demands patience, dedication, and a student must know how to research.

In this example, three elements form a series: *patience, dedication,* and *a student must know how to research.* The first two elements are nouns, but the third element is a clause. Because all the elements in the series do not have the same form, the sentence lacks parallelism. Here is the sentence revised to achieve parallelism:

> This course demands patience, dedication, and research ability. (three nouns)

Practice 7.30

In each list of words, one element is not parallel because it does not have the same form as the other elements. Circle the element that is not parallel. On the blank, rewrite the circled element to make it parallel with the rest. The first one is done as an example.

1. graceful

   strong

   quick

   (versatility) *versatile* _____

2. to swim

   to sail

   surfing

   to snorkle _____

3. pleasant

   helpful

   has charm

   witty _____

4. blown by the wind

   sunburned

   soaked by the rain

   frozen by the cold _____

5. the evening

   before noon

   after breakfast

   during the afternoon _____

6. small, private parties

   large, crowded restaurants

   noisy, hot cafeterias

   going to flashy, loud nightclubs _____

7. attend class

   be sure to take notes

   ask questions

   listen carefully _____

8. she never lies

   she is always fair

   she is usually optimistic

   dependability is one of her traits _____

Practice 7.31

The underlined element in the pair or series is not parallel. Rewrite the sentence to achieve parallelism. The first one is done as an example.

1. Joan's aptitude test revealed ability in math and <u>learning foreign languages</u>.

   Joan's aptitude test revealed ability in math and foreign languages.

2. The citizen's committee criticized the mayor's proposal because of its complexity and <u>it was expensive</u>.

   _____

   _____

3. To save money on his living expenses, Lawrence got a roommate, ate out less often, <u>he fired his cleaning person</u>, and <u>he clipped coupons to use at the grocery store</u>.

   _____

   _____

4. Before agreeing to the surgery, Delores decided she would get a second opinion and <u>to see if she feels better in two weeks</u>.

   _____

   _____

5. The proposal for renovating the downtown business district suggests eliminating one-way streets, instituting on-street parking, and <u>we should reface some of the other buildings</u>.

   _____

   _____

6. My family decided we prefer a week at the ocean in a condominium to <u>spending a week in the mountains in a cabin</u>.

   _____

   _____

7. By three months, most infants will recognize their mother's voice, hold their heads up unassisted, and <u>three-month-old infants will grasp at objects placed within their reach.</u>

_____

_____

8. My piano teacher gave me a choice between playing one difficult piece or <u>I could play two less difficult ones.</u>

_____

_____

9. Geography 102 was canceled because the enrollment was low and <u>because of the illness of the instructor.</u>

_____

_____

10. The Emmy Awards broadcast was criticized for boring speeches, <u>because the production numbers were lackluster,</u> and for several tasteless jokes.

_____

_____

Practice 7.32

Complete each sentence with a parallel element. The first one is done as an example.

1. Tony swaggered in, tipped his hat, and *smiled at everyone in*

   the room. _____

2. Most people expect Gregory to win the race for Student Government president because of his intelligence, integrity, and

   _____

3. I like spending a quiet Saturday evening alone better than

   _____

4. Maria approached the stage with her heart pounding, her palms sweating, and _____

_____

5. To pass the course, Professor Lloyd explained that we would have to write a research paper, that we would have to pass a midterm examination, and that _____

_____

6. Several committee members wanted to raise money with a rummage sale, but most wanted_____

_____

7. Chez enjoyed the novel, but I found it predictable, sluggish, and

_____

8. The new president of Little League is having trouble finding coaches, cleaning the fields, and _____

_____

9. Lee has always liked small, informal weddings better than _____

_____

10. If you are not sure what courses to take next semester, you can consult the college catalog or_____

_____

PARALLELISM: PAIRS OF CONJUNCTIONS

Some conjunctions work in pairs. These conjunctions are:

either . . . or	not only . . . but [also]
neither . . . nor	whether . . . or
both . . . and	if . . . then

When you use these conjunctions, put the words that follow the second conjunction in the same form as the words that follow the first conjunction. In this way, you will achieve parallelism. Here is an example:

Either I will earn enough money to pay my tuition, or I will ask my parents for a loan.

The words that follow *either* take the same form as the words that follow *or* (both word groups are clauses). Thus, parallelism is achieved.

Here is another example:

Working full-time while going to school full-time is both tiring and foolish.

In this example, the word that follows *both* takes the same form as the word that follows *and* (both words are modifiers). As a result, the sentence has balance, and parallelism is achieved.

Now here is an example of a sentence that lacks parallelism:

This stretch of beach is not only beautiful, but it is private as well.

In this example, *not only* is followed by *beautiful* (a descriptive word), and *but* is followed by *it is private as well* (a clause). Because each conjunction is not followed by words in the same form, the sentence lacks parallelism. To achieve parallelism, follow each conjunction with words in the same form:

This stretch of beach is not only beautiful but private as well.

Practice 7.33

Complete each of the following sentences with a parallel element. The first one is done as an example.

1. To pass Calculus II either I must get a tutor, or *I must go to the math lab.*

2. Luis will either trade his car in for a new model or _____

    _____

3. Either I will ask my parents for a loan to pay tuition, or _____

    _____

4. Professor Amin decided both to postpone the examination for a week and_____

    _____

5. Tyler hopes not only to graduate a semester early but_____

_____

6. The principal can neither enforce the dress code to the board of education's satisfaction nor_____

_____

7. To improve economic conditions, the governor must not only attract new industry to our state but also _____

_____

8. Jonathan is either helping those less fortunate than he or_____

_____

9. Juanita is not only a good listener but _____

_____

10. I disagree both with the mayor's decision to fire the police chief and_____

_____

Practice 7.34 Practice with Parallelism

On a separate sheet, rewrite the following paragraph to eliminate problems with parallelism.

Friendships at work have their own set of guidelines. You should understand the difference between work friends and friends who are personal. Conversations with work friends focus mostly on office personalities, politics, and they center on work-related problems. You should neither confide personal information nor problems to work friends. To avoid complications, try to socialize mostly with coworkers who are at your level in the hierarchy. Unequal status can lead to envy, suspicion, or sometimes cause favoritism. Proceed carefully with office friendships with members of the opposite sex. Avoid any hint of romance, either during work hours or there should be no hint after work hours. If you follow these guidelines, you can enjoy friendships at work without unpleasant complications.

USING TRANSITIONS

Transitions help your reader understand the order and relationship of your ideas. In addition, transitions help your sentences flow smoothly. Here is an example:

> The health commissioner told the board of health that asbestos had to be removed from three schools. *Also,* he told the board that asbestos may be a problem in two libraries.

The transition *also* tells the reader that the idea in the second sentence functions in addition to the idea in the first sentence. The transition also helps the first sentence flow smoothly into the second. To appreciate this, read the sentences without the transition and notice the gap or abrupt shift:

> The health commissioner told the board of health that asbestos had to be removed from three schools. He told the board that asbestos may be a problem in two libraries.

Because transitions show how ideas relate to each other and improve the flow of writing, they make your sentences more effective.

Here is a chart that gives you many of the commonly used transitions:

Transition Chart

Transitions that Signal Addition	also, and, and then, in addition, too, furthermore, further, moreover, equally important, another, first, second, third . . .
	If the school levy does not pass, some teachers will be laid off. *Furthermore,* band and choir will be eliminated.
Transitions that Signal Illustration	for example, for instance, an illustration of this is, to illustrate
	Chuck became very irritable when he quit smoking. *For example,* when James asked to borrow his chemistry notes, Chuck yelled at him and called him irresponsible.

Transitions that Signal Emphatic Order	more important, most important, most of all, best of all, of greatest importance, least of all, even better, the best [worst] case (example, instance, time, etc.)

Mayor DeSalvo has been working hard to bring new industry to our area. *More important,* she has devised a plan to restore confidence in local government.

Transitions that Signal Spatial (Space) Order	near, nearby, far, alongside, next to, in front of, to the rear, above, below, over, across, under, around, beyond, beneath, on one side, to the left.

The high school is centrally located, and *directly behind* it is the football stadium.

Transitions that Signal Cause and Effect	so, therefore, since, if . . . then, thus, as a result, because, hence, consequently

Only five hundred students bought tickets to the spring concert. *As a result,* the concert had to be canceled.

Transitions that Signal Contrast (Differences)	but, yet, still, however, in contrast, on the other hand, nevertheless

David sprained his knee in practice; *however,* he plans to be in shape for Saturday's game.

Transitions that Signal Comparison (Similarities)	similarly, likewise, in the same way, in like manner

Most of today's movies are unsuitable for young viewers. *Similarly,* many television shows are not appropriate for children.

Transitions that Signal Purpose	for this reason, for this purpose, in order to

Theresa hopes to make the women's basketball team. *For this reason,* she is training very hard.

Transitions that Signal Chronological (Time) Order	now, then, later, after, before, soon, suddenly, next, afterward, earlier, at the same time, meanwhile, often, suddenly

Before buying a used car, a person should have it checked over by a reliable mechanic.

Transitions that Signal Emphasis	indeed, in fact, truly, certainly, to be sure, surely, without a doubt, undoubtedly

Our basketball team has the best record in our division. *Undoubtedly,* we will win a spot in a postseason tournament.

Transitions that Signal Summary or Clarification	in conclusion, in summary, to sum up, in other words, in brief, that is, all in all

I cannot support a candidate who is opposed to women's rights. *In other words,* I will not vote for Nathaniel Q. Wisherwaite.

Transitions that Signal Admitting a Point	although, even though, while it is true, granted

Although the temperature is rising quickly, I am still going skiing this weekend.

A second way to achieve transition is to repeat a key word or idea. Here is an example with a key word repeated:

The doctor put Maria on a special diet. This diet required her to restrict her intake of fats and proteins.

The second sentence repeats the word diet, which appears in the first sentence. This repetition helps the reader understand the relationship of the ideas in the two sentences, and it helps the first sentence flow smoothly into the second.

Now here is an example with a key idea repeated:

The senior class raised five thousand dollars for the homeless. Such an effort should not go unnoticed.

In this example, the second sentence opens with Such an effort. These words repeat the key idea of the first sentence: that the class raised five thousand dollars for the homeless. Repeating the key idea shows how the ideas in the two sentences relate to each other; it also helps the first sentence flow smoothly into the second.

Practice 7.35

1. Read "Able-bodied but Addle-brained" on p. 81. Cite two transitions that signal chronological (time) order.

    _____

    _____

2. Read "One Step Forward and Two Steps Back" on p. 162. Cite one transition that signals illustration, one that signals cause and effect, and one that signals emphasis. Also, cite an example of repetition of a key word to achieve transition.

    _____

    _____

    _____

    _____

3. Read "Let's Hear It for Tradition" on p. 117. Cite one transition that signals chronological (time) order, one that signals admitting a point, and one that signals contrast. Also cite an example of repetition of a key idea.

    _____

    _____

    _____

    _____

Practice 7.36

Fill in the blanks with a transitional word or phrase from the chart beginning on p. 234. The first one is done as an example.

1. Douglas is the biggest practical joker I know. *For example,* _____ last week he glued Dana's shoes together.

2. I refuse to speak to Alonzo unless he learns to control his temper. _____ I refuse to be in the same room with him.

3. Diana was not expecting to be transferred to Houston. _____ she needs some time to adjust to the idea.

4. The novelty shop in the mall rarely advertises.

   _____ not many people realize what unusual items are sold there.

5. Television shapes our thinking more than we realize.

   _____ it can influence our emotions.

6. First I will make myself the most valuable employee I can be.

   _____ I will ask my boss for a raise.

Practice 7.37

Fill in the blanks with suitable transitions. Use the words and phrases from the chart beginning on p. 234 and repetition of key words and ideas.

The idea that the number 13 is unlucky is a superstition. _____, it is probably the most widely held superstition there is. In one way or another, it is observed all over the world. _____ hotels everywhere do not have a 13th floor. _____, their rooms are not numbered with 13. Many people will not have 13 guests at the dinner table.

Strangely, there is no single explanation for the superstition. _____ has many different stories behind it. _____, some experts say that 13 was unpopular from the time when people learned to count. By using their ten fingers and two feet as a unit, people came up with the number 12. _____ 13 became unlucky because it was unknown and frightening—beyond 12. In religious circles, the 13 superstition is traced to the Last Supper. In attendance were Jesus and the twelve Disciples—13 in all. Others trace the superstition to the story of the Valhalla banquet in Greek mythology, to which twelve gods were invited. _____, Loki, the Spirit of Strife and Mischief, intruded to make 13. _____ Balder, the favorite of the gods, was killed. _____ 13 is generally regarded as unlucky, the number was considered lucky by the ancient Chinese and Egyptians.

CHAPTER
8

Avoiding Sentence Fragments

To be a sentence, a word group must have a subject, a verb, and enough information to create a sense of completeness. If any one of these elements is missing, the word group cannot be a sentence. (See also p. 173.) A *sentence fragment* is a word group being passed off as a sentence because it has a capital letter and a period. However, a fragment cannot really stand as a sentence because it lacks a subject, a complete verb, or enough information for completeness.

The italicized words in the following examples are fragments.

fragment (subject missing):   The gale force wind toppled power lines. *And interrupted radio communications.*

fragment (complete verb missing): *The mother wondering what the children could be up to.* She quietly peeked into the bedroom.

fragment (lacks completeness): *When the band played their last song.* The audience cheered wildly.

If you have a tendency to write fragments, this chapter will help you. You will learn:

1. what a fragment is
2. how to identify fragments in your own writing
3. how to eliminate fragments from your writing

Pretest

Write *S* on the blank if the pair of word groups includes only sentences, and write *F* if the pair includes a fragment. Do not guess. If you are unsure, do not write anything. When you are done, check your answers in Appendix III.

1. _____ I enjoy one activity more than any other. Eating Mexican food.

2. _____ Terri's dog likes playing hide-and-seek. And playing with balls too.

3. _____ Although many people do not appreciate Sondra's sense of humor. I think she is very funny.

4. _____ After I took a study skills course, I learned to take better notes. Now my grades are improving steadily.

5. _____ One thing will convince Marion to study. The threat of flunking out of school.

6. _____ Jane having spoken too soon. Regretted her action.

7. _____ Apologizing for the misunderstanding. Jeffrey asked for another chance.

8. _____ Before you go on a job interview, you should learn something about the company offering the job. This information will enable you to ask intelligent questions.

9. _____ Bitten by the acting bug. My sister went to New York to try for a career on the stage.

10. _____ Some people refuse to believe the earth's resources are dwindling. Even though the evidence is all around them.

FRAGMENTS THAT RESULT FROM MISSING SUBJECTS

To be a sentence, every word group must have its own subject. A fragment results when a word group depends on another word group for its subject.

The salesclerk told us she would be with us in a minute. *But spent ten minutes with another customer.*

The italicized words are a fragment because they contain no subject for the verb *spent.* The subject in the preceding sentence (*salesclerk*) cannot operate outside its own sentence. (If you need help finding subjects and verbs, study the material beginning on p. 181.)

Here is another example:

Dr. Fine passed out the exam papers. *Then announced we would have one hour to complete the questions.*

The italicized words are a fragment because they contain no subject for the verb *announced.* The subject in the preceding sentence (*Dr. Fine*) cannot operate outside its own sentence.

To correct fragments that result from missing subjects, you have two options.

Method 1

Join the fragment to the sentence preceding it.

fragment:	The salesclerk told us she would be with us in a minute. *But spent ten minutes with another customer.*
sentence:	The salesclerk told us she would be with us in a minute but spent ten minutes with another customer.

Now the verb *spent* has a subject: *salesclerk.*

Method 2

Add a subject so the fragment becomes a sentence.

fragment:	Dr. Fine passed out the exam papers. *Then announced we would have one hour to complete the questions.*
sentence:	Dr. Fine passed out the exam papers. Then he announced we would have one hour to complete the questions.

Now the verb *announced* has a subject: *he.*

Practice 8.1

Each pair of word groups has one sentence and one fragment. Underline the fragment. Then rewrite to eliminate the fragment, using the correction method given in parentheses. (Method 1 is joining the fragment to the preceding sentence; method 2 is adding the missing subject.) The first one is done as an example.

1. (method 1) Alexander enrolled in a CPR course. <u>And learned valuable lifesaving techniques.</u>

   Alexander enrolled in a CPR course and learned valuable

   lifesaving techniques.

2. (method 1) I quit smoking for three months. But started again when I changed jobs.

   _____

   _____

3. (method 1) During the depression, my grandmother raised four daughters alone. And sold insurance to keep food on the table.

   _____

   _____

4. (method 2) Dr. Juarez described the requirements for the research project. Then answered questions from the class.

   _____

   _____

5. (method 2) The movers gently positioned the antique sofa against the wall. However, dropped the oil lamp that has been in my family for generations.

   _____

   _____

6. (method 1) The cruel children made fun of their new classmate's accent. And caused her to feel like an outcast.

   _____

   _____

7. (method 2) The comedy special earned the highest ratings for a program in that time slot. Still, offended many people because of the profanity used by three of the comedians.

_____

_____

Practice 8.2

On a separate sheet, rewrite the following paragraph to eliminate the two fragments that are created by missing subjects. If you have trouble finding the fragments, try reading the paragraph slowly, from last sentence to first sentence.

When a child turns eleven, a difficult period begins. It is a time of insecurity and a period of pulling away from parental control. The child wants to strike out alone. Yet is uncertain of his or her ability to do so. As a result, the child alternately rebels against the parents. And clings to them for support and reassurance. At this time, the child is a preadolescent. Some say preadolescence can be more difficult than adolescence. From what I've seen of my own eleven-year-old, I believe it.

FRAGMENTS THAT RESULT FROM INCOMPLETE VERBS

A fragment will result if you do not include a helping verb that belongs with an action verb. (See p. 176 on action and helping verbs.)

fragment: Jane going to the store.

sentence: Jane is (or was) going to the store. [The helping verb *is* (or *was*) is added.]

In general, *-ing* verb forms and past participle verb forms (see p. 312 and p. 321 for an explanation of past participles) must appear with a helping verb, or the result will be a fragment.

-ing fragment:	The baby sleeping soundly in the crib.
sentence:	The baby is (or was) sleeping soundly in the crib.
past participle fragment:	The police officer angered by the driver's attitude.
sentence:	The police officer was (or is) angered by the driver's attitude.

To correct fragments that result from incomplete verbs, you have two options.

<u>Method 1</u>

Add the missing helping verb. Choose from *is, are, was, were, have, has,* or *had*—whichever is appropriate.

fragment:	The sun setting in the west.
sentence formed by adding helping verb:	The sun is setting in the west.

<u>Method 2</u>

Change the *-ing* or past participle form to the present or past tense, whichever is appropriate.

fragment:	The baby sleeping soundly in the crib.
sentence with simple present tense verb:	The baby sleeps soundly in the crib.
fragment:	The police officer angered by the driver's attitude.
sentence with simple past tense verb:	The driver's attitude angered the police officer.

Practice 8.3

Change each fragment to a sentence using the method of correction given in parentheses. Method 1 is adding the missing helping verb; method 2 is changing the verb to the simple present or past tense form. The first two are done as examples.

1. (method 1) The university's faculty promotions committee considering the promotion requests of fifty instructors.

The university's faculty promotions committee is considering the

promotion requests of fifty instructors.

2. (method 2) The adolescent boys devouring everything in the refrigerator.

    The adolescent boys devoured everything in

    the refrigerator.

3. (method 2) Before the second half began, the coach reminding the front line to avoid off-sides penalties.

    _____

    _____

4. (method 2) The President's speech was enthusiastically received. Both Democrats and Republicans vowing to help pass the legislation requested.

    _____

    _____

5. (method 1) The hijackers want to call attention to their political agenda. Therefore, they taken a hardline stand during the negotiations.

    _____

    _____

6. (method 1) Many people believe that we are not the only life forms in the universe. They noting frequent UFO sightings and other unexplained events as proof.

    _____

    _____

7. (method 2) A female named Hatshepsut being an ancient Egyptian Pharoah.

    _____

    _____

8. (method 1) The hawk riding the air currents and soaring majestically.

    _____

    _____

Practice 8.4

On a separate sheet, rewrite the following paragraph to correct the three fragments that result from incomplete verbs. If you have trouble finding the fragments, try reading the paragraph slowly from last sentence to first.

In France there is a computer network with 1.4 million subscribers. In fact, more people joining every day. The network called "Minitel." Subscribers get a screen and a keyboard to log on to the system. The system does not run programs or do word processing, but subscribers can use it to find out what is playing in theatres and what is on sale at department stores. Minitel also employed to pay bills and get weather forecasts. Minitel is so successful that similar systems are predicted for other countries in the not too distant future.

FRAGMENTS THAT RESULT FROM MISSING SUBJECTS AND VERBS

Some fragments are word groups that lack both a subject and a complete verb. In the examples that follow, the fragments are the italicized word groups.

Gloomy weather always depresses me. *Also snowy weather.*

All the Smiths are very considerate. *Particularly in times of trouble.*

Unable to assemble Leo's bike. Dad was frustrated.

I walked across campus. *Reading my biology notes.*

To correct fragments that result from missing subjects and verbs, you have two options.

<u>Method 1</u>

Some fragments can be corrected by joining them to preceding or following sentences.

fragment:	*Unable to assemble Leo's bike.* Dad was frustrated.
sentence:	Unable to assemble Leo's bike, Dad was frustrated.
fragment:	I walked across campus. *Reading my biology notes.*
sentence:	I walked across campus reading my biology notes.

<u>Method 2</u>

Some fragments can be corrected by adding the missing subject and verb.

fragment:	Gloomy weather always depresses me. *Also snowy weather.*
sentence:	Gloomy weather always depresses me. Also I am depressed by snowy weather.
fragment:	All the Smiths are very considerate. *Particularly in times of trouble.*
sentence:	All the Smiths are very considerate. They are particularly considerate in times of trouble.

Practice 8.5

Each set of word groups contains one fragment and one sentence. First underline the fragment. Then rewrite to eliminate the fragment, using either method 1 (joining the fragment to the sentence) or method 2 (adding the missing subject and verb). The first one is done as an example.

1. <u>Fearing she would not get a satisfactory grade in physics.</u> Joanie hired a tutor.

   Fearing she would not get a satisfactory grade in physics, Joanie

   hired a tutor.

2. Hoping to confuse the opposition. The coach switched defensive strategies.

   _____

   _____

3. Because of his high cholesterol level, Rudy began a lowfat, high carbohydrate diet. At the advice of his physician and at the urging of his wife.

   _____

   _____

4. To score high on the Law School Admissions Test. A person must have strong verbal skills.

_____

_____

5. All the starting players are sophomores. Except Morrison, who is a graduating senior.

_____

_____

6. Caffeine is found in many everyday foods. Including candy, soft drinks, and coffee.

_____

_____

7. A wide range of idea-generation techniques is available to writers. Facing writer's block and searching for ideas to write about.

_____

_____

8. Before beginning any exercise program. You should have a complete physical. With a blood pressure screening.

_____

_____

9. Surprisingly, some fruits are a prime cause of tooth decay. Raisins, for example, with their high sugar content.

_____

_____

Practice 8.6

On a separate sheet, rewrite the paragraph, eliminating the five fragments that result from missing subjects and verbs. If you have trouble finding the fragments, read the paragraph slowly from last sentence to first.

There are fundamental differences between the alligator and the crocodile. The head of the alligator is shaped like a spade. The crocodile has a pointy nose. With protruding teeth. Living in swampy areas of the southeastern United States. The alligator is particularly numerous in Louisiana and parts of Florida. The crocodile, however, likes salt water, and in the United States is found only in south Florida. The alligator is dark brown. Also yellow markings. The crocodile is olive green and black. While there are differences, both animals benefit the ecology. Offering refuge to many species during floods. Their nests are important. Also, their droppings add vital nutrients to the water. Thus, these animals, which offer little threat to humans, should be protected. To preserve the balance of nature.

FRAGMENTS THAT RESULT FROM LACK OF COMPLETENESS

To be a sentence a word group must have a subject and a complete verb. However, it must also have a sense of completeness. The following has both a subject and a complete verb. It is not a sentence, however, because it lacks a sense of completeness.

                s.   v.
When George was a child.

When you read this word group, you do not have a sense of completeness. You need to know what happened when George was a child. Now read the following word group and notice that there *is* a sense of completeness. For this reason, the word group can stand as a sentence.

When George was a child, he had several health problems.

The following fragments are caused by lack of completeness. Read them aloud to hear that something is missing.

After the meeting was over.

Before we can leave on our vacation.

Although Jessie admitted he made a mistake.

Since I have begun taking college courses.

Word groups with subjects and complete verbs but insufficient completeness to be sentences are called *subordinate clauses.* (See p. 190 for more on subordinate clauses.) Subordinate clauses begin with *subordinating conjunctions,* one of the words or short phrases in the list that follows. When you check your work for fragments, pay special attention to word groups that begin with one of these words or short phrases. Be sure the necessary completeness is there.

after	before	when
although	even though	whenever
as	if	where
as if	in order to	wherever
as long as	since	whether
as soon as	so that	while
as though	unless	
because	until	

Some subordinate clause fragments begin with *who, where, which,* or *that,* so watch for word groups that begin with one of these words.

fragment:	Who lives next door to my parents.
fragment:	Where the Allegheny River meets the Monongahela.
fragment:	That I told you about.

To correct fragments that result from lack of completeness, you can often join the fragment to a sentence that appears before or after it.

fragment:	*After the meeting was over.* We all went out for coffee.
sentence:	After the meeting was over, we all went out for coffee.
fragment:	My self-esteem has improved. *Since I have begun taking college courses.*
sentence:	My self-esteem has improved since I have begun taking college courses.
fragment:	This is the Italian restaurant. *That I told you about.*
sentence:	This is the Italian restaurant that I told you about.

Practice 8.7

Each pair of word groups includes one fragment that results from lack of completeness and one sentence. Underline the fragment and correct it by joining it to the sentence. The first one is done as an example.

1. Because Terry's grades are so good. He is an excellent candidate for the humanities scholarship.

   Because Terry's grades are so good, he is an excellent candidate for the humanities scholarship.

2. If it snows another two inches. We will be able to go skiing in the morning.

3. Gail is an interesting person. Who understands how to relate to people.

4. Voter turnout is expected to reach an all-time high. Because the Senate race is so hotly contested.

5. By the time the box office opened at 6:00. A line had already formed halfway around the block.

6. If schoolchildren do not eat a nutritious lunch. Their schoolwork in the afternoon will suffer.

7. Professor Weinblatt is a talented teacher. Whose lectures hold everyone's attention.

8. If I were you. I would reconsider dropping out of school.

Practice 8.8

On a separate sheet, rewrite the following paragraph to eliminate the four fragments that result from lack of completeness. If you have trouble finding the fragments, try reading the paragraph slowly from last sentence to first.

Desktop publishing is the newest advance in office communications. If a company has a personal computer, the right software, and a laser printer. It can produce under its own roof in weeks what it used to take months to produce using outside publishing support. Desktop publishing has a variety of uses for both small businesses and large corporations. It can be used to produce manuals, operations reports, in-house newsletters, and sales letters. Many people think it will replace computer printouts. Which are unattractive and therefore hard to understand. Since desktop publishing is so new. It is hard to predict all the uses people will discover. One thing is certain, however. Because desktop publishing is proving versatile and inexpensive. There will certainly be a revolution in the publishing industry.

□ **TIPS FOR FINDING SENTENCE FRAGMENTS** □

1. Read your essay backwards, from last sentence to first. You may notice fragments easier this way because you will be less likely to join them mentally to other sentences.

2. Isolate each word group you are calling a sentence by placing one finger of one hand at the beginning capital letter and a finger of the other hand at the period. Now study the words between your fingers to be sure they generate the sense of completeness needed for sentence status.

3. Pay special attention to word groups with *-ing* and *-ed* verb forms. Be sure the verb is complete.

4. Be sure that each word group beginning with one of the subordinating conjunctions on page 204 has a sense of completeness.

5. Be sure word groups beginning with *who, which, where,* or *that* have the sense of completeness needed to be a sentence.

Post Test

On a separate sheet, rewrite the paragraphs to eliminate the fragments.

A. All families should plan and practice how to escape from their homes in the event of a fire. Especially at night. Because every minute spent in a burning house means extra danger. Escape routes should be planned and practiced periodically. Family members should practice crawling through the house in the event rooms are filled with smoke. Also learning how to move through the house in darkness. In addition, family members should plan where to meet outdoors. And what to do when they get there. If families plan and practice their escape, a house fire does not have to mean complete tragedy. To learn more about fire safety in the event of a house fire. Contact your local fire department.

B. The California condor looks very strange. When perched in a tree. It has a bald head and a wrinkled neck. And a large black, feathered body. Near the ground, the bird is hilariously awkward. It lumbers on takeoffs, and it crashes on landings. In the air, however, the bird is a breathtaking sight. Its wings spreading out nine feet. It can soar at an amazing 80 miles an hour.

At one time, one wild condor was left in California. Scientists managed to capture it when it swooped down to feed on a dead goat. The scientists took it to the San Diego Zoo. Where it lived with thirteen other condors. These condors, along with fourteen in the Los Angeles Zoo, the only remaining California condors in the world. Scientists captured these birds. To protect them from being shot or poisoned.

CHAPTER
9

Avoiding Run-On Sentences and Comma Splices

A single sentence can be made up of two word groups, each capable of being a sentence, *only if* these word groups are correctly separated. If the word groups are not separated at all, the result is a *run-on sentence*. If the word groups are separated by just a comma, the result is a *comma splice*. Run-on sentences and comma splices interfere with communication because they confuse sentence boundaries.

Here are two word groups that can be sentences:

    A. Randy could not wait to tell everyone his good news.

    B. He got the job he wanted so badly.

If you fail to separate these word groups, the result is a problem called a *run-on sentence:*

    run-on: Randy could not wait to tell everyone the good news he got the job he wanted so badly.

If you separate these word groups with just a comma, the result is a problem called a *comma splice:*

    comma splice: Randy could not wait to tell everyone the good news, he got the job he wanted so badly.

> NOTE: Word groups that can be sentences are also called *main clauses.* Therefore, another way to define run-on sentences and comma splices is to call them main clauses that are not correctly separated. (Main clauses are discussed on p. 190.)

If you write run-on sentences or comma splices, this chapter will help you. You will learn:

1. how to identify run-ons and comma splices
2. how to eliminate run-ons and comma splices from your writing

Pretest

If the word group is a run-on, write *RO* in the blank; if it is a comma splice, write *CS* in the blank; if it is correct, write *C* in the blank.

1. _____ I heard a siren, I pulled my car to the edge of the road.
2. _____ The sudden spring rains caused flash flooding the towns-people moved to higher ground.
3. _____ Charlie's singing career is going very well he has signed a contract with an important talent agent.
4. _____ If I had the opportunity, I would travel to Europe.
5. _____ The last day of the month is the best time to buy a car at that time dealers are anxious to reduce their inventory.
6. _____ People are changing their eating habits, more of us are restricting fat and cholesterol.
7. _____ Because I spilled bleach on it, the shirt is ruined.
8. _____ I do all my grocery shopping on Sunday to avoid the crowds.
9. _____ Martha subscribes to ten magazines she doesn't know where to put them all.
10. _____ To be sure that your car runs well, change the oil regularly.

CORRECTING RUN-ONS AND COMMA SPLICES WITH A PERIOD AND CAPITAL LETTER

One way to eliminate a run-on sentence or comma splice is to use a period and capital letter to make each main clause (word group that can stand as a sentence) a separate sentence.

run-on:	I left the party at 11:00 then I went to a movie.
sentence:	I left the party at 11:00. Then I went to a movie.
comma splice:	Darla is the perfect person for the job, she is reliable, intelligent, and efficient.
sentence:	Darla is the perfect person for the job. She is reliable, intelligent, and efficient.

Practice 9.1

Eliminate each run-on or comma splice by adding a period and capital letter. The first one is done as an example.

1. The city is recovering from its hard times, one sign of the recovery is the number of buildings under construction.

   The city is recovering from its hard times. One sign of the recovery

   is the number of buildings under construction.

2. The state finally approved the completion of Interstate 90, now there will be an exit near our business district.

   _____

   _____

3. Imran has won dozens of track trophies they are on display in the trophy case near the school auditorium.

   _____

   _____

4. A winter storm is forecast for later this evening, we plan to drive to Akron anyway.

   _____

   _____

5. I watched *West Side Story* on my VCR, it was very sad.

   _____

   _____

6. Be sure to arrive at the theater early there is certain to be a crowd.

Practice 9.2

On a separate sheet, rewrite the following paragraph; eliminate the three run-on sentences and comma splices by using periods and capital letters. If you have trouble finding the run-ons and comma splices, study each word group with a period and capital letter. Ask yourself how many main clauses (word groups that can stand as sentences) there are. If there is more than one, be sure they are correctly separated.

Bill Haley was the first real rock and roll star, his recording of "Crazy Man Crazy" was the first rock and roll record to make *Billboard's* pop music charts. Although he started out as a country singer, Haley decided to make a bid for teen appeal in the mid-1950s. When his "Rock Around the Clock" became the theme song for the movie *The Blackboard Jungle* in 1955, Haley scored big with teen audiences he was at this point a genuine rock and roll star. For the next two years he had a dozen top-40 hits, these included "See You Later Alligator" and "Burn That Candle." When Haley died in 1981, he was 55, and he had sold 60 million records.

CORRECTING RUN-ONS AND COMMA SPLICES WITH A SEMICOLON

A second way to eliminate a run-on or comma splice is to use a semicolon to separate the main clauses (word groups that can stand as sentences).

run-on:	None of us wanted to go out we were all too tired.
sentence:	None of us wanted to go out; we were all too tired.
comma splice:	Jim and Clarice bought a house that is a hundred years old, they will have to work hard to fix it up.

| sentence: | Jim and Clarice bought a house that is a hundred years old; they will have to work hard to fix it up. |

A run-on or comma splice can also be corrected with one of the following (see also p. 198):

| ; however, | ; furthermore, | ; consequently, |
| ; nevertheless, | ; therefore, | ; moreover, |

run-on:	The examination was harder than I expected I believe I passed it.
sentence:	The examination was harder than I expected; however, I believe I passed it.
comma splice:	On April Fools' Day my son put a rubber snake in my bed, he poured salt in my coffee.
sentence:	On April Fools' Day my son put a rubber snake in my bed; furthermore, he poured salt in my coffee.

CAUTION: When you use a semicolon, to avoid a run-on sentence or comma splice, be sure you have a main clause on *both sides* of the semicolon.

| Incorrect: | Carol decorated the Christmas tree; before Philippe got home from work. (There is no main clause after the semicolon.) |
| Correct: | Carol decorated the Christmas tree before Philippe got home from work. |

Practice 9.3

Eliminate the run-ons and comma splices by inserting semicolons.

1. Mother got three purses for her birthday, she will probably take two of them back.
2. The local tax base has been reduced, the city is forced to cut spending.
3. At first I did not like the movie, then I became interested in the main character and the plot.
4. I have tried to learn how to play bridge three times, however, each time I lost interest and gave up.

5. On his sixteenth birthday, Gregory took his driver's examination he passed with a very high score.

Practice 9.4

Insert semicolons to eliminate the three run-on sentences and comma splices. If you have trouble finding the run-ons and comma splices, study every word group with a period and capital letter and decide how many main clauses there are. If there is more than one main clause, be sure the clauses are correctly separated.

An increasing number of employers are providing day-care centers at their places of business they have learned that employees are more productive when they do not have to worry about baby-sitting arrangements for their children. In addition, when child-care is on company premises, employees do not have to call off work when the baby-sitter fails to show up. Many companies are learning that on-site day-care is a valuable fringe benefit. Employees are less likely to change their places of employment when day-care is available this means companies do not have to worry about rapid employee turnover. Undoubtedly, more and more companies will be providing day-care facilities, they are a benefit to both employer and employee.

CORRECTING RUN-ONS AND COMMA SPLICES WITH A COMMA AND COORDINATING CONJUNCTION

The words in the following list are *coordinating conjunctions*. These words are explained on p. 192. Now is a good time to review that explanation.

and	or	so
but	for	yet

You can eliminate a run-on sentence or comma splice by separating the main clauses (word groups that can stand as sentences) with a comma and coordinating conjunction.

run-on: The hamburger was not completely cooked I asked the waiter to take it back to the kitchen.

sentence:	The hamburger was not completely cooked, so I asked the waiter to take it back to the kitchen.
comma splice:	The compact disc player costs more than a tape player, it is worth the added expense.
sentence:	The compact disc player costs more than a tape player, but [yet] it is worth the added expense.

Practice 9.5

Eliminate the run-ons and comma splices with a comma and coordinating conjunction. The first one is done as an example.

1. Both candidates for the school board favor raising teacher salaries only Kelly has figured out a way to fund the raises.

    Both candidates for the school board favor raising teacher salaries,

    but only Kelly has figured out a way to fund the raises.

2. Carlo is an excellent pianist he has no desire to study music in college.

    _____

    _____

3. Dr. Stein explained the material on our exam then she dismissed class a little early.

    _____

    _____

4. My glasses are not strong enough, I cannot get to the eye doctor until next week.

    _____

5. You can clean your room before supper, you can do it after supper.

    _____

    _____

6. Interest rates are beginning to decline more young couples are buying a house.

    _____

    _____

Practice 9.6

On a separate sheet, rewrite the paragraph, using commas and co-ordinating conjunctions to eliminate the four run-ons and comma splices. If you have trouble finding the run-ons and comma splices, study every word group with a period and capital letter. Ask yourself how many main clauses there are. If there is more than one, be sure they are properly separated.

Exercise does not have to be unpleasant. If you follow some simple guidelines, you can enjoy the road to fitness. First pick a form of exercise you like, walking, swimming, running, bicycling, or whatever. You should set goals for yourself, you should make those goals a little harder as you move along. You should swim a bit further you should run a little longer each day. It is important to go slowly at first, you might sustain an injury. To avoid injuries, you should also do warm-up and cool-down stretching exercises. Finally, exercise with a friend you can encourage each other and enjoy the companionship.

RUN-ON AND COMMA SPLICE WORDS OF WARNING

Pay special attention to the words and short phrases in the list that follows. These words often begin main clauses. When you are editing and come across one of these words, check the number of main clauses in the sentence. If there is more than one, be sure the clauses are correctly separated.

however	then	moreover	nevertheless
therefore	thus	furthermore	similarly
hence	finally	consequently	next
as a result	in addition	on the contrary	for example

Practice 9.7

Each word group includes a run-on and comma splice word of warning. However, not all the word groups are run-ons or comma splices. If the word group is a run-on, write *RO* on the blank; if it is a comma splice, write *CS;* if it is a correct sentence, write *S.*

1. _____ Harry completed the committee report for his fraternity, then he took it to the chapter president.

2. _____ Carla's cavity was so deep she had to have two shots of novocaine consequently she couldn't feel the right side of her face for three hours.

3. _____ We waited most of the morning for Jeff to arrive; finally, we just left without him.

4. _____ Not everyone understands Dad's sarcastic sense of humor; as a result, some people feel insulted when he teases them.

5. _____ In addition to losing my keys last week, I misplaced my good leather gloves.

6. _____ First you should choose an advisor in your major field of study, next you should select an advisor in your minor field of study.

7. _____ Dr. Schultz is sick with the flu therefore our midterm has been postponed until next week.

8. _____ The football team lost three games in a row as a result of errors by the defensive squad.

□ TIPS FOR FINDING RUN-ON SENTENCES □ AND COMMA SPLICES

1. Study every word group with a capital letter and a period. Determine the number of main clauses. If there are two or more, be sure these clauses are correctly separated with a semicolon or with a comma and coordinating conjunction.

2. Focus on every word group that contains a comma. Check before and after the comma. If there is a main clause on *both* sides of the comma, be sure to include a coordinating conjunction with the comma.

3. Pay special attention to word groups with words of warning. If these words are separating main clauses, be sure a semicolon is used before the warning word.

4. Do not assume a long sentence is a run-on or comma splice. The only true test is whether main clauses are correctly separated—length is not a factor.

Post Test

On a separate sheet, rewrite the following paragraphs to eliminate the run-on sentences and comma splices. You may use any or all of the correction methods discussed in this chapter.

A.   Margaret Chase Smith was the first woman elected to both the United States House of Representatives and the United States Senate. Her husband, a Republican congressman from Maine, died in 1940, Mrs. Smith replaced him in the House of Representatives. She served in the House for eight years. She was elected to the Senate in 1948 she was reelected in 1954 and 1960. In 1950 she was one of the first senators to oppose Senator Joseph McCarthy. In 1965 she campaigned for the Republican presidential nomination, she was the first woman to do so. Smith was an influential legislator during her years in Congress, moreover, she was not put off by the fact that at the time, politics was largely the domain of males. In fact, Smith helped pave the way for other women to enter the political arena at the national level.

B.   Many schools have alcohol-awareness programs to steer children away from drinking, however, parents need to be involved as well. Parents can do a number of things, for example, they can discuss drinking scenes in programs and movies they watch with their children. Parents should ask questions such as "Why do you think grown-ups drink?" and "Can grown-ups have fun without drinking?" Because children may become confused seeing adults drink when they have been told to say no, parents should explain the health risks associated with alcohol and the fact that the legal drinking age is 21. It is also a good idea to emphasize positive reasons for saying no: Children need to keep their heads clear for school, they also need to keep their bodies healthy for athletics. Parents can also role-play with their children. Give them a glass of water and have them practice saying "No thanks." Parents must be actively involved, they cannot leave the full responsibility for alcohol prevention to the schools.

CHAPTER
10

Choosing Words Carefully

Writers must choose their words carefully so they communicate clearly and create a positive impression. In this chapter, you will learn principles of effective word choice, including:

1. using specific words
2. using simple words
3. building your vocabulary
4. using idioms
5. distinguishing between frequently confused words
6. avoiding slang
7. avoiding clichés
8. eliminating wordiness
9. avoiding double negatives
10. improving your spelling

SPECIFIC WORD CHOICE

To communicate your ideas as clearly and exactly as possible, choose specific words rather than general ones. Study the following chart to understand the difference between specific and general words:

General	Specific
car	red Camaro
book	*Gone with the Wind*
shoe	loafer
aunt	Aunt Millie
math course	Algebra II

sweater	yellow pullover sweater
walk	swagger
eat	gobble

As you can tell from the chart, specific words give a more exact idea than the general ones do because they provide more specific information. Here are two sentences to consider. The first one includes general words, and the second includes specific ones. Which sentence communicates more precisely?

The girl sat on the chair feeling bad.

Susan slumped into the chair, worried about losing her job.

Clearly, the second sentence communicates more exactly because the words are more specific; they provide more detailed information.

Chapter 3 discusses specific word choice in more detail. Now is the time to review that material, which begins on p. 63. In addition, Chapter 3 includes several *Practice* exercises to help you learn to use specific words. If you have not already done so, complete these exercises.

□ **TIP FOR SPECIFIC WORD CHOICE** □

Do not worry too much about specific word choice when you are writing a first draft. Instead, when you revise the draft, underline every general noun, verb, and modifier. Then substitute more specific words for some or all of what you underlined.

SIMPLE WORD CHOICE

Sometimes people think that the bigger and fancier their words are, the better their writing is. However, this is not true at all. In fact, if you consistently choose fancy, twenty-dollar words, your writing will seem unnatural.

The truth is, effective writing is clear writing. To be clear, you probably know most of the words you need. Your job is to choose the right, specific words that convey your meaning as directly, simply, and exactly as possible. Consider, for a moment, this sentence taken from "Wear a Helmet" on p. 135:

For example, many times I have seen the flash of a helmet before I have seen the motorcycle itself.

This sentence is effective, in part because it communicates with clear, specific, *simple* language. Any reader will appreciate the natural style that comes from the simple, specific word choice.

Now consider how you react to this revision of the sentence, a revision that relies on overblown, fancy words:

> By way of illustrative clarification, allow me to interject that on numerous occasions I have visually detected the sudden display of light from a helmet prior to visually acknowledging the two-wheeled, engine-propelled vehicle itself.

Like most readers, you probably find this sentence wordy and unclear. It shows, however, that you should not reach for high-sounding words to get your message across. Instead, be specific and be simple in your word choice.

Practice 10.1

1. Read "Wear a Helmet" on p. 135. Copy a sentence with specific yet simple word choice. Underline the simple, specific word(s).

    _____

    _____

2. Read "The Plant" on p. 87. Copy three sentences with specific, simple word choice. Underline the simple, specific words.

    A. _____

    _____

    B. _____

    _____

    C. _____

    _____

3. Read "Let's Hear It for Tradition" on p. 117. Copy two sentences with specific, simple word choice. Underline the specific, simple words.

    A. _____

    _____

    B. _____

    _____

4. Read "Different Kinds of Shoppers" on p. 168. Copy two sentences with specific, simple word choice. Underline the specific, simple words.

A. _____

_____

B. _____

_____

VOCABULARY BUILDING

"I know what I want to say, but I don't know how to say it." If you often speak something like this, you probably need to build up your vocabulary. To be an effective writer, you must know enough words to express a wide range of ideas with precision. Furthermore, studies show that successful people are likely to have rich, varied vocabularies. If you need to add to your storehouse of words, *now* is the time to begin.

To improve your vocabulary, you must understand one point: there is no quick, easy way. You must dedicate yourself to the task from this point forward. You must become interested in words, study words each day, and review the words you learn often. The rewards will be great, however. You will become a more effective writer, speaker, listener, and reader.

Finding Words to Learn

Vocabulary lists for study are available in any vocabulary-building book in your campus bookstore, study skills center, or library. However, more learning will occur if *you* decide on the words to learn.

To develop your own list, write down every unfamiliar word you hear or read that you want to learn. Pay particular attention to unfamiliar words in your textbooks and class lectures. Make note of words you see in the newspaper and magazines and words you hear on television and radio. Also write down unfamiliar words you hear friends and family use. In addition, write the sentence you saw or heard the word used in. If you develop your list of words this way, you will be more motivated than you would be with a list of words developed by someone else. Also, it will be easier to learn words you already have heard or read.

Learning New Words

You can take these steps to improve your vocabulary.

1. Keep a small notebook with you. Each time you hear or read an unfamiliar word you wish to learn, write the word in the notebook with the sentence in which the word was used. If you do not want to interrupt your reading to write words in your notebook, underline the unfamiliar words and record them in your notebook after you have finished reading.

2. *Each day* transfer each new word in your notebook to its own index card. On the front of the card write the word, correctly spelled, and the sentence the word was used in. If you do not know how to pronounce the word, copy the dictionary pronunciation on the front of the card. Check a dictionary, and on the back of the card write the meaning of the word. If there is more than one meaning, record the one that fits the use of the word in the sentence on the front of the card. Then write a sentence of your own on the back of the card that uses the word correctly.

3. Study your cards *every day.* Learn each new word and review several from previous days.

4. When possible, learn meanings through association. For example, to learn that *ostracize* means "to banish or expel," you may associate it with an ostrich, which banishes itself by poking its head in the sand.

5. Learn clusters of words. For example, once you have learned what *luminous* means, learn *luminance, illuminate, luminary,* and *luminosity.* To discover word clusters, look for related words around each word you check in the dictionary.

6. Use the words you learn as you speak, write, and think, so they become a natural part of your vocabulary.

7. Work on vocabulary building with a friend or classmate. Quiz each other, trade words, try to stump each other, use your new words in conversation with each other, and study your cards together. With a partner, the learning is more fun, and your motivation may be greater.

8. Buy two good dictionaries: a fat paperback and a hardbound collegiate dictionary. Carry the paperback with you to check words as they come up. Keep the hardbound dictionary where you study or read so it will be convenient to check words.

9. After studying vocabulary awhile, you may discover that many words share common prefixes (beginnings) and suffixes (endings). At this point, study the meanings of prefixes and suffixes as an aid to learning meanings. To do this, consult a vocabulary book in the library or study skills center.

Practice 10.2

1. For a day, record in a small notebook any words you see or hear that you do not know. At the end of the day, make index cards for the words according to the directions given in the previous discussion.

2. Find a vocabulary-building partner. Arrange a specific time and place to meet during the week to work on vocabulary according to the suggestions in the previous discussion.

3. Buy a copy of *Time* or *Newsweek* and read three articles. Underline every word that is not familiar to you. Add some of these words to your index cards. Read at least one article in the magazine each day and add unfamiliar words to your cards. When you are through with the magazine, buy another and begin again.

Idioms

An *idiom* is an expression whose meaning cannot be determined from the meaning of its individual words. Consider, for example, the idiom "drop someone a line." The four individual words in that expression do not add up to its rightful meaning, which is to write a letter or correspond in writing: As soon as I move in to my new apartment, I will *drop you a line* with my address.

You are probably familiar with a great many idioms already. Others, however, may be new to you, particularly if you speak English as a second language. As you work to build your vocabulary, pay particular attention to idioms. When you look up a word in your dictionary, any idioms associated with the word will be noted for you for easy reference. To become familiar with ten frequently occurring idioms, review the following list.

make allowance for—excuse; allow for

I can *make allowances for* Carla's bad behavior because she is very tense right now.

call the shots—be in charge

Joel is not happy unless he is *calling the shots.*

[out] in the cold—ignored

After I missed three committee meetings, all the members left me *out in the cold,* so I did not know what was happening.

to land on one's feet—to recover from a dangerous or difficult situation

Although Jacob lost his job last year, he has *landed on his feet* and found a better job.

go to any lengths—do anything to reach a goal

Lizette wants a graduate assistantship so badly that she will *go to any lengths* to get it.

make one's mark—achieve success

As the most honored coach in the school's history, Rich Morales has *made his mark* in our community.

To play by ear—to go ahead without a plan

I am not sure what I will tell Katrina. I will have to *play it by ear.*

on the ropes—close to failure

I am really *on the ropes* on this project. It is due in two days, and I still have no ideas.

strike a blow for—further the cause of

Forcing the dictator to leave the country *struck a blow* for democracy.

carry weight—have importance

Because of her reputation in scientific circles, Dr. Wang's opinion *carries considerable weight.*

Practice 10.3

From the following list, pick eight idioms that you are unsure of. Look up their meanings in your dictionary by checking under the italicized key word in the idiom. Then, on a separate sheet, write the meaning of each of the idioms and use each one in a sentence that you compose. If you are unfamiliar with more than eight idioms, learn two or three each day until you know them all.

chew the fat	*rub* off on
chew the scenery	*rub* out

kick the bucket

stay put

steer clear of

still and all

grasp at straws

goof off

talk back to

take it upon oneself

take five

take responsibility

clear the air

up in the *air*

do or die

in the *cards*

lay (put) one's *cards*
  on the table

free and easy

be in someone's *shoes*

fix up

try one's hand at

keep a *hand* in

put one's best foot forward

put something over on

put oneself out

in *store*

set *store* by

get out of line

draw the line at

tough it out

keep *track* (lose *track*)

off the *track*

over a *barrel*

off *base*

touch *base*

make *ends* meet

give up the *ghost*

give and take

keep one's *head*

lose one's *head*

be of one *mind*

FREQUENTLY CONFUSED WORDS

The words given here sometimes present problems for writers. However, errors with these words will distract or annoy a reader, so you should check your usage carefully.

A/An

1. *A* is used before a consonant sound. (See p. 297 on vowels and consonants.)

    a tree, *a* friendly face, *a* unicycle (despite the opening vowel, this word begins with a consonant *sound*)

2. *An* is used before a vowel sound.

    an apple, *an* ice cream cone, *an* hour (despite the opening consonant, this word begins with a vowel *sound*)

Practice 10.4

A. Fill in the blanks with *a* or *an*.

1. ____ friendly stranger gave us directions.

2. Troy suggested ____ interesting interpretation of the short story.

3. ____ uncle of mine is ____ sheriff in ____ county west of here.

4. Laughter is ____ universal language.

5. ____ sink full of dirty dishes awaited me when I returned from ____ meeting of the Art Guild.

6. ____ unicorn is ____ mythical beast.

B. On a separate sheet, write two sentences using *a* and two using *an*.

Accept/Except

1. *Accept* means "to receive."

   I *accept* your offer of help with thanks.

2. *Except* means "leaving out" or "excluding."

   All the votes *except* those from Precinct Z have been counted.

> TIP: Think of the *ex* in *ex*cept and *ex*cluding.

Practice 10.5

A. Fill in the blanks with *accept* or *except*.

1. I cannot _____ your explanation.

2. It is not easy to _____ defeat with dignity.

3. Everyone _____ Joanie found the movie dull.

4. No teacher will _____ a paper as sloppy as this.

5. _____ for the first number, the concert was very good.

6. The examination was easy _____ for the last essay question.

B. On a separate sheet, write two sentences using *accept* and two using *except*.

Advice/Advise

1. *Advice* is a noun meaning a suggestion or opinion.

   In her column, Ann Landers gives *advice*.

2. *Advise* is a verb meaning to give advice.

   The doctor *advised* Harriet to quit smoking.

TIP: If you have a vice, you need *advice.*

Practice 10.6

A. Fill in the blanks with *advice* or *advise.*

1. You should follow my _____ and go back to school.

2. Why should I _____ you if you won't do as I say?

3. If you reject my _____, I will offer no more help.

4. Anton's _____ is always sound because he thinks problems through so carefully.

5. I cannot _____ you without more information.

6. No one can _____ you on matters of the heart.

B. On a separate sheet, write two sentences with *advice* and two with *advise.*

Affect/Effect

1. *Affect* is a verb meaning to influence.

   The steelworkers' strike has begun to *affect* the local economy.

2. *Effect* is usually a noun meaning result.

   The *effects* of the plant layoffs will be serious.

3. *Effect* is sometimes a verb meaning to bring about.

   Councilman Page will try to *effect* a change in the city charter.

Practice 10.7

A. Fill in the blanks with *affect* or *effect.*

1. The _____ of the drought will be felt in the marketplace early this fall.

2. I hope my decision to resign from the committee will not have a negative _____ on the committee's work.

3. The store owners petitioned the mall management to _____ a change in Christmas shopping hours.

4. What people eat for breakfast can _____ how they perform all morning.

5. An immediate _____ of an oil shortage is increased gasoline prices.

6. Childhood traumas _____ us as adults.

B. On a separate sheet, write two sentences using *affect* and two using *effect*.

All ready/Already

1. *All ready* means "all set," or "prepared."

   The crew was *all ready* to set sail.

2. *Already* means "by this time."

   Do not apply for the job because the position has *already* been filled.

TIP: *All ready* and *all set* are both two words.

Practice 10.8

A. Fill in the blanks with *all ready* or *already.*

1. The party was _____ over, and the guest of honor had not arrived.

2. I just cleaned this closet, and _____ it is cluttered.

3. The water skier waved his hand to the driver to signal he was _____ .

4. Harry and Alice were _____ to go, but I still had to make a phone call.

5. _____ Hank is whining, and we just got here.

6. As soon as Martha completes her last economics course, she will be _____ to graduate.

B. On a separate sheet, write two sentences using *all ready* and two using *already.*

All right/Alright

In formal usage, *all right* is considered the acceptable form. *Alright* is not acceptable in college papers.

Among/Between

1. Use *between* for two people or things.

There are many differences *between* working in a fast food restaurant and working in a fancy restaurant.

2   Use *among* for more than two people or things.

The argument *among* the students lasted most of the class period.

> TIP: *Between* refers to two people or things, and there are two *e*'s in the second syllable of the word.

Practice 10.9

A.   Fill in the blanks with *among* or *between.*

1.   _____ the students in the class, only Mario earned an A on the final exam.

2.   It is difficult for me to choose _____ teaching and research for my career.

3.   The competition _____ the three teams is friendly.

4.   My antique necklace is _____ my most prized possessions.

5.   Ten-year-old Anna could not decide _____ the red bicycle and the green one.

6.   Just _____ you and me, I do not trust Lee.

B.   On a separate sheet, write two sentences using *among* and two using *between.*

Been/Being

1.   *Been* is the past participle of *be.* It is usually used after *have, has,* or *had.*

It has *been* years since I have seen Joel.

2.   *Being* is the *-ing* (present participle) form of *be.* It is usually used after *am, is, are, was,* or *were.*

Wanda is *being* careless when she leaves her purse there.

> TIP: Do not use *been* without *have, has,* or *had.*

Incorrect: I been working hard.

Correct: I have been working hard.

Practice 10.10

A. Fill in the blanks with *being* or *been*.

1. Although I have _____ absent, I studied the assignments.

2. The child does not understand that she is _____ rude.

3. The Chens had _____ gone a week before they remembered they forgot to stop their mail.

4. I am _____ inducted into the honor society tonight.

5. Ned has _____ more than patient.

6. Six families are _____ relocated to make way for the new road.

B. On a separate sheet, write two sentences with *been* and two with *being*.

Beside/Besides

1. *Beside* means "alongside of."

   Park the car *beside* the garage.

2. *Besides* means "in addition to."

   Besides being too small, the house was poorly located.

Practice 10.11

A. Fill in the blanks with *beside* or *besides*.

1. _____ the garage, the dog buried its bones.

2. _____ the creek, the collie lay sleeping peacefully.

3. Mother hid the children's Christmas presents in the chest _____ the bed.

4. Few people _____ you and me realize that Randy is insecure.

5. _____ having a headache, I feel sick to my stomach.

6. What is the restaurant's specialty, _____ pasta?

B. On a separate sheet, write two sentences using *beside* and two using *besides*.

Can/Could

1. *Can* is used for the present tense to mean "am/is/are able to."

   If I get an income tax refund, I *can* buy a stereo.

2. *Could* is used for the past tense to mean "was/were able to."

   I thought I *could* finish by noon, but I was wrong.

Practice 10.12

A. Fill in the blanks with *can* or *could*. To determine if you need present or past tense, check the tense of the other verb in the sentence, or look for clues such as *yesterday* or *now*.

1. Before I _____ walk, I was reading.

2. When I was sixteen, I _____ stay up all night and feel great the next day; now I _____ sleep for eight hours and still be tired.

3. The photographer was certain he _____ restore the old family picture I found in Grandma's steamer trunk.

4. I _____ never be sure if Sam is telling the truth or lying.

5. Jenny is sure she _____ help us draft a petition to circulate.

6. Last year I _____ not afford a vacation, but this year I _____ manage a week at the ocean.

B. On a separate sheet, write two sentences using *can* and two using *could*.

Fewer/Less

1. Use *fewer* for things that can be counted.

   Fewer than half the class passed the midterm.

2. Use *less* for something considered as a unit, and for something that cannot be counted.

   There is *less* concern for the homeless than there should be.

> TIP: Think of the word *countless*. It contains *count* and *less*. Then remember that *less* is used for things that are not counted.

Practice 10.13

A. Fill in the blanks with *fewer* or *less*.

1. The older I get, the _____ I worry about minor matters.

2. If you take vitamin C, you may get _____ colds.

3. _____ accidents occurred on Fifth Avenue this year than last year.

4. The movie had _____ violent scenes than I expected.

5. If more people would exercise, there would be _____ depression in the world.

6. With _____ sex discrimination in the workplace, more women are executives.

B. On a separate sheet, write two sentences using *fewer* and two using *less*.

Good/Well

1. *Good* is an adjective, so it only describes nouns and pronouns.

   Lester is a *good* drummer. (*Good* describes the noun, *drummer.*)

2. *Well* is an adverb, so it describes verbs.

   Bonnie sings *well.* (*Well* describes the verb, *sings.*)

3. *Well* also refers to health.

   Tanya does not feel *well* enough to join us.

Practice 10.14

A. Fill in the blanks with *good* or *well*.

1. This is a _____ time to congratulate you on how you played.

2. I hope I do as _____ as you did in the time trials.

3. I did not do very _____ on my chemistry exam because I did not understand covalent bonding _____ enough.

4. The movie was not as _____ as I expected it to be.

5. Carol played a _____ tennis match today; I wish I had played as _____.

6. The _____ behavior of the children earned them a treat.

7. After eating five cookies, I do not feel _____.

B. On a separate sheet, write two sentences with *good* and two with *well.*

It's/Its

1. *It's* is the contraction form and means "it is" or "it has."

   It's time to head for home.

   It's been a pleasure serving you.

2. *Its* is the possessive form, so it shows ownership.

   The rubber tree plant is dropping *its* leaves.

> TIP: Do not use *it's* unless you can substitute *it is* or *it has*.

Practice 10.15

A. Fill in the blanks with *it's* or *its*.

1. _____ a sure bet that the store will close if _____ merchandising policies don't improve.

2. The head librarian announced that the library has increased _____ holdings by 30 percent.

3. _____ hard to believe, but _____ been three years since we met.

4. If _____ work you want, you have come to the right place.

5. _____ a shame, but Cinema Sixty has changed _____ policy of showing only first-run features.

6. The company decided to reduce _____ costs by switching from television to direct-mail advertising.

B. On a separate sheet, write two sentences using *it's* and two using *its*.

Of/Have

Do not substitute *of* for *have. Have* is a helping verb (see p. 177), and *of* is a preposition (see p. 182).

Incorrect	Correct
could of	could have or could've
will of	will have
would of	would have or would've
should of	should have or should've
may of	may have
must of	must have
might of	might have or might've

Passed/Past

1. *Past* refers to a previous time. It can also mean "by."

   It is not possible to change the *past.*

Past experiences affect us in the present.

I drove *past* your house yesterday.

2. *Passed* is the past tense of the verb *to pass,* and means "went by" or "handed."

As John *passed* Cathy's desk, he gave her a rose.

The teacher *passed* the specimen around so all could see it.

> TIP: Think of the letters *p* and *t,* as in *past* and *previous time.*

Practice 10.16

A. Fill in the blanks with *past* or *passed.*

1. When the police officer _____ the warehouse, she saw the flames.

2. The _____ too often intrudes on the present.

3. As the marching band _____ the reviewing stand, thunderous applause erupted.

4. We should forgive Kurt for his _____ mistakes.

5. The relay runner _____ the baton to his teammate, who quickly _____ the runner in first place.

6. In times _____ it was safe to walk at night.

B. On a separate sheet, write two sentences with *past* and two with *passed.*

Quiet/Quit/Quite

1. *Quiet* means "silence/silent" or "calm."

Some people can work with a radio on, but I need *quiet.*

2. *Quit* means "stop" or "give up."

Even if I wanted to *quit* school, my parents would not let me.

3. *Quite* means "very" or "exactly."

I am *quite* sure no one lives here.

That is not *quite* the point I am making.

Practice 10.17

A. Fill in the blanks with *quiet, quit,* or *quite.*

1. If you are _____ certain you can remain _____ for an hour, I can get my work done.

2. If you do not _____ smoking soon, it is _____ likely that you will have health problems.

3. The _____ in this room is almost eerie.

4. Martha returned the paint because it was not _____ the color she wanted.

5. If you are not _____ certain that you can finish this project, you should probably _____.

6. Alonzo _____ his fraternity because the parties were too _____.

B. On a separate sheet, write two sentences using *quiet,* two using *quit,* and two using *quite.*

Suppose/Supposed

1. *Suppose* means "assume" or "guess."

   I *suppose* I can be done by six if I hurry.

2. *Supposed* means "ought" or "should." In this case, it is preceded by a form of *be* and is always followed by *to. Supposed* is also the past tense form of *suppose.*

   We are *supposed* to clear the cafeteria tables when we are through eating. (should)

   The mayor *supposed* he would win the election by a large margin. (past tense of *suppose,* meaning *assume*)

TIP: Always use *supposed* (with the *-ed*) to mean "ought" or "should." *I am suppose to go* is an incorrect form written when the *t* in *to* is allowed to function as the *d* in *supposed* in spoken English.

Practice 10.18

A. Fill in the blanks with *suppose* or *supposed.*

1. Eric is _____ to drive everyone to the party, but where do you _____ he will get a car?

2. We all _____ Matthew would go on to graduate school.

3. What do you _____ will happen if the research council does not get the grant it is _____ to?

4. Cathy was _____ to meet me here an hour ago.

5. Lorenzo is _____ to bring the chips to the party, but I _____ he will forget.

6. Do you _____ it is possible to finish the cleaning before our guests arrive?

B. On a separate sheet, write two sentences using *suppose* and two using *supposed.*

Then/Than

1. *Then* refers to a certain time.

   I asked Sylvia what she meant; *then* she yelled at me.

2. *Than* is used to compare.

   The chicken is tastier *than* the veal.

> TIP: *Then* and *time* have an *e; than* and *compare* have an *a.*

Practice 10.19

A. Fill in the blanks with *then* or *than.*

   1. My new apartment is less noisy _____ my previous one.

   2. If you arrive _____, you will be able to meet my sister.

   3. _____ she said that she would rather arrive late _____ not at all.

   4. You asked for my advice and _____ refused to take it.

   5. Diana would rather quit school _____ sell her stamp collection for tuition money.

   6. It is easier to get a campus job _____ people realize.

B. On a separate sheet, write two sentences using *then* and two using *than.*

There/Their/They're

1. *There* shows direction. It can also come before *are, was, were, is,* or *will be.*

   Put the boxes down over *there.*

   There are twelve of us helping out at the senior citizens' center.

2. *Their* is a possessive form; it shows ownership.

   The students opened *their* test booklets and began to work.

3. *They're* is the contraction form of *they are.*

   If *they're* leaving now, I should go with them.

> TIP: Use *they're* only when you can substitute *they are.*

Practice 10.20

A. Fill in the blanks with *there, their,* or *they're.*

    1. According to the evening paper, _____ will be a serious wheat shortage next year.

    2. Henri and Tom said _____ not going unless they can bring _____ boom boxes with them.

    3. If you put the couch over _____, then _____ will be enough room for _____ record collection.

    4. The police officers are concerned because the levy that would grant _____ pay raises may not get on the November ballot.

    5. _____ asking five hundred dollars for _____ used piano.

    6. I looked _____, but I couldn't find _____ coats.

B. On a separate sheet, write two sentences using *there,* two using *their,* and two using *they're.*

Through/Though/Threw

    1. *Through* means "in one side and out the other." It also means "finished."

        It was hard for Grandma to pass the thread *through* the needle.

        I'll be *through* proofreading my essay in an hour.

    2. *Though* means "although"; *as though* means "as if."

        Though Alan has never taken lessons, he plays the piano well.

        Maria acts *as though* she is mad at the world.

    3. *Threw* is the past tense of *throw.*

        The quarterback *threw* an incomplete pass.

Practice 10.21

A. Fill in the blanks with *through, though,* or *threw.*

    1. When she was _____ studying, Eleni rested for an hour.

    2. _____ Hank pretends he doesn't care, anyone can see _____ his act.

3. Cal won a stuffed rabbit when he _____ the baseball at the milk bottles on the midway.

4. _____ Lionel made a basket, the shot didn't count because he _____ the ball after the buzzer.

5. Diane strolled _____ the park as _____ she did not have any worries.

6. If we elect Smith we will have a better chance to work _____ the police labor dispute.

B. On a separate sheet, write two sentences using *through,* two using *though,* and two using *threw.*

To/Too/Two

1. *To* means "toward." It can also be part of a verb, as in *to run.*

I was going *to* class when I saw Rhonda.

I wanted *to* ask you a favor.

2. *Too* means "excessively" or "also."

The movie was *too* violent for me.

I would like a piece of that cake *too.*

3. *Two* is the number.

Only two candidates for the school board have experience.

Practice 10.22

A. Fill in the blanks with *to, too,* or *two.*

1. Before beginning _____ exercise, stretch for ten minutes.

2. _____ much smoking and _____ little exercise make Dan a prime candidate _____ get a heart attack.

3. The car needed _____ new tires and a water pump _____.

4. _____ tell you the truth, I was not _____ pleased _____ be headed _____ the mall _____ days before Christmas.

5. The highlight of the trip was going _____ Disney World for _____ days.

6. A week is _____ long for me _____ be gone.

B. On a separate sheet, write two sentences using *to,* two using *too,* and two using *two.*

Use/Used

1. *Use* is a noun that means "purpose." It is also a verb that means "make use of."

   What possible *use* could this have?

   How do you *use* this gadget?

2. *Used* is the past tense and past participle form of the verb *to use*. It also means "adjusted" or "accustomed"; in this case, it is followed by *to*.

   The child *used* the towel and threw it on the floor.

   I have *used* this product successfully before.

   I am not *used* to this kind of treatment.

TIP: *I am use to* is an incorrect form written when the *t* in *to* is allowed to function as the *d* in *used*. The correct form is *I am used to*.

Practice 10.23

A. Fill in the blanks with *use* or *used*.

1. I am not _____ to the idea that I am now an adult.
2. I _____ that shampoo, but I did not like the results.
3. This school does not make sufficient _____ of computers.
4. A person _____ to feel safe walking alone at night.
5. We have _____ that textbook in our English class.
6. I _____ to wear braces on my teeth.

B. On a separate sheet, write two sentences using *use* and two using *used*.

Where/Were/We're

1. *Where* refers to location.

   Home is *where* a person should feel safe.

2. *Were* is the past tense form of *are*.

   The Raiders *were* ahead until the third quarter.

3. *We're* is the contraction form of *we are*.

   We're certain that Mom will do well in school.

Practice 10.24

A. Fill in the blanks with *where, were,* or *we're.*

1. If you ask me, we do not know _____ we are going.

2. The plans _____ changed because _____ uncertain about how long it will take us to drive to Cleveland.

3. The new federal building will be built _____ the old courthouse now stands.

4. _____ all uncertain about what the future holds and _____ we will be this time next year.

5. Debbie and Lenny _____ the best-behaved children at the party.

6. _____ going, but _____ not happy about it.

B. On a separate sheet, write two sentences using *were,* two using *where,* and two using *we're.*

Will/Would

1. *Will* looks to the future from the present tense.

   Dr. Schwartz believes [present tense] he *will* [at a later date] get his book published.

2. *Would* looks to the future from the past tense.

   Dr. Schwartz believed [past tense] he *would* [at a later date] get his book published.

3. *Would* is sometimes used to mean "will."

   Would you help me with this?

Practice 10.25

A. Fill in the blanks with *will* or *would.*

1. Councilwoman Drucker promised that she _____ not vote to raise city taxes.

2. The regional basketball tournament _____ be played on our campus this spring.

3. If you do not stop snapping at people, no one _____ want to be around you.

4. The fans wondered who _____ pitch the crucial last inning.

5. The Academic Council plans to announce that graduation requirements _____ change in the near future.

6. The child _____ not leave unless he could take his toy.

B. On a separate sheet, write two sentences using *will* and two using *would.*

Whose/Who's

1. *Whose* indicates possession.

   The person *whose* car is double-parked got a ticket.

2. *Who's* is the contraction form of *who is* or *who has.*

   Who's on the telephone?

   Who's been watching the game?

> TIP: Use *who's* only when you can substitute *who is* or *who has.*

Practice 10.26

A. Fill in the blanks with *whose* or *who's.*

1. _____ umbrella was left on the desk?

2. Dr. Berringer is a teacher _____ lectures are always stimulating.

3. It is impossible to know _____ been here in the last hour.

4. They are the couple _____ children broke our window.

5. _____ the instructor for this course?

6. I cannot be sure _____ coming to Luis's surprise party.

B. On a separate sheet, write two sentences using *whose* and two using *who's.*

Your/You're

1. *Your* is a possessive form and therefore shows ownership.

   Remember to bring *your* ticket when you come.

2. *You're* is the contraction form of *you are.*

   You're the only person I can trust with this secret.

> TIP: Use *you're* only when you can substitute *you are.*

Practice 10.27

A. Fill in the blanks with *your* or *you're*.

  1. If you really don't want _____ bicycle anymore, Jane will buy it from you.

  2. _____ never really certain what _____ future holds.

  3. _____ best bet is to give Luigi a gift certificate because _____ never going to find something he doesn't already have.

  4. The key to _____ success will be hard work, not _____ parents' money.

  5. _____ my best friend, so I know you will help me.

  6. I felt _____ prose was a bit too wordy, so I took the liberty of revising some of _____ phrasing.

B. On a separate sheet, write two sentences with *your* and two with *you're*.

SLANG

Slang expressions are very informal usages unsuitable for most formal writing. Slang can originate with one group of people, say musicians or artists, and spread to the larger population. Slang often originates with young people and makes for colorful, vital speech. However, until a slang expression works its way into the language of the general population (if it ever does), avoid it in your college writing, unless you need it to create a special effect.

Here are examples of slang expressions. Because slang changes quickly, many of them may not be current slang by the time you read them.

grossed out	awesome
dude	get my act together
bummed out	off the wall
wired (for nervous)	chill out

Practice 10.28: Working Together

With some classmates, make a list of as many slang expressions as you can think of. Limit your list to the slang that you and your friends currently use. Your instructor may want to share some of the slang that was current when he or she was in college.

Practice 10.29: Working Together

With your group members, pick two of the slang expressions from *Practice 10.28* and use each of them in a separate sentence. Then rewrite the sentences, eliminating the slang and substituting language more appropriate to formal writing.

Practice 10.30

Rewrite the following sentences to eliminate the underlined slang. The first one is done as an example.

1. There is no sense even asking Denise to help because she is such an airhead.

   There is no sense even asking Denise to help because she is so

   scatterbrained.

2. When Dad heard that I had wrecked the car, he freaked.

   _____

   _____

3. I'd like to ask Doug to help, but he's totally out to lunch.

   _____

   _____

4. Marvin told Denise she better chill out or she would never make it through the exam.

   _____

   _____

5. I better study because my grades are going down the tubes.

   _____

   _____

6. Elaine got really ticked off when I told her I lost her biology notes.

   _____

   _____

CLICHÉS

Clichés are overworked expressions. At one time they were fresh and interesting, but years of overuse have made them tired and dull. Eliminate clichés when you revise because an experienced reader will find them annoying.

Here is a partial list of clichés. Studying it will help you become sensitive to the kinds of expressions to avoid.

over the hill	sadder but wiser	crack of dawn
free as a bird	last but not least	busy as a beaver
cold as ice	fresh as a daisy	light as a feather
spring chicken	love conquers all	green with envy
hour of need	shadow of a doubt	slowly but surely
white as snow	high as a kite	sharp as a tack

Practice 10.31

Write three clichés not on the list.

1. _____

2. _____

3. _____

Practice 10.32

Underline the clichés in the following sentences.

1. One thing I learned as a result of the experience is that it is better to be safe than sorry.

2. This summer has been as hot as blazes.

3. Janine worked like a dog finishing her senior paper in time.

4. To make a long story short, the mayor promised to consider removing the parking meters in front of the Red Cross office.

5. Trapped like a rat, the burglar was forced to surrender.

Practice 10.33

Rewrite the sentences, substituting fresh phrasings for the under-lined clichés. The first one is done as an example.

1. I dread going shopping with Dotty because she is <u>like a bull in a china shop</u>.

   I dread going shopping with Dotty because she is so clumsy she is

   always bumping into displays and breaking things.

2. If I were you, I would not <u>bet the rent</u> that Julian will keep his promise.

   _____

   _____

3. The comedian is not very funny because his jokes are <u>as old as the hills</u>.

   _____

   _____

4. Trying to find my contact lens in the dark was like <u>looking for a needle in a haystack</u>.

   _____

   _____

5. It is <u>a crying shame</u> that more is not being done to help the homeless.

   _____

   _____

6. Nina and Jacob were <u>busy as beavers</u> completing their wedding plans.

   _____

   _____

WORDINESS

Unnecessary words weaken your style. Therefore, when you revise, prune away words that add no meaning (deadwood) and words that repeat meaning (repetition).

Deadwood

Words that add no meaning are *deadwood* and should be eliminated.

Sentences with Deadwood	Revisions
Two different kinds of cake were offered.	Two different cakes were offered. (*Kinds of* adds no meaning.)
	or
	Two kinds of cake were offered
Diane's new Corvette is brown in color.	Diane's new Corvette is brown. (Can brown be anything *but* a color?)
We rushed quickly to see what was wrong.	We rushed to see what was wrong. (Rushing has to be done quickly.)

Practice 10.34

Underline the deadwood, and then revise the sentence to eliminate it. The first one is done as an example.

1. Pat has a <u>past</u> history of lying to make himself look important.

    Pat has a history of lying to make himself look important.

2. Sigfried and Roy, the world-famous magicians, make a tiger disappear from view.

    _____

    _____

3. I want to be alone by myself for a while, to decide what to do.

    _____

    _____

4. The end result of Dale's hard work was a successful career and a promising future in politics.

    _____

    _____

5. Luis is the type of person who likes to stay home and watch old movies on television.

_____

_____

6. In our modern society, urban decay is a serious problem.

_____

_____

Repetition

Another form of annoying wordiness is purposeless repetition. Consider this sentence:

To relax before my exam, I watched and viewed a movie.

Viewed repeats the idea included in *watched,* so *viewed* is needless repetition. Here is the sentence revised to eliminate the repetition:

To relax before my exam, I watched a movie.

Here are more examples to study:

Sentences with Repetition	Revisions
Carol finally came to the realization and understanding that she had to help herself.	Carol finally came to the realization that she had to help herself.
	or
	Carol finally came to the understanding that she had to help herself. (*Realization* and *understanding* mean the same.)
Some people think and believe that drug abuse is our nation's most serious problem.	Some people think that drug abuse is our nation's most serious problem.
	or
	Some people believe that drug abuse is our nation's most serious problem. (*Think* and *believe* mean the same.)

Practice 10.35

Revise the following sentences to eliminate the purposeless repetition. The first one is done as an example.

1. The prize-winning rose was distinctive for its unusual color and hue.

   The prize-winning rose was distinctive for its unusual color.

2. The big, huge coat dwarfed Marnie.

   _____

   _____

3. Collette's biggest wish and desire is to go and visit China.

   _____

   _____

4. The president of the city council is completely obsessed and absorbed with the core center of town.

   _____

   _____

5. In my opinion, I think that the government should fund day-care centers in all metropolitan areas.

   _____

   _____

6. The necessary funding was essential because without it St. Mark's Church would have to close its soup kitchen.

   _____

   _____

DOUBLE NEGATIVES

These words are negatives (they communicate the idea of *no*):

no	none	hardly
not	nowhere	scarcely
no one	nobody	

never   nothing

any contraction form with *not* (*can't, don't, won't,* etc.)

In English, only one negative is used to express a single negative idea.

Incorrect (two negatives):	I *can't* see *no* reason to go.
Correct (one negative):	I can see *no* reason to go.
Correct (one negative):	I *can't* see any reason to go.

Incorrect (two negatives):	Dee would *never* tell *no one.*
Correct (one negative):	Dee would *never* tell anyone.
Correct (one negative):	Dee would tell *no one.*

Incorrect (two negatives):	The boys could *not hardly* eat.
Correct (one negative):	The boys could *hardly* eat.
Correct (one negative):	The boys could *not* eat.

If you study the preceding examples, you will notice that eliminating one negative may mean changing *no one* to *anyone, nowhere* to *anywhere, never* to *ever,* and *no* or *none* to *any.*

Practice 10.36

The following sentences contain double negatives. First underline each negative. Then revise each sentence by eliminating one negative. The first one is done as an example.

1. The board member came under attack because he is <u>not never</u> at the meetings.

   The board member came under attack because he is never at

   the meetings.

2. Paul didn't do nothing to start the fight.

   _____

   _____

3. I gave the cashier $20.00, but I didn't get no change.

   _____

   _____

4. Mom couldn't find nowhere to hide the Christmas presents.

_____

_____

5. Some people won't ask nobody for nothing.

_____

_____

6. The street department hardly never swept the streets this fall.

_____

_____

SPELLING

A reader will lose confidence in your ability if your writing contains misspellings, even if your ideas are excellent. If spelling is a serious problem for you, the tips and rules that follow will help.

□   TIPS FOR IMPROVING YOUR SPELLING   □

1. Study your draft word by word, very slowly. Each time you encounter a word that might be misspelled, underline it. Then check every underlined word in a dictionary. Never overlook a word even if your suspicion is very slight. If you have the smallest doubt, underline and check.

2. Keep a list of words you misspell, and study your list daily. Ask someone to quiz you on the words once a week, and study even harder any words you miss on the quiz. You may find it helpful to underline the troublesome parts of words like this:

    foreign

3. Learn the correct pronunciation of words. You may misspell *disastrous* if you pronounce it incorrectly as "disas*ter*ous."

4. Break words into parts when you spell, like this:

with*hold	class*room	under*standing
under*statement	break*fast	table*cloth
room*mate	shoe*lace	beach*front

5. Some words may be easier to handle if you spell them syllable by syllable. For example, *organization* may be easier to spell if you say each syllable as you go: "or∗gan∗i∗za∗tion."

6. Be aware of prefixes (word beginnings) like *un, inter, mis,* and *dis.* When they are added to words, the spelling of the base word is not likely to change.

dis∗satisfaction   inter∗related   mis∗spell

un∗noticed   dis∗engage   un∗nerve

7. Use tricks to help you remember correct spellings. For example, *instrument* contains the word *strum,* and you strum a guitar, which is an instrument; *tragedy* contains the word *rage.*

8. Study the frequently confused words beginning on p. 302 and learn the spellings and meanings given.

9. Learn the spelling rules that follow.

Spelling Rules

To apply many of the spelling rules, you must know the difference between vowels and consonants.

VOWELS: *a, e, i, o, u*

CONSONANTS: *b, c, d, f, g, h, j, k, l, m, n, p, q, r, s, t, v, w, x, z*

NOTE: *Y* can be a vowel or a consonant, depending on how it sounds.

y as a vowel: *funny, shy*

y as a consonant: *yellow, yesterday*

Rule 1:   *I* before *e* except after *c,* or when sounding like long *a* as in *neighbor* and *weigh.*

The *i* comes before the *e:*

niece, field, grief, believe, friend, relieve, belief

The *e* comes before the *i* because the letters are after *c:*

conceive, ceiling, deceive, receipt, conceit, receive

The *e* comes before the *i* because of the long *a* sound:

neighbor, weight, weigh, sleigh

Words with a *shin* sound are spelled *ie* after *c:*

ancient, conscience, efficient, sufficient

Some exceptions to the rule:

either, neither, seize, weird, height, foreign, society

TIP: The following nonsense sentence contains five of the most common exceptions to the ie/ei rule: Either foreigner seized weird leisure.

Rule 2:   Before adding an ending other than *ing,* change *y* to *i* if there is a consonant before the *y.*

Change *y* to *i* because there is a consonant before the *y:*

study + ed	= studied	plenty + ful	= plentiful
happy + ness	= happiness	cry + ed	= cried
pretty + est	= prettiest	lovely + er	= lovelier

Keep the *y* because there is a vowel before it:

enjoy + ment	= enjoyment	stay + ed	= stayed
play + s	= plays	toy + s	= toys
employ + ed	= employed	destroy + er	= destroyer

Keep the *y* because the ending is *ing:*

hurry + ing	= hurrying	study + ing	= studying
employ + ing	= employing	cry + ing	= crying
fly + ing	= flying	imply + ing	= implying

Some exceptions to the rule:

dry + ly	= drily	say + ed	= said
day + ly	= daily	lay + ed	= laid
pay + ed	= paid	sly + ness	= slyness
shy + ly	= shyly	gay + ly	= gaily

Rule 3:   When you add an ending to a word that ends with a silent *e,* drop the *e* if the ending begins with a vowel, but keep the *e* if the ending begins with a consonant.

Drop the *e* because the ending begins with a vowel:

hope	+ ing	= hoping	dine	+ ing	= dining
pleasure	+ able	= pleasurable	write	+ er	= writer
dine	+ er	= diner	dense	+ ity	= density
praise	+ ing	= praising	rhyme	+ ed	= rhymed
time	+ ed	= timed			

Keep the *e* because the ending begins with a consonant:

hope	+ ful	= hopeful	complete	+ ly	= completely
loose	+ ly	= loosely	state	+ ment	= statement
hate	+ ful	= hateful	home	+ less	= homeless
time	+ less	= timeless	move	+ ment	= movement
rude	+ ness	= rudeness			

Some exceptions to the rule:

acknowledge	+ ment	=	acknowledgment
judge	+ ment	=	judgment
mile	+ age	=	mileage
notice	+ able	=	noticeable
argue	+ ment	=	argument
nine	+ th	=	ninth
acre	+ age	=	acreage
awe	+ ful	=	awful
true	+ ly	=	truly
courage	+ ous	=	courageous

Rule 4:   When adding an ending that begins with a vowel to a one-syllable word, double the final consonant if the last three letters of the word are consonant-vowel-consonant (c-v-c).

Double the final consonant because the one-syllable word ends c-v-c:

swim	+ ing	= swimming	fat	+ est	= fattest
thin	+ er	= thinner	skip	+ ing	= skipping
drop	+ ed	= dropped	run	+ er	= runner

Do not double the final consonant because the one-syllable word does not end c-v-c:

eat + ing = eating   burn + er = burner   boil + ed = boiled

An exception to the rule:

bus + ing = busing (bussing means "kissing")

Rule 5:   When adding an ending that begins with a vowel to a word of more than one syllable, double the final consonant if the last three letters of the word are consonant-vowel-consonant (c-v-c) *and* if the stress is on the last syllable.

Double the final consonant because the word ends c-v-c, and the stress is on the last syllable:

begin + er = beginner   regret + ed = regretted
admit + ing = admitting

Do not double the final consonant because the stress is not on the last syllable:

pardon + ed = pardoned   ripen + ing = ripening
labor   + er = laborer

Do not double the final consonant because the word does not end c-v-c:

evict + ing = evicting   pretend + er = pretender
ordain + ed = ordained

Do not double the consonant if the stress shifts from the last syllable when the ending is added.

prefer (stress on last syllable)
confer (stress on last syllable)
                        but
preference (stress shifts to first syllable)
conference (stress shifts to first syllable)

Rule 6:   Most nouns form the plural by adding *s*. However, if the noun ends in *ch, sh, s, x, z,* or *o,* add *es* to form the plural.

genius + es = geniuses   mix   + es = mixes

potato + es = potatoes   church + es = churches

Some exceptions to the rule:

memos   radios   solos

Rule 7:   When you change the final *y* to *i*, add *es* to form the plural
(see p. 298).

candy + es = candies   party + es = parties   fly + es = flies

but

key   + s   = keys   boy + s   = boys   toy + s = toys

Practice 10.37

1. To check your understanding of spelling rule 1, fill in the blanks
   with either *ie* or *ei*. If you are unsure, check a dictionary.

   a. ch __ __ f   **g.** perc __ __ ve

   b. br __ __ f   **h.** sh __ __ ld

   c. fr __ __ ght   **i.** r __ __ gn

   d. ach __ __ ve   **j.** v __ __ n

   e. w __ __ gh   **k.** th __ __ r

   f. c __ __ ling

2. To check your understanding of spelling rules 2–5, add the given
   endings to the words below. If you are unsure, consult the rule
   given in parentheses or look up the word in a dictionary.

   a. sorry + er _____ (rule 2)

   b. bat + er _____ (rule 4)

   c. make + s _____ (rule 3)

   d. hammer + ing _____ (rule 5)

   e. hop + ed _____ (rule 4)

   f. enjoy + able _____ (rule 2)

   g. advertise + ment _____ (rule 3)

   h. ask + ing _____ (rule 4)

   i. sense + ible _____ (rule 3)

   j. slip + ed _____ (rule 4)

   k. gossip + ed _____ (rule 5)

l. omit + ing _____ (rule 5)

m. wealthy + er _____ (rule 2)

n. rake + ing _____ (rule 3)

o. ship + ment _____ (rule 4)

p. permit + ed _____ (rule 5)

q. bite + ing _____ (rule 3)

r. marry + ed _____ (rule 2)

s. big + er _____ (rule 4)

t. lazy + ness _____ (rule 2)

3. To check your understanding of rules 6 and 7, write the plural of each noun. If you are unsure, check a dictionary.

   a. toy _____

   b. brush _____

   c. jelly _____

   d. mosquito _____

   e. television _____

   f. veto _____

   g. tax _____

   h. girl _____

   i. enemy _____

   j. match _____

Frequently Misspelled Words

The following seventy-five words are often misspelled. Learn to spell every word on the list by making flash cards to study. Have someone quiz you until you can spell all of these words with ease.

1. absence	11. belief	21. embarrass
2. across	12. business	22. especially
3. actually	13. coming	23. existence
4. a lot	14. committee	24. February
5. analyze	15. criticism	25. foreign
6. appreciate	16. definitely	26. government
7. argument	17. dependent	27. grammar
8. athlete	18. develop	28. guarantee
9. awkward	19. discuss	29. guidance
10. beginning	20. eighth	30. height

31. hoping	46. ninety	61. religious
32. immediately	47. ninth	62. rhythm
33. independent	48. occasionally	63. sacrifice
34. intelligence	49. opinion	64. safety
35. knowledge	50. parallel	65. scene
36. laboratory	51. persuade	66. schedule
37. leisure	52. physical	67. separate
38. length	53. planned	68. severely
39. library	54. pleasant	69. success
40. marriage	55. preferred	70. surprise
41. mathematics	56. prejudice	71. thoroughly
42. meant	57. privilege	72. through
43. medicine	58. pursue	73. until
44. necessary	59. receipt	74. weight
45. neither	60. receive	75. written

The Hyphen

Hyphens are most often used to form compound words and to show that a word continues from the end of one line to the beginning of the next. If you are at the typewriter or word processor, use one horizontal line for the hyphen (-) and two lines for the dash (—).

1. Use a hyphen between words that form a single adjective before a noun.

state-of-the-art stereo	well-known speaker
comparison-contrast essay	run-of-the-mill Sunday
strong-willed woman	so-called advice

   Do not use a hyphen when the compound comes after the noun:

   Fran is a success because she is strong willed.

   Do not use a hyphen with an -*ly* word:

   The slowly moving traffic made me an hour late.

2. Use hyphens between compound numbers from twenty-one through ninety-nine.

thirty-six   seventy-seven

forty-two   fifty-eight

3. Use a hyphen between the numerator and denominator in written fractions.

one-fourth   two-thirds

4. Use a hyphen after the prefixes *self-, all-, ex-* (meaning *former*), and before the suffix *-elect.*

self-assured   ex-governor

all-inclusive   mayor-elect

5. Use a hyphen with a prefix before a word that begins with a capital letter.

un-American   pro-Cuban   mid-January

6. Use a hyphen to divide a word at the end of a line, but remember these cautions:

a. Do not divide one-syllable words.

b. You should not leave a single letter at the end of the line, so do not divide a word such as *a-void.*

Practice 10.38

Add hyphens where they are needed in the following paragraph.

My mother in law is a first rate artist who will show her paintings at a gallery on the twenty first of the month. Her show will last until mid May. In addition to being a highly acclaimed artist, my mother in law is the ex chair of the United Way campaign in our city and an energetic fundraiser for anti drug campaigns. At sixty seven, she is a remarkable, self possessed, high powered woman whom I admire greatly.

CHAPTER
11

Using Verbs Correctly

In this chapter you will learn important information about using verbs correctly. In particular, you will learn how to:

1. use correct verb forms
2. make subjects and verbs agree
3. avoid tense shifts

VERB FORMS

The following pages will help you use standard English verb forms correctly. If your instructor marks verb errors on your compositions, pay careful attention to this material. Also, you can help yourself improve by reading daily and noticing the verb forms used and by paying careful attention to the verb forms your instructors use in class.

Pretest

If the underlined verb is correct, write *C* on the blank. If it is incorrect, write *I* on the blank. If you are unsure, do not guess; leave the space blank. Check your answers in Appendix III.

1. _____ Six weeks ago Joe <u>decide</u> to move out of the dorm.

2. _____ The sun <u>shone</u> so brightly I couldn't see to drive.

3. _____ Maria <u>be</u> the one to ask about that.

4. _____ I don't <u>understand</u> a thing Alfie says.

5. _____ We <u>had driven</u> two hundred miles when the fuel pump broke.

6. _____ Larry explained, "A man <u>do</u> what he has to do."

7. _____ I <u>hopes</u> I can get a part-time job this summer.

8. _____ We <u>have did</u> everything you asked.

9. _____ Mother <u>has worn</u> that old coat for ten years.

10. _____ The teachers <u>began</u> their strike the day after Christmas vacation.

11. _____ They <u>has told</u> me they do not plan to go with us.

12. _____ My sister Hannah <u>decided</u> to join the navy.

13. _____ The movie was so sad that Hank <u>starts</u> to cry.

14. _____ Lois <u>brang</u> her botany notes for me to copy.

15. _____ I <u>sings</u> when I'm working hard.

Regular Verb Forms

Most English verbs are *regular verbs*. Regular verbs form the past tense by adding *d* or *ed*. Here are some examples of regular verbs:

Present Tense	Past Tense
walk	walked
yell	yelled
study	studied
love	loved
smell	smelled

Sometimes people use regular verbs incorrectly because they do not use the verb endings correctly. Study the charts on the pages that follow to learn how endings are used with regular verbs.

REGULAR VERB FORMS: PRESENT TENSE

(Use these forms when you want to write or speak of events occurring in the present time.)

I play.   We play.

You play.   They play.

He plays.   }   The children (or *more than*
She plays.   }Watch for the *s*   *one* person or thing) play.
It plays.   }or *es* ending here.

Watch for the
The child (or any *one* person or thing) plays. }   *s* or *es* ending
here.

CAUTION: A common error is forgetting the *s* or *es* ending for a regular, present tense verb used with *he, she, it,* or any singular noun subject.

Incorrect: Mary *like* chocolate pudding.

Correct: Mary *likes* chocolate pudding.

Practice 11.1

Rewrite the sentences, changing the underlined past tense verbs to present tense forms. Be careful to use the *s* or *es* ending when needed. The first sentence is done as an example.

1. Martha often <u>asked</u> me to baby-sit on Saturday afternoons.

    Martha often asks me to baby-sit on Saturday afternoons.

    _____

2. The bank clerk <u>computed</u> the interest on my car loan.

    _____

    _____

3. In literature class, we <u>analyzed</u> the poetry of Walt Whitman.

    _____

    _____

4. After the Thanksgiving meal, I <u>walked</u> two miles.

    _____

    _____

5. The Post Office <u>returned</u> the letters I <u>mailed</u> without stamps.

    _____

    _____

6. You <u>composed</u> your thesis sentence before you <u>drafted</u> your essay.

    _____

    _____

7. Left alone in the yard, the dog <u>howled</u> all afternoon.

    _____

    _____

8. Most of the passengers <u>boarded</u> the bus on time, but Jim <u>arrived</u> late.

    _____

    _____

Practice 11.2

Complete each of the sentences by using a present tense form of a regular verb from the list and any other words you want. Do not use the same verb in more than one sentence. Be sure to use *s* or *es* endings where needed. The first one is done as an example.

play	laugh	organize
smile	move	follow
study	practice	learn
worry	joke	collect

1. The excited children *play happily in the school yard* *during recess.*

2. My best friend_____

   _____

3. Professor Bauer_____

   _____

4. We _____

   _____

5. The homecoming committee _____

   _____

6. You_____

   _____

7. I _____

   _____

8. He _____

   _____

9. My younger sister _____

   _____

Practice 11.3

Fill in the blanks with the correct present tense form of the verb in parentheses. The first blank is filled in as an example.

Because of my cold, my nose no longer (to function) ____*functions*____ as part of my respiratory system. I (to inhale) _____ deeply, but no air (to penetrate) _____ the blocked passages. I (to race) _____ to the bathroom and (to grab) _____ a tissue before I (to sneeze) _____ myself to the floor. Pulling myself up, I (to head) _____ for the kitchen. My throat (to rust) _____ out, and my mouth (to enter) _____ the drought season. Switching on the light, I (to tug) _____ at the refrigerator door, which (to seem) _____ like wrenching a two-ton vault. Struggling for strength, I (to open) _____ the door, (to grab) _____ the orange juice, and (to pour) _____ the liquid. The juice (to burn) _____ my aching throat. I (to reach) _____ for a cold tablet and (to pop) _____ it in. To clear my nose, I (to reach) _____ for the nasal spray. I (to squirt) _____ twice in each nostril and (to tilt) _____ my head back. I (to head) _____ back to bed, but I (to toss) _____ and (to turn) _____ for hours until exhausted I (to drift) _____ off to sleep, hoping not to awaken until the cold (to burn) _____ itself out.

REGULAR VERB FORMS: PAST TENSE

(Use these forms when you want to write or speak of events that occurred in the past.)

I played.	We played.
You played.	They played.
He played.	The children (or *more than one* person or thing) played.
She played.	
It played.	

The child (or any *one* person or thing) played.

CAUTION: A common error is forgetting the *d* or *ed* ending for a regular, past tense verb.

Incorrect:	Yesterday I *walk* to work.
Correct:	Yesterday I *walked* to work.

Practice 11.4

Fill in the blanks with the past tense forms of the regular verbs in parentheses. Circle the past tense endings. The first one is done as an example.

1. (enjoy) The fifth-grade class ___enjoyed___ the ballet's performance of *The Nutcracker.*

2. (to burn) Because the oven was set at the wrong temperature, I _____ the chicken.

3. (to rush; to arrive) The alarm did not go off, so we _____ across campus and _____ ten minutes late to our 8:00 class.

4. (to clean) After the movie, the theater usher _____ the trash from the floor.

5. (to remove; stop) She _____ the speck of dust from my

eye, and the pain _____.

6. (to look) They _____ everywhere for you before leaving.

Practice 11.5

On a separate sheet, write a sentence using the regular verb in parentheses in its past tense form. Circle the past tense ending. The first one is done as an example.

1. (start) *The referee started the sudden death overtime play.*
2. (look)
3. (want)
4. (talk)
5. (expect)
6. (discover)

Practice 11.6

On a separate sheet, rewrite *Practice 11.3*. This time fill in the blanks with past tense forms of the verbs given.

REGULAR VERB FORMS: PAST PARTICIPLE

The *past participle* is the verb form that can be used with the helping verbs *has, have,* and *had.* The past participle of regular verbs is formed in the same way the past tense of regular verbs is formed: by adding *d* or *ed.*

I have played.	We have played.
I had played.	We had played.
You have played.	They have played.
You had played.	They had played.
He has played.	The children (or *more than one* person or thing) have played.
He had played.	
She has played.	The children (or *more than one* person or thing) had played.

She had played.

It has played.

It had played.

The child (or any *one* person or thing) has played.

The child (or any *one* person or thing) had played.

NOTE: As you can tell from the preceding examples, the past participle form does not change even though the form of the helping verb changes.

CAUTION: A common error is forgetting the *d* or *ed* ending for the past participle form of a regular verb.

Incorrect: The union *has decide* to accept the
                         wage offer.

Correct: The union *has decided* to accept the
                         wage offer.

Practice 11.7

Fill in the blank with the past participle form of the regular verb in parentheses. The first one is done as an example.

1. (help) As a social worker, Lenny has ___*helped*___ many people solve their problems.

2. (turn) After three weeks in the refrigerator, this cider has _____ to vinegar.

3. (realize, call) Tony and Maria have _____ that they are not compatible, so they have _____ off their wedding.

4. (play) The theater had _____ *The Rocky Horror Picture Show* every Saturday for five years.

5. (stop) The First National Bank had _____ payment on my check.

6. (earn) The scout has _____ three awards from the mayor for community service.

Practice 11.8

On a separate sheet, write a sentence using the helping verb and past participle form of the regular verb in parentheses. The first one is done as an example.

1. (has + walk) *For the past year, Jill has walked three miles a day.*
2. (had + jump)
3. (has + change)
4. (had + open)
5. (has + work)
6. (had + apply)

Irregular Verb Forms

A *regular verb* forms the past and past participle by adding *d* or *ed*. If you have not studied regular verbs, go back to p. 306 and read so you understand what present, past, and past participle forms are.

An *irregular verb* does not add *d* or *ed* to form the past and past participle forms. Instead, irregular verbs form the past and past participle a variety of ways.

A list of some irregular verbs with their past and past participle forms follows. Study the list and place a star next to the forms you do not already know. Then memorize these forms.

Present	Past	Past Participle
become(s)	became	become
begin(s)	began	begun
bend(s)	bent	bent
bite(s)	bit	bitten
blow(s)	blew	blown
break(s)	broke	broken
bring(s)	brought	brought
buy(s)	bought	bought
catch(es)	caught	caught
choose(es)	chose	chosen
come(s)	came	come
cost(s)	cost	cost
draw(s)	drew	drawn

Present	Past	Past Participle
drink(s)	drank	drunk
drive(s)	drove	driven
eat(s)	ate	eaten
fall(s)	fell	fallen
feed(s)	fed	fed
feel(s)	felt	felt
fight(s)	fought	fought
find(s)	found	found
fly(flies)	flew	flown
forget(s)	forgot	forgotten
forgive(s)	forgave	forgiven
freeze(s)	froze	frozen
get(s)	got	got *or* gotten
give(s)	gave	given
go(goes)	went	gone
grow(s)	grew	grown
hang(s)—a picture	hung	hung
hang(s)—a person	hanged	hanged
hear(s)	heard	heard
hide(s)	hid	hidden
hold(s)	held	held
hurt(s)	hurt	hurt
keep(s)	kept	kept
know(s)	knew	known
lay(s)—to place	laid	laid
lead(s)	led	led
leave(s)	left	left
lend(s)	lent	lent
lie(s)—to rest	lay	lain
light(s)	lit	lit
lose(s)	lost	lost
make(s)	made	made
meet(s)	met	met

Present	Past	Past Participle
pay(s)	paid	paid
read(s)	read	read
ride(s)	rode	ridden
ring(s)	rang	rung
rise(s)	rose	risen
run(s)	ran	run
say(s)	said	said
see(s)	saw	seen
sell(s)	sold	sold
send(s)	sent	sent
set(s)	set	set
shake(s)	shook	shaken
shine(s)—to give light	shone	shone
shine(s)—to polish	shined	shined
shrink(s)	shrank	shrunk
sing(s)	sang	sung
sit(s)	sat	sat
sleep(s)	slept	slept
speak(s)	spoke	spoken
spend(s)	spent	spent
stand(s)	stood	stood
steal(s)	stole	stolen
sting(s)	stung	stung
strike(s)	struck	struck
swim(s)	swam	swum
take(s)	took	taken
teach(es)	taught	taught
tear(s)	tore	torn
tell(s)	told	told
think(s)	thought	thought
throw(s)	threw	thrown
wake(s)	woke *or* waked	woken *or* waked
wear(s)	wore	worn

Present	Past	Past Participle
win(s)	won	won
write(s)	wrote	written

To understand how irregular verb forms are used, study the charts that follow.

IRREGULAR VERB FORMS: PRESENT TENSE

(Use the present tense form in the first column of the chart beginning on p. 314 when you want to write or speak of events occurring in the present time.)

I drink.   We drink.

You drink.   They drink.

He drinks. ⎱   The dogs (or *more than*
She drinks. ⎰ Watch for the   *one* person or thing) drink.
It drinks.   *s* or *es* ending
              here.

                                          Watch for the
The dog (or any *one* person or thing) drinks. }   *s* or *es* ending
                                          here.

CAUTION: A common error is forgetting the *s* or *es* ending for an irregular present tense verb used with *he, she, it,* or any singular noun subject.

Incorrect:	Hank *sing* beautifully.
Correct:	Hank *sings* beautifully.

Practice 11.9

Rewrite the sentences, changing the underlined past tense verbs to present tense forms. Be careful to use the *s* or *es* ending when needed. If you are unsure of the correct form, check the chart beginning on p. 314. The first one is done as an example.

1. The golden sun <u>rose</u> over the Atlantic Ocean.

   The golden sun rises over the Atlantic Ocean.

2. Nancy always <u>forgot</u> to meet me at the library after class.

_____

_____

3. The thoughtful dinner guest <u>brought</u> the hostess a bottle of wine.

_____

_____

4. For a moment the center fielder <u>lost</u> the ball in the sun, but he <u>caught</u> it anyway.

_____

_____

5. I <u>knew</u> you <u>drove</u> because I <u>saw</u> your car.

_____

_____

6. Jannine <u>left</u> her car keys in the ignition.

_____

_____

7. When the church bells <u>rang</u>, the congregation <u>rose</u> and <u>sang</u> a hymn.

_____

_____

8. The Jefferson Tigers <u>won</u> most of their games because their star forward <u>made</u> most of his shots.

_____

_____

Practice 11.10

Complete each sentence with a present tense form of an irregular verb from the list beginning on p. 314 and any other words. Use *s* or *es* endings where needed. The first one is done as an example.

1. The scouts and their leader *take a group of senior citizens* _____

   shopping every week. _____

2. She _____

   _____

3. During the meeting, Boris and I _____

   _____

4. Before leaving for work, Luis _____

   _____

5. They _____

   _____

6. The customer _____

   _____

IRREGULAR VERB FORMS: PAST TENSE

(Use the past tense form in the second column of the chart beginning on p. 314 when you are speaking or writing of events that occurred in the past.)

I drank.	We drank.
You drank.	They drank.
He drank.	The dogs (or *more than one* person or thing) drank.
She drank.	
It drank.	

The dog (or any *one* person or thing) drank.

CAUTION: A common error is using the past participle form (in the third column) for the simple past tense. Remember, the past participle appears with a helping verb (see p. 177).

Incorrect: Jim *done* the work. (past participle without helping verb)

Correct:	Jim *did* the work. (past tense form)
Incorrect:	I *seen* her yesterday. (past participle without helping verb)
Correct:	I *saw* her yesterday. (past tense form)

Practice 11.11

Fill in the blank with the past tense form of the irregular verb in parentheses. If you are unsure of the form, check the chart beginning on p. 314. The first one is done as an example.

1. (hold) As Grandma __*held*__ the quilt I made for her, she smiled gratefully.

2. (forget) Michael was embarrassed because he _____ his sister's birthday.

3. (hear) When Eleni _____ about the earthquake in California, she raced home to call her relatives in San Diego.

4. (lend) Jake is sorry he _____ Lenny $50.00 because Lenny never repaid the loan.

5. (begin) Once everyone was seated, the orchestra _____ the overture.

6. (steal) As Aaron Cohen released the pitch, Brett Butler _____ second base.

7. (wake) The alarm on the clock radio sounded at 6:45, and I _____ with a start.

8. (teach) Yesterday Professor Morales _____ us several techniques for successful revising.

9. (buy) The angora sweater I _____ for Sue is one size too large.

Practice 11.12

Pick five irregular verbs that you do not already know the parts of (use the chart beginning on p. 314). Then, on a separate sheet, use the past tense form of each of these verbs in a sentence.

IRREGULAR VERB FORMS: PAST PARTICIPLE

The *past participle* is the verb form used with the helping verbs *has, have,* and *had.* The past participle of irregular verbs is the form in the third column of the chart beginning on p. 314.

I have drunk.	We have drunk.
I had drunk.	We had drunk.
You have drunk.	They have drunk.
You had drunk.	They had drunk.
He has drunk.	The dogs (or *more than one* person or thing) have drunk.
He had drunk.	
She has drunk.	The dogs (or *more than one* person or thing) had drunk.
She had drunk.	
It has drunk.	
It had drunk.	

The dog (or any *one* person or thing) has drunk.

The dog (or any *one* person or thing) had drunk.

NOTE: As you can tell from the preceding examples, the past participle form does not change even though the form of the helping verb changes.

CAUTION: The past participle form must be used with a helping verb; it is not used alone.

Incorrect:	I *seen* Nancy. (past participle without helping verb)
Correct:	I *have seen* Nancy. (past participle and helping verb)
Correct:	I *had seen* Nancy. (past participle and helping verb)

> Correct: I *saw* Nancy. (simple past tense form)
>
> CAUTION: Do not use "would have" for "had."
>
> Incorrect: If I *would have* known, I could have
>   helped.
> Correct: If I *had* known, I could have helped.

Practice 11.13

Fill in the blank with the past participle form of the irregular verb in parentheses. The first one is done as an example.

1. (bring) Fortunately, Gina has ___*brought*___ a first-aid kit.

2. (blow) The strong winds have _____ since early this morning.

3. (choose) Jeremy has _____ to attend St. Bonaventure.

4. (go) The stray dogs had _____ by the time the dog warden arrived.

5. (lie) Doreen has _____ down for awhile to try to get rid of her headache.

6. (ride) After Peter and Dolly had _____ the merry-go-round for the fifth time, they wanted some cotton candy.

7. (write) Thousands of angry consumers have _____ the Better Business Bureau to complain about the faulty appliance.

Practice 11.14

Write a sentence using the helping verb and past participle form of the irregular verb in parentheses. If you are unsure, check the chart beginning on p. 314. The first one is done as an example.

1. (has + teach) *Dr. Yurak has taught both English and history for twenty years.*

2. (had + wake) _____

3. (has + go) _____

_____

4. (had + sting) _____

_____

5. (has + stand) _____

_____

6. (had + see) _____

_____

7. (has + meet) _____

_____

Verb Forms for *Be, Have,* and *Do*

The charts that follow will help you learn the forms for the three common irregular verbs, *be, have,* and *do:*

BE

Present Tense Forms

I am.	We are.
You are.	They are.
He is.	The toys (or *more than* one person or thing) are.
She is.	
It is.	

The toy (or any *one* person or thing) is.

Past Tense Forms

I was.	We were.
You were.	They were.
He was.	The toys (or *more than one* person or thing) were.
She was.	
It was.	

The toy (or any *one* person or thing) was.

Past Participle Forms

I have been.	We have been.
I had been.	We had been.
You have been.	They have been.
You had been.	They had been.
He has been.	The toys (or *more than one* person
He had been.	or thing) have been.
She has been.	The toys (or *more than one* person
She had been.	or thing) had been.
It has been.	
It had been.	

The toy (or any *one* person or thing) has been.

The toy (or any *one* person or thing) had been.

CAUTION: The past participle form must be used with another helping verb; do not use the past participle form alone for the past tense.

Incorrect:	I *been* alone too long. (past participle without helping verb)
Correct:	I *have been* alone too long. (helping verb and past participle)
Correct:	I *had been* alone too long. (helping verb and past participle)
Correct:	I *was alone* too long. (past tense form)

HAVE

Present Tense Forms

I have.	We have.
You have.	They have.
He has.	The children (or *more than one*
She has.	person or thing) have.
It has.	

The child (or any *one* person or thing) has.

Past Tense Forms

I had.	We had.
You had.	They had.
He had.	The children (or *more than one* person or thing) had.
She had.	
It had.	

The child (or any *one* person or thing) had.

Past Participle Forms

I have had.	We have had.
I had had.	We had had.
You have had.	They have had.
You had had.	They had had.
He has had.	The children (or *more than one* person or thing) have had.
He had had.	
She has had.	The children (or *more than one* person or thing) had had.
She had had.	
It has had.	
It had had.	

The child (or any *one* person or thing) has had.

The child (or any *one* person or thing) had had.

DO

Present Tense Forms

I do.	We do.
You do.	They do.
He does.	The children (or *more than one* person or thing) do.
She does.	
It does.	

The child (or any *one* person or thing) does.

CAUTION: Use the contraction forms *don't* and *doesn't* carefully. A common mistake is to use *don't (do not)* when *doesn't (does not)* is needed.

Incorrect:	The toy *don't* work anymore.
Correct:	The toy *doesn't* work anymore.
Incorrect:	He *don't* want to work outside in the summer heat.
Correct:	He *doesn't* want to work outside in the summer heat.

Past Tense Forms

I did.	We did.
You did.	They did.
He did.	The children (or *more than one* person or thing) did.
She did.	
It did.	
The child (or any *one* person or thing) did.	

Past Participle Forms

I have done.	We have done.
I had done.	We had done.
You have done.	They have done.
You had done.	They had done.
He has done.	The children (or *more than one* person or thing) have done.
He had done.	
She has done.	The children (or *more than one* person or thing) had done.
She had done.	
It has done.	
It had done.	
The child (or any *one* person or thing) has done.	
The child (or any *one* person or thing) had done.	

CAUTION: *Done* must appear with a helping verb. Do not use it alone as a past tense form.

Incorrect:	I *done* the dishes. (past participle without a helping verb)
Correct:	I *have done* the dishes. (helping verb and past participle)

Correct:	I *had done* the dishes. (helping verb and past participle)
Correct:	I *did* the dishes. (past tense form)

Practice 11.15

Change the underlined past tense verb forms to present tense forms. The first one is done as an example.

1. Teenage unemployment <u>was</u> a major problem in this state.

   Teenage unemployment is a major problem in this state.

2. High school dances <u>were</u> always a disappointment for me.

   _____

   _____

3. Many parents <u>didn't</u> understand their teenage children.

   _____

   _____

4. I <u>had</u> the information you asked for.

   _____

   _____

5. The books I <u>had</u> for you <u>were</u> on the coffee table.

   _____

   _____

6. Sheila <u>didn't</u> understand today's psychology lecture, but I <u>did</u>.

   _____

   _____

7. I <u>was</u> sure he <u>was</u> here.

   _____

   _____

8. You <u>were</u> wrong to accuse Jake of lying.

_____

_____

9. Sam and I <u>had</u> the dean's approval to take extra courses.

_____

_____

10. You <u>did</u> well, but I <u>did</u> not because I <u>had</u> exam anxiety.

_____

_____

Practice 11.16

Fill in the blank with the correct past tense form of the verb in parentheses.

1. (have) The house _____ a security system.

2. (do) The children _____ exactly what they have always _____.

3. (have) We _____ heard that you _____ the flu.

4. (be) The doctor _____ certain that rest and a better diet _____ all you needed.

5. (do) Jamal _____ the best he could, but I _____ not always recognize that fact.

6. (be) I _____ here if you needed help, and your parents _____ too.

Practice 11.17

On a separate sheet, write sentences with the following past participle forms.

1. have + been

2. had + been

3. have + done

4. had + done

5. has + done

6. has + been

7. have + had

8. has + had

Post Test

Fill in the blank with the correct form of the verb in parentheses. You must draw upon everything you have learned about verb forms.

1. (draw—past tense) Carlotta _____ the picture that hangs over her fireplace.

2. (prevent) The new influenza vaccine has _____ many deaths among the elderly.

3. (do) I wish you had _____ what you promised you would do.

4. (sing—past tense) The vocalist who _____ at Pete and Mary's wedding is a student in the school of music.

5. (occur) It should have _____ to you by now that no one will help you unless you help yourself.

6. (be—present tense) The teachers and students _____ not the only ones affected by the teachers' strike.

7. (swim) Meg has _____ in over fifty swim meets.

8. (do—present tense) Louise _____ not believe in taking pills, not even aspirin.

9. (peel—present tense) Carefully, Mother _____ the sweet potatoes for the pie.

10. (have—present tense) Marcus and Denzel _____ all the GI Joe action dolls ever made.

On a separate sheet, write a sentence for each of the following verb forms.

1. the present tense of *smile*
2. the past tense of *escape*
3. the past participle of *go*
4. the past tense of *be*
5. the past participle of *talk*
6. the present tense of *be*
7. the past participle of *take*
8. the past tense of *do*
9. the present tense of *move*
10. the past tense of *think*

SUBJECT-VERB AGREEMENT

Subject-verb agreement means a singular subject must be paired with a singular verb, and a plural subject must be paired with a plural verb. The issue of subject-verb agreement only comes up with present tense verbs and with the past tense forms *was* and *were*.

Pretest

Fill in the blank with the correct present tense form in parentheses. Do not guess. If you are unsure, do not fill in the blank. When you are done, check your answers in Appendix III.

1. (means/mean) My collection of shells from Ocean City _____ a great deal to me.

2. (visits/visit) Either Mother or Aunt Harriet _____ Grandma in the nursing home every day.

3. (plans/plan) Both Brian and his best friend _____ to attend Ohio State University.

4. (likes/like) Everyone _____ a good mystery.

5. (practices/practice) The football team _____ twice a day in August.

6. (decides/decide) The personnel committee _____ who to hire for the teaching positions.

7. (is/are) Here _____ the papers you lost.

8. (wants/want) Each of the children _____ to take karate lessons.

9. (works/work) Stavros is one of those people who _____ harder than necessary.

10. (sleeps/sleep) The cat, along with her kittens, _____ in the garage.

Making Subjects and Verbs Agree

A word that refers to one person or thing is *singular;* a word that refers to more than one person or thing is *plural.*

Singular (refers to one person or thing)		Plural (refers to more than one person or thing)	
dog	month	dogs	months
desk	I	desks	we
box	he	boxes	they
cup	she	cups	they

To achieve subject-verb agreement, use a singular verb with a singular subject and a plural verb with a plural subject. Subject-verb agreement is only an issue with present tense verb forms and the past tense forms *was* (singular) and *were* (plural).

Look back at the verb form charts on p. 307 and p. 317. Notice that present tense verb forms add *s* or *es* when used with *he, she, it,* or a singular noun. Now look at the chart on p. 323. Notice that *was* is used with singular nouns and *I, he, she,* and *it.* This is much of what you have to remember to achieve subject-verb agreement. The following charts summarize this subject-verb agreement rule.

PRESENT TENSE—MOST VERBS

Singular Subject/ Singular Verb	Plural Subject/ Plural Verb
I move slowly.	We move slowly.
You move slowly.	You move slowly.
He moves slowly.	They move slowly

She moves slowly.   The dogs (or any plural noun) move slowly.

It moves slowly.

The dog (or any singular noun) moves slowly.

NOTE: Add *s* or *es* to the verb only when the subject is *he, she, it,* or a singular noun.

PAST TENSE: WAS/WERE

I was here.   We were here.

You were here.   They were here.

He was here.   The dogs (or any plural noun) were here.

She was here.

It was here.

The dog (or any singular noun) was here.

NOTE: Use *was* only when the subject is *I, he, she, it,* or a singular noun.

Practice 11.18

Fill in each blank with the correct present tense form of the verb in parentheses.

1. (bark) My neighbor's dog _____ almost all night.

2. (lose) I _____ my car keys once a week.

3. (sleep) On hot summer evenings, Grandfather _____ on the front porch.

4. (move) Each winter, Chad's parents _____ to Florida for three months.

5. (listen) I _____ as carefully as I can, but I still have trouble understanding the words to that song.

6. (hope) As soon as she graduates, Sheila _____ to land a job with a prestigious advertising firm.

7. (expect) You _____ a great deal from people, but I _____ very little.

8. (solve) We _____ the hard problems before the easy ones, but Luis _____ the easy problems before the hard ones.

9. (believe) Harry _____ that any obstacle can be overcome with effort, but I _____ an element of luck is also involved.

10. (exaggerate) Too often, television commercials _____ the benefits of a product.

Practice 11.19

Fill in the blanks with either *was* (singular) or *were* (plural).

1. We _____ certain that Charles _____ not here yet.

2. You _____ the best person for the job because Joyce _____ not available.

3. This class _____ difficult, but they _____ able to handle it.

4. Jane _____ new in town, but she _____ making friends easily.

5. It _____ too early to leave, but we _____ too tired to stay.

6. The spring rains _____ over, but the summer heat _____ not here yet.

Compound Subjects

A *compound subject* is a two-part subject with the parts connected by *and, or, either . . . or, neither . . . nor,* or *not only . . . but [also].*

1. If the subjects are joined by *and,* the verb will usually be plural. Here is an example:

My best friend and I *spend* spring break in Florida.

2. If the subjects are joined by *or, either . . . or, neither . . . nor,* or *not only . . . but [also],* the verb agrees with the closer subject. Here are two examples:

Either my brothers or my sister *is* going. (singular verb to agree with the singular *sister*)

Neither my hat nor my gloves *are* where I left them. (plural verb to agree with the plural *gloves*)

NOTE: If you do not like the sound of "Either my brothers or my sister is going," reverse the order to place the plural subject second, so you can use a plural verb:

Either my sister or my brothers *are* going.

Practice 11.20

Follow each compound subject with the correct present tense form of the verb in parentheses. Then finish the sentence with any other words you care to add. The first one is done as an example.

1. (taste) The meat and the potatoes *taste overcooked and bland.*

2. (know) Neither the club president nor the treasurer _____

   _____

3. (grow) Cotton and tobacco_____

   _____

4. (sing) The choir or the choir master _____

   _____

5. (visit) The children and their teacher _____

   _____

6. (taste) Neither the meat nor the potatoes _____

   _____

7. (plan) Not only Sue but also Helen _____.

   _____

8. (volunteer) Either Mr. Chen or his wife _____

   _____

Collective Nouns

A *collective noun* refers to a group. They are words like these:

congregation	committee	band	faculty
group	team	jury	flock
herd	audience	family	class

1. If the collective noun is thought of as one group acting as a whole, a singular verb is used. Here is an example:

   At noon, the band *boards* the bus for the trip to the Rose Parade. (The singular verb is used because *band* is acting as a whole.)

2. If the members of the group are acting individually, the collective noun takes a plural verb. Here is an example:

   The faculty *have* debated that issue for years. (The plural verb is used because the individual members of the faculty are acting individually.)

Practice 11.21

On a separate sheet, write sentences using the given collective nouns as subjects and the correct present tense forms of the verbs in parentheses. Be prepared to explain why you used the verb form that you did. The first one is done as an example.

1. flock (migrate) *The flock migrates to a warmer climate for the winter.*
2. **army** (attack)
3. **family** (eat)
4. **jury** (argue)
5. **committee** (decide)
6. **team** (practice)

Indefinite Pronouns

Indefinite pronouns refer to a group without specifying the specific members.

1. These indefinite pronouns always take a singular verb:

anyone	anybody	anything	each
everyone	everybody	everything	one

no one	nobody	nothing	none
someone	somebody	something	

Anyone *is* welcome to attend the open house.

Everything *works* out eventually.

Each student *writes* a term paper during the senior year.

Somebody *helps* Grandma clean her house every week.

2. These indefinite pronouns always take a plural verb:

both	many	few	several

Many *believe* that Congress will defeat the budget proposal.

3. These indefinite pronouns take either a singular or plural verb, depending on whether the sense of the subject is singular or plural:

all	more	some
any	most	

Some of my homework *is* missing. (The verb is singular because the sense of the subject is that one unit is missing.)

Some of the puzzle pieces *are* missing. (The verb is plural because the sense is that more than one unit is missing.)

Practice 11.22

Fill in the blanks with the correct present tense form of the verb in parentheses. The first one is done as an example.

1. (be) All of the lost money ____*is*____ in the back of the drawer.

2. (believe) Each of us _____ the tax increase will improve the economy.

3. (find) Many of the band members _____ the new director enthusiastic and creative.

4. (be) Everyone _____ invited to the tailgate party before the homecoming game.

5. (be) All of the hem _____ torn from the skirt.

6. (seem) None of the proposals _____ adequate to solve the problem.

7. (be) Some of the desserts _____ low in fat and sugar.

8. (go) Everything _____ wrong when you are in a hurry.

9. (taste) All of the items _____ underseasoned to me.

10. (expect) Nobody _____ you to be perfect.

Phrases between the Subject and Verb

Phrases (word groups) that come between the subject and verb do not affect subject-verb agreement. Your verb should agree with the subject and not some other word positioned nearby.

Prepositional phrases often come between a subject and verb. Go back now to p. 182 and review the material on prepositional phrases. Remember, the subject will not be part of a prepositional phrase.

The theme of the stories *is* middle-class greed. (A singular verb is used to agree with the singular subject *theme*. The phrase *of the stories* does not affect agreement.)

Practice 11.23

After each subject and phrase that follows, write a present tense verb and any other words you want to add. Underline the subject once and the verb twice; draw a line through the phrase between the subject and verb. The first one is done as an example.

1. The <u>carton</u> ~~of records~~ <u><u>*is blocking the entrance to the room.*</u></u> _____

2. The people on the bus_____

_____

3. Many paintings by that artist_____

_____

4. The students from Sri Lanka _____

_____

5. The scouts, along with their scoutmaster,_____

_____

6. The group of children _____

_____

7. The mistakes on the last page of the essay _____

    _____

8. The seats in the tenth row _____

    _____

9. The ragweed in the fields _____

    _____

10. One of the kittens _____

    _____

Inverted Order

When a sentence has *inverted order,* the subject comes *after* the verb. (See p. 184 for more on inverted order.) Inverted order often occurs when a sentence begins with *here* or *there.* The following sentences have inverted order. The subjects are underlined once, and the verbs are underlined twice.

Here <u>are</u> the <u>items</u> for the charity garage sale.
There <u>is</u> only <u>one movie</u> suitable for children.

Even if a sentence has inverted order, the subject and verb must agree. If you have trouble finding the subject and verb, find the word or words that change form to show tense—that's the verb. Then ask "who or what?" before the verb—your answer will be the subject. (See p. 184 and p. 185 on this procedure.)

Practice 11.24

Complete the following sentences, being sure your subjects and verbs agree. The first one is done as an example.

1. Here is *an unusual painting.* _____

2. Here are_____

    _____

3. There is _____

    _____

4. There are _____

_____

5. There were _____

_____

6. There was _____

_____

Who, Which, That

Who, Which, and *That* are *relative pronouns* that refer to nouns. (See p. 208.) Use a singular verb when *who, which,* or *that* refers to a singular noun; use a plural verb when *who, which,* or *that* refers to a plural noun. Study these two examples:

Peter is one of those students who *study* constantly. (The plural verb is used because *who* refers to the plural noun *students.*)

This is the book that *has* the surprise ending. (The singular verb is used because *that* refers to the singular noun *book.*)

Practice 11.25

Draw an arrow from *who, which,* or *that* to the noun referred to. Then fill in the blank with the correct present tense form of the verb in parentheses. The first one is done as an example.

1. (follow) Corrine is a person who ___*follows*___ every rule to the letter.

2. (do) A person who _____ not understand trigonometry will have trouble with physics.

3. (support) The beams which _____ this section of roof are beginning to rot.

4. (believe) Dr. Perni is one of those instructors who _____ her students can succeed.

5. (divide) This is the lake that _____ the property in half.

6. (scare) This is the kind of movie that always _____ me.

Post Test.

A. Drawing on everything you have learned about subject-verb agreement, fill in the blanks with the correct verb in parentheses.

1. (was/were) There _____ three accidents at the corner of Broadway and Elm Street last month.

2. (needs/need) The rose bush in the middle of the petunias _____ more sun.

3. (stands/stand) A bookcase and a record cabinet _____ against the wall opposite the fireplace.

4. (has/have) Some of the mess _____ been straightened up.

5. (belongs/belong) Every six-year-old _____ in school.

6. (makes/make) Either magazines or a mystery novel _____ a suitable gift to someone in the hospital.

7. (is/are) Some of my family members _____ not able to attend this year's annual Thanksgiving reunion.

8. (has/have) The decision of the three judges _____ been disputed by the skater and her coach.

9. (was/were) There _____ no question about the wisdom of electing Lynne president of student council.

10. (makes/make) Maureen is one of those people who _____ friends wherever she goes.

11. (is/are) Here _____ the supplies you need to complete the project.

12. (dislikes/dislike) The Beast, a roller coaster at King's Island, is not for people who _____ speed and heights.

13. (speaks/speak) The chief of police and two police officers _____ about drug abuse at local schools.

14. (decides/decide) A panel of writing instructors _____ who wins the senior essay award.

15. (drives/drive) Either Jesse or Mike _____ me to school every morning.

B. On a separate sheet, rewrite the following paragraphs, changing the underlined past tense verbs to present tense verbs. Pay careful attention to subject-verb agreement.

After the noon rush hour, Leo's Pizzeria <u>was</u> a mess. The once clean, stainless steel table where pizzas <u>were</u> made <u>was</u> splattered with sauce and flooded with oil. On the table, crusty dough and hardening strands of mozzarella <u>con-tributed</u> to the mess, which <u>included</u> crumbled plastic dough bags dripping with oil. A mountain of dirty dishes <u>sat</u> in wait, threatening to topple if someone <u>did</u> not come soon to wash them. A collection of torn pizza boxes, strewn across the counter, <u>hid</u> spatulas used and abandoned. Blackened pizzas, burned and forgotten during the rush, <u>filled</u> the air with the scent of charcoal. Added to this smell <u>were</u> the watering onions near the ovens. The flour used to make the crusts <u>covered</u> everything in the room with a fine dust. Anyone who <u>entered</u> the kitchen would surely think twice before eating at Leo's.

Everything <u>seemed</u> to be shrinking, even the size of the incisions doctors <u>made</u> for certain kinds of back surgery. For some kinds of herniated spinal disks, for example, doc-tors <u>used</u> "microdiskectomy." This <u>was</u> one of those proce-dures that <u>allowed</u> surgeons to use a a very thin tool that <u>cut</u> and <u>removed</u> the damaged part of the disk. A possible drawback of such procedures <u>was</u> that surgeons <u>didn't</u> have as wide a view of what they <u>were</u> operating on. To balance this problem <u>was</u> the fact that patients <u>went</u> home sooner and <u>got</u> back to work earlier than people who <u>had</u> tradi-tional surgery. Either microdiskectomy or traditional surgery <u>was</u> recommended in many cases. Thus, there <u>were</u> good reasons to consult with your physician before decid-ing what to do. The medical community <u>believed</u> that the final decision <u>rested</u> with you, the patient.

TENSE SHIFTS

Verb tenses show time (see p. 174). A writer must be careful to use the tense (present, past, or future) that correctly shows the time of an event. Moving from one tense to another without a good reason cre-ates a problem called *tense shift.*

Pretest

If there is a tense shift, write, *TS* on the blank; if the sentence is correct, write *C* on the blank. Do not guess. If you are unsure, do not write anything. You can check your answers in Appendix III.

1. _____ After I took my algebra midterm examination, I walk to the student union to relax for a while.

2. _____ Chuck is a man with a dream, and he planned to make it come true.

3. _____ When I finished the novel, I felt enriched by what I had read.

4. _____ Dr. Juarez explains difficult points in detail and was always glad to answer student questions patiently.

5. _____ I was struggling to get the top up on my convertible when the storm hits and the downpour starts.

6. _____ The doctor explained that the child's tonsils were badly infected and that they had to be surgically removed when the infection was gone.

7. _____ All of us are prepared for an emergency. We have first-aid kits, flashlights, waterproof clothing, and extra food.

8. _____ When the nature guide turned over the leaf, the scouts see the monarch butterfly egg.

9. _____ The killer whale feeds on seals, fish, and other whales. It did not attack human beings.

10. _____ The blue whale can grow to be 100 feet long, although it eats only microscopic animals.

Avoiding Inappropriate Tense Shifts

Verbs show time (tense). A writer uses a present tense verb form to show that an event is occurring now, a past tense verb form to show that an event occurred before the present, and a future tense verb form to show that an event will occur after the present. For more information on verb tenses, turn back to p. 174. Writers should use the same verb tense throughout the composition unless they want to show a change in time. A writer who changes verb tense without a valid reason creates a problem called *tense shift*. Here is an example:

tense shift: When I *left* the house this morning, I *go* to school.

explanation: The first verb (*left*) is in the past tense to show that an event occurred before the present. However, the second verb (*go*) shifts to the present tense for no reason.

correction: When I *left* the house this morning, I *went* to school.

explanation: Both verbs are now in the past tense, so the shift in tense is eliminated.

Some tense shifts are not a problem because a change of time is called for. Consider the following example:

appropriate tense shift: "Frankfurters" *are* named for the city where they *were* first made: Frankfurt, Germany.

explanation: The present tense *are* is used because frankfurters are named *in the present.* The past tense *were* is used because frankfurters were first made *in the past.*

Practice 11.26

Underline the verbs and then eliminate each inappropriate tense shift by crossing out the problem verb and writing the correct form above it. The first one is done as an example.

1. After I <u>completed</u> my research paper for sociology class, I ~~treat~~ *treated* myself to dinner and a movie.

2. My high school teachers always asked for an outline whenever I submit my final essay.

3. As I drive into my old neighborhood, I saw that the house I grew up in was no longer standing.

4. Painting the walls in my bedroom went quickly, but painting the ceiling takes most of the day.

5. The eager science students collect specimens in the park. Then they mounted them on slides and view them under the microscope.

6. Before leaving the house, I make sure the stove is turned off, and then I checked the security locks.

Practice 11.27

On a separate sheet, rewrite the paragraphs eliminating inappropriate tense shifts by changing verb tenses where necessary. Remember not all tense changes are a problem. Eliminate only the inappropriate shifts.

A.   The smallest deer in the world live on islands off the southern tip of Florida. They are called key deer, and each one is only the size of a Great Dane dog. The key deer thrived for thousands of years, and then Columbus stops at the islands on one of his trips to the New World. Soon explorers are coming and discovering the deer. Eventually, settlers move on the island, and the deer were hunted. By the 1940s, only several dozen of these small creatures were left. The deer remained unprotected until the late 1950s, when Congress passes a law establishing a refuge for the key deer. Now the number of these endangered animals is 350, up from fewer than 30 in 1948.

B.   In 1937, pilot Amelia Earhart and Fred Noonan, her navigator, were attempting an around-the-world flight. They planned to land and refuel on Howland Island. However, Earhart's plane is lost over the Pacific Ocean, although she gave compass readings over the plane's radio, hoping to be guided to a safe landing. "We're on the line of 157–337. . . . We are running north and south," the pilot says. These were the last words the outside world heard Earhart speak. The ground crew on Howland listens in vain for the twin-engine plane, but Earhart and Noonan are never heard from again. Still, Earhart lives in the memory of millions of Americans who admire her as a pioneer who, as the first woman to fly the Atlantic Ocean alone, is not afraid of adventure.

Post Test

On a separate sheet, rewrite the following paragraph, eliminating inappropriate tense shifts by changing verb forms where necessary.

Scientists raise fleas in laboratories to learn more about how these pests caused disease in humans and to learn more about effective ways to control the insects. The fleas are kept in special jars that contain sieves. The fleas lay eggs in the jars, and these eggs drop through the sieves. The scientists collected the eggs so they can raise more fleas from them. The jars also have tubes that carry warm water to heat blood that is contained underneath a skinlike sheath. The fleas bit through this sheath to drink the blood, which served as their food. Interestingly, these laboratory breeding grounds for fleas are called fake pups.

CHAPTER
12

Using Pronouns Correctly

A *pronoun* takes the place of a noun or refers to a noun (a noun names a person, place, idea, emotion, or thing). Pronouns allow us to avoid unpleasant repetition, as the following example illustrates:

repeated noun:	Harry said Harry could bring extra chairs to the party.
pronoun used to avoid repeated noun:	Harry said he could bring extra chairs to the party.

The noun the pronoun stands for or refers to is the *antecedent*. In the following examples an arrow is drawn from the pronoun to the noun antecedent:

Some consumers do not understand their legal rights.

Michelle understood that if she did not find a suitable baby-sitter, she would not be able to return to college.

The oak tree must be diseased, for it is dropping its leaves.

In this chapter you will learn much about pronouns, including:

1. how to ensure that pronouns agree with their antecedents
2. how to avoid unclear reference to antecedents
3. how to avoid distant reference to antecedents
4. how to avoid reference to unstated antecedents

5. when to use subject pronouns and when to use object pronouns

6. how to avoid problems with person shift

Pretest

Fill in the blanks with the correct pronoun form in parentheses, and then check your answers in Appendix III. Do not guess; if you are unsure, do not put anything in the blank.

1. (I, me) My sister and _____ are attending the same college.

2. (they, them) Each morning I jog farther than _____

3. (I, me) Because there was a fly in the soup, the manager gave my date and _____ a free dinner.

4. (her, their) Each of the mothers complained that _____ children watched too much television.

5. (his or her, their) All of the students were instructed to bring _____ books and notes to the examination.

6. (its, their) The book of old photographs fell off _____ shelf.

7. (its, their) The committee felt _____ authority should be extended to making and enforcing rules.

8. (his, their) Most of the football players have memorized _____ playbooks.

9. (I, me) The police officer told the other driver and _____ that it was impossible to determine who caused the accident.

10. (its, their) One of the dresses has lost _____ shape.

PRONOUN-ANTECEDENT AGREEMENT

A pronoun must be singular if the word it refers to (the antecedent) is singular. The pronoun must be plural if the antecedent is plural. Matching singular pronouns with singular antecedents and plural pronouns with plural antecedents creates *subject-verb agreement.*

singular pronoun/singular antecedent: The child cried because she broke her favorite toy.

plural pronoun/plural antecedent: The basketball players cheered when they won the game in double overtime.

Here is a chart of singular and plural pronouns.

Singular Pronouns	*Plural Pronouns*
I, me, my, mine	we, us, our, ours
he, she, it, him, her	they, their, theirs
his, hers, its	them

Pronouns That Are Both Singular and Plural

you, your, yours

Practice 12.1

Draw an arrow from each underlined pronoun to its antecedent. Then on the blank write *S* if the pronoun and antecedent are singular; write *P* if the pronoun and antecedent are plural. The first one is done as an example.

1. __*P*__   The students were disappointed to learn that their tests had not been graded yet.

2. ____   The Children's Hospital is having its annual fundraiser.

3. ____   Lillian dropped her folder, and its contents spilled all over the floor.

4. ____   Stavros said that he needed a ride home because his car had a flat tire.

5. ____   Mario said that he didn't like potatoes, but he would eat them anyway.

6. ____   The noise was distracting, but the students concentrated on their work in spite of it.

7. ____   Too many people believe that money will buy them happiness, but they will eventually learn the truth.

Compound Subject Antecedents

A *compound subject* is a two-part subject with the parts connected by *and, or, either . . . or,* or *neither . . . nor.* Follow these rules when a pronoun refers to all or part of a compound subject.

1. When the noun antecedents are joined by *and,* the pronoun will usually be plural.

   My father and mother sold their house and moved into an apartment. (Their is plural because it refers to two people, father and mother.)

2. If the noun antecedents are joined by *or, either . . . or,* or *neither . . . nor,* the pronoun agrees with the closer antecedent.

   Ivan or Ralph will lend me his car to use while mine is in the shop. (The singular his is used to agree with Ralph, the closer antecedent.)

   Neither the president nor his advisors believe they can get the disarmament bill through Congress. (The plural they is used to agree with advisors, the closer antecedent.)

   Either Jeff or his brothers will bring their extension ladder over so I can clean the gutters around the house. (The plural their is used to agree with brothers, the closer antecedent.)

NOTE: To avoid an awkward-sounding (but grammatically correct) pronoun usage, place the plural part of a compound subject last.

Correct (but awkward):	Either the scouts or the scout leader will bring *his* leaf identification manual.
Correct and natural sounding:	Either the scout leader or the scouts will bring *their* leaf identification manual.

Practice 12.2

Fill in the blank with the correct pronoun. The first one is done as an example.

1. The students and their teacher decorated __*their*__ classroom for the Martin Luther King memorial celebration.

2. Joyce and Burt handed in _____ research papers early.

3. Either my mother or my grandmother will bake _____ secret chocolate chip cookie recipe for the family reunion.

4. Neither the teachers nor the school board members changed _____ positions after hours of negotiating.

5. I thought Michael or Elliot would offer to bring _____ Coleman stove on the camping trip.

6. The Hummel figurine and the Royal Copenhagen plate were knocked from _____ shelves during the brief earth tremor.

Collective Noun Antecedents

A *collective noun* refers to a group. These words are examples of collective nouns:

band	committee	jury
group	family	team
herd	audience	faculty

1. If the sense of the collective noun is that the group is acting as one unit, the pronoun that refers to the collective noun will be singular:

   The committee was unsure of its assignment. (The committee is acting as one unit, so the singular its is used.)

NOTE: If you find it awkward to use the singular *its,* add "members of" before the collective noun and use a plural verb and pronoun:

The members of the committee were unsure of their assignment.

---

2. If the members of the group are acting individually, the pronoun that refers to the collective noun will be plural:

   The committee argued about their differing opinions. (The plural their is used because the members of the committee are arguing as individuals, as more than one unit.)

Practice 12.3

Circle the collective noun antecedent. Then fill in the blank with the correct pronoun (choose the singular *its* or the plural *their*). The first one is done as an example.

1. The women's softball (team) scored ___*its*___ third upset of the season against the top-ranked team in the league.

2. The jury debated all night in order to resolve _____ differences of opinion.

3. The audience shouted _____ approval by calling for an encore.

4. After the curtain fell on the third act, the cast came out and took _____ bow.

5. The coach reminded the team to bring _____ playbooks to every practice.

6. The orchestra lifted _____ instruments, signaling that the concert was about to begin.

7. At the general membership meeting, the committee reported _____ findings.

Indefinite Pronoun Antecedents

An *indefinite pronoun* refers to a part of a group without mentioning the specific members. An indefinite pronoun can be an antecedent for another pronoun.

1. These indefinite pronouns are always singular, so any pronoun that refers to one of them will also be singular:

anyone	everybody	nothing
everyone	nobody	something
no one	somebody	each
someone	anything	one
anybody	everything	none

Everyone should bring his or her notebook to the lecture.

Each priest is volunteering his time to help at the battered persons' shelter.

None of the mothers brought her children to the meeting.

NOTE: As the last example illustrates, a prepositional phrase that comes after the indefinite pronoun does not affect pronoun-antecedent agreement. (See also "Phrases after the Antecedent" on p. 354.)

2. These indefinite pronouns are always plural, so any pronoun that refers to them should also be plural:

both   many   few   several

Few understand all <u>their</u> rights under the law.

Many believe <u>their</u> educational backgrounds are not adequate.

3. These indefinite pronouns are either singular or plural, depending on the meaning. Any pronoun that refers to one of them will be singular if the meaning of the indefinite pronoun is singular, and plural if the meaning of the indefinite pronoun is plural.

all   more   some

any   most

All of the class finished <u>their</u> research papers. (The plural pronoun is used because the antecedent <u>all</u> has a plural sense.)

All of the report fell out of <u>its</u> folder. (The singular pronoun is used because the antecedent <u>all</u> has a singular sense.)

Using Nonsexist Language

In the past, writers would use the masculine forms *he, his, him,* and *himself* to refer to nouns and indefinite pronouns that included both males and females. Thus, sentences like the following were frequently written and spoken:

Each student is expected to bring <u>his</u> book to class.

Every person has <u>his</u> own opinion.

Everybody described <u>his</u> career goals.

Today more writers and speakers understand that this use of the masculine pronoun is grammatically correct, but it excludes women. To avoid using a masculine pronoun to refer to groups that include both men and women, you have three options.

1. Use *he or she, him or her, his or hers, himself or herself.*

Everybody described his or her career goals. (*Instead of:* Everybody described his career goals.)

Using pairs of pronouns works in many situations. However, when this solution becomes awkward, it is better to use one of the two solutions that follow.

2. Use plural forms.

All students are expected to bring their books to class. (*Instead of:* Each student is expected to bring his book to class.)

3. Reshape the sentence to avoid the masculine reference.

Every person has an opinion. (*Instead of:* Every person has his own opinion.)

Practice 12.4

Fill in the blanks with the correct pronoun; choose *his, her, its, they,* or *their.* The first one is done as an example.

1. All of the contestants hoped _____*their*_____ entries would be judged the best of the show.

2. None of the girl scouts had trouble finding _____ way out of the woods during the survival training exercise.

3. Most of the curtain has slipped off _____ rod.

4. Many of the protesters shouted that _____ civil rights had been violated.

5. To pass inspection, you must be sure that everything is in _____ place.

6. Each of the boys on the varsity basketball team is expected to keep _____ grades up to a B average.

7. The salesclerk was alarmed because one of the expensive designer dresses was missing from _____ hanger.

8. Very few of the contestants believed _____ had much of a chance to win.

Practice 12.5

Rewrite each sentence so it has nonsexist language. Refer to the three preceding suggestions for how to do this, and try to use each suggestion twice. The first one is done as an example.

1. None of the people who entered the writing contest had his manuscript returned.

    The people who entered the writing contest did not have their

    manu-scripts returned.

2. Anyone who cannot reach his goal is sure to feel frustrated.

    _____

    _____

3. Everyone who entered the poetry contest is convinced that his poem will win the $500 prize.

    _____

    _____

4. Anyone who puts his money in a money market fund now will earn an average of 4 percent interest.

    _____

    _____

5. None of the audience felt the play was worth the price he paid.

    _____

    _____

6. Each of the investment brokers advised his clients to avoid the risks of penny stocks.

    _____

    _____

7. Someone has left his chemistry book and notes on the desk.

    _____

    _____

Phrases after the Antecedent

Sometimes a prepositional phrase comes after the antecedent (see p. 182 for an explanation of prepositional phrases). When this happens, the phrase will not affect pronoun-antecedent agreement.

The can of sardines fell off its shelf in the cupboard. (The prepositional phrase of sardines does not affect agreement. The singular its is used to agree with the singular can.)

Each of the windows had slipped off its track. (The prepositional phrase of the windows does not affect agreement. The singular its is used to agree with the singular each.)

The students in the class asked if their test would be given on Wednesday. (The prepositional phrase in the class does not affect agreement. The plural their is used to agree with the plural students.)

Practice 12.6

Draw a line through each prepositional phrase. Then fill in the blanks with the correct pronoun (choose *its* or *their*). The first one is done as an example.

1. Each of the birds spread _____*its*_____ wings and flew from the nest.

2. The last two cars in the caravan lost _____ way after taking a wrong turn north of Cincinnati.

3. Each of the items for the experiment is in _____ proper place on the counter.

4. The baby birds in the nest opened _____ mouths to be fed.

5. The box of Christmas presents fell from _____ hiding place on the shelf in the back of the closet.

6. Two of the women sold _____ stereo systems to buy a one-way ticket to Toronto.

☐ TIPS FOR SOLVING ☐ PRONOUN-ANTECEDENT AGREEMENT PROBLEMS

1. When you edit, underline every pronoun once. Then draw an arrow from the pronoun to the antecedent. Compare each pronoun and antecedent to be sure they are both singular or they are both plural.

2. Memorize the group of indefinite pronouns that is singular, the group that is plural, and the group that can be either singular or plural, so you can use pronouns correctly with them.

3. Edit one extra time, just looking for pronoun-antecedent agreement errors.

4. Find a pattern to your errors. Maybe you usually make mistakes with collective noun antecedents. If this is the case, you can pay special attention to your use of pronouns with collective nouns. If you are not sure whether there is a pattern to your errors, ask your instructor.

Post Test

Cross out each incorrect pronoun and write the correct one above it.

A person who lives in constant fear of becoming a victim of crime can solve their problem easily—by turning off their television. Several years ago, a set of studies was done. They showed that when people watch a great deal of television, they suffer an exaggerated sense of fear. Apparently, all the murder and mayhem on the small screen makes frequent TV-viewers feel at risk. Thus, someone who spends most of their time in front of the set will worry far more about being victimized by crime than someone who watches little or no television. Women and children may find his or her fears even greater. This is because women on television are most often shown as the victims of violent crime, and young children do not recognize the unrealistic nature of much programming. Thus, women and children feel more threatened than adult male viewers. Obviously, the studies show that parents of a young child should limit his or her child's viewing time.

PRONOUN REFERENCE

In general, three kinds of pronoun reference problems are common:

1. unclear reference
2. distant reference
3. unstated reference

The next pages will explain these pronoun reference problems.

Unclear Reference

When the reader cannot tell which antecedent a pronoun refers to, the problem is *unclear reference*. Here is a sentence that has unclear reference because the pronoun could refer to two nouns:

Kathy was having lunch with Thelma when she heard the news.

Because the pronoun reference is unclear, the reader cannot tell whether Kathy or Thelma heard the news. Here is another example:

After I put the cereal and orange juice on the table, my dog jumped up and spilled it.

What was spilled, the cereal or the orange juice? Because the pronoun reference is unclear, the reader cannot tell for sure.

To solve a problem with unclear reference, you may have to use a noun instead of a pronoun:

Kathy was having lunch with Thelma when Thelma heard the news.

After I put the cereal and orange juice on the table, my dog jumped up and spilled the juice.

Practice 12.7

Rewrite the following sentences to solve problems with unclear pronoun reference. The first one is done as an example.

1. Lenny told Jake that he would have to return the book by Friday.

Lenny told Jake that Jake would have to return the book

by Friday.

2. I put the chicken in the oven and the broccoli in the microwave. An hour later it burned.

_____

_____

3. Sasha carefully removed the vase from the coffee table before dusting it.

_____

_____

4. My mother explained to my sister that she had to leave for school in an hour.

_____

_____

5. Before Jack could give Marvin his class notes, he fell asleep.

_____

_____

6. As I was placing the ceramic bowl on the glass table, it broke.

_____

_____

Distant Reference

If a pronoun is too far away from the noun it refers to (its antecedent), the problem is *distant reference.* Distant reference can create confusion for a reader, so replace the pronoun with the appropriate noun. Here is an example of distant reference:

Monica set her purse on the chair next to her and started studying. When she realized she needed a dictionary, she crossed the room to get one. She looked up three words, and when she returned, she discovered that it was gone.

The pronoun *it* in the last sentence is meant to refer to the noun antecedent *purse*. However, *purse* is far from the pronoun. The result is confusing. To solve the problem, replace the pronoun with a noun:

Monica set her purse on the chair next to her and started studying. When she realized she needed a dictionary, she crossed the room to get one. She looked up three words, and when she returned, she discovered that <u>her purse</u> was gone.

Practice 12.8

Cross out the pronoun that creates a problem with distant reference and write in a correction. The first one is done as an example.

1. I put the rolls in the oven and started preparing the salad. Just then my son came into the kitchen and announced he was out of notebook paper for his homework, and he had to have it immediately. I was annoyed, but I got in the car to drive to the drugstore. Ten minutes later when I emerged from the drugstore, I realized ~~they~~ *the rolls* were still in the oven.

2. Using a power drill, I put a hole in the roof of the porch and inserted a t-hook. Carefully, I hung the delicate windchimes from the hook. Just then a gentle breeze sent the ceramic pieces nudging into each other, and a pleasant tinkling filled the air. I descended the ladder, pleased with my work, but just as I stepped off the last rung, they fell and shattered in hundreds of fragments.

3. I set the book on the desk and went off to tell Rita I was leaving the library. When I found her, she was waist-deep in reference books, looking for information for her research paper. I helped her for an hour, and when I returned to the desk, it was gone.

4. Ben cut himself a piece of chocolate cake and then went to the refrigerator and poured himself a glass of milk. The milk overflowed the glass, so Ben tried to clean up the counter and floor. When he finished, he turned to see that Rags, his collie, had eaten it.

Unstated Reference

Unstated reference occurs when a pronoun refers to an unstated antecedent. To solve the problem, add the unstated form.

unstated reference: Carter is known as a patient tutor. It is a trait the other tutors admire. [<u>It</u> is meant to refer to *patience,* but that word does not appear—<u>patient</u> does.]

correction:	Carter is known as a patient tutor. <u>His pa</u>tience is a trait the other tutors admire.
unstated reference:	Because Joel is so insecure, he has very few friends. It causes him to seek constant approval. [It is meant to refer to <u>insecurity</u>, but that word does not appear—<u>insecure</u> does.]
correction:	Because Joel is so insecure, he has very few friends. <u>His insecurity</u> causes him to seek constant approval.

Unstated reference also occurs when *this, that, which, it,* or *they* has no stated antecedent. To solve the problem, add the missing word or words.

unstated reference:	During my last physical examination, the doctor urged me to lower my salt intake. This means my food tastes bland. [<u>This</u> has no stated antecedent.]
correction:	During my last physical examination, the doctor urged me to lower my salt intake. <u>This change</u> means my food tastes bland.
unstated reference:	The auto workers and GM negotiated all night, but it failed to produce a contract. [<u>It</u> has no stated antecedent.]
correction:	The auto workers and GM negotiated all night, but <u>the session</u> failed to produce a contract.

Unstated reference will occur when *they* or *you* has no stated antecedent. To solve the problem, add the missing word or words.

unstated reference:	I called the billing office to complain about my bill, but they said it was correct. [<u>They</u> has no stated antecedent.]
correction:	I called the billing office to complain about my bill, but <u>the clerk</u> said it was correct.
unstated reference:	Worker dissatisfaction occurs when you do not let employees participate in decision-making. [<u>You</u> has no stated antecedent.]
correction:	Worker dissatisfaction occurs when <u>employ</u>ers do not let employees participate in decision-making.

NOTE: *You* and *your* address the reader directly. Avoid these pronouns unless you mean to address the reader; do not use them for general statements that apply to more people than the reader.

no:	At election time, <u>you</u> always see politicians promising things they can't deliver.
yes:	At election time, politicians are always promising things they can't deliver.

Unstated reference occurs when a pronoun refers to a possessive form (a form that designates ownership). To solve the problem, rewrite to eliminate the possessive form.

unstated reference:	The speaker's words were inspirational because he was so emotional. [The antecedent of <u>he</u> is <u>speaker</u>, not <u>speaker's</u>, but <u>speaker</u> does not appear.]
correction:	The speaker's words were so inspirational because the speaker was so emotional. [<u>Speaker</u> is substituted for <u>speaker's</u>.]
unstated reference:	Janet's library books are three months overdue. She will have to pay a stiff fine. [<u>She</u> cannot refer to <u>Janet's</u>.]
correction:	Janet's library books are three months overdue. Janet will have to pay a stiff fine. [<u>Janet</u> is substituted for <u>she</u>.]

▢   TIPS FOR SOLVING PROBLEMS   ▢
WITH PRONOUN REFERENCE

1. Underline every pronoun. Next find the specific antecedent for each pronoun. If you cannot find a stated antecedent, you have a problem with unstated reference, which you can correct by supplying the missing antecedent.

2. Check to be sure the pronoun does not have two possible antecedents. If it does, use a noun instead of a pronoun. Check once again to be sure the antecedent is close enough to the pronoun. If there is too much distance between the pronoun and antecedent, use a noun instead of the pronoun.

3. Check your use of *you, it,* and *they.* Be sure these pronouns have stated antecedents. If they do not, supply the missing antecedents.

Practice 12.9

Revise the sentences to eliminate the unstated reference problems. The first one is done as an example.

1. Because he had a tension headache, Nick was irritable. It made him very difficult to be around.

   Because he had a tension headache, Nick was irritable.

   His irritability made him very difficult to be around.

2. The comedian told several ethnic jokes. It annoyed most of the audience.

3. The movie was excessively violent and too long. This caused most of the critics to review it badly.

4. The paint had a few blisters in it near the ceiling, but for the most part, they did an excellent job.

5. My mechanic explained that my car's starter and shock absorbers must be replaced, so I am thinking of trading it in.

6. I went to see my advisor, but they said that he was sick.

7. Ivan felt nervous about the upcoming examination. It made sleep difficult for him.

8. Betty's problem will not be easy to solve. She will probably have to get professional help.

_____

_____

9. During finals week, you always know that students are working hard.

_____

_____

10. The police officer explained to the suspects that they had a right to an attorney, which is guaranteed by law.

_____

_____

11. Corrine is a very talented artist. It helped her earn a scholarship to the state art institute.

_____

_____

SUBJECT AND OBJECT PRONOUNS

A pronoun can be the *subject* of a sentence. That is, it can be the word that shows who or what the sentence is about (see p. 181 for more on identifying subjects). In the following sentences, the italicized pronouns act as subjects:

He slammed the car door on John's finger.

During summer school, *she* took a word processing course.

They ate quickly and left.

In the spring and summer, *I* walk five miles a day.

A pronoun can also be the *object of a verb*. That is, it can be the word that receives the action the verb expresses.

Diana carried *it* upstairs.

In this example, the verb is *carried*. When we ask "carried whom or what?" we get the answer *it*. Thus, *it* receives the action of the verb *carried*.

To find the object of a verb, ask "whom or what?" *after* the verb. Here are some examples:

Pat ate *it.* (Ask "ate whom or what?" and the answer is *it,* so *it* is the object of the verb.)

Ida always understands *him.* (Ask "understands whom or what?" and the answer is *him,* so *him* is the object of the verb.)

The ending of the book surprised *me.* (Ask "surprised whom or what?" and the answer is *me,* so *me* is the object of the verb.)

You may remember from an earlier chapter that asking "who or what?" is a good way to find the subject of a sentence. Just keep in mind that to find the subject you ask "who or what?" *before* the verb, and to find the object you ask "whom or what?" *after* the verb.

I invited them to the party.

In this sample sentence, the verb is *invited.* (If you are unsure about how to find the verb in a sentence, see p. 174.) Ask "who or what invited?" and you get the answer *I,* so *I* is the subject. Ask "invited whom or what?" and you get the answer *them,* so *them* is the object of the verb.

In addition to being the subject of a sentence or the object of a verb, a pronoun can be the *object of a preposition.* That is, a pronoun can come after prepositions—words like *to, in, at, near, around.* (If you do not know what a preposition is, turn to p. 182.) In the sentences that follow, the italicized pronouns function as objects of prepositions:

Janine put the chair next to *us.* (The preposition is *to.*)

The annoyed pitcher threw the ball at *me.* (The preposition is *at.*)

Raul always wants to be near *her.* (The preposition is *near.*)

Sometimes the preposition is not stated. Instead it is understood to be *to* or *for.* This often happens after the verbs *give, tell, buy, bring,* and *send.*

The instructor gave *him* the answer. (The instructor gave the answer *to him.*)

Mother sent *me* a rose for my birthday. (Mother sent a rose *to me* for my birthday.)

I bought *him* the book. (I bought the book *for him.*)

The particular pronoun used depends on whether the pronoun is functioning as a subject or object (either the object of a verb or the object of a preposition). The chart that follows shows you which pronouns can be subjects and which can be objects.

Subject Pronouns	Object Pronouns
I	me
you	you (the form does not change)
he	him
she	her
it	it (the form does not change)
we	us
they	them
who	whom
whoever	whomever

Practice 12.10

Above each italicized pronoun, write *S* if the pronoun is a subject, or write *O* if the pronoun is an object. The first one is done as an example.

    S   *O*
1. *I* asked Molly to lend *me* her car while mine was in the shop.

2. *We* asked *him* to come with *us.*

3. *I* gave *you* my answer yesterday.

4. Before leaving the house, *he* checked with *me* to learn what my plans were.

5. *You* bought *her* just the right present for the occasion.

6. On the bus, *they* sat behind *them* and in front of *us.*

7. *I* bought *it,* but now *you* must return *it.*

Practice 12.11

Fill in the blanks with a correct subject or object pronoun. Write *S* if you have used a subject pronoun or *O* if you have used an object pronoun. The first one is done as an example.

Roy was a promising high school quarterback in 1985. As a sophomore ___*he*___ broke the school passing records, and as a junior _____ led his team to a conference championship. Many college scouts were watching _____, and _____ were ready to offer _____ rather impressive scholarships. Unfortunately, an incident occurred in Roy's senior year. Two hefty players on an opposing team sacked Roy at the line of scrimmage. _____ tackled _____ so hard that _____ was knocked unconscious and rushed to the hospital. He had a concussion, but _____ came out of it just fine. However, when I went to see Roy in the hospital, he told _____ that he had no desire to play football again. When Roy got out of the hospital, his friends and coaches tried to change his mind, but _____ were unable to persuade _____ to go back to the game. Roy was just too afraid of getting hurt again. Roy went to college, but _____ had to give up his athletic scholarship. He does not seem to have any regrets, though. In fact, when I last spoke to _____, he told _____ he was sure he had done the right thing.

Choosing Subject and Object Pronouns in Compounds

And or *or* can link a pronoun to a noun to form a *compound*.

Bob and *me*	the children and *us*
the boy and *I*	Gloria and *he*

Sometimes writers are unsure whether to use subject or object pronouns in compounds. They wonder whether to use "Bob and *me*" or "Bob and *I*," "Gloria and *he*" or "Gloria and *him*," and so forth. Whether to use a subject or object pronoun depends on how the pronoun is used in the sentence. If the pronoun is part of a compound that acts as a subject, then a subject pronoun is used. If the pronoun is part of a compound that acts as the object of a verb or the object of a preposition, then an object pronoun is used.

Bob and I bought season tickets to the Steelers' games. (The italicized compound is the subject of the sentence, so the subject pronoun is used.)

The car almost hit *Bob and me.* (The italicized compound is the object of the verb, so the object pronoun is used.)

The coach was angry with *Bob and me.* (The italicized compound is the object of the preposition *with,* so the object pronoun is used.)

□   TIP FOR SELECTING PRONOUNS   □
IN COMPOUNDS

An easy way to decide if a subject or object pronoun is needed in a compound is to cross out everything in the compound except the pronoun. Then decide if the remaining pronoun is a subject or an object.

~~The children and~~ I went to the movie.

~~The children and~~ me went to the movie.

When everything but the pronoun is crossed out in each compound, it is clear that the pronoun is part of the subject. Thus, the subject form *I* is needed:

The children and I went to the movies.

Here is another example:

Professor Hernandez explained to ~~Colleen, Louise, and~~ I that our project was well researched and informative.

Professor Hernandez explained to ~~Colleen, Louise, and~~ me that our project was well researched and informative.

With everything in the compound except the pronoun crossed out, it is easier to see that the pronoun is part of the object of the preposition *to.* Therefore an object pronoun is needed:

Professor Hernandez explained to Colleen, Louise, and me that our project was well researched and informative.

NOTE: When a noun and pronoun form a compound, place the pronoun at the end of the compound.

Avoid: I and the teacher disagreed about the correct answer.

Use: The teacher and I disagreed about the correct answer.

Avoid: The boat belongs to me and Joyce.

Use: The boat belongs to Joyce and me.

Practice 12.12

Fill in each blank with the correct subject or object pronoun in parentheses. If you have trouble choosing, cross out everything in the compound except the pronoun and decide whether a subject or object pronoun is needed. The first one is done as an example.

1. (I, me) The salesclerk gave ~~Jim and~~ _me_ the wrong packages.

2. (we, us) The band was too loud for Dale and _____ so we left.

3. (I, me) Molly and _____ searched the piles of sweaters for my size.

4. (we, us) The movers or _____ will pack the dishes in the kitchen.

5. (they, them) I gave you and _____ the directions to the farm that sells fresh produce.

6. (he, him) Dr. Amin wants Julia and _____ as lab assistants.

7. (she, her) To make money for college, Wanda and _____ worked all summer as table servers.

8. (I, me) Give the library books to Hans or _____ to return for you.

Choosing Subject and Object Pronouns with Appositives

An *appositive* renames the noun or pronoun it follows.

My brother Brian is a business administration major.

Brian is an appositive because it renames *my brother.*

If an appositive follows a pronoun, you can decide whether a subject or object pronoun is needed by crossing out the appositive and deciding whether the remaining pronoun is a subject or object. For example, crossing out the appositives in the following sentences will help you choose the correct pronoun:

We ~~nonsmokers~~ favor banning smoking in public places.

Us ~~nonsmokers~~ favor banning smoking in public places.

With the appositives crossed out, it is easier to see that the pronoun acts as a subject, so the subject pronoun *we* is needed. This makes the first example the correct sentence. Now look at these sentences:

Smokers are sometimes inconsiderate of we ~~nonsmokers~~.

Smokers are sometimes inconsiderate of us ~~nonsmokers~~.

With the appositives crossed out, we can see that the pronoun is the object of the preposition *of,* so the second sentence is correct because it uses the object pronoun *us.*

Practice 12.13

For each pair of sentences, cross out the appositive and decide if a subject or object pronoun is needed. Then place a check mark next to the correct sentence. The first one is done as an example.

1. _√_ We ~~students~~ believed that the tuition hike was unfortunate but necessary in light of increasing costs.

    _____ Us ~~students~~ believed that the tuition hike was unfortunate but necessary in light of increasing costs.

2. _____ Some of we golfers were unhappy with the condition of the course.

    _____ Some of us golfers were unhappy with the condition of the course.

3. _____ None of the legislators considered the impact of the tax increase on we, the middle-class property owners.

    _____ None of the legislators considered the impact of the tax increase on us, the middle-class property owners.

4. ____ Dr. Wren asked I, the only one who did not understand the problem, to put my answer on the board.

____ Dr. Wren asked me, the only one who did not understand the problem, to put my answer on the board.

5. ____ We new pledges must stick together if we are going to make it through the fraternity initiation.

____ Us new pledges must stick together if we are going to make it through the fraternity initiation.

6. ____ The club charter prevents we new members from holding office for a year.

____ The club charter prevents us new members from holding office for a year.

Choosing Subject and Object Pronouns in Comparisons

The words *than* and *as* can be used to show comparisons.

Marta is friendlier *than* Lorraine. (Marta's friendliness is being compared with Lorraine's friendliness.)

Larry is not as good at math *as* John. (Larry's math ability is being compared with John's math ability.)

Notice that when *than* or *as* is used to show comparison, words that could finish the comparison go unstated.

Marta is friendlier than Lorraine.

> *could be*

Marta is friendlier than Lorraine *is.*

Larry is not as good at math as John.

> *could be*

Larry is not as good at math as John *is.*

When a pronoun follows *than* or *as* in a comparison, decide whether to use a subject or object pronoun by adding the unstated words. Which sentence uses the correct pronoun?

Marcus is a better basketball player than *I.*

Marcus is a better basketball player than *me.*

To decide which pronoun is correct, add the unstated word or words:

Marcus is a better basketball player than I am.

Marcus is a better basketball player than me am.

With the unstated *am* added, you can see that the pronoun functions as the subject of the verb *am*. Since *I* is a subject pronoun, the first example is correct. Here is another example:

The news report disturbed Harriet as much as *I*.

The news report disturbed Harriet as much as *me*.

To decide on the correct pronoun, add the unstated words:

The news report disturbed Harriet as much as it disturbed *I*.

The news report disturbed Harriet as much as it disturbed *me*.

With the unstated words *it disturbed* added, you can see that the pronoun functions as the object of the verb *disturbed*. Since *me* is an object pronoun, the second example is correct.

Correct pronoun choice in comparisons is important because the pronoun can affect meaning. Here is an example:

Carol always liked Julio more than I.

Carol always liked Julio more than me.

The first sentence means that Carol like Julio more than I liked Julio. The second sentence means that Carol liked Julio more than she liked me.

Practice 12.14

Rewrite each sentence supplying the unstated words. Then fill in the blank with the correct pronoun in parentheses. The first one is done as an example.

1. (we, us) Carol and I were annoyed to discover that Ted and Janet had better seats for the concert than ___*we*___.

   Carol and I were annoyed to discover that Ted and Janet had better

   seats for the concert than we did.

2. (I, me) Making friends has always been easier for Eleni than ___.

   _____

   _____

3. (he, him) Studying together helps you as much as _____

_____

_____

4. (she, her) I believe in the power of positive thinking more than
_____.

_____

_____

5. (we, us) On opening night, Francis was less nervous than_____.

_____

_____

6. (I, me) Since you do not care for classical music as much as _____,
you should meet me after the concert for dinner.

_____

_____

PERSON SHIFT

When you write or speak about yourself, you use these pronouns:
I, we, my, mine, our, ours, me, and *us.* They are called *first person
pronouns.*

I hated to leave, but *I* had to get *my* car home by 10:00. (The pronouns *I* and *my* are first person pronouns; they allow the writer or
speaker to refer to himself or herself.)

When you write or speak directly to a person, you use these pronouns: *you, your,* and *yours.* They allow you to address directly the person you are writing or speaking to. These pronouns are *second person
pronouns.*

You should bring *your* dictionary to class on Thursday. (The pronouns *you* and *your* are second person pronouns; they allow the
speaker or writer to refer to the person spoken to or written to.)

To write about people or things that do not include yourself or a person you are addressing, you use *he, she, it, they, his, hers, its, their,
theirs, him, her,* and *them.* These are *third person pronouns.*

She told *him* to pick *her* up at 7:00. (The pronouns *she, him,* and *her* are third person pronouns; they allow writers or speakers to refer to someone or something other than themselves or the person addressed.)

Here is a chart of first, second, and third person pronouns.

First Person Pronouns (These Refer to the Speaker or the Writer)

> I, we, me, us, my, mine, our, ours

Second Person Pronouns (These Refer to the Person Spoken to or Written to)

> you, your, yours

Third Person Pronouns (These Refer to Someone or Something Other Than the Speaker or Writer or Person Addressed)

> he, she, it, they, his, her, hers, its, their, theirs, him, them

---

If you move unnecessarily from one person to another person within a sentence or longer passage, you create a problem called *person shift:*

I attend aerobics classes three times a week. The exercise helps *you* relax. (shift from the first person *I* to the second person *you*)

Here is the example rewritten to eliminate the person shift:

I attend aerobics classes three times a week. The exercise helps *me* relax. (Both *I* and *me* are first person pronouns.)

To avoid person shifts, remember that nouns are always third person, so pronouns that refer to nouns should also be third person.

person shift:	*Salesclerks* have a difficult job. *You* are on *your* feet all day dealing with the public. (shift from the third person *salesclerks* to the second person *you* and *your*)
shift eliminated:	*Salesclerks* have a difficult job. *They* are on *their* feet all day dealing with the public. (The third person pronouns *they* and *their* refer to the third person *salesclerks.*)

> NOTE: The most frequent problems with person shift occur when writers shift from the first person or third person to the second person *you*. For this reason, be sure when using *you* that you are really addressing the reader and not shifting from a first or third person form.

Practice 12.15

Rewrite the sentences to eliminate troublesome person shifts. The first one is done as an example.

1. Chemistry was not as hard as I thought it would be. You just had to keep up with the reading and ask questions when you did not understand.

    Chemistry was not as hard as I thought it would be. I just had to

    keep up with the reading and ask questions when I did not

    understand.

2. It was a mistake for me to try to teach my son to drive because you lose patience so quickly when working with your own children.

    _____

    _____

3. Learning to use a computer was not difficult for me. You just had to study the user's manual and practice a bit.

    _____

    _____

4. I realize too much sun is not good for your skin, but every summer I still try to get the perfect tan.

    _____

    _____

5. Before high school seniors select a college, you should visit several campuses and speak to the admissions counselors.

    _____

    _____

6. Many doctors believe women should take calcium supplements. Doing this can help you guard against osteoporosis.

_____

_____

Practice 12.16

Cross out pronouns that create troublesome person shifts and write the correction above the line.

Some people are saying that men are less willing to mentor women in the workplace because they fear charges of sexual harassment. However, male employees can still coach and support women to help them advance their careers. First, companies should have formal mentor programs. You should assign experienced employees to show newer employees the ropes. That way, no one will suspect that the mentoring is anything other than a professional work arrangement. Second, employers should draw up rules for people in the mentoring program. Then, you do not have to wonder if your behavior will be seen as inappropriate. You just follow the rules for mentoring and you will know that your behavior is acceptable. Finally, new employees should have more than one mentor when possible to avoid the suspicion that people are pairing up. If these guidelines were introduced into the workplace, both employees and employers would be comfortable with mentoring. You would not have to worry that charges of sexual harrassment would be leveled.

Post Test

A. Fill in the blanks with the correct pronoun in parentheses.

1. (its, their) After days of discussion, the jury felt confident _____ verdict was the correct one.

2. (his or her, their) The instructor told everyone to bring _____ dictionary to class each day for the next two weeks.

3. (her, their) Several of the mothers agreed that _____ preschool children would benefit from a play group.

4. (its, their) Some of the essay strays from _____ topic.

5. (its, their) When he was through playing, Tommy put his bag of marbles on _____ shelf.

6. (her, their) Each of the kindergarten girls brought _____ favorite toy for sharing day.

7. (I, me) Between you and _____, I am sure that Janet is planning to break up with Phil.

8. (he, him) Carla and _____ are sure to take first prize in the science fair, just as they did last year and the year before that.

9. (I, me) Even though Eduardo is stronger than _____, he rarely pins me in a wrestling match.

10. (we, us) Some of _____ fans felt the official's call was incorrect.

11. (we, us) _____ students should insist that the administration explain why tuition was raised 20 percent.

12. (we, you) Last weekend I went camping with three of my friends. However, it was not very relaxing because _____ had to work too hard setting up and maintaining the camp.

B. Cross out each incorrect pronoun, and write in the correction.

Most volunteer youth coaches find it a rewarding experience because you can make an important contribution to the lives of young people. To make coaching a positive experience, coaches must remember several points. First, successful coaches' priorities should be fun and learning—they should not emphasize winning above all. You should remember that the players are kids first and athletes second. Coaches should know the players and respect their limits. For example, ten-year-olds should not be asked to lift weights. This could harm young bodies. They say that successful coaches allow for a wide range of abilities and resist the temptation to field only the best players. Most important of all, however, is making sure that the kids feel they are a valued part of a team.

CHAPTER
13

Modifiers

A word or word group that describes another word or word group is a *modifier.* In the following sentences, the modifiers are italicized. An arrow is drawn from the modifier to the word it describes.

The *cloudy* sky threatened rain. (*Cloudy* describes *sky.*)

The pitcher threw a *sinker* ball. (*Sinker* describes *ball.*)

The *marathon* runner was breathing *heavily.* (*Marathon* describes *runner,* and *heavily* describes *breathing.*)

In this chapter, you will learn a great deal about modifiers, including:

1. when to use adjectives and when to use adverbs
2. when to use *good* and when to use *well*
3. how to use comparative and superlative forms
4. how to avoid dangling modifiers
5. how to avoid misplaced modifiers

Pretest

If the underlined modifier is used correctly, write *yes* on the blank. If the underlined modifier is not used correctly, write *no* on the blank. Do not guess; if you are unsure, do not write anything. You can check your answers in Appendix III.

1. _____ Chuyen has a lovely voice, but she sings too <u>loud</u>.

2. _____ Professor Smith <u>quickly</u> explained the directions before he passed out the exam questions.

3. _____ The splinter in Fluffy's paw caused her to limp <u>bad</u>.

4. _____ The <u>frustrated</u> toddler pounded her fists against the floor and screamed in rage.

5. _____ Les is <u>more happier</u> now that he has changed his major to physical therapy.

6. _____ Diana plays the cello <u>good</u>.

7. _____ Ivan felt his history midterm was the <u>easiest</u> test he had taken this semester.

8. _____ <u>Whistling as he walked down the street</u>, Tom's mood could not have been better.

9. _____ <u>Wondering which route to take</u>, Karen pulled to the side of the road and studied the map.

10. _____ The second day I had the flu, I felt <u>worser</u> than I did the day before.

ADJECTIVES AND ADVERBS

Words or word groups that describe nouns and pronouns are *adjectives*. In the following sentences, the adjectives are italicized and an arrow is drawn from the adjective to the word it describes:

Janet spilled *hot* coffee.   (*Hot* describes the noun *coffee*.)

Michael is *shy*.   (*Shy* describes the noun *Michael*.)

She seems *angry*.   (*Angry* describes the pronoun *she*.)

Adverbs are words or word groups that describe verbs, adjectives, or other adverbs. Adverbs often tell *how, when,* or *where*. Here are some examples:

The lecturer spoke *briefly.*   (*Briefly* describes the verb *spoke;* it tells *how* the lecturer spoke.)

The lecturer spoke *very* briefly.   (*Very* describes the adverb *briefly;* it tells *how* briefly.)

I just finished an *extremely* difficult job.   (*Extremely* describes the adjective *difficult;* it tells *how* difficult.)

I just finished an extremely difficult job *yesterday.*   (*Yesterday* describes the verb *finished;* it tells *when* the job was finished.)

The car stalled *in my driveway.*   (*In my driveway* describes the verb *stalled;* it tells *where* the car stalled.)

Practice 13.1

Draw an arrow from each bracketed modifier to the word described. Above each bracketed modifier, write *adj* if the modifier is an adjective (if it describes a noun or pronoun) or *adv* if the modifier is an adverb (if it describes a verb, adjective, or adverb). The first one is done as an example.

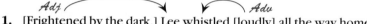

1. [Frightened by the dark,] Lee whistled [loudly] all the way home.

2. The [experimental] therapy relieved Jan's [painful] symptoms [in twenty-four hours.]

3. [Briefly] the waiter explained the specials [of the day], and then he turned and walked away [quickly].

4. The [silver] tinsel sparkled [brightly] in the [colorful] lights of the Christmas tree.

5. The [elderly] man spoke [fondly] of his [childhood] days on a farm [in Indiana].

6. The [high] [academic] standards of the university are [well] known throughout the country.

-ly Adverbs

Many adjectives can be made into adverbs by adding an *-ly* ending. Here are some examples:

Adjective	Adverb
glad	gladly
painful	painfully
quick	quickly
loud	loudly
quiet	quietly

The *painful* tooth kept me awake all night. (*Painful* is an adjective describing the noun *tooth.*)

The dog limped *painfully* into the garage. (*Painfully* is an adverb describing the verb *limped.*)

Be careful to use the adverb form when the modifier describes a verb, adjective, or adverb.

Incorrect:	Marvin ran *quick* into the house.
Correct:	Marvin ran *quickly* into the house. (The adverb form is needed because the modifier is describing a verb.)

Practice 13.2

The first form in parentheses is an adjective, and the second form is an adverb. First draw a line under the word the modifier describes. If the underlined word is a noun or pronoun, fill in the blank with the adjective; if the underlined word is a verb, adjective, or adverb, use the adverb. The first one is done as an example.

1. (quiet, quietly) Angela tiptoed __*quietly*__ into the house because she did not want to wake up her parents.

2. (eager, eagerly) The _____ student raised his hand to answer every question.

3. (slow, slowly) _____, Anne traced the pattern onto the delicate material.

4. (happy, happily) The personnel director _____ explained that I got the job and would start to work on Monday.

5. (loud, loudly) The person who lives upstairs plays the stereo too _____ at night.

6. (patient, patiently) The _____ children sat quietly, waiting for the school play to begin.

7. (soft, softly) Aware that others were sleeping, Marco played the stereo very _____.

8. (heated, heatedly) Allison and Kelly had a _____ debate over who the best Democratic candidate is.

9. (silent, silently) Louisa offered up a _____ prayer of thanks after she stopped the car before it hit the collie.

10. (harsh, harshly) The umpire spoke _____ to the coach who shouted an obscenity to the players.

Practice 13.3

On a separate sheet, use each adjective and adverb in its own sentence. Draw an arrow from the adjective or adverb to the word it describes.

1. easy
2. easily
3. comfortable
4. comfortably
5. fearful
6. fearfully

Good/Well

Good and *well* sometimes give people trouble. Just remember that *good* is an adjective, so it describes nouns and pronouns. *Well*—except when it means "healthy"—is an adverb, so it describes verbs, adjectives, and other adverbs.

It saddens me that Jordan is moving because he is a *good* friend. (*Good* is an adjective describing the noun *friend*.)

Two weeks after my surgery, I felt *well* again. (Here, *well* means "healthy" and is an adjective describing the pronoun *I*.)

For a beginner, you skate very *well.* (*Well* is an adverb describing the verb *skate.*)

Be careful not to use *good* as an adverb.

Incorrect: Marla did good on her test.

Correct: Marla did well on her test. (*Well* is an adverb describing the verb *did.*)

NOTE: *Good* is used as an adjective after verbs like *feel* and *taste:*

I feel good today. (Here, *good* suggests "in good spirits" and describes the pronoun *I.*)

The food tastes good. (*Good* describes the noun *food;* no action is being described.)

The cool breeze feels good. (Again, no action is described; *good* describes *breeze.*)

Practice 13.4

Fill in each blank with *good* or *well,* whichever is correct.

1. The children's production of *Hansel and Gretel* was _____ staged, and the sets were particularly _____.

2. The horse I bet on ran _____ until the home stretch, and then she did not do very _____.

3. Although I have been taking my allergy medicine, I still do not feel _____.

4. Howard plays the clarinet _____ enough to have his first recital, even though he has had only a dozen lessons.

5. With her red hair, Marsha looks _____ in green.

Comparative and Superlative Forms

Adjectives and adverbs can be used to show how two or more things compare to each other. Here are some examples:

Katherine is *thinner* than Mario. (The adjective *thinner* compares how thin Katherine and Mario are.)

The audience is cheering *more loudly* now. (The adverb *more loudly* compares how loudly the audience is cheering now with how loudly it cheered at some point in the past.)

Lee is the *tallest* member of the basketball team. (The adjective *tallest* compares Lee's height with the height of the other team members.)

The form of an adjective or adverb that compares two things is the *comparative*. The form of an adjective or adverb that compares more than two things is the *superlative*.

The comparative form of adjectives and adverbs is usually made by adding *-er* or using the word *more* before the modifier. The superlative form is usually made by adding *-est* or using the word *most* before the modifier.

Modifier	Comparative (compares two things)	Superlative (compares more than two things)
loud	louder	loudest
heavy	heavier	heaviest
fast	faster	fastest
young	younger	youngest
annoyed	more annoyed	most annoyed
beautiful	more beautiful	most beautiful
intelligent	more intelligent	most intelligent

modifier:	Joy and Ned bought a *large* house. (no comparison here)
comparative:	Joy and Ned bought a *larger* house than Kay and Tom. (two houses are compared)
superlative:	Joy and Ned bought the *largest* of the three houses they looked at. (more than two houses are compared)
modifier:	Etty told a *ridiculous* story. (no comparison here)
comparative:	Etty told a *more ridiculous* story than Carl did. (two stories are compared)
superlative:	Etty told the *most ridiculous* story I have ever heard. (more than two stories are compared)

Keep the following guidelines in mind when you form the comparative and superlative forms of modifiers:

1. With one-syllable modifiers, *-er* and *-est* are usually used.

sad	sadder	saddest
loud	louder	loudest
near	nearer	nearest

2. With three-syllable words, use *more* and *most*.

usual	more usual	most usual
rapidly	more rapidly	most rapidly
important	more important	most important

3. With adverbs of two or more syllables, use *more* and *most*.

quickly	more quickly	most quickly
clearly	more clearly	most clearly
freely	more freely	most freely

4. With two-syllable adjectives ending in *-y*, change the *y* to *i* and add *-er* and *-est*.

happy	happier	happiest
angry	angrier	angriest
easy	easier	easiest

5. Some two-syllable adjectives that do not end in *-y* use *-er* and *-est* and some use *more* and *most*. Many of these you know; the others you will learn with experience.

foolish	more foolish	most foolish
careful	more careful	most careful
quiet	quieter	quietest

6. The following comparative and superlative forms are irregular. Memorize them or check this chart each time you use them.

good	better	best
well	better	best
bad	worse	worst
badly	worse	worst
many	more	most
much	more	most

some	more	most
little	less	least

7. Never use an *-er* form with *more* or an *-est* form with *most.*

Incorrect: Maria is *more happier* now that she quit her job.

Correct: Maria is *happier* now that she quit her job.

Incorrect: Lionel is the *most foolhardiest* child I know.

Correct: Lionel is the *most foolhardy* child I know.

Practice 13.5

The base form of a modifier appears in parentheses. Fill in the blank with the correct comparative or superlative form of the modifier (whichever is called for). The first one is done as an example.

1. (young) My sister is two years __*younger*__ than I.

2. (loud) When I banged on the wall to request quiet, the person in the next apartment turned the radio up _____.

3. (quickly) Of all the runners in the race, Dana is expected to run the _____.

4. (talented) Of the two actors auditioning for the role, Stavros is the _____.

5. (easy) John drew Henry a map showing an _____ way to get to the lake than taking Route 11.

6. (bad) Christmas is the _____ holiday for those who have no friends or family.

Practice 13.6

The base form of a modifier appears in parentheses. Fill in the blank with the correct comparative or superlative form. If you are unsure of the correct form, check the list of irregular forms beginning on p. 385.

1. (good) I like studying in the library _____ than studying in my room.

2. (bad) Of all the movies playing in town this week, you selected the _____ one to see.

3. (well) Since I began to exercise regularly, I feel _____ than I ever did before.

4. (some) _____ of us are going to our twenty-year reunion than went to the ten-year reunion.

5. (good) The score Jamie got on his third algebra quiz was the _____ one he has earned this term.

6. (bad) Lying to a friend is bad; refusing to admit the lie is _____.

Dangling Modifiers

If you use a modifier without providing a word for it to describe, you have written a *dangling modifier.* Dangling modifiers are a problem because they create silly or confusing sentences. Here is an example:

Standing at the street corner, a car splashed mud all over my new coat. (There is no word for *standing at the street corner* to describe. Therefore, it seems that the *car* was standing at the street corner.)

Standing at the street corner is a dangling modifier because it has no stated word to describe. Here is another sentence with a dangling modifier:

Tired after a hard day of classes, sleep was needed. (There is no word for *tired after a hard day* of classes to describe. Therefore, it seems that *sleep* was tired.)

Dangling modifiers can be eliminated two ways. First, you can supply a word for the modifier to describe just after the modifier.

dangling modifier:	Feeling depressed, an evening with friends was needed. (Was the evening depressed?)
correction:	Feeling depressed, Colleen needed an evening with friends. (Now *feeling depressed* has a word to describe—*Colleen.*)
dangling modifier:	Unsure of which choice to make, an academic advisor was needed. (Was the advisor unsure of which choice to make?)
correction:	Unsure of which choice to make, I needed an academic advisor. :(Now *unsure of which choice to make* has a word to describe—*I.*)

A second way to eliminate a dangling modifier is to change the modifier to a subordinate clause. (Subordinate clauses are discussed on p. 190.)

dangling modifier:	Walking across the street, a truck turned the corner and narrowly missed me. (Was the truck walking across the street?)
correction:	While I was walking across the street, a truck turned the corner and narrowly missed me. (The opening modifier is rewritten as a subordinate clause.)
dangling modifier:	When entering the bar, an ID must be shown. (Does the ID enter the bar?)
correction:	When a person enters the bar, an ID must be shown. (The opening modifier is rewritten as a subordinate clause.)

☐ TIP FOR FINDING DANGLING MODIFIERS ☐

When you edit, double-check all sentences you open with an *-ing* or *-ed* form. Be sure these forms are closely followed by words they can logically describe.

Practice 13.7

On a separate sheet, rewrite each sentence to eliminate the dangling modifier.

1. Tired after a full day of yard work, a nap was what I needed.
2. Feeling the chill in the air, a roaring fire in the fireplace sounded perfect.
3. Before beginning to make the Mississippi mud cake, all the ingredients were assembled on the kitchen counter.
4. Frightened by the menacing dog, my knees began to shake.
5. Unsure of the best course of action, the decision was difficult.
6. Making no errors in the field and batting the best they have all season, the game was easily won by the Meadville Tigers.

Misplaced Modifiers

A modifier placed too far away from the word it describes is a *misplaced modifier.* Misplaced modifiers are a problem because they create confusing or silly sentences.

misplaced modifier:	Andrea bought a silk dress at a thrift shop with a broken zipper. (Did the thrift shop have a broken zipper? It seems so because *with a broken zipper* is too far from *dress,* the word the modifier is meant to describe.)
misplaced modifier:	The decorator suggested buying the chair to place against the wall that was upholstered in plaid fabric. (Was the wall upholstered in plaid fabric? It seems so because *that was upholstered in plaid fabric* is too far from *chair,* the word the modifier is meant to describe.)
misplaced modifier:	The litterbug threw a plastic wrapper out of the car window driving down Route 11. (Was the car window driving down Route 11? It seems so because *driving down Route 11* is too far from *litterbug,* the word the modifier is meant to describe.)

To eliminate a misplaced modifier, move the modifier as close as possible to the word it describes. Here are the corrections for the previous sentences with misplaced modifiers:

Andrea bought a silk dress with a broken zipper at a thrift shop. (*With a broken zipper* is now next to *dress,* the word the modifier describes.)

The decorator suggested buying the chair that was upholstered in plaid fabric to place against the wall. (*That was upholstered in plaid fabric* is now next to *chair,* the word the modifier describes.)

Driving down Route 11, the litterbug threw a plastic wrapper out of the car window. (*Driving down Route 11* is now next to *litterbug,* the word the modifier describes.)

Practice 13.8

Rewrite the sentences to eliminate the misplaced modifiers.

1. The children stuck in the hospital for Halloween got candy from the visiting clown that was chocolate.

    _____

    _____

2. Carlo asked Henry to help him fix his flat tire in the restaurant.

    _____

    _____

3. At a garage sale, I bought a lovely end table for my apartment with drawers.

    _____

    _____

4. Gregory gave an electronic keyboard to his brother with a memory and playback functions.

    _____

    _____

5. For the New Year's Eve celebration, Tony borrowed noise makers from his roommate with colored streamers.

    _____

    _____

Post Test

Eliminate the incorrect use of modifiers by crossing out and writing above the line.

Johnny Heisman, for whom the Heisman Trophy is named, was one of football's inventivest coaches. One of his most odd inventions was the hidden-ball trick. Once a player asked him if it was illegal to hide a ball during a play in 1895. Heisman knew it was not against the rules, and he wondered how it could be done. Thinking the ball could be hidden under a running back's jersey, a play was devised by Heisman and two of his players. As the ball was snapped to "Tick" Tichenor, the rest of the team would drop back and form a circle around him. Then Tichenor would drop to one knee and slip the ball quick under his jersey. The team would run to the right, and the defenders would follow them. Then Tichenor would get up quick and run the other way. Trying the trick against Vanderbilt, a touchdown was scored. More tighter uniforms and more faster play have made the hidden-ball trick more hard to perform. The bizarre play is rarely used today.

CHAPTER
14

Capitalization and Punctuation

Because readers expect correct punctuation and capitalization, you should take the time to learn the rules. Until you have mastered them, check these pages often to be sure you are applying the rules correctly. This chapter will explain the rules governing the use of

1. capital letters
2. periods, question marks, and exclamation points
3. commas
4. semicolons
5. colons
6. parentheses
7. dashes
8. apostrophes
9. quotation marks

CAPITALIZATION

Most often, capital letters are used to identify something specific. The capital letters in *Fifth Avenue* signal that Fifth Avenue is a specific street; the capital letters in *General Motors* signal that General Motors is a specific car manufacturer.

Pretest

If all the necessary capital letters appear, write *yes* on the blank; if one or more capitals are missing, write *no.* Do not guess; if you are unsure, do not write anything. Check your answers in Appendix III.

1. _____ My dog, Laddie, ran away last week, but he was seen near lake jewel.

2. _____ My favorite holiday is memorial day because it signals the start of summer.

3. _____ This semester my favorite class is psychology, although I am also enjoying Western Civilization 303.

4. _____ Ever since I was a child, I have eaten Kellogg's Rice Krispies for breakfast along with Minute Maid orange juice.

5. _____ Last summer I was sure the Cleveland indians would be in the pennant race.

6. _____ After Brian graduated with his degree in spanish, he went to Central America to work with the poor.

7. _____ I asked dad to lend me five hundred dollars so I could take the trip to Lake Michigan.

8. _____ Thomas Jefferson died fifty years after the signing of the declaration of independence.

9. _____ Julia bought her Pontiac after her Buick was stolen near the South Avenue interchange.

10. _____ At the student gallery there is a new exhibition of african art that will be on display until January.

Using Capital Letters

1. Capitalize the first word of a sentence.

   The door slammed shut on Henry's finger.

2. Capitalize the first word of a direct quotation.

   Doreen explained, "You must get an advisor's signature before you can register for this course."

   BUT

   "You must get an advisor's signature," Doreen explained, "before you can register for this course." (Do not capitalize *before* because it does not begin a *sentence* that is a direct quotation.)

3. Capitalize the names of people and animals.

Lucy	Fido	Madonna
Douglas	Rover	Bill Clinton

BUT

Do not capitalize words such as *man, boy, girl, woman, cat, rock star, collie,* and *child.*

My sister Gail bought a sheepdog she named Hairy.

4. Always capitalize *I.*

Curt and I felt I had a good chance of winning the competition.

5. Capitalize titles before people's names.

Mayor Morales	Judge Fulks	Senator Glenn
Reverend Jones	Rabbi Mendel	Captain McKenna
Professor O'Brien	Uncle Raymond	President Clinton

BUT

Do not capitalize titles used without the names.

a mayor	the judge	a senator
a reverend	a rabbi	the captain
a professor	my uncle	a president

The instructor, Professor Chang, introduced the guest lecturer, Councilman Luntz, who used to be a senator.

6. Capitalize months, days of the week, and holidays.

January	Tuesday	Easter
May	Saturday	Labor Day

The first Monday in September is Labor Day.

7. Capitalize specific geographic locations, including specific cities, states, countries, bodies of water, roads, and mountains.

Georgia	Columbus, Ohio	Lake Erie
Route 86	Stark County	Atlantic Ocean
Mt. Rushmore	Grand Canyon	France
Colorado River	Northwest Territory	Pike's Peak

BUT

Do not capitalize general geographic locations.

state	city	the country
a lake	the mountain	north of town
the ocean	a river	my county

We left the city at ten in the morning and headed west; by late afternoon, we had arrived in St. Louis and were ready to see the Mississippi River.

8. Capitalize the names of nationalities, religions, languages, and the adjective forms of these words.

English	Judaism	Spanish
Catholic	Thai food	Chinese
African dance	French restaurant	Latin American music

This town has excellent Japanese restaurants and art galleries with extensive European collections.

9. Capitalize names of organizations, companies, colleges, and buildings.

Fraternal Order of Police	General Foods
Democratic Party	Yale University
Empire State Building	American Cancer Society

BUT

organization	university
political party	building

When I was in New York for the Modern Language Association conference, I stayed near the World Trade Center.

10. Capitalize historic events and documents.

Gettysburg Address	the Roaring '20s
the Reformation	Battle of the Bulge
the Declaration of Independence	the Korean War
World War I	the Constitution

The television show *MASH* was set in the Korean War, but it was first shown during the Vietnam War.

11. Capitalize the names of sacred books, and words referring to God. Also capitalize pronouns that refer to God.

the Lord	the Talmud	the Scriptures
the Trinity	the Koran	Jehovah
the Old Testament	the Torah	the Bible

The man prayed to the Almighty for His help.

12. Capitalize the names of specific course titles, but not the general names of courses unless they are languages.

| History 101 | French | Survey of English Literature |
| Chemistry 709 | Italian | Business Management II |

BUT

| sociology | accounting | mathematics |

My geography course was not as difficult as I expected it to be, but Child Psychology 303 and German were very hard.

13. Capitalize the brand names of products but not the general names of product types.

| Aim toothpaste | Jell-O | Tretorn sneakers |
| Marlboro | Chevrolet | London Fog |

BUT

| toothpaste | gelatin | tennis shoes |
| cigarettes | car | raincoat |

At the grocery store, I remembered to get the Roman Meal bread, but I forgot the ice cream and Hershey's syrup.

14. Always capitalize the first and last word of a title. In between, capitalize everything *except* articles (*a, an,* and *the*), conjunctions (words like *and, but, or, for, so, if, as*), and prepositions (words like *of, at, in, near, by*). If the title has a colon, capitalize the first word after the colon.

Gone with the Wind	*Star Trek II: The Wrath of Khan*
"A Modest Proposal"	*Around the World in Eighty Days*
A Farewell to Arms	"Politics and the English Language"

In English class we read *Tender Is the Night.*

15. Capitalize words that show family relationships if these words are used in place of names.

Ask Mother what she wants for her birthday. (*Mother* can be used in place of a name, such as *Lucille:* Ask Lucille what she wants for her birthday.)

During World War II, Grandpa was a medic. (*Grandpa* can be used in place of a name, such as *Charles:* During World War II, Charles was a medic.)

BUT

Ask my mother what she wants for her birthday. (We do not say *Ask my Lucille what she wants for her birthday.*)

During World War II, my grandpa was a medic. (We do not say *During World War II, my Charles was a medic.*)

Practice 14.1

Fill in the blanks according to the directions given in parentheses. The first one is done as an example.

1. (Use a street.) For most of my life, I lived on ____*Elm Avenue*____ .

2. (Use the title of a television show or movie; underline the title.) If you are interested in good entertainment, be sure to see

    _____

3. (Use the title of a book; underline the title.)

    In literature class, I read _____.

4. (Use the specific title of a course.)

    Besides composition, this term I am taking _____.

5. (Use the general name of a course other than a language.)

    So far in college, my favorite course has been _____.

6. (Use a holiday.)

    The holiday that I enjoy the least is_____.

7. (Use a date.)

    My birthday is _____.

8. (Use the brand names of three specific products and use the general name of one other product.)

    At the grocery store, I spent twenty dollars on_____

    _____

9. (Use a specific geographic location.)

This summer, I would very much like to see_____

_____.

10. (Use a specific historic period or event.)

In history, I enjoyed studying about _____.

11. (Use a congressperson's title and last name.)
When I learned that the legislature was considering raising the

speed limit, I wrote a letter of protest to _____.

12. (Use *mother* or *father* as a substitute for a name.)

As I was growing up, _____ taught me to take
responsibility for my actions.

13. (Use *mother* or *father.*)

As I was growing up, my _____ taught me to
take responsibility for my actions.

PUNCTUATION

By signaling complete stops, pauses, possession, conversation, and such, punctuation helps writers express meaning. In the next pages, you will learn rules for using a number of punctuation marks.

Ending Sentences

To end a sentence, writers can use a period (.), question mark (?), or exclamation point (!). These marks signal a full stop at the end of one sentence to let the reader know there is a complete break between ideas in that sentence and the ideas in the following sentence.

Pretest

Add a period, question mark, or exclamation point, whichever is most appropriate. Check your answers in Appendix III.

1. My advisor asked me when I planned to graduate

2. The hysterical child screamed, "My dog has been hit by a car " (Put the punctuation inside the quotation mark.)

3. I wondered why Janie never introduced me to her family

4. How many eggs do you add to the cake batter

5. My parents wanted to know when I would get a part-time job to help with college expenses

6. Close the door before the cat gets out

7. Is there any way I can help you finish your project on time

8. Call 911; the kitchen is on fire

9. If you ask me, Paul should major in psychology because he understands people so well

10. Which of your cousins will be at the reunion

The Period, Question Mark, and Exclamation Point

The period (.), question mark (?), and exclamation point (!) are all used to end sentences.

1. Use a period to end a sentence that makes a statement, makes a request, or issues an order.

   Because of the heavy rains, the lowlands are flooded. (This sentence makes a statement.)

   Bring me the evening paper, please. (This sentence makes a request.)

   Leave me alone so I can study. (This sentence issues an order.)

2. Use a question mark to end a sentence that asks a direct question.

   Will you lend me your history notes?

   Is this seat taken?

   How can I help you if you refuse my advice?

NOTE: Use a period—not a question mark—to end a sentence with an indirect question. An <u>indirect question</u> is a statement, even though it notes that someone asked a question.

indirect question:	I wonder where I will be in ten years.
direct question:	Where will I be in ten years?
indirect question:	The waiter asked whether we wanted dessert.

direct question:	The waiter asked, "Do you want dessert?"
indirect question:	Kevin wanted to know if he could borrow my car.
direct question:	May I borrow your car?

3. Use an exclamation point after a statement or command that shows strong feeling or surprise.

Get out of the car before the engine catches on fire! (a command with strong feeling)

I will get even with you if it is the last thing I do! (a statement with strong feeling)

I couldn't believe I earned the highest grade ever scored on the exam! (a statement with surprise)

NOTES: 1. Be careful not to overuse exclamation points. If you must use them often, your words are not conveying the message; it is a mistake to rely on punctuation to say what your words are supposed to.
2. Do not use an exclamation point with a period or question mark.

no:	Are you sure you want to go?!
yes:	Are you sure you want to go?
no:	I am amazed at her nerve.!
yes:	I am amazed at her nerve.
yes:	I am amazed at her nerve!

3. Do not use more than one exclamation point at a time.

| no: | I hate you!! |
| yes: | I hate you! |

Practice 14.2

On a separate sheet, write sentences according to the directions given, ending each sentence with a period, question mark, or exclamation point—whichever is appropriate.

1. Write a sentence you might hear spoken on campus; be sure the sentence makes a statement.

2. Write a direct question you might ask a waiter in a restaurant.

3. Write a sentence that asks an indirect question. Begin the sentence with "Shelly asked whether."

4. Write a sentence that expresses great anger or fear.

5. Write a sentence that expresses a request a parent might make of a child.

6. Write a sentence that expresses a command a fire chief might give to fire fighters; the command should express strong emotion.

Post Test

In the following paragraph, the punctuation has been omitted at the ends of most of the sentences. On the blanks, add the end punctuation. Be prepared to explain why you have used each mark.

I used to wonder what I would do in an emergency __1__ Unfortunately, I recently learned that I do not know what I should do to handle a crisis situation __2__ Two weeks ago I was having lunch at Chico's Restaurant with my friend Sally __3__ As we chatted, Sally nibbled on her taco __4__ Suddenly, Sally stopped talking and started clutching her throat __5__ Instantly I knew she was choking, but I did not know what to do __6__ In desperation, I screamed, "Somebody help her __7__" A waiter came running from across the room __8__ When he reached Sally, he asked her, "Can you talk __9__" As soon as Sally shook her head no, he stood her up and performed the Heimlich maneuver. A piece of taco shell popped out. Sally is fine, but I was unnerved because I did not know what to do to help my friend__10__ Because I was helpless in this emergency, I have enrolled in a Red Cross CPR class to learn lifesaving techniques, including the Heimlich maneuver __11__ Would you know what to do in an emergency __12__ If not, call your local Red Cross to enroll in a CPR class __13__

Using Commas

Some writers place commas wherever they would pause or draw a breath in speech. However, this is not a reliable way to determine when commas are needed. If you are not sure how to use commas, promise yourself to learn the rules now.

Pretest

If commas are used correctly, write *yes* on the blank; if they are not used correctly, write *no*. Do not guess; if you are unsure, do not write anything. You can check your answers in Appendix III.

1. ____ After storming onto the floor and arguing with the referee Coach Bennett was given a technical foul.

2. ____ The withered, ivy plant could not be saved, so I tossed it in the trash.

3. ____ I left for Nashville, Tennessee, on August 22, 1983.

4. ____ Uncertain yet eager, Josh began his first day as a camp counselor.

5. ____ When we have children of our own we come to understand how our own parents worried, sacrificed, and planned to ensure our own futures.

6. ____ Without telling the children where they were going, we picked them up at school, put them in the car, and headed for Virginia Beach Virginia.

7. ____ Rosa was well prepared for the test and feeling confident, so she was sure she did well.

8. ____ Suddenly, and unexpectedly, the string snapped, and the kite was carried off.

9. ____ George in my opinion is trustworthy, and he is certainly a hard worker.

10. ____ Because the spring was unusually dry the crop yield was low, and produce prices rose.

11. ____ Michael, I need you to help me unload the car.

12. ____ In the heat of the afternoon, Louise fell asleep in the sun, and got a bad burn.

Dates, Places, and Addresses

1. With dates, place a comma between the day and the year.

   I expect to graduate June 14, 1995.

   OR

   I expect to graduate 14 June 1995.

Note: You may use either form, but be consistent; do not mix the two forms.

2. If no day is given, there is no comma between the month and the year.

Julia began working for the United Parcel Service in January 1985.

3. Do not use a comma between the month and the day.

no: My birthday is May, 4, 1949.

yes: My birthday is May 4, 1949.

4. Use commas to separate the names of cities and states.

When they retired, my parents moved to Naples, Florida.

OR

My parents moved to Naples, Florida, when they retired.

5. Place a comma between the street address and the city. There is no comma before the zip code.

Garth's Flower Shop is located at 311 West Palm Lane, Warren, Ohio 44484.

Practice 14.3

On a separate sheet, write sentences as directed.

1. Write a sentence that begins with *I live at.* Include your complete street address, city, state, and zip code.

2. Write a sentence that gives the city and state of a place you want to visit. Begin the sentence with *I would like to visit.*

3. Write a sentence that gives the month and year you began college. Begin the sentence with *I began college.*

4. Write a sentence that gives your complete date of birth. Begin the sentence with *I was born.*

Words, Phrases, and Clauses in a Series   A *series* is three or more words, phrases, or clauses. (See p. 182 and p. 223 on phrases; see p. 189 on clauses.) All but the last item in a series should be followed by a comma.

When I arrived at my hotel, I realized I had forgotten my *shampoo, brush, and pajamas.* (words in a series)

Since beginning my exercise program, I have *lost weight, toned my muscles, and increased my flexibility.* (phrases in series)

If you want to help me, *you can take these books back to the library, you can pick up my dry cleaning, and you can wash the car.* (clauses in a series)

NOTE: When all the items in a series are separated by *and* or *or,* no comma is used.

The dessert cart held fancy *pies and cakes and tortes.*

Place the plant *in the kitchen window or on the television or on the coffee table.*

Practice 14.4

Use each series or pair in a sentence, being careful to use commas correctly. The first one is done as an example.

1. the spaghetti   the veal   and the broiled chicken

The waiter explained that the specials of the day were the spaghetti, the veal, and the broiled chicken.

2. the hardback   or the paperback

_____

_____

3. the noise   the pollution   and the crowds

_____

_____

4. a fever   a sore throat   a stuffy nose   and body aches

_____

_____

5. the food was overpriced   the service was slow   and the seating was uncomfortable

_____

_____

6. a relaxing bath   or an invigorating shower

_____

_____

7. swept the downstairs   and washed the clothes   and cleaned the garage

_____

_____

8. on the shelf   in the car   or in my room

_____

_____

Post Test

Place commas where they are needed in the following sentences. Some sentences are correct as they are.

1. For winning the contest, Dean had his choice of a trip to Bermuda or two thousand dollars.

2. When my boss came for dinner, I served eye of round roast rice pilaf ginger carrots and fruit salad.

3. Bring two pencils several sheets of paper and a folder to the exam.

4. To improve the quality of the lawn, you must aerate the soil and lay down some fertilizer and use a pesticide.

5. The coat the radio and the necklace are all good choices for Grandma's birthday present.

6. To get material for my research paper, I wrote to the Government Printing Office interviewed a physician and checked books and articles in the library.

7. The child's mother said she could have an ice cream cone or a popsicle or an ice cream sandwich.

8. With my pay raise, I will buy a stereo new clothes or a fancy watch.

Coordination   *Coordination* means that two word groups that can stand alone as sentences (*main clauses*) are joined by *and, but, or, for, so,* or *yet* (*coordinating conjunctions*). Coordination is explained more fully on p. 192.

Place a comma before a coordinating conjunction (*and, but, or, for, so,* or *yet*) that joins two main clauses.

I would ask you to join me, but I know that you are busy.

Jillian gently picked up the baby chick, and she stroked it lovingly.

Our current basketball coach will probably be fired, for he has won only a fourth of his games the past two years.

The corporate offices of Raphael Industries will move to our town, so we can expect a decrease in our unemployment rate.

Do not place a comma every time you use a coordinating conjunction. Many times these conjunctions do not connect word groups that can stand as sentences (main clauses). When they do not, no comma is used.

The Corvette raced down the street and sped around the corner. (No comma is used because *and* does not join *two* main clauses, only two verb phrases.)

Be sure to remember that main clauses cannot be joined by a comma alone—the comma must be used with the coordinating conjunction. If you join main clauses with just a comma, you have written a comma splice. (See p. 254.)

Practice 14.5

Circle each coordinating conjunction. If the conjunction joins word groups that can be sentences (main clauses), place a comma before the conjunction. Otherwise, do not place a comma.

1. I canceled the subscription months ago but the magazines keep arriving in my mailbox.

2. Several colleges are recruiting Kwame yet he is unsure if he wants to attend any of them.

3. The mechanic explained that the water pump was broken and had to be replaced immediately.

4. The cable television company raised its rates for the third time in two years so consumers protested vigorously.

5. The awards Lorraine received for her writing did not turn her head or cause her to overestimate her abilities.

6. We left the beach three days early for the temperature was twenty degrees below normal and heavy rains were predicted.

Introductory Words, Phrases, and Clauses.

1. In most cases, use a comma after an introductory word (a word that comes before the subject of the sentence).

   Carefully, the child placed the precious china doll on the shelf.

   Whistling, Kobina sanded the cupboard doors.

   Thoughtfully, Louise chewed on her pencil as she considered topics for her essay.

2. In most cases, use a comma after a pair of introductory words (words that come before the subject of the sentence).

   Quickly and easily, Dan completed the employment application.

   Exhausted and discouraged, I could not complete the marathon.

   Disappointed but hopeful, Sue vowed to do better next time.

3. Use a comma after an introductory phrase (a phrase that comes before the subject of the sentence).

   Playing both offense and defense, Mario was the most valuable member of the football team.

   In the middle of the night, the smoke alarm went off and roused all of us from our beds.

   After borrowing ten thousand dollars from private investors, Lynette opened her own children's clothing store.

NOTE: You may omit the comma after an introductory phrase of two or three words.

By morning I was not angry with Joe any longer.

In the yard the children built a snowperson.

or

By morning, I was not angry with Joe any longer.

In the yard, the children built a snowperson.

---

4. Use a comma after an introductory subordinate clause (a subordinate clause that comes before the subject of the sentence). (Subordinate clauses are discussed on p. 190.)

   When the steel mills closed, over a thousand people were out of work.

   Before you leave, please say good-bye to Grandpa.

   If the union does not get a pay raise, its members will take a strike vote.

Practice 14.6

On a separate sheet, write a sentence that begins with each of the openers given. Use commas after the introductory words, phrases, and subordinate clauses. The first one is done as an example.

1. While I was studying for my algebra test

While I was studying for my algebra test, I was distracted by

the stereo playing across the hall.

2. Interestingly

3. Frustrated and angry

4. In the corner behind the couch

5. According to the latest news reports

6. If you do not mind

7. Although I disagree with you

Interrupters   An *interrupter* is a word or phrase that interrupts the flow or main idea of a sentence. Some common interrupters are:

I believe	it seems to me
incidentally	as a matter of fact
in fact	to tell the truth
believe it or not	I am sure
by all means	if you ask me
by the way	without a doubt

1. Interrupters are set off from the rest of the sentence with commas.

    The physical education requirement, *if you ask me,* should be abolished. (The interrupter comes in the middle of the sentence, so there is a comma *before and after it.*)

    By the way, Charles has decided to run for a seat on the student council. (The interrupter comes at the beginning of the sentence, so a comma is placed *after* it.)

    Mayor Juarez has no choice but to lay off some city workers, *it seems to me.* (The interrupter comes at the end of the sentence, so a comma is placed *before* it.)

2. Transitions are often considered interrupters and are set off from the rest of the sentence with commas. (Transitions are explained on p. 234.)

As a result, Donofrio won the election by a fifty percent margin. (The transition comes at the beginning of the sentence, so a comma is placed *after* it.)

Dr. Wright, *however,* disagrees with my view. (The transition comes in the middle of the sentence, so a comma is placed *before and after* it.)

3. Nonessential elements are set off from the rest of the sentence with commas. A *nonessential element* is a word, phrase, or clause that is *not* essential for identifying the person or thing referred to. Here are some examples of sentences with nonessential elements:

Asa, *my oldest brother,* joined the Air Force. (*My oldest brother* is nonessential because it is not needed to identify who joined the Air Force: *Asa* does that.)

The woman next door, *determined to strike out on her own,* quit her job and moved to Tennessee. (*Determined to strike out on her own* is nonessential because it is not needed to identify who quit her job and moved to Tennessee; *the woman next door* does that.)

Xenia, Ohio, *which was once devastated by a tornado,* is now back on its feet. (*Which was once devastated by a tornado* is nonessential because it is not needed to identify what is now back on its feet; *Xenia, Ohio* does that.)

4. The same word group can be nonessential in one sentence and essential in another. Here is an example:

Alexis Ellington, *who won three major poetry contests,* will read some of her poems on campus this Friday night. (*Who won three major poetry contests* is nonessential for identifying who will read her poems, so commas are used.)

A woman *who won three major poetry contests* will read some of her poems on campus this Friday night. (*Who won three major poetry contests* is now essential for identifying who will read her poems; therefore, no commas are used.)

Practice 14.7

Place commas to set off each interrupter. Remember to use a comma *before* an interrupter at the end of a sentence, *after* an interrupter at the beginning of a sentence, and *before and after* an interrupter in the middle of a sentence. One sentence is correct as it is.

1. One of the candidates however chose not to participate in the debate.

2. Officer Suarez who rescued a child from a burning car was awarded a medal of valor.

3. Olympic athletes it seems to me deserve more support from the government.

4. The figure skater who won the gold medal is known for her triple jumps.

5. Final examinations are not a true test of students' knowledge in my opinion.

6. Nonetheless most colleges require final examinations.

7. For the most part the pace of the movie was sluggish, and the acting was wooden.

8. Dr. Alexander who studied medicine in China is an expert in the use of acupuncture for anesthesia.

Coordinate Modifiers   Use a comma to separate coordinate modifiers not already separated by *and*. *Coordinate modifiers* describe the same word equally. Here are some examples:

> Be careful on the *wet, slippery* floor. (*Wet* and *slippery* are coordinate modifiers because they both describe *floor,* so a comma is placed between them.)

> The *tough, stringy* meat was difficult to chew. (*Tough* and *stringy* are coordinate modifiers because they both describe *meat,* so a comma is placed between them.)

If *and* is used between the coordinate modifiers, no comma is used.

> The *long and boring* movie made me restless.

> or

> The *long, boring* movie made me restless.

To test if modifiers are coordinate, try placing *and* between them. If the result sounds natural, the modifiers are coordinate.

> Davey could not part with his *old, faded* shorts because he wore them in the state basketball championships. (*Old and faded shorts* sounds natural, so the modifiers are coordinate, and a comma is used.)

> I asked the waiter for *fresh apple* pie for dessert. (*Fresh and apple*

pie does not sound natural, so the modifiers are not coordinate, and no comma is used.)

Another way to test if modifiers are coordinate is to reverse their order. If the result sounds natural, the modifiers are coordinate. In the preceding examples, *old, faded shorts* can be changed to *faded, old shorts* so the modifiers are coordinate. However, *fresh apple pie* cannot be changed to *apple fresh pie,* so the modifiers are not coordinate.

NOTE: Do not use a comma between coordinate modifiers separated by *and.*

no: The speaker was given a warm, and enthusiastic welcome.

yes: The speaker was given a warm and enthusiastic welcome.

Practice 14.8

Use each pair of modifiers and the noun in a sentence of your own. If the modifiers are coordinate and *not* already separated by *and,* place a comma between them. The first one is done as an example.

1. hot blinding sun

   It was difficult to see the horizon because of the hot, blinding sun.

2. cut bleeding knee

   _____

   _____

3. elegant silk scarf

   _____

   _____

4. steaming chicken soup

   _____

   _____

5. sensitive and caring nurse

_____

_____

6. warm gentle breeze

_____

_____

Direct Address   In *direct address,* you use the name of the person or animal you are speaking or writing to. Names used in direct address are set off with commas.

> Marvin, I need to borrow your class notes. (*Marvin* is a noun of direct address at the beginning of a sentence, so it is followed by a comma.)
>
> If you ask me, Harriet, we should leave now. (*Harriet* is a noun of direct address that comes in the middle of the sentence, so a comma is placed before and after it.)
>
> Stop rolling in the clean laundry, you silly cat. (*You silly cat* is a phrase of direct address that comes at the end of the sentence, so a comma is placed before it.)

Do not set off the name of a person or animal spoken *about;* set off only the names of persons or animals spoken *to.*

> direct address: Carla, let me use your car for an hour.
>
>   (Carla is spoken *to.*)

> no direct address: Carla will let me use her car for an hour.
>
>   (Carla is spoken *about.*)

Practice 14.9

On a separate sheet, write six sentences of your own. Two sentences should have direct address at the beginning, two should have direct address in the middle, and two should have direct address at the end. Remember, a comma is used *after* direct address at the beginning, *before* direct address at the end, and *before and after* direct address in the middle.

Direct Quotations   In *direct quotations,* commas are used to separate the words that identify the speaker from the words that are spoken.

> Dr. Herndon explained, "High blood pressure is serious, but it can be treated."

> "High blood pressure is serious, but it can be treated," Dr. Herndon explained.

> "High blood pressure is serious," Dr. Herndon explained, "but it can be treated."

For more on punctuating quotations, see p. 428.

Post Test

Place commas where they are needed in the following paragraph.

When I woke up I knew it was going to be "one of those days." First I heard my roommate cry, "Ryan come quick." I sprinted to the living room and saw the cause of Ralph's scream: We had been robbed. Amazed I scanned the room. The stereo was gone the television was gone and the VCR was gone. The couch was gone and the coffee table was gone. In fact the only thing that was not taken was the laundry basket which stood alone in the middle of the room. Ralph and I just looked at each other in disbelief. Not knowing what else to do we started to laugh for we both realized at the same moment that this was the day we were going to put new locks on the doors. Timing I guess is everything.

Using Semicolons

A semicolon (;) can be used instead of a period to separate main clauses (word groups that can stand alone as sentences). The semicolon can also be used to separate items in a series when the series already contains commas.

Pretest

If the semicolon is used correctly, write *yes* on the blank; if it is not used correctly, write *no.* Do not guess; if you are unsure, do not write anything. Check your answers in Appendix III.

1. ____ I told you not to go; it's too bad you didn't listen to me.

2. ____ People who do not vote; do not understand how a democracy functions.

3. ____ My mother was born in Alexandria, Virginia; my father was born in Denver, Colorado; my sister was born in Tucson, Arizona; and I was born in Detroit, Michigan.

4. ____ The wedding was a disaster; by the end of the evening, the bride and groom were not speaking to each other.

5. ____ When the lifeguard put up the gale warning flags; everyone left the beach.

6. ____ The honored guests included Marie Sanchez, president of Willit Industries; Paul Romeo, director of the local mental health center; and Lee Myers, mayor of the city.

Semicolons to Separate Main Clauses   Semicolons can separate main clauses (word groups that can stand alone as sentences). For a discussion of main clauses, see p. 190.

> The table has been in my family for four generations; it was given to me by my mother. (The word groups on *both* sides of the semicolon are main clauses.)

> The fund-raising drive was a success; we collected enough pledges to keep the soup kitchen open another year. (The word groups on *both* sides of the semicolon are main clauses.)

When you use a semicolon, be sure you have main clauses on *both* sides. A semicolon cannot separate a main clause from a word group that is not a main clause.

> no: Because Hank was having trouble with math; he decided to hire a tutor. (The word group before the semicolon is not a main clause that can stand alone as a sentence.)

Semicolons can also be used with conjunctive adverbs to join main clauses. This rule is discussed in detail on p. 198.

> Some people agreed with the speaker's remarks; however, most seemed to disagree.

> State aid to public schools has been cut drastically; therefore, it will be necessary to pass a school levy.

Practice 14.10

Place semicolons where they are needed in the following sentences:

1. The December snowfall set a record however, it was never necessary to close the schools.

2. A person who runs for public office must endure considerable scrutiny every facet of a politician's life is subject to examination.

3. Louisa was finally realizing her dream she was about to open her own toy and hobby shop.

4. I took my complaint to three company officials nonetheless, no one was sure how to help me.

5. The driver failed to see the stop sign partially hidden by the bushes as a result, he narrowly missed hitting an oncoming van.

6. My son studied ecology in his fourth grade science class he then convinced me to recycle aluminum and paper.

Semicolons with Items in a Series   A semicolon can be used instead of a comma to separate items in a series when the series already has commas in it.

> The menu featured omelets, pancakes, and sausage for breakfast; hero sandwiches, soup, and burgers for lunch; and pasta, steak, and fish for dinner.

Practice 14.11

Place semicolons where they are needed in the following sentences. In some cases, you will replace commas with semicolons.

1. The team's infield is strong: Jakes, a senior, plays first base Juarez, a sophomore, plays second Wallace, a junior, plays third and Sniderman, a freshman, plays shortstop.

2. Tony looked for his Christmas presents in the linen closet, where they were hidden last year, in the attic, where years of castoffs were stored and in the garage, where Dad has his workroom.

3. At the flea market I bought an old chair, which should fit in my living room a weathered porch swing, which I plan to refinish and a broken record player, which I have no use for at all.

4. On the cruise, my parents met a couple from Juneau, Alaska, a woman from Nashville, Tennessee, and a family from Great Neck, New York.

Post Test

Place semicolons where needed. One sentence is correct.

1. Three-year-old Sally wanted nothing to do with her baby brother she was convinced he was totally worthless.

2. Speaking at the awards banquet will be Frank Osborne, coach of a local high school football team Judith Silverstein, a track star and Luis Gomez, athletic director of the Central Conference.

3. Although more women are working outside the home, they still do not have the same employment opportunities that men do.

4. The trouble with Helen is that she has no goals she just does not know what she wants in life.

5. We all make mistakes however, we do not all learn from our mistakes.

6. My favorite teachers are Lorraine Booth, who teaches American history Joseph Dull, who teaches anthropology and Kelly McGuire, who teaches biology.

7. According to the map, the road forks in a mile we should turn left at that point.

8. He turned and left the room he did not have the courage to tell her the truth.

Using Colons, Parentheses, and Dashes

The colon (:) introduces a long list, a quotation, or an explanation. Parentheses [( )] enclose material that is downplayed. Dashes (—) signal long pauses for emphasis or dramatic effect.

Pretest

If the colon, parentheses, or dash is used correctly, write *yes* on the blank. If the mark is used incorrectly, write *no.* If you are unsure, do not write anything. Check your answers in Appendix III.

1. _____ We went to the restaurant at eight o'clock, but it was closed. (I'm not really sure why.)

2. ____ Joey was voted the most valuable player of the game—he scored 26 points, he had 19 rebounds, and he made 10 assists.

3. ____ The topic of my research paper is: why eating disorders are more common among females than males.

4. ____ Franklin Roosevelt said this: "We have nothing to fear except fear itself."

5. ____ My earliest memory of my father—and it is indeed a pleasant one—is of him putting me on his shoulders and parading around the house.

6. ____ Drexel (what an unusual name) has a sister named Drexine (good grief!).

7. ____ I told you not to go: but you would not listen to me.

8. ____ The audience was growing restless—they had already waited two hours for the show to start—and they began stomping their feet and chanting.

The Colon

1. Use a colon to introduce a list.

    The doctor told me to avoid the following: salt, chocolate, caffeine, and artificial preservatives.

    I got a job for these reasons: bills, bills, and more bills.

NOTE: Do not use a colon after a linking verb (see p. 176), after a preposition (see p. 182), or between a verb and its object (see p. 363).

no:	Michael is: bright, motivated, and talented. (The colon appears after a linking verb.)
yes:	Michael is bright, motivated, and talented.
no:	I looked for my lost wallet in: the house, the car, and the office. (The colon appears after a preposition.)
yes:	I looked for my lost wallet in the house, the car, and the office.
no:	At the outlet mall Karen bought: pottery, baskets, and shoes. (The colon comes between the verb and its object.)
yes:	At the outlet mall Karen bought pottery, baskets, and shoes.

---

2. Use a colon to introduce material that explains something in the main clause or to introduce an example of something in the main clause.

Joyce has only one goal: to graduate in three years. (The colon introduces an explanation.)

The evening ended on a bad note: a prankster pulled the fire alarm, and the building had to be evacuated. (The colon introduces an explanation.)

Jake has become a compulsive buyer: just yesterday he spent a hundred dollars on a silk shirt and fifty dollars on a leather belt. (The colon introduces an example.)

3. Use a colon to introduce a quotation in a formal way.

Herman Melville wrote one of the most famous opening sentences in literature: "Call me Ishmael."

There is one question that parents have asked since the dawn of time: "If Johnny jumped off a bridge, would you jump off a bridge?"

Practice 14.12

Place colons where they are needed in the following sentences. Two sentences are correct.

1. Jamie prized one thing above all money.

2. Most business forecasters agree on the year's economic outlook consumer prices will rise.

3. The topics we will be covering in Introduction to Psychology are defense mechanisms, organic psychoses, and behavioral disorders.

4. The instructor's meaning was clear students who cut class will not do well in the course.

5. There are seven colors in the spectrum red, orange, yellow, green, blue, indigo, and violet.

6. We frantically searched for the missing file in my office, the secretary's desk, and the file cabinets.

7. Lynette is my kind of woman, determined, smart, and focused.

Parentheses   Parentheses enclose material that you want to downplay or deemphasize because it is not essential to the main idea of the sentence. Often material in parentheses is a side comment.

My physics teacher (Dr. Garner) has agreed to give me extra help before the final exam.

Translators (the unsung heroes of the literary world) must preserve the meaning and intent of the original work.

Before beginning assembly, check to be sure you have all the parts (a parts list can be found in the owner's manual).

NOTE: Often commas can be used in place of parentheses, if you do not want to downplay the material as much.

Translators, the unsung heroes of the literary world, must preserve the meaning and intent of the original work.

Often dashes can be used in place of parentheses, if you want to emphasize rather than downplay.

Translators—the unsung heroes of the literary world—must preserve the meaning and intent of the original work.

Practice 14.13

Place parentheses where appropriate in the following sentences:

1. My grandfather a Russian immigrant speaks heavily accented English.

2. Natasha's science project which she spent a month working on won a blue ribbon in the science fair.

3. The dinner for four at Serendipity cost eighty dollars I'm glad I wasn't picking up the check.

4. When I graduated 1967 our country was in a period of political unrest.

5. Dean's father a distinguished attorney advised me to sue the company for negligence.

Dashes   A dash signals a long pause for emphasis or dramatic effect.

My flight was canceled because of bad weather—what an annoyance that proved to be.

Eight of us—all wearing heavy winter coats—squeezed into the car.

Carla—an extremely talented violinist—was asked to be the youngest member of the symphony orchestra.

NOTE: If you want to downplay rather than emphasize, use parentheses.

Carla (an extremely talented violinist) was asked to be the youngest member of the symphony orchestra.

If the material is an interrupter or nonessential element (these are explained on p. 408 and p. 409), you can also use commas.

Carla, an extremely talented violinist, was asked to be the youngest member of the symphony orchestra.

Practice 14.14

Place dashes where appropriate in the following sentences. Use two dashes to set off something in the middle of the sentence.

1. A teacher, a surgeon, a magician, a carpenter, and an actor were at the cocktail party what a strange assortment of people.

2. I dreamed I had won a million dollars in the lottery too bad I had to wake up.

3. I felt betrayed when Lee who is supposed to be my best friend refused to help me.

4. The midway of the country fair held all the usual attractions games, a bearded lady, the world's fattest man, and a person who guesses people's weight.

5. Michael don't ask me why decided to drop out of school and work as a plumber's apprentice.

Post Test

On a separate sheet, write two sentences that use the colon correctly, two sentences that use parentheses correctly, and two sentences that use the dash correctly. Be prepared to explain why you have used each punctuation mark.

Using Apostrophes

Apostrophes serve two main purposes: they signal ownership, and they signal that letters or numbers have been omitted in contractions and other forms.

Pretest

If apostrophes are used correctly, write *yes* on the blank; if they are used incorrectly, write *no.* If you are unsure, do not write anything. Check your answers in Appendix III.

1. _____ The hat I found belongs to one of the boy's.

2. _____ I can't understand why Julie is so angry at Ralph.

3. _____ Its' been quite some time since I've had a vacation.

4. _____ In the '50s life was simpler.

5. _____ Both senators' bills died in committee.

6. _____ Someone's car is double-parked and sure to be ticketed.

7. _____ My boss's top priority right now is increasing efficiency in all departments.

8. _____ My father-in-law's condominium in Florida is for rent.

9. _____ All of her *e*'s look like *i*'s to me.

10. _____ The childrens' Christmas play was canceled because the roads were snow-covered and slippery.

Apostrophes for Possession   *Possession* means ownership. One way to show possession is with a phrase beginning with *of,* and the other way is with an apostrophe.

The brightness *of the sun* makes it difficult to drive. (The brightness belongs to the sun.)

The *sun's* brightness makes it difficult to drive. (The brightness belongs to the sun.)

The office *of the vice president* is on the second floor. (The office belongs to the vice president.)

The *vice president's* office is on the second floor. (The office belongs to the vice president.)

The paw *of the dog* is badly cut. (The paw belongs to the dog.)

The *dog's* paw is badly cut. (The paw belongs to the dog.)

A number of rules govern how to use the apostrophe to show possession. These are given for you in the following pages.

1. Add an apostrophe and an *s* to all singular nouns and to plural nouns that *do not* end in *s.*

Noun Is Singular or Does Not End in *s*	Add *'s*	Possessive Form
Bill (singular)	Bill's	Bill's coat
car (singular)	car's	car's drive shaft
children (plural, does not end in *s*)	children's	children's toys
teacher (singular)	teacher's	teacher's desk
men (plural, does not end in *s*)	men's	men's clothing
Doris (singular)	Doris's	Doris's job

2. Add an apostrophe to plural nouns ending in *s.*

Plural Noun Ending in *s*	Add an Apostrophe	Possessive Form
brothers (two brothers)	brothers'	brothers' room
shoes (two shoes)	shoes'	shoes' laces
babies (two babies)	babies'	babies' diapers

3. When a word is hyphenated, add the apostrophe after the last part of the word.

    This is my mother-in-law's car.

    All of my editor-in-chief's decisions were carefully made.

4. With two or more nouns, use the apostrophe after the last noun to show joint possession. Use the apostrophe after each noun to show individual possession.

    Carol and Dan's son will go to Italy this summer as part of the Children's International Summer Village program. (The son belongs to both Carol and Dan; this is joint ownership.)

    Carol's and Dan's businesses are enjoying excellent growth. (Carol and Dan each have a business; this is individual ownership.)

5. Use an apostrophe and *s* to make indefinite pronouns posses-

sive. *Indefinite pronouns* refer to members of a group without specifying the particular members. (Indefinite pronouns are explained more fully on p. 335.)

Someone's car is parked so closely to mine that I cannot get in on the driver's side.

Everyone's responsibility is to help the poor.

6. Do not use apostrophes with possessive pronouns. These words already show ownership, so no apostrophe is needed. Here is a list of possessive pronouns:

hers	my
his	ours
its	theirs
mine	yours

yes: The winning number is *his*.

no: The winning number is *his'*.

NOTE: *Its* is a possessive pronoun, so no apostrophe is needed to show ownership. *It's* is a contraction form that means "it is" or "it has." There is no form *its'*.

yes: The dog keeps licking *its* paw as if something is wrong. (*Its* is the possessive form; the paw belongs to the dog.)

yes: *It's* difficult to predict who will win the Democratic presidential nomination. (*It's* is the contraction form meaning "it is.")

Practice 14.15

Fill in the blank with the correct possessive form; use the information in parentheses as a guide. The first one is done as an example.

1. (The dog belongs to Mona.) _____*Mona's*_____ dog will weigh over a hundred pounds when it is grown.

2. (The questions belong to the students.) The instructor was careful to answer all the _____ questions.

3. (The mattress belongs to the bed.) I have trouble sleeping in the dorm because my _____ mattress is too soft.

4. (The blades belong to the knives.) All of the steak _____ blades are too dull to cut easily.

5. (The paycheck belongs to Phyllis.) A mistake was made in _____ paycheck, and she was shorted twenty dollars.

6. (The laces belong to the shoes.) Both of the _____ laces broke when I tried to tie them.

7. (The ring belongs to my sister-in-law.) My _____ square-cut emerald ring is a family heirloom worth a great deal of money.

8. (The help belongs to everyone.) _____ help is needed if the fundraiser is to be a success.

9. (Rhonda and Helen made different mistakes.) _____ and _____ mistakes are easy to correct.

10. (Rhonda and Helen have the same expectations.) _____ and _____ expectations are too high.

11. (The van belongs to Morris.) _____ van has 100,000 miles on it, but he has no plans to trade it in.

12. (The fillings belong to the teeth.) Most of my _____ fillings are loose.

13. (The natural resources belong to the country.) The _____ natural resources must be protected.

14. (The leg belongs to the table.) The _____ leg is marred because the cat uses it as a scratching post.

15. (The gloves belong to several boys.) The _____ gloves were left in a pile to dry by the radiator.

Apostrophes for Contractions   A *contraction* is formed when two words are joined to make one. When the words are joined, at least one letter is omitted. An apostrophe stands for the missing letter or letters. Here are some common contractions:

Two Words	Contraction	Missing Letter(s)
are not	aren't	o
is not	isn't	o
does not	doesn't	o
have not	haven't	o
can not	can't	no
could not	couldn't	o
they will	they'll	wi
she will	she'll	wi
he will	he'll	wi
who is	who's	i
who has	who's	ha
will not	won't	irregular: ill/o
would not	wouldn't	o
we are	we're	a
they are	they're	a
she had	she'd	ha
he would	he'd	woul

> NOTE: Avoid contractions in formal writing, although they are acceptable in semiformal and informal writing.

Practice 14.16

Fill in the blank with the contraction form of the words in parentheses. The first one is done as an example.

1. (I am) _____*I'm*_____ changing my major to computer technology because the job opportunities are excellent in that field.

2. (we are) Although Higgins is a longshot candidate, _____ still planning to campaign for him.

3. (do not) _____ look now, but the person you are talking about just walked in the room.

4. (I am) If I do not get at least a *C* in my circuits class, _____ going to change my major to computer science.

5. (would not) Juanita turned down the job offer because she knew she _____ like the hours.

6. (does not) Now that he has had a year of physical therapy, Lee _____ have trouble with his back.

7. (it is) _____ possible to be happy living anywhere as long as you have good friends.

8. (she will) Marge called to say _____ be an hour late.

9. (I will) _____ help you in any way I can as long as you cooperate with me.

10. (who is) Jamison is the attorney _____ likely to be appointed a municipal judge.

11. (who has) _____ been borrowing my tapes without my permission?

Other Uses for the Apostrophe

1. The apostrophe can stand for missing numbers.

    My father was born in '44. (The apostrophe stands for the missing *19.*)

    I graduated with the class of '71. (The apostrophe stands for the missing *19.*)

2. The apostrophe can stand for missing letters in words that are not contractions. This is often the case in quotations that include informal speech or dialect.

    Grandpa always said, "Feelin' sorry fer yourself is a waste of time."

    "Bring 'em with ya," Mike shouted.

3. The apostrophe is used with an *s* to form the plural of letters. No apostrophe is used to form the plural of numbers, symbols, abbreviations, and words used as terms.

    How many *s*'s are in *embarrass?*

    Be more careful about how you make your 4s.

    All your *theres* are used incorrectly.

    Write out the word *number* instead of using #s.

    There are three M.D.s here tonight.

Practice 14.17

Place apostrophes where needed. Some sentences are correct.

1. In the 90s, anyone who cannot operate a computer is at a serious disadvantage.

2. The second grader was having trouble learning how to make *r*s.

3. Gary announced, "The best things in life are eatin, sleepin, and partyin."

4. The English department hired three new Ph.Ds to teach full time.

5. Martha was having trouble with her *then*s and *than*s.

Post Test

Place apostrophes where they are needed in the following sentences. One sentence requires an apostrophe and an *s.*

1. The quarterbacks spectacular pass sparked the offenses scoring drive.

2. Once youve owned a car with a tape deck, youll never buy a car without one again.

3. Chris short story was accepted for publication by one of this countrys leading magazines.

4. The *C*s that Dana earned kept her off of the Deans list.

5. Johns and Marthas problems arent going to be solved overnight; it will take years of counseling before theyre able to understand and alter their behavior.

6. Three companies employees were honored with Chamber of Commerce awards of excellence.

7. My sister-in-laws business, which she started in the late 70s, is now grossing over two hundred thousand dollars a year.

8. Dave snapped, "Were comin; dont be so impatient."

9. The teams locker room was jammed with reporters, following their upset victory over the Division I champs.

10. The cab drivers strike is a problem for those visiting the city.

11. The Reading Labs speed-reading class is designed for students whose reading rate is very low.

12. The three doctors opinions were the same: my tonsillectomy cant be postponed.

Using Quotation Marks

Quotation marks are most frequently used to enclose someone's spoken or written words or the titles of short published writings.

Pretest

If quotation marks are used correctly, write *yes* on the blank; if they are used incorrectly, write *no.* If you are unsure, do not write anything. Check your answers in Appendix III.

1. ____ "Dad said, If you decide to go to graduate school, I will pay half of your tuition."

2. ____ One of the best novels I have read is John Jakes's "Love and War."

3. ____ "Before writing your research paper," Dr. Jones explained, "examine at least three books and ten articles on your topic."

4. ____ The salesman in the pet store said that "the goldfish we bought will not live very long unless we buy a filter for the water."

5. ____ I remember thinking to myself, "If I get out of this mess, I will never take an unnecessary risk again."

6. ____ "Ma'am, you were traveling 50 miles per hour in a school zone," the police officer snapped.

7. ____ "They Also Wait Who Stand and Serve Themselves" is a delightful essay written by Andrew Ward.

8. ____ "Slow down the pace," the coach shouted from the sidelines.

Quotation Marks with Exact Spoken or Written Words   When you reproduce the exact words someone spoke or wrote, enclose the words in quotation marks. A sentence with someone's exact words usually has two parts: a statement of who spoke or wrote the words and the words themselves. The sentence is punctuated according to where in the sentence the exact words appear.

1. Exact words after the statement of who spoke or wrote the words:

    Judy warned me, "Be sure to study hard for the chemistry exam because it's a real killer."

A Tale of Two Cities begins, "It was the best of times. It was the worst of times."

I asked Mario, "Will you join me for lunch tomorrow?"

The preceding examples illustrate the following points about punctuating sentences with the exact words after the statement of who spoke or wrote them:

a. A comma separates the statement of who spoke from the exact words.

b. The first word of the exact words is capitalized.

c. The period or question mark appears inside the final quotation marks.

2. Exact words before the statement of who spoke or wrote the words:

"There is a reason for everything," Julia always said.

"Take me to your leader," the alien ordered.

"Will I ever be promoted?" the weary office worker wondered.

The preceding examples illustrate the following points about punctuating sentences with the exact words before the statement of who spoke or wrote them:

a. If the exact words do not ask a question, a comma appears before the final quotation marks.

b. If the exact words ask a question, a question mark appears before the final quotation marks.

c. The first word after the exact words is not capitalized unless it is a person's name.

3. Exact words before and after the statement of who spoke or wrote the words:

"Before we begin today's lecture," said Dr. Sanchez, "let's review yesterday's material."

"I think we can go now," I said. "The rain has stopped."

"Are you sure," I asked, "that we can come along?"

The preceding examples illustrate the following points about punctuating sentences with exact words before and after the statement of who spoke or wrote them:

a. A comma appears after the first group of exact words, inside the quotation marks.

b. If the first group of exact words does not form a sentence, a comma appears after the statement of who spoke or wrote the words. The second group of exact words does not begin with a capital letter.

c. If the first group of exact words forms a sentence, a period appears after the statement of who spoke or wrote the words. The second group of exact words begins with a capital letter.

d. A period or question mark appears inside the final quotation marks.

4. A person's thoughts are punctuated like exact words:

I asked myself, "How did I get into this mess?"

"I know I can do it," I thought.

5. Before using quotation marks, be sure you really have someone's exact words.

use quotation marks:	Jane said, "I hate snow."
do not use quotation marks:	Jane said that she hates snow. (No one's exact words are repeated here.)
use quotation marks:	The lawyer said, "The case will be settled out of court."
do not use quotation marks:	The lawyer said that the case will be settled out of court. (No one's exact words are repeated here.)

Practice 14.18

Write sentences according to the directions given. The first one is done as an example.

1. Write a sentence that you recently heard spoken on campus. Place the exact words after the statement of who spoke.

   Harry replied, "I'll meet you in the library at 2:00."

2. Write a sentence you recently spoke to a friend. Place the exact words after the statement of who spoke.

3. Write a sentence that includes a question a teacher has asked you. Place the exact words before the statement of who spoke.

_____

_____

4. Write a sentence that includes words a waiter might say. Place the exact words before the statement of who spoke.

_____

_____

5. Write two sentences that you might speak to a classmate before an exam. Place the exact words before and after the statement of who spoke.

_____

_____

6. Write a sentence a grandparent might speak. Use the words *When I was young* to begin the exact words. Place the exact words before and after the statement of who spoke.

_____

_____

7. Write a sentence that includes a question you might ask your doctor. Place the exact words after the statement of who spoke.

_____

_____

8. Write a sentence that includes words you would think to yourself after waiting for fifteen minutes in a traffic jam.

_____

_____

Quotation Marks with Short Published Titles Quotation marks enclose the titles of *short* published works: the titles of magazine and newspaper articles, essays, short stories, short poems, songs, and book chapters.

Titles of longer works, such as books, magazines, newspapers, record albums, television shows, plays, and movies are underlined, or placed in italics (slanted type).

Use Quotation Marks	Underline
"Araby" (a short story)	Gone with the Wind (a novel/film)
"That Lean and Hungry Look" (an essay)	Arsenic and Old Lace (a play)
"Art at Its Best" (newspaper article)	Wall Street Journal (a newspaper)
"Ode to the West Wind" (a short poem)	Twentieth Century American Poets (a book)
"Rootbeer Rag" (a song)	Streetlife Serenade (an album)

Post Test

On a separate sheet, write the sentences, punctuating and capitalizing the quoted material correctly. One sentence is already correct.

1. The magician raised his arms and said there is nothing up my sleeves.

2. I couldn't possibly have been at the scene of the crime the defendant told the attorney because I was in the dentist's office.

3. I asked myself do I really want to go to graduate school?

4. Congressman Howard explained that because population has decreased significantly in our state, one congressional district might be eliminated.

5. The professional writer who visited our classroom said keep a journal and you will never be at a loss for ideas to write about.

6. The ozone layer must be protected, or planet Earth will be in big trouble the environmentalist explained.

7. If I were you Louise cautioned I would not be so quick to judge others.

8. In poetry class we are reading Robert Browning's My Last Duchess.

9. My favorite short story is Young Goodman Brown, but I also enjoy Flannery O'Connor's story Good Country People.

10. Kevin wondered out loud is all this effort going to pay off?

CHAPTER

15

Writing in Response to Reading

As a college student you read a great deal: studying textbooks, preparing research assignments, and reading required books are routine tasks that call upon you to read frequently and thoughtfully. What you may not realize is that reading is also important to college students working to improve their writing skills. If you read often, paying attention to the characteristics of what you read and observing how other writers handle their tasks, you will learn about writing—and you can bring what you learn to your own writing tasks.

Therefore, the focus of this chapter is on reading because reading is an important part of college life and because reading can help you improve your writing. Also, because much of your writing in college will be written responses to reading material, much of this chapter is devoted to writing in response to reading. You will learn

1. how to interact with a text through active reading
2. what to look for when you read
3. how to write a summary of what you have read
4. how to write essay examination answers

ACTIVE READING

When you read for your own enjoyment, all that matters is that you are having a good time, so if you skip a paragraph or fail to understand a word or read with the television on, it does not matter—as long as you are enjoying yourself. However, when you read for your college classes, more is expected of you. You must read attentively for full comprehension. To do this, you must follow a different reading procedure than you follow when you read for pleasure alone; you must follow a process called *active reading.*

As the name suggests, *active reading* gets the reader *actively* involved in what is being read. It helps the reader understand what is read, and it helps the reader form judgments about what is read. Active readers do not consider their job done until they have answered a number of questions about what they are reading. These questions appear in the following box.

QUESTIONS AN ACTIVE READER ASKS

1. What is the author's main idea (thesis)?
2. What main points support the thesis?
3. Is the support for the thesis adequate and convincing?
4. Is the author expressing facts, opinions, or both?
5. What is the author's tone or attitude (serious, sarcastic, preachy, humorous, angry, insulting, etc.)?
6. What is the author's purpose (to share, inform, entertain, and/or persuade)?
7. Who is the author's intended audience?
8. What is the source of the author's detail (observation, personal experience, research, and/or reasoning)?

A reader who has the answers to the preceding questions understands what has been read and has an awareness of the techniques the writer used to communicate.

HOW TO BE AN ACTIVE READER

To be an active reader, you must do more than let the words sound in your ears. You must become actively involved by focusing on what you are reading. The steps described in the following pages—*surveying, uninterrupted reading, studied reading,* and *testing yourself*—will show you how to do this. Keep in mind, however, that the key to your success will be *reading the material more than once.*

Step 1—Surveying

Find a quiet place free of distractions and get comfortable, but not so comfortable that you will nod off or daydream. Make sure the light is good. Now you are ready to survey your reading material to get an idea of what to expect.

First check the title. What does it suggest the reading will be about? Who is the author? Have you read anything by this person before? If so, what might you expect based on your past experience? Has your instructor said anything about this material? If so, what can you expect based on these comments?

Now look through the material. Are there headings, boldface type, italics, lists, or pictures with captions? If so, what do these suggest you can expect from the reading?

Now read the opening and closing paragraphs quickly. What clues do these provide to content and the writer's purpose? Read the first sentence of each paragraph. What clues to content do these provide?

Once you have surveyed the material, you will have a sense of what to expect when you read. You will probably know what the writer's general subject is and whether the author is expressing feelings, explaining something, or trying to convince you of something. Just as important, you will form some questions about the reading. When you are through surveying and move on to reading, you should look for the answers to your survey questions.

Step 2—Uninterrupted Reading

Read the material quickly but attentively, without stopping. If you encounter a word you do not understand, circle it to check later; if there is a passage you do not understand, place a question mark next to it. The important thing is to keep going, getting as much as you can without laboring over anything. As you read, try to establish the writer's main point (thesis).

After this reading, write the answers to as many of the active-reader questions as you can. Then look up every word you circled, and write the meanings in the margin near the circled word. Now take a break if you feel the need.

Step 3—Studied Reading

Pick up your pen and read again. This time underline the author's thesis (if it is stated) and the main points to support the thesis (these are often found in topic sentences). Be careful not to underline too much—just go for the thesis and main points. As you read, use your pen to write your reactions in the margins. Record your observations (even personal comments like "This makes me think of Chris"); note strong agreement or disagreement ("how true" or "absolutely not"); indicate where more detail is needed ("this isn't proven"). In addition, put stars next to passages you particularly like and question marks next to parts you do not understand. (See p. 437 for an example of how to mark up an essay.) After this reading, return to the active-reading questions and answer the ones that remain.

If the material is long or difficult, take a break and then read it one more time, again using your pen to record your observations and underline main points. If you are unable after this reading to answer all the questions an active reader asks, or if there is anything you do not understand, write your questions down, take them to class, and ask your teacher.

Step 4—Testing Yourself

Close the book after your studied reading and write a brief summary of the material. Or recite a summary to yourself or to another person. This testing helps lock the main points in your memory.

> NOTE: Do not confuse active reading with speed-reading. Speed is not the issue here. Rather, your goal is to understand the form and content of what you read and to make judgments about its truth and effectiveness.

A Sample Active Reading

The following essay has been marked the way an active reader might mark it. After the essay are the answers to the questions an active reader asks. Studying this material will help you appreciate how an active reader interacts with a text.

The Trouble with Television

Robert MacNeil

It is difficult to escape the influence of television. If you fit the sta- (1)
tistical averages, by the age of 20 you will have been exposed to at least
20,000 hours of television. You can add 10,000 hours for each decade
you have lived after the age of 20. The only things Americans do more
than watch television are work and sleep.

Calculate for a moment what could be done with even a part of (2)
those hours. Five thousand hours, I am told, are what a typical college
undergraduate spends working on a bachelor's degree. In 10,000
hours you could have learned enough to become an astronomer or engineer. You could have learned several languages fluently. If it appealed
to you, you could be reading Homer in the original Greek or Dos-
toyevsky in Russian. If it didn't, you could have walked around the
world and written a book about it.

The trouble with television is that it discourages concentration. Al- (3)
most anything interesting and rewarding in life requires some con-
structive, consistently applied effort. The dullest, the least gifted of us
can achieve things that seem miraculous to those who never concentrate on anything. But television encourages us to apply no effort. It
sells us instant gratification. It diverts us only to divert, to make the time
pass without pain.

Television's variety becomes a narcotic, not a stimulus. Its serial, (4)
kaleidoscopic exposures force us to follow its lead. The viewer is on a
perpetual guided tour: 30 minutes at the museum, 30 at the cathedral,
30 for a drink, then back on the bus to the next attraction—except on
television, typically, the spans allotted are on the order of minutes or
seconds, and the chosen delights are more often car crashes and people killing one another. In short, a lot of television usurps one of the
most precious of all human gifts, the ability to focus your attention
yourself, rather than just passively surrender it.

Capturing your attention—and holding it—is the prime motive of (5)
most television programming and enhances its role as a profitable ad-

Source: From a speech "Is Television Narrowing Our Minds?" by Robert Mac-
Neil delivered at the President's Leadership Forum, SUNY, Purchase, NY.
Reprinted by permission from the author and the 1985 *Reader's Digest*.

Sesame Street is like this) and it's an educational show.

vertising vehicle. Programmers live in constant fear of losing anyone's attention—anyone's. The surest way to avoid doing so is to keep everything brief, not to strain the attention of anyone but instead to provide constant stimulation through [variety, novelty, action and movement.] Quite simply, television operates on the appeal to the short attention span.

An order sacred willed

(6)   It is simply the easiest way out. But it has come to be regarded as a given, as inherent in the medium itself; as an imperative, as though General Sarnoff, or one of the other august pioneers of video, had bequeathed to us tablets of stone commanding that nothing in television shall ever require more than a few moments' concentration.

spreading through

(7)   In its place that is fine. Who can quarrel with a medium that so brilliantly packages escapist entertainment as a mass-marketing tool? [But I see its values now pervading this nation and its life. It has become fashionable to think that, like fast food, fast ideas are the way to get to a fast-moving, impatient public.] *– interesting!*

How about an example or some proof?

(8)   In the case of news, this practice, in my view, results in inefficient communication. I question how much of television's nightly news effort is really absorbable and understandable. Much of it is what has been aptly described as "machine-gunning with scraps." I think the technique fights coherence. I think it tends to make things ultimately boring and dismissible (unless they are accompanied by horrifying pictures) because almost anything is boring and dismissible if you know almost nothing about it.

There's no proof in this ¶.

How did grammar get into this?

(9)   I believe that TV's appeal to the short attention span is not only inefficient communication but decivilizing as well. Consider the casual assumptions that television tends to cultivate: that complexity must be avoided, that visual stimulation is a substitute for thought, that verbal precision is an anachronism. It may be old-fashioned, but I was taught that thought is words, arranged in grammatically precise ways.

something that is in the wrong time.

(10)   There is a crisis of literacy in this country. One study estimates that some 30 million adult Americans are "functionally illiterate" and cannot read or write well enough to answer a want ad or understand the instructions on a medicine bottle.

can't be transferred

(11)   Literacy may not be an inalienable human right, but it is one that the highly literate Founding Fathers might not have found unreasonable or even unattainable. We are not only not attaining it as a nation, statistically speaking, but we are falling further and further short of attaining it. And, while I would not be so simplistic as to suggest that television is the cause, I believe it contributes and is an influence.

Maybe T.V. does cause illiteracy) but where's the proof?

(12)   Everything about this nation—the structure of the society, its forms of family organization, its place in the world—has become more complex, not less. Yet its dominating communications instrument, its principal form of national linkage, is one that sells neat resolutions to human problems that usually have no neat resolutions. It is

all symbolized in my mind by the hugely successful art form that television has made central to the culture, the 30-second commercial: the
tiny drama of the earnest housewife who finds happiness in choosing
the right toothpaste.

Yes, I agree

When before in human history has so much humanity collectively
surrendered so much of its leisure to one toy, one mass diversion?
When before has virtually an entire nation surrendered itself wholesale
to a medium for selling?

(13)

J.V.

as Joy

nice!

Some years ago Yale University law professor Charles L. Black, Jr.,
wrote: ". . . forced feeding on trivial fare is not itself a trivial matter." I
think this society is being force-fed with trivial fare, and I fear that the
effects on our habits of mind, our language, our tolerance for effort,
and our appetite for complexity are only dimly perceived. If I am
wrong, we will have done no harm to look at the issue skeptically and
critically, to consider how we should be resisting it. [I hope you will
join with me in doing so.]

(14)

*Not me, buddy.
I think you're making
a big deal out of
nothing.*

Answers to Active-Reader Questions for "The Trouble with Television"

1. What is the author's main idea (thesis)?

   "The trouble with television is that it discourages concentration."

2. What main points support the thesis?

   The variety on television is a narcotic.
   Television appeals to a short attention span.
   Television's values have spread throughout our lives.
   Television causes inefficient communication.
   The appeal to the short attention span is decivilizing.
   Television contributes to illiteracy.
   Television sells simple solutions to complex problems.

3. Is the support for the thesis adequate and convincing?

   *I don't think so because so many points appear without proof. The
   author seems more like he is yelling than persuading. It's
   emotional without proof.*

4. Is the author expressing facts, opinions, or both?

   opinions

5. What is the author's tone or attitude (serious, sarcastic, preachy, humorous, angry, insulting, etc.)?

   The author seems angry and preachy to me. He doesn't really give facts. Just his anger shows through. He even seems a little snobby, like TV is just for the "lower classes."

6. What is the author's purpose (to share, inform, entertain, and/or persuade)?

   to persuade the reader that television is bad and to inform the reader of why it is bad

7. Who is the author's intended audience?

   Because the essay seems a little stuffy and intellectual, I think his audience is very educated and probably already agrees that television is a problem.

8. What is the source of the author's detail (observation, personal experience, and/or reasoning)?

   observation and reasoning

On Being 17, Bright, and Unable to Read

David Raymond

Because all of us have felt inadequate at one time or another, we sympathize with the following account of the pain the author felt because he could not read, and we rejoice in his victory when he confronts his learning disability and triumphs. As you read the selection, ask yourself what can be learned from the author's experience.

You will notice that the essay is a narration *(it tells a story). Like most narrations, it answers the questions who? what? when? where? why? and how? Notice the answers to these questions and decide which answers are emphasized the most.*

You will also notice that the narration lacks a stated thesis and that some supporting paragraphs lack topic sentences. Often narrations do not have stated thesis sentences and topic sentences because the time sequence provides an adequate organizational framework and topic sentences are not required as an ordering device.

Before reading the essay, study the following vocabulary:

dyslexia—a learning disability

potter's wheel—a device with a rotating horizontal dish upon which clay is molded

cross-country team—a track team that runs over fields and through woods, etc., rather than on a track

Leonardo da Vinci—a brilliant Italian painter, sculptor, architect, engineer, and scientist who lived from 1452 to 1519

One day a substitute teacher picked me to read aloud from the text- (1)
book. When I told her "No, thank you," she came unhinged. She
thought I was acting smart, and told me so. I kept calm, and that got
her madder and madder. We must have spent 10 minutes trying to solve
the problem, and finally she got so red in the face I thought she'd blow
up. She told me she'd see me after class.

(2)   Maybe someone like me was a new thing for that teacher. But she wasn't new to me. I've been through scenes like that all my life. You see, even though I'm 17 and a junior in high school, I can't read because I have dyslexia. I'm told I read "at a fourth-grade level," but from where I sit, that's not reading. You can't know what that means unless you've been there. It's not easy to tell how it feels when you can't read your homework assignments or the newspaper or a menu in a restaurant or even notes from your own friends.

(3)   My family began to suspect I was having problems almost from the first day I started school. My father says my early years in school were the worst years of his life. They weren't so good for me, either. As I look back on it now, I can't find the words to express how bad it really was. I wanted to die. I'd come home from school screaming, "I'm dumb. I'm dumb—I wish I were dead!"

(4)   I guess I couldn't read anything at all then—not even my own name—and they tell me I didn't talk as good as other kids. But what I remember about those days is that I couldn't throw a ball where it was supposed to go, I couldn't learn to swim, and I wouldn't learn to ride a bike, because no matter what anyone told me, I knew I'd fail.

(5)   Sometimes my teachers would try to be encouraging. When I couldn't read the words on the board they'd say, "Come on, David, you know that word." Only I didn't. And it was embarrassing. I just felt dumb. And dumb was how the kids treated me. They'd make fun of me every chance they got, asking me to spell "cat" or something like that. Even if I knew how to spell it, I wouldn't; they'd only give me another word. Anyway, it was awful, because more than anything I wanted friends. On my birthday when I blew out the candles I didn't wish I could learn to read; what I wished for was that the kids would like me.

(6)   With the bad reports coming from school, and with me moaning about wanting to die and how everybody hated me, my parents began looking for help. That's when the testing started. The school tested me, the child-guidance center tested me, private psychiatrists tested me. Everybody knew something was wrong—especially me.

(7)   It didn't help much when they stuck a fancy name onto it. I couldn't pronounce it then—I was only in second grade—and I was ashamed to talk about it. Now it rolls off my tongue, because I've been living with it for a lot of years—dyslexia.

(8)   All through elementary school it wasn't easy. I was always having to do things that were "different," things the other kids didn't have to do. I had to go to a child psychiatrist, for instance.

(9)   One summer my family forced me to go to a camp for children with reading problems. I hated the idea, but the camp turned out pretty good, and I had a good time. I met a lot of kids who couldn't read and somehow that helped. The director of the camp said I had a higher I.Q. than 90 percent of the population. I didn't believe him.

About the worst thing I had to do in fifth and sixth grade was go to   (10)
a special education class in another school in our town. A bus picked
me up, and I didn't like that at all. The bus also picked up emotionally
disturbed kids and retarded kids. It was like going to a school for the
retarded. I always worried that someone I knew would see me on that
bus. It was a relief to go to the regular junior high school.

Life began to change a little for me then, because I began to feel bet-   (11)
ter about myself. I found the teachers cared; they had meetings about
me and I worked harder for them for a while. I began to work on the
potter's wheel, making vases and pots that the teachers said were
pretty good. Also, I got a letter for being on the track team. I could always run pretty fast.

At high school the teachers are good and everyone is trying to help   (12)
me. I've gotten honors some marking periods, and I've won a letter on
the cross-country team. Next quarter I think the school might hold a
show of my pottery. I've got some friends. But there are still some embarrassing times. For instance, every time there is writing in the class,
I get up and go to the special education room. Kids ask me where I go
all the time. Sometimes I say, "to Mars."

Homework is a real problem. During free periods in school I go   (13)
into the special ed room and staff members read assignments to me.
When I get home my mother reads to me. Sometimes she reads an
assignment into a tape recorder, and then I go into my room and listen to it. If we have a novel or something like that to read, she reads
it out loud to me. Then I sit down with her, and we do the assignment. She'll write, while I talk my answers to her. Lately I've taken
to dictating into a tape recorder, and then someone—my father, a
private tutor or my mother—types up what I've dictated. Whatever homework I do takes someone else's time, too. That makes me
feel bad.

We had a big meeting in school the other day—eight of us, four from   (14)
the guidance department, my private tutor, my parents and me. The
subject was me. I said I wanted to go to college, and they told me about
colleges that have facilities and staff to handle people like me. That's
nice to hear.

As for what happens after college, I don't know and I'm worried   (15)
about that. How can I make a living if I can't read? Who will hire me?
How will I fill out the application form? The only thing that gives me
any courage is the fact that I've learned about well-known people who
couldn't read or had other problems and still made it. Like Albert Ein-
stein, who didn't talk until he was 4 and flunked math. Like Leonardo
da Vinci, who everyone seems to think had dyslexia.

I've told this story because maybe some teacher will read it and go   (16)
easy on a kid in the classroom who has what I've got. Or, maybe some
parent will stop nagging his kid, and stop calling him lazy. Maybe he's

not lazy or dumb. Maybe he just can't read and doesn't know what's wrong. Maybe he's scared, like I was.

Study Questions

1. "On Being 17, Bright, and Unable to Read" is a narration (it tells a story). Paragraph 1 tells a brief narration, but it is not the main story. Where does the main narration begin?

2. The essay does not have a sentence that states exactly what the essay is about (a thesis), but the thesis is implied in paragraph 2. Write a sentence that expresses the thesis idea.

3. In his last paragraph, Raymond explains his purpose for writing, and he mentions his intended audience. What is his purpose? Who is his intended audience?

4. Are all the who? what? when? where? why? how? questions answered? Which ones get the most emphasis?

5. Raymond's time sequence (his chronology) begins with his early years of school. What are the next three time periods discussed in the narration?

6. Is Raymond's detail adequate enough to fulfill his purpose? Explain.

7. Can "On Being 17, Bright, and Unable to Read" be viewed as a definition essay? Explain.

Writing Assignments

1. Raymond's narration explains how his dyslexia affected him. In a narrative paragraph, tell about a time you were unable to do something. For example, tell about what happened one time when you could not sing, play a sport, speak in front of a group, dance, handle yourself well in a job interview, etc. (See p. 81 on writing a narrative paragraph.)

2. Raymond's opening paragraph tells a brief story (called an *anecdote*) about a time a teacher became angry with him. In a paragraph, narrate an account of time a teacher became angry or frustrated with you or someone you know. (See p. 81 on writing a narrative paragraph.)

3. Raymond was treated cruelly by his classmates. In a paragraph, explain why you think the other kids in school made fun of him. (See p. 119 on the cause-and-effect paragraph.)

4. Raymond's dyslexia has had a profound impact on his life. In an essay of 4–5 paragraphs, use cause-and-effect analysis to explain the effects of one fact of your life (being tall or short, overweight or underweight, rich or poor, an only child or part of a large family, having allergies, etc.). (See p. 119 for the characteristics of cause-and-effect analysis.)

5. Raymond expresses concern for his future. Are you concerned about yours? In an essay of 4–5 paragraphs, explain what you are concerned about and why.

6. Were your school years happy or unhappy ones? In an essay of 4–5 paragraphs, write a narration that expresses your happiness or unhappiness. Like Raymond, begin with the early years and progress to the present focusing on 3–4 periods in the time sequence (for example, first grade, eighth grade, and twelfth grade). (See p. 81 for the characteristics of narration.)

Expecting Friends

Gary Soto

Poet and essayist Gary Soto is a Mexican-American who lives in Fresno, California. In the following selection from his 1986 collection, Small Faces, *the author describes his eager anticipation of the arrival of two old friends. The result is a loving portrait of friends and friendship.*

As you read, notice that although the description is restrained, specific word choice still allows the reader to form mental pictures of the author's friends. Notice, too, how carefully Soto chooses examples of each friend's behavior so the reader can appreciate each one's special appeal.

Before reading, review the following vocabulary.

Estonian—native of Estonia, a country once a part of the USSR

naive—lacking worldly wisdom

clammy—cool and damp

half-eclipsed—half covered

Lord Byron (1788–1824)—an English poet

acid—LSD, a drug popular in the sixties and seventies

cowpoke—cowboy

(1)   My friends are coming—Jon the Estonian and Omar the Mexican—and what we want is to sit under the apricot tree in the backyard and talk about friends who couldn't come—Chris the one-book scholar and Leonard the two-beat drummer. We're going to talk poetry, ours mostly, and open beers one after another until we're a little drunk and a little wiser than the chairs we're sitting on. But we're going to take this slowly. We may, in fact, not sit under that tree but first take a drive to Tilden Park, where we'll hike as if there's a place to go and maybe sit waist-deep in wild grass, chewing long stalks that are springboards for

the ants. Later we could go to the Country Club and slouch in leather chairs that overlook the green and its small rise of hills. Men in plaid kneeling over golf balls. Clouds over the trees. Trees like pieces of the sea standing up. The day will be so open, so filled with blue air, that we won't believe it's all for us.

But who are these friends? Jon was a classmate in poetry, room-   (2) mate in Laguna Beach, and the best man in my wedding, a guy who drank to all the causes of the heart. A friend writes of Jon and the day of the wedding:

> The best man, lifting
> at least his fifth bottle of champagne,
> stands on a table in his white tuxedo;
> and turning slowly toward us, like Tommy Dorsey
> to the band, invites us to toast the moon,
> the clear Fresno moon, which he finds gone.

And the moon did disappear, for my wife and I married on a night of an eclipse that comes every twenty years, a rare treat for the astronomer's wife. We didn't know. We planned the wedding from an old calendar, sent out homemade invitations, and stood in front of a churchroom of relatives who gave money, clock radios, vases, a quilt, and a new bed to wear down over the years. Here are sensible gifts, they were saying. Now make a home. Make a laughing baby in your arms.

And Omar? He was already a poet when I was a naive college stu-   (3) dent who carried books under both arms when we first met in a hall-way at Fresno State in 1972. I put down my books and asked, "Are you really Omar?" He smiled, offered a clammy hand, and said, "Keep read-ing, young man," when I told him how much I admired his poetry. And I did. I read lines like "Someone is chasing me up my sleeve" and "If I remember the dying maybe I'll be all right."

Later in the year I saw him with friends in front of the student union.   (4) Omar looked tattered, like a sailor roughed up by the sea, for his face was stubbled, his eyes red and milky in the corners, and his hair stiff as a shirt collar. I joined him and his friends who were hunched in old trench coats, feet moving a little because it was a gray December. No one was talking or about to talk. They looked around like sparrows, heads turning nervously left and then right, and shivered the cold from their shoulders. I looked around too and shivered, shaking off the cold. Trying to be friendly, I asked Omar how he was doing. He turned to me with a crazed look and said, "Go ask the dead!" I was taken back, surprised by his tone and half-eclipsed eye. Then he relaxed and chuckled; his friends chuckled. I opened my mouth into a stiff smile, stood with them for a while longer, and finally said goodbye as I hur-ried away with my sophomore books under my arms.

(5)   Omar the Crazy Gypsy, Lord Byron in Mexican clothes, cheerleader of the acid set of the late 60s, is now a quiet poet in the rural town of Sanger where, on weekends with an uncle, he sells pants, shirts, cowboy hats, and whatever workers buy from the back of a station wagon or sweaty tents at swap meets. He is a merchant, he says, and when I ask jokingly if he sells his poetry too, he says, "Yes, they cost too. Right here." He touches his heart, and I know what he means.

(6)   These friends are coming to visit. We may drive to Tilden Park; we may drive across the San Rafael Bridge and search the water for migrating whales through binoculars. We'll pass the C&H Sugar Refinery in Hercules, then San Quentin, and finally come to the moss-green hills of Sonoma. We'll drive talking and looking left, then right, between bites of apples and slapped-together sandwiches. We may stop to take pictures of cows; we may stop at a roadside bar with a name like The South Forty or The Trail's End and stand drinking frosty beers. After a beer or two we may become so at ease that we invite a cowpoke who, after two or three or four beers, may call us city queers and hit us on our silly grins.

(7)   If we were smart we'd only drink one beer and get out—or just stay home, my home in Berkeley, under that apricot tree in the feathery light of an early spring day. The world is in blossom: apple and apricot, the tulip and yellow daffodil that is broken by wind. The sky is like no other: blue over the garage and silver-blue where the sun is coming through behind a rack of clouds. The breeze is doing things in the trees; my neighbor's dog is wagging his tail against the fence.

(8)   This will be Saturday. I will get my winter wish: to sit with friends who mean much to me and talk about others who mean much to us. I've been waiting for this moment. I've been waiting months to open up to others, laugh, and flick beer tops at kidding friends who have drunk too much. We'll carry chairs from the kitchen and set them under the tree. My wife may join us; I'll slap my lap and she'll sit with a sparkling wine glass in her hand. And our daughter may come out with her flying dolphin, a stuffed animal that's taped together and just hanging on. This will be Saturday, the weather faintly remembered from another time. In the back yard we may talk, or not talk, but be understood all the same.

Study Questions

1. Soto chooses specific words to help his reader form mental pictures and to keep his description lively. For example, in paragraph 1, he uses the specific "Tilden Park" rather than the less specific "park." In paragraph 6, he refers to "slapped-together sandwiches" rather than the less specific "sandwiches." Cite

four other examples of specific word choice that helps the reader form a mental picture or that adds liveliness.

2. *Similes* compare two things using the words "like" or "as." Descriptive writers often use similes. For example, in paragraph 4, Soto says "They looked around like sparrows," in order to help the reader visualize how the people were behaving. Find two other similes in the essay.

3. *Metaphors* compare two things without using the words "like" or "as." Descriptive writers often use metaphors. For example, in paragraph 1, Soto compares the stalks of grass to "springboards for the ants" to help the reader form a mental picture. Find two other metaphors in the essay.

4. Soto uses examples to help the reader learn about his friends. What does the example of Jon's behavior reveal about him?

5. What does the example of Omar's behavior reveal about him?

Writing Assignments

1. In a paragraph, describe the appearance of a close friend. (See p. 87 on writing a descriptive paragraph.)

2. Select one of your friends, and in a paragraph, illustrate one characteristic of that friend with one or more examples of that person's behavior. (See p. 93 on writing an illustration paragraph.)

3. If you could be friends with any person, past or present, who would you pick? Explain why in a paragraph.

4. In an essay of 4–5 paragraphs, explain one or more traits of the ideal friend, using examples to illustrate the trait(s). For example, if the ideal friend is loyal, give an example of a time a friend displayed loyalty.

5. In a paragraph of 4–5 paragraphs, describe one of your favorite holidays and what it is like to look forward to that holiday.

6. Soto writes about his friends Jon and Omar, who are very different from each other. In an essay of 4–5 paragraphs, describe two friends of yours, focusing on their differences.

Living with My VCR

Nora Ephron

"Living with My VCR" is a light-hearted account of the author's love-hate relationship with her video-cassette recorder. Like many modern devices, the VCR can have a measure of frustration attached to the pleasure and convenience it provides. Do any modern devices cause you frustration at the same time they offer convenience and pleasure?

Ephron's thesis is not stated, so as you read, look for clues to the implied thesis. Notice too how Ephron uses illustration, comparison and contrast, and cause and effect analysis to make her points. The elements of humor make the essay entertaining. Try to identify those humorous elements.

Before you read, review the following vocabulary:

compulsive—having an irresistible need to do something

Cuisinart—a small kitchen appliance for chopping and slicing

rebuke—to express disapproval

obsessive—completely preoccupied with something

(1)   When all this started, two Christmases ago, I did not have a video-cassette recorder. What I had was a position on video-cassette recorders. I was against them. It seemed to me that the fundamental idea of the VCR—which is that if you go out and miss what's on television, you can always watch it later—flew in the face of almost the only thing I truly believed—which is that the whole point of going out is to miss what's on television. Let's face it: Part of being a grown-up is that every day you have to choose between going out at night or staying home, and it is one of life's unhappy truths that there is not enough time to do both.

(2)   Finally, though, I broke down, but not entirely. I did not buy a video-cassette recorder. I rented one. And I didn't rent one for myself—I my-

self intended to stand firm and hold to my only principle. I rented one for my children. For $29 a month, I would tape "The Wizard of Oz" and "Mary Poppins" and "Born Free," and my children would be able to watch them from time to time. In six months, when my rental contract expired, I would re-evaluate.

For quite a while, I taped for my children. Of course I had to sub-   (3)
scribe to Home Box Office and Cinemax in addition to my normal cable service, for $19 more a month—but for the children. I taped "Oliver" and "Annie" and "My Fair Lady" for the children. And then I stopped taping for the children—who don't watch much television, in any case—and started to tape for myself.

I now tape for myself all the time. I tape when I am out, I tape when   (4)
I am at home and doing other things, and I tape when I am asleep. At this very moment, as I am typing, I am taping. The entire length of my bedroom bookshelf has been turned over to video cassettes, mostly of movies; they are numbered and indexed and stacked in order in a household where absolutely nothing else is. Occasionally I find myself browsing through publications like Video Review and worrying whether I shouldn't switch to chrome-based videotape or have my heads cleaned or upgrade to a machine that does six or seven things at once and can be set to tape six or seven months in advance. No doubt I will soon find myself shopping at some Video Village for racks and storage systems especially made for what is known as "the serious collector."

How this happened, how I became a compulsive videotaper, is a   (5)
mystery to me, because my position on video-cassette recorders is very much the same as the one I started with. I am still against them. Now, though, I am against them for different reasons: Now I hate them out of knowledge rather than ignorance. The other technological breakthroughs that have made their way into my life after my initial pigheaded opposition to them—like the electric typewriter and the Cuisinart—have all settled peacefully into my home. I never think about them except when I'm using them, and when I'm using them I take them for granted. They do exactly what I want them to do. I put the slicing disk into the Cuisinart, and damned if the thing doesn't slice things up just the way it's supposed to. But there's no taking a VCR for granted. It squats there, next to the television, ready to rebuke any fool who expects something of it.

A child can operate a VCR, of course. Only a few maneuvers are re-   (6)
quired to tape something, and only a few more are required to tape something while you are out. You must set the time to the correct time you wish the recording to begin and end. You must punch the channel selector. You must insert a videotape. And, on my set, you must switch the "on" button to "time record." Theoretically, you can then go out and have a high old time, knowing that even if you waste the evening, your video-cassette recorder will not.

(7)   Sometimes things work out. Sometimes I return home, rewind the tape, and discover that the machine has recorded exactly what I'd hoped it would. But more often than not, what is on the tape is not at all what I'd intended; in fact, the moments leading up to the revelation of what is actually on my video cassettes are without doubt the most suspenseful of my humdrum existence. As I rewind the tape, I have no idea of what, if anything, will be on it; as I press the "play" button, I have not a clue as to what in particular has gone wrong. All I ever know for certain is that something has.

(8)   Usually it's my fault. I admit it. I have mis-set the timer or channel selector or misread the newspaper listing. I have knelt at the foot of my machine and methodically, carefully, painstakingly set it—and set it wrong. This is extremely upsetting to me—I am normally quite competent when it comes to machines—but I can live with it. What is far more disturbing are the times when what has gone wrong is not my fault at all but the fault of outside forces over which I have no control whatsoever. The program listing in the newspaper lists the channel incorrectly. The cable guide inaccurately lists the length of the movie, lopping off the last 10 minutes. The evening's schedule of television programming is thrown off by an athletic event. The educational station is having a fund-raiser.

(9)   You would be amazed at how often outside forces affect a video-cassette recorder, and I think I am safe in saying that video-cassette recorders are the only household appliances that outside forces are even relevant to. As a result, my video-cassette library is a raggedy collection of near misses: "The Thin Man" without the opening; "King Kong" without the ending; a football game instead of "Murder, She Wrote"; dozens of PBS auctions and fund-raisers instead of dozens of episodes of "Masterpiece Theater." All told, my success rate at video-taping is even lower than my success rate at buying clothes I turn out to like as much as I did in the store; the machine provides more opportunities per week to make mistakes than anything else in my life.

(10)   Every summer and at Christmastime, I re-evaluate my six-month rental contract. I have three options: I can buy the video-cassette recorder, which I would never do because I hate it so much; I can cancel the contract and turn in the machine, which I would never do because I am so addicted to videotaping; or I can go on renting. I go on renting. In two years I have spent enough money renting to buy two video-cassette recorders at the discount electronics place in my neighborhood, but I don't care. Renting is my way of deluding myself that I have some power over my VCR; it's my way of believing that I can still some day reject the machine in an ultimate way (by sending it back)—or else forgive it (by buying it)—for all the times it has rejected me.

In the meantime, I have my pathetic but ever-expanding collection (11)
of cassettes. "Why don't you just rent the movies?" a friend said to me
recently, after I finished complaining about the fact that my tape of
"The Maltese Falcon" now has a segment of "Little House on the
Prairie" in the middle of it. Rent them? What a bizarre suggestion. Then
I would have to watch them. And I don't watch my videotapes. I don't
have time. I would virtually have to watch my videotapes for the next
two years just to catch up with what my VCR has recorded so far; and
in any event, even if I did have time, the VCR would be taping and
would therefore be unavailable for use in viewing.

So I merely accumulate video cassettes. I haven't accumulated any- (12)
thing this mindlessly since my days in college, when I was obsessed
with filling my bookshelf, it didn't matter with what; what mattered
was that I believed that if I had a lot of books, it would say something
about my intelligence and taste. On some level, I suppose I believe that
if I have a lot of video cassettes, it will say something—not about my
intelligence or taste, but about my intentions. I intend to live long
enough to have time to watch my videotapes. Any way you look at it,
that means forever.

Study Questions

1. What is the first clue to the humorous tone of the essay?

2. What purpose do the first four paragraphs serve?

3. What is the primary method of development in paragraphs 1–3? In paragraph 6? In paragraphs 7–9?

4. Which paragraph relies heavily on illustration?

5. Cite three examples of Ephron's humorous tone.

6. What approach does Ephron take to her conclusion?

7. Is Ephron to be taken seriously when she says in the conclusion, "I intend to live long enough to have time to watch my videotapes. Any way you look at it, that means forever"? Explain.

Writing Assignments

1. In a paragraph, tell about a time when a modern appliance or gadget caused you a problem. (See p. 81 on writing a narrative paragraph.)

2. In a paragraph, provide examples to illustrate one way some modern device (a car, a television, a computer, the telephone, etc.) can cause us problems. (See p. 93 on writing an illustration paragraph.)

3. Are you compulsive about something the way Ephron is compulsive about videotaping? In a paragraph, describe your compulsion and its effects on you. (See p. 119 on writing a cause-and-effect analysis.)

4. Ephron says, "Renting is a way of deluding myself that I have some power over my VCR. . . ." Do you have any behaviors that allow you to delude yourself? Describe one and tell how it helps you delude yourself.

5. In an essay of 4–5 paragraphs, explain what life would be like without some modern device (the car, the television, the telephone, the typewriter, the radio, the alarm clock, etc.). (See p. 119 for characteristics of cause-and-effect analysis.)

6. Ephron says that her "position on video-cassette recorders" changed after she began to rent one. In an essay of 4–5 paragraphs, contrast your view of something before and after you had experience with it. (See p. 110 for the characteristics of comparison and contrast.)

7. Like Ephron, do you have a love-hate relationship with some modern device? In an essay of 4–5 paragraphs, tell about it. Consider using some touches of humor, as Ephron does.

8. Invent a gadget you believe is needed to make life easier or more pleasant. Give the gadget a name, and in an essay of 4–5 paragraphs, describe your invention, explain how it works, and tell how it will benefit people. Let your imagination fly.

Green Frog Skin

John Lame Deer

John Lame Deer, a tribal priest of the Sioux, has strong views about the way whites feel about money and nature, and the way they treat the land. He expresses these views in "Green Frog Skin." As you read, try to decide why he expresses these views. Also, ask yourself how the process analysis in the essay helps the author achieve his purpose.

Despite Lame Deer's serious purpose, you will likely find "Green Frog Skin" an entertaining piece, largely because of the relaxed, energetic language and the interest-holding opening narration. Before you read, however, review the following vocabulary.

gally-hooting—racing

gully—ditch

buffalo chips—dried manure

strychnine—a poison used to kill rodents

THE GREEN FROG SKIN—that's what I call a dollar bill. In our attitude (1)
toward it lies the biggest difference between Indians and whites. My
grandparents grew up in an Indian world without money. Just before
the Custer battle the white soldiers had received their pay. Their
pockets were full of green paper and they had no place to spend it.
What were their last thoughts as an Indian bullet or arrow hit them? I
guess they were thinking of all that money going to waste, of not having had a chance to enjoy it, of a bunch of dumb savages getting their
paws on that hardearned pay. That must have hurt them more than the
arrow between their ribs.

The close hand-to-hand fighting, with a thousand horses gallyhoot- (2)
ing all over the place, had covered the battlefield with an enormous
cloud of dust, and in it the green frog skins of the soldiers were
whirling around like snowflakes in a blizzard. Now, what did the Indi-

Source: Copyright © 1972 by John Fire/Lame Deer and Richard Erdoes.
Reprinted by permission of Simon & Schuster, Inc.

ans do with all that money? They gave it to their children to play with, to fold those strange bits of colored paper into all kinds of shapes, making them into toy buffalo and horses. Somebody was enjoying that money after all. The books tell of one soldier who survived. He got away, but he went crazy and some women watched him from a distance as he killed himself. The writers always say he must have been afraid of being captured and tortured, but that's all wrong.

(3)   Can't you see it? There he is, bellied down in a gully, watching what is going on. He sees the kids playing with the money, tearing it up, the women using it to fire up some dried buffalo chips to cook on, the men lighting their pipes with green frog skins, but mostly all those beautiful dollar bills floating away with the dust and the wind. It's this sight that drove that poor soldier crazy. He's clutching his head, hollering, "Goddam, Jesus Christ Almighty, look at them dumb, stupid, red sons of bitches wasting all that dough!" He watches till he can't stand it any longer, and then he blows his brains out with a six-shooter. It would make a great scene in a movie, but it would take an Indian mind to get the point.

(4)   The green frog skin—that was what the fight was all about. The gold of the Black Hills, the gold in every clump of grass. Each day you can see ranch hands riding over this land. They have a bagful of grain from their saddle horns, and whenever they see a prairie-dog hole they toss a handful of oats in it, like a kind little old lady feeding the pigeons in one of your city parks. Only the oats for the prairie dogs are poisoned with strychnine. What happens to the prairie dog after he has eaten' this grain is not a pleasant thing to watch. The prairie dogs are poisoned, because they eat grass. A thousand of them eat up as much grass in a year as a cow. So if the rancher can kill that many prairie dogs he can run one more head of cattle, make a little more money. When he looks at a prairie dog he sees only a green frog skin getting away from him.

(5)   For the white man each blade of grass or spring of water has a price tag on it. And that is the trouble, because look at what happens. The bobcats and coyotes which used to feed on prairie dogs now have to go after a stray lamb or a crippled calf. The rancher calls the pest-control officer to kill these animals. This man shoots some rabbits and puts them out as bait with a piece of wood stuck in them. That stick has an explosive charge which shoots some cyanide into the mouth of the coyote who tugs at it. The officer has been trained to be careful. He puts a printed warning on each stick reading, "Danger, Explosive, Poison!" The trouble is that our dogs can't read, and some of our children can't either.

(6)   And the prairie becomes a thing without life—no more prairie dogs, no more badgers, foxes, coyotes. The big birds of prey used to feed on prairie dogs, too. So you hardly see an eagle these days. The bald eagle is your symbol. You see him on your money, but your money is killing him. When a people start killing off their own symbols they are in a bad way.

The Sioux have a name for white men. They call them *wasicun*—   (7)
fat-takers. It is a good name, because you have taken the fat of the land.
But it does not seem to have agreed with you. Right now you don't look
so healthy—overweight, yes, but not healthy. Americans are bred like
stuffed geese—to be consumers, not human beings. The moment
they stop consuming and buying, this frog-skin world has no more use
for them. They have become frogs themselves. Some cruel child has
stuffed a cigar into their mouths and they have to keep puffing and puffing until they explode. Fat-taking is a bad thing, even for the taker. It
is especially bad for Indians who are forced to live in this frog-skin
world which they did not make and for which they have no use.

Study Questions

1. In paragraphs 1–3, Lame Deer tells a brief story about a battle
   between Native Americans and General Custer. What purpose
   does the narration serve? What does it contribute to the essay?

2. Which paragraphs include process analysis (an explanation of
   how something is made or done)? What purpose does this
   process analysis serve?

3. In your own words, write out the thesis of "Green Frog Skin."

4. For what purpose do you think the author wrote "Green Frog
   Skin?"

5. Who do you think the author's intended audience is?

6. Lame Deer does not specifically explain what happens to a
   prairie dog after it eats strychnine. He simply says that its death
   is "not a pleasant thing to watch" (paragraph 4). Why do you
   think he omits the specific details?

7. Lame Deer uses informal language. For example, he refers to
   the Native Americans' hands as "their paws" (paragraph 1). Cite
   two other examples of informal language. What does this language contribute to the essay?

Writing Assignments

1. In a paragraph, summarize John Lame Deer's opinion about
   whites and how they have affected Native Americans.

2. Lame Deer says that Americans are "consumers, not human beings" (paragraph 7). In a paragraph, agree or disagree with this
   statement, citing at least two examples to support your view.

3. In a paragraph, explain what Lame Deer means when he says, "When a people start killing off their own symbols they are in a bad way" (paragraph 6). What point is the author making?

4. In an essay of 4–5 paragraphs, agree or disagree with Lame Deer's view that Americans are "fat-takers" (paragraph 7). Be sure to cite examples to support your view.

5. In an essay of 4–5 paragraphs, agree or disagree with Lame Deer's view of whites. Be sure to cite examples to support your view.

6. Which would you choose if given the chance: a $100,000 a year job that involved harm to the environment or a $20,000 a year job that involved helping the environment? Be sure to explain the reasons for your choice.

How Dictionaries Are Made

S. I. Hayakawa

When you consult a dictionary, do you believe you are checking an authority—the source that will give you the "correct" meaning of a word? If so, you are not alone. However, in the following essay, Hayakawa explains that dictionaries are not authorities that present the "correct" way—they are historical records of customary usage.

Hayakawa combines process analysis with contrast to explain how dictionaries are made. The process may surprise you. As you read, try to discover why the author explains the process and notice how he uses contrast along with some illustration and narration to achieve his purpose.

Study the following vocabulary list before you begin:

eccentric—odd or peculiar

disseminate—spread widely

compelling—forcing

context—the parts just before and after a word or passage that determine its meaning

prophecy—predictions of the future

It is widely believed that every word has a correct meaning, that we (1) learn these meanings principally from teachers and grammarians (except that most of the time we don't bother to, so that we ordinarily speak "sloppy English"), and that dictionaries and grammars are the supreme authority in matters of meaning and usage. Few people ask by what authority the writers of dictionaries and grammars say what they say. I once got into a dispute with an Englishwoman over the pronunciation of a word and offered to look it up in the dictionary. The Englishwoman said firmly, "What for? I am English. I was born and brought up in England. The way I speak *is* English." Such self-assurance about one's own language is not uncommon among the English. In the United States, however, anyone who is willing to quarrel with the dictionary is regarded as either eccentric or mad.

Source: From *Language in Thought and Action,* Fourth Edition, by S. I. Hayakawa, copyright © 1978 by Harcourt Brace Jovanovich, Inc. Reprinted by permission of the publisher.

(2)   Let us see how dictionaries are made and how the editors arrive at definitions. What follows applies, incidentally, only to those dictionary offices where first-hand, original research goes on—not those in which editors simply copy existing dictionaries. The task of writing a dictionary begins with reading vast amounts of the literature of the period or subject that the dictionary is to cover. As the editors read, they copy on cards every interesting or rare word, every unusual or peculiar occurrence of a common word, a large number of common words in their ordinary uses, and also the sentences in which each of these words appear, thus:

pail
The dairy *pails* bring home increase of milk

Keats, *Endymion* I, 44–45

(3)   That is to say, the context of each word is collected, along with the word itself. For a really big job of dictionary-writing, such as the *Oxford English Dictionary* (usually bound in about twenty-five volumes), millions of such cards are collected, and the task of editing occupies decades. As the cards are collected, they are alphabetized and sorted. When the sorting is completed, there will be for each word anywhere from two or three to several hundred illustrative quotations, each on its card.

(4)   To define a word, then, the dictionary-editor places before him the stack of cards illustrating that word; each of the cards represents an actual use of the word by a writer of some literary or historical importance. He reads the cards carefully, discards some, rereads the rest, and divides up the stack according to what he thinks are the several senses of the word. Finally, he writes his definitions, following the hard-and-fast rule that each definition *must* be based on what the quotations in front of him reveal about the meaning of the word. The editor cannot be influenced by what *he* thinks a given word *ought* to mean. He must work according to the cards or not at all.

(5)   The writing of a dictionary, therefore, is not a task of setting up authoritative statements about the "true meanings" of words, but a task of *recording,* to the best of one's ability, what various words *have meant* to authors in the distant or immediate past. *The writer of a dictionary is a historian, not a lawgiver.* If, for example, we had been writing a dictionary in 1890, or even as late as 1919, we could have said that the word "broadcast" means "to scatter" (seed, for example), but we could not have decreed that from 1921 on, the most common meaning of the word should become "to disseminate audible messages, etc., by radio transmission." To regard the dictionary as an "authority," therefore, is to credit the dictionary-writer with gifts of prophecy which neither he nor anyone else possesses. In choosing our words

when we speak or write, we can be *guided* by the historical record afforded us by the dictionary, but we cannot be *bound* by it, because new situations, new experiences, new inventions, new feelings are always compelling us to give new uses to old words. Looking under a "hood," we should ordinarily have found, five hundred years ago, a monk; today, we find a motorcar engine.

Study Questions

1. The thesis of "How Dictionaries Are Made" (the statement of what the essay is about) appears in paragraph 2. What is the thesis?

2. Paragraph 1 explains what many people believe about dictionaries. What is this commonly held belief?

3. The final paragraph explains that the commonly held belief is untrue. What does this last paragraph say *is* true about the nature of dictionaries?

4. What is the purpose of the story in paragraph 1?

5. What methods of development are used in paragraph 1? In paragraphs 2, 3, and 4? In paragraph 5?

6. What purpose do the examples serve in paragraphs 2 and 5?

7. What do you judge to be Hayakawa's purpose for writing "How Dictionaries Are Made"? Who do you think was his intended audience?

Writing Assignments

The following assignments rely on process analysis. See p. 99 for information on this method of development.

1. In a paragraph, use process analysis to explain how to spend a relaxing Sunday afternoon.

2. In a paragraph, use process analysis to explain how to postpone studying until the last minute. Your purpose is to entertain.

3. In a paragraph, use process analysis to explain how to look up a word in the dictionary. Your purpose is to convince your instructor that you know how to perform this task.

4. In an essay of 4–5 paragraphs, use process analysis to explain how to register for courses at your university. Your purpose is to inform a freshman new to your campus.

5. In an essay of 4–5 paragraphs, use process analysis to explain how to flunk a test. Your purpose is to entertain.

6. In an essay of 4–5 paragraphs, use process analysis to explain how to do something you do well (bake bread, interview for a job, serve a tennis ball, baby-sit, plan a party, etc.). Your purpose is to help a reader perform the task as well as you do.

Cinematypes

Susan Allen Toth

Can movie dates be classified according to the movies they prefer and the behavior they exhibit? English professor Susan Allen Toth does so in "Cinematypes," an amusing essay that also makes a statement about relationships.

You will notice that the essay lacks a traditional introduction and stated thesis. Instead, the author launches immediately into her classification. As you read, decide how you feel about this approach. Also, you will notice a number of references to movies and actors that may not be familiar to you. Do these references interfere with your appreciation of the essay?

Before reading, review the following vocabulary.

reputable—respected

cinematography—movie photography

military-industrial complex—a nation's armed services together with the industries that supply them

propaganda—material, often slanted, that promotes a cause

beating a tattoo—tapping rhythmically

peccadilloes—slight offenses

convivial—friendly

Aaron takes me only to art films. That's what I call them, anyway: (1) strange movies with vague poetic images I don't always understand, long dreamy movies about a distant Technicolor past, even longer black-and-white movies about the general meaninglessness of life. We do not go unless at least one reputable critic has found the cinematography superb. We went to *The Devil's Eye,* and Aaron turned to me in the middle and said, "My God, this is *funny.*" I do not think he was pleased.

When Aaron and I go to the movies, we drive our cars separately and (2) meet at the box office. Inside the theater he sits tentatively in his seat, ready to move if he can't see well, poised to leave if the film is disappointing. He leans away from me, careful not to touch the bare flesh of his arm against the bare flesh of mine. Sometimes he leans so far I am afraid he may be touching the woman on his other side. If the movie is very good, he leans forward, too, peering between the heads of the couple in front of us. The light from the screen bounces off his glasses; he gleams with intensity, sitting there on the edge of his seat, watching the screen. Once I tapped him on the arm so I could whisper a comment in his ear. He jumped.

(3)   After *Belle de Jour* Aaron said he wanted to ask me if he could stay overnight. "But I can't," he shook his head mournfully before I had a chance to answer, "because I know I never sleep well in strange beds." Then he apologized for asking. "It's just that after a film like that," he said, "I feel the need to assert myself."

(4)   Pete takes me only to movies that he thinks have redeeming social value. He doesn't call them "films." They tend to be about poverty, war, injustice, political corruption, struggling unions in the 1930s, and the military-industrial complex. Pete doesn't like propaganda movies, though, and he doesn't like to be too depressed, either. We stayed away from *The Sorrow and the Pity;* it would be, he said, just too much. Besides, he assured me, things are never that hopeless. So most of the movies we see are made in Hollywood. Because they are always topical, these movies offer what Pete calls "food for thought." When we saw *Coming Home,* Pete's jaw set so firmly within the first half-hour that I knew we would end up at Poppin' Fresh Pies afterward.

(5)   When Pete and I go to the movies, we take turns driving so no one owes anyone else anything. We leave the car far from the theater so we don't have to pay for a parking space. If it's raining or snowing, Pete offers to let me off at the door, but I can tell he'll feel better if I go with him while he finds a spot, so we share the walk too. Inside the theater Pete will hold my hand when I get scared if I ask him. He puts my hand firmly on his knee and covers it completely with his own hand. His knee never twitches. After a while, when the scary part is past, he loosens his hand slightly and I know that is a signal to take mine away. He sits companionably close, letting his jacket just touch my sweater, but he does not infringe. He thinks I ought to know he is there if I need him.

(6)   One night, after *The China Syndrome,* I asked Pete if he wouldn't like to stay for a second drink, even though it was past midnight. He thought a while about that, considering my offer from all possible angles, but finally he said no. Relationships today, he said, have a tendency to move too quickly.

(7)   Sam likes movies that are entertaining. By that he means movies that Will Jones in the *Minneapolis Tribune* loved and either *Time* or *Newsweek* rather liked; also movies that do not have sappy love stories, are not musicals, do not have subtitles, and will not force him to

think. He does not go to movies to think. He liked *California Suite* and *The Seduction of Joe Tynan,* though the plots, he said, could have been zippier. He saw it all coming too far in advance, and that took the fun out. He doesn't like to know what is going to happen. "I just want my brain to be tickled," he says. It is very hard for me to pick out movies for Sam.

When Sam takes me to the movies, he pays for everything. He thinks   (8) that's what a man ought to do. But I buy my own popcorn, because he doesn't approve of it; the grease might smear his flannel slacks. Inside the theater, Sam makes himself comfortable. He takes off his jacket, puts one arm around me, and all during the movie he plays with my hand, stroking my palm, beating a small tattoo on my wrist. Although he watches the movie intently, his body operates on instinct. Once I inclined my head and kissed him lightly just behind his ear. He beat a faster tattoo on my wrist, quick and musical, but he didn't look away from the screen.

When Sam takes me home from the movies, he stands outside my   (9) door and kisses me long and hard. He would like to come in, he says regretfully, but his steady girlfriend in Duluth wouldn't like it. When the *Tribune* gives a movie four stars, he has to save it to see with her. Otherwise her feelings might be hurt.

I go to some movies by myself. On rainy Sunday afternoons I often   (10) sneak into a revival house or a college auditorium for old Technicolor musicals, *Kiss Me Kate, Seven Brides for Seven Brothers, Calamity Jane,* even, once *The Sound of Music.* Wearing saggy jeans so I can prop my feet on the seat in front, I sit toward the rear where no one can see me. I eat large handfuls of popcorn with double butter. Once the movie starts, I feel completely at home. Howard Keel and I are old friends; I grin back at him on the screen. I know the sound tracks by heart. Sometimes when I get really carried away I hum along with Kathryn Grayson, remembering how I once thought I would fill out a formal like that. I am rather glad now I never did. Skirts whirl, feet tap, acrobatic young men perform impossible feats, and then the camera dissolves into a dream sequence I know I can comfortably follow. It is not, thank God, Bergman.

If I can't find an old musical, I settle for Hepburn and Tracy, vintage   (11) Grant or Gable, on adventurous days Claudette Colbert or James Stewart. Before I buy my ticket I make sure it will all end happily. If necessary, I ask the girl at the box office. I have never seen *Stella Dallas* or *Intermezzo.* Over the years I have developed other peccadilloes: I will, for example, see anything that is redeemed by Thelma Ritter. At the end of *Daddy Long Legs* I wait happily for the scene when Fred Clark, no longer angry, at last pours Thelma a convivial drink. They smile at each other, I smile at them, I feel they are smiling at me. In the movies I go to by myself, the men and women always like each other.

Study Questions

1. What is Toth classifying? According to what behavior does she group the elements in her classification?

2. "Cinematypes" lacks an introduction designed to stimulate the reader's interest and present the thesis. Instead, it begins right off with the classification. Do you think the essay would be improved if an introduction were added? Explain.

3. The thesis of the essay is implied rather than stated. In your own words, write out the thesis.

4. Toth uses topic sentences to introduce each category in her classification. What are those topic sentences?

5. In the first nine paragraphs, Toth's sentences are short, with little vivid descriptive language. After that, she uses more descriptive, flowing sentences. How do you explain this shift in style? What does the shift reveal about Toth's attitude?

6. How does Toth use examples in the essay?

7. Does Toth prefer going to the movies alone or with a date? Why does she have this preference?

Writing Assignments

1. In a paragraph, evaluate the relationship between Toth and her dates. Do they like each other? How can you tell?

2. In a paragraph, explain what your favorite type of movie is (musicals, westerns, horror films, romance movies, mysteries, and so forth). Be sure to explain why you like this type of movie.

3. In a paragraph, write a review of a television program you particularly like or dislike. Be sure to give specific reasons for your view.

4. Consider the movies you have watched on television and in theaters over the past year. In an essay of 4–5 paragraphs, describe these movies and explain what your choices reveal about your personality and interests. For example, a preference for science fiction movies may reveal a very active imagination.

5. Consider the dates you have had over the years and in an essay of 4–5 paragraphs, classify them according to some specific behavior, preference, or activity (preferred restaurants, telephone behavior, willingness to spend money, and so forth).

6. Moves are an immensely popular form of entertainment. People watch them often on television, on VCRs, and in theaters.

In an essay of 4–5 paragraphs, explain why people are so fascinated with movies.

WRITING A SUMMARY

A *summary* is a restatement—*in your own words*—of an author's main ideas. When you summarize, you record an author's major points and major supporting details using your own wording and style.

Students must often summarize readings or chapters in textbooks. This is one way an instructor can check whether you understand reading assignments. In addition, when you write research papers, you may have to include summarized material.

The Characteristics of a Summary

To write a successful summary keep the following points in mind:

1. *Include only the author's main points and major supporting details.* Do not include minor details, examples, or explanation unless these are necessary to clarify a main point.

2. *Include only the author's ideas.* You may be tempted to comment on something the author has said, but you must resist because a summary should not contain anything that is not in the original.

3. *Keep the summary shorter than the original.* Because you are including only the main ideas, your summary is bound to be shorter than the original. As a general guideline, a summary runs about one-third the length of the original.

4. *Preserve the author's meaning.* Do not alter the author's meaning in any way.

original:	Some states still have not enacted legislation mandating barrier-free structures.
unacceptable restatement:	There are no laws requiring barrier-free buildings in many states.
explanation:	*Many* in the restatement changes the meaning of the original because the author said *some*.
acceptable restatement:	There are no laws requiring barrier-free buildings in a number of states.
explanation:	Use of *a number of* does not alter the author's meaning.

original:	Unless states raise the drinking age to 21, they will lose their federal highway funds.
unacceptable restatement:	States are being pressured to make 21 the legal age to drink.
explanation:	The restatement alters meaning by omitting important information: the fact that states that do not raise the drinking age will lose federal highway funds.
acceptable restatement:	States that do not make 21 the legal drinking age face the loss of federal highway funds.
explanation:	All the important information is in the restatement.

5. *Use your own wording and sentence style.* You must preserve the author's meaning, but you should restate the author's ideas in your own way. Here is an example:

| original: | The trouble with Little League is that the coaches have emphasized winning at the expense of skill acquisition and having fun. |
| restatement: | Little League coaches stress winning rather than enjoyment and learning, which creates problems. |

When you summarize, do not merely substitute synonyms (words with similar meaning) for the original words. Substituting synonyms is *not* restating in your own style because sentence structure is not altered.

| original: | The trouble with Little League is that the coaches have emphasized winning at the expense of skill acquisition and having fun. |
| unacceptable restatement: | The problem (synonym) with Little League is that the managers (synonym) have stressed (synonym) beating the opponent (synonym) at the cost of (synonym) acquiring skills (synonym) and having a good time (synonym). |

explanation:	The preceding restatement is un-acceptable because sentence structure has not been changed. Instead, synonyms have been sub-stituted for words in the original.

6. *You may use the author's words when there is no acceptable substitute, or when you particularly like the author's phrasing.* In the Little League example, a restatement may use the words *Little League* because no other words will do. However, if you use original words that are not part of your normal vocabulary or that are part of the author's distinctive phrasing, use quotation marks around the words. Here is an example:

original:	The trouble with Little League is that the coaches have empha-sized winning at the expense of skill acquisition and having fun.
restatement:	*Little League coaches* (no quota-tion marks because there is no substitute and the words are part of my vocabulary) stress *winning* (no quotation marks because there is no substitute and the word is part of my vocabulary) but do not stress "*skill acquisi-tion*" (quotation marks because the words are part of the author's distinctive phrasing) and the en-joyment of the game.

Use quotations when necessary, but do not overuse them. Most of the summary should be in your own words.

7. *The opening sentence of a summary should include the au-thor's name, the title of the material being summarized, and the author's focus, purpose, and/or thesis.* Here are sample openings for summaries of the essays beginning on pages 441, 437, 446, and 459.

   A. In "On Being 17, Bright, and Unable to Read," David Raymond narrates an account of the difficulties he faced in school because of his dyslexia. (author's focus presented)

   B. In "The Trouble with Television," Robert MacNeil asserts that television "discourages concentration." (author's thesis presented)

C. Gary Soto's "Expecting Friends" is a warm tribute to friendship and the joys of anticipating a visit from old friends. (author's focus presented)

D. S. I. Hayakawa explains the process of dictionary making in "How Dictionaries Are Made" to show that the function of dictionaries is not what many people believe it to be. (author's purpose and thesis presented)

Notice that in each of the examples the verb that functions with the author's name is in the present tense. Even though the work was written in the past, use the present tense:

Raymond *narrates* . . .

Robert MacNeil *asserts* . . .

Gary Soto's "Expecting Friends" *is* . . .

Hayakawa *explains* . . .

8. *To achieve transition, repeat the author's name with a present tense verb.* Use phrases like these:

MacNeil also explains . . .

Soto continues by describing . . .

Hayakawa goes on to show . . .

A Sample Summary

The essay that follows, "If You Had to Kill Your Own Hog," was written by Dick Gregory. The main ideas and important supporting details have been underlined to mark them for inclusion in the summary that follows.

Read through the essay, paying particular attention to the underlined material. Then read the summary that follows the essay. Notes in the margin of the summary call your attention to important features.

If You Had to Kill Your Own Hog

Dick Gregory

My momma could never understand how white folks could twist the (1) words of the Bible around to justify racial segregation. Yet she could read the Ten Commandments, which clearly say, "Thou shalt not kill," and still justify eating meat. Momma couldn't read the newspaper very well, but she sure could interpret the Word of God. "God meant you shouldn't kill people," she used to say. But I insisted, "Momma, He didn't say that. He said, 'Thou shalt not kill.' If you leave that statement alone, a whole lot of things would be safe from killing. But if you are going to twist the words about killing to mean what you want them to mean, then let white folks do the same thing with justifying racial segregation."

"You can't live without eating meat," Momma would persist. "You'd (2) starve." I couldn't buy that either. You get milk from a cow without killing it. You do not have to kill an animal to get what you need from it. You get wool from the sheep without killing it. Two of the strongest animals in the jungle are vegetarians—the elephant and the gorilla. The first two years are the most important years of a man's life, and during that period he is not involved with eating meat. If you suddenly become very ill, there is a good chance you will be taken off a meat diet. So it is a myth that killing is necessary for survival. The day I decide that I must have a piece of steak to nourish my body, I will also give the cow the same right to nourish herself on human beings.

There is so little basic difference between animals and humans. The (3) process of reproduction is the same for chickens, cattle, and humans. If suddenly the air stopped circulating on the earth, or the sun collided with the earth, animals and humans would die alike. A nuclear holocaust will wipe out all life. Life in the created order is basically the same and should be respected as such. It seems to me the Bible says it is wrong to kill—period.

If we can justify *any* kind of killing in the name of religion, the door (4) is opened for all kinds of other justifications. The fact of killing animals

Source: From *The Shadow that Scares Me,* by Dick Gregory. Copyright © 1968 by Dick Gregory. Used by permission of Doubleday, a division of Bantam Doubleday Dell Publishing Group, Inc.

(5)

is not as frightening as our human tendency to justify it—to kill and not even be aware that we are taking life. It is sobering to realize that when you misuse one of the least of Nature's creatures, like the chicken, you are sowing the seed for misusing the highest of Nature's creatures, man.

Animals and humans suffer and die alike. If you had to kill your own hog before you ate it, most likely you would not be able to do it. To hear the hog scream, to see the blood spill, to see the baby being taken away from its momma, and to see the look of death in the animal's eye would turn your stomach. So you get the man at the packing house to do the killing for you. In like manner, if the wealthy aristocrats who are perpetrating conditions in the ghetto actually heard the screams of ghetto suffering, or saw the slow death of hungry little kids, or witnessed the strangulation of manhood and dignity, they could not continue the killing. But the wealthy are protected from such horror. They have people to do the killing for them. The wealthy profit from the daily murders of ghetto life but they do not see them. Those who immerse themselves in the daily life of the ghetto see the suffering—the social workers, the police, the local merchants, and the bill collectors. But the people on top never really see.

(6)

By the time you see a piece of meat in the butcher shop window, all the blood and suffering have been washed away. When you order a steak in the restaurant, the misery has been forgotten and you see the finished product. You see a steak with butter and parsley on it. It looks appetizing and appealing and you are pleased enough to eat it. You never even consider the suffering which produced your meal or the other animals killed that day in the slaughterhouse. In the same way, all the wealthy aristocrats ever see of the black community is the finished product, the window dressing, the steak on the platter—Ralph Bunche and Thurgood Marshall. The United Nations or the Supreme Court bench is the restaurant and the ghetto street corner is the slaughterhouse.

(7)

Life under ghetto conditions cuts short life expectancy. The Negro's life expectancy is shorter than the white man's. The oppressor benefits from continued oppression financially; he makes more money so that he can eat a little better. I see no difference between a man killing a chicken and a man killing a human being, by overwork and forcing ghetto conditions upon him, both so that he can eat a little better. If you can justify killing to eat meat, you can justify the conditions of the ghetto. I cannot justify either one.

(8)

Every time the white folks made my momma mad, she would grab the Bible and find something bitter in it. She would come home from the rich white folks' house, after they had just called her "nigger," or patted her on the rump or caught her stealing some steaks, open her Bible and read aloud, "It is easier for a camel to pass through the eye of a needle than for a rich man to get into Heaven." When you get involved with distorting the words of the Bible, you don't have to be bitter. The same tongue can be used to bless and curse men.

Summary of "If You Had to Kill Your Own Hog"

[1]In "If You Had to Kill Your Own Hog," Dick Gregory argues that the continued practice of eating meat is like the continued practice of segregation. He makes this point by showing a contradiction in the way his mother viewed the Bible. [2]Gregory says that his mother could not understand how whites could use the Bible [3]"to justify racial segregation," but she herself failed to see that the commandment "Thou shalt not kill" prohibits the killing of animals for food.

[4]Gregory explains that his mother believed that people needed meat to live. [5]Gregory counters this argument, however, by noting that it is untrue. Further, he contends that all life is to be [6]respected, and, thus, killing animals is wrong. In fact, taking animal life is [7]"sowing the seed for misusing the highest of Nature's creatures, man."

[8]Gregory believes that if people had to kill the animals they ate, they would not eat animals. [9]The fact that people do not watch the suffering allows it to continue—just as ghetto conditions persist because the wealthy do not witness the suffering there. [10]Gregory extends the comparison between the suffering of animals and the suffering of blacks in the ghetto when he says, [11]"If you can justify killing to eat meat, you can justify the conditions of the ghetto. . . ." [12]Gregory finds them both wrong.

[1]Opening sentence includes author, title, and thesis. Notice the present tense of the verb *argues*.

[2]Author's name repeated for transition. Note the present tense verb. Restatement of first main point.

[3]Quotation marks because phrase is the author's distinctive style.

[4-5]Author's name repeated for transition. Note the present tense verbs. Restatement of main points.

[6]No quotation marks around *respected* because not part of author's distinctive style.

[7]Quotation marks around exact words.

[8]Author's name repeated for transition. Verb in present tense. Restatement of main point.

[9]Restatement of main point.

[10]Author's name repeated for transition. Verb is in present tense. Restatement of main point.

[11]Exact words in quotation marks.

[12]Final point restated.

How to Write a Summary

Step 1.

Read the material as many times as necessary to understand everything the author says. Look up any words you do not understand.

Step 2.

Underline the thesis, topic sentences, and main points. Underline *only* those supporting details necessary for clarifying main points. If a main point is clear enough, do not underline supporting details.

Step 3.

On a separate sheet, write the underlined ideas in your own words, being careful not to change meaning in any way. Avoid substituting synonyms for every key word. Keep a dictionary nearby to look up alternatives for words you are having trouble with. A good way to restate an underlined idea in your words is to read the idea until you are sure you understand it. Then look away from your book, imagine how you would explain that idea to a friend in your own words, and write the idea the same way you would explain it to your friend. If you cannot satisfactorily restate something in your own words, use the author's words in quotation marks. However, use the author's words sparingly. Most of the summary should be your own restatement.

Step 4.

Write a first draft, opening with a sentence that includes the author, title, and the author's thesis, focus, or purpose. Use a present tense verb with the author's name. Then go to your list of restatements and write these in the same order the ideas appear in the original.

Step 5.

Read your summary out loud. If you hear an awkward gap, add a transition and/or repeat the author's name with a present tense verb. If an idea is not clear, add a restatement of a clarifying detail.

Step 6.

Review the summary to be sure you can answer yes to these questions:

Did you open with the author, title, and thesis, focus, or purpose?

Did you include only main points and major supporting details?

Did you alter the author's sentence structure and wording?

Did you preserve the author's meaning?

Have you used quotation marks around words that are part of the author's special phrasing?

Have you avoided adding meaning not in the original?

Is the summary significantly shorter than the original?

Did you avoid substituting synonyms?

Step 7.

Edit your summary carefully for mistakes.

Three Essays to Summarize

Summarizing the three essays that follow (or summarizing the ones your instructor assigns) will give you practice.

What Mothers Teach Their Daughters

Ellen Goodman

Ellen Goodman is a Pulitzer Prize winning author who has written a syndicated column for the Boston Globe *since 1972. In "What Mothers Teach Their Daughters," she explains what she calls "the politics of housekeeping"—the way household chores are assigned in American culture. The essay was first written in 1982. As you read, consider how much of it is still true today. First, however, review the following vocabulary.*

maternalistic—like a mother	*wrenchingly—with a painful strain*
eternal—endless; enduring	*legacy—inheritance*
inane—senseless	*excoriate—to denounce or attack severely*

(1)   The TV ad is cheerfully maternalistic, a mother and daughter special. In a mere 60 seconds, we see the passing of eternal wisdom from one generation of women to the next. It begins as we discover that the girl has bought—gasp!—a bargain bleach. This turns out to be more a cause for pity than for censure. Mother, who knows best about washing, explains gently that a bargain is not always a bargain, especially when it is being used on a favorite blouse. By the end of the commercial, the girl has become wise in the ways of brand-name bleaches and we have become wise in the ways we really live in our changing families.

(2)   The commercial is no more inane than any other, but there is a new character in the advertising soap opera: the commercial geared to the teen-age girl as family shopper. The advertising people are hip to something. As more and more mothers go to work, we are looking for more and more help at home . . . from our daughters.

For all of our talk about training kids differently, of raising a whole   (3)
new generation of men and women who will share their adult lives easily instead of wrenchingly, we haven't changed the realities of young
life very much at all. In this laundry-room scene, there is neither father
nor brother. Mother and daughter share the laundry and the shopping.
It is still women's work . . . and girl's work . . . and you don't have to
be a social scientist to know how close this advertising fiction is to fact.

I see it every day on the streets where teen-age girls are in charge   (4)
of their brothers and sisters, while teen-age boys are involved in sports
or "real" jobs. I see it in homes where girls are more likely to carry the
weight of the housekeeping chores than their brothers. I see it even
in people who have easy expectations of help from their daughters and
self-conscious requests of help from their sons.

Of course, all families are not alike in this. There are differences among   (5)
homes that have boys, girls, or both. Differences among homes with two
parents or one, fathers who share and fathers who don't. Differences
among homes where parents and children are conscious or unconscious
of the politics of housekeeping. But the majority of women in this country still carry the double burden—doing half the work outside the home
and three-quarters of the work inside it. The majority of men still resist
household tasks—adding one hour a week of this home work over a
decade. Willy-nilly, they both pass on the legacy to their children.

It is always more difficult to change the next generation, without   (6)
changing our own. We all seem to end up caught at times in the assorted traps of the evolving family, especially on the issue of husbands
and wives, daughters and sons and housekeeping.

One mother I talk with describes her choices. She can fight with her   (7)
husband over housework in front of the children. Or do it herself . . .
in front of the children. She worries about either message. Another
tries to teach her son what she calls "survival skills," only to hear him
lovingly reply: "I won't need them, Mommy, I'm going to marry someone just like you." A third struggles to assign work equally between her
children. Too often her sons asks, "Why should I do that? Daddy
doesn't." If he refuses, her daughter also rebels, "Why should I do anything my brother doesn't have to do?"

Teen-agers target hypocrisy like sharp shooters. In our own families we   (8)
hold up a bulls-eye, that huge space between what we say and how we
behave. When we excoriate smoking, they point to our cigarettes. And
when we uphold equality they point to our own less-than-equal lives. In
the end, a host of working mothers describe feeling stuck in their daily lives
between carrying a heavy burden or sloughing off more of it . . . to their
daughters. A host of daughters feel caught: between taking on a load that
isn't fairly shared with brothers or fathers, or leaving it on their mothers.

And in that scenario, a great deal more is passed down from mother   (9)
to daughter than the brand name of a bleach.

Abortion, Right and Wrong

Rachel Richardson Smith

Abortion is a hotly debated issue, and emotions run high on both sides. The issue is complex in its own right, but it is made even more so by the fact that it has legal, moral, religious, social, and political aspects. Despite its complexity, though, people usually argue the issue in black and white terms: they are either for it or against it. Rachel Richardson Smith, however, sees the gray areas of the issue. As the following essay reveals, she sees right and wrong on both sides.

Before reading, review the following vocabulary.

contraceptives—forms of birth control

alienated—indifferent or hostile

articulate—capable of speaking well

absolutes—certainties

languishing—lingering in distress

flagrant—glaring

fundamentalist—the belief that the Bible is without any errors

vigilant—watchful

sanctity—holiness

ambivalence—uncertainty

(1)   I cannot bring myself to say I am in favor of abortion. I don't want anyone to have one. I want people to use contraceptives and for those contraceptives to be foolproof. I want people to be responsible for their actions; mature in their decisions. I want children to be loved, wanted, well cared for.

(2)   I cannot bring myself to say I am against choice. I want women who are young, poor, single or all three to be able to direct the course of their lives. I want women who have had all the children they want or can afford or their bodies can withstand to be able to decide their future. I want women who are in bad marriages or destructive relationships to avoid being trapped by pregnancy.

(3)   So in these days when thousands rally in opposition to legalized abortion, when facilities providing abortions are bombed, when the

Source: Reprinted by permission of the author, Rachel Richardson Smith.

president speaks glowingly of the growing momentum behind the anti-abortion movement, I find myself increasingly alienated from the pro-life groups.

At the same time, I am overwhelmed with mail from pro-choice (4) groups. They, too, are mobilizing their forces, growing articulate in support of their cause, and they want my support. I am not sure I can give it.

I find myself in the awkward position of being both anti-abortion and (5) pro-choice. Neither group seems to be completely right—or wrong. It is not that I think abortion is wrong for me but acceptable for someone else. The question is far more complex than that.

Part of my problem is that what I think and how I feel about this is- (6) sue are two entirely different matters. I know that unwanted children are often neglected, even abandoned. I know that many of those seeking abortions are children themselves. I know that making abortion illegal will not stop all women from having them.

Absolutes

I also know from experience the crisis an unplanned pregnancy can (7) cause. Yet I have felt the joy of giving birth, the delight that comes from feeling a baby's skin against my own. I know how hard it is to parent a child and how deeply satisfying it can be. My children sometimes provoke me and cause me endless frustration, but I can still look at them with tenderness and wonder at the miracle of it all. The lessons of my own experience produce conflicting emotions. Theory collides with reality.

It concerns me that both groups present themselves in absolutes. (8) They are committed and they want me to commit. They do not recognize the gray area where I seem to be languishing. Each group has the right answer—the only answer.

Yet I am uncomfortable in either camp. I have nothing in common (9) with the pro-lifers. I am horrified by their scare tactics, their pictures of well-formed fetuses tossed in a metal pan, their cruel slogans. I cannot condone their flagrant misuse of Scripture and unforgiving spirit. There is a meanness about their position that causes them to pass judgment on the lives of women in a way I could never do.

The pro-life groups, with their fundamentalist religious attitudes, (10) have a fear and an abhorrence of sex, especially premarital sex. In their view abortion only compounds the sexual sin. What I find incomprehensible is that even as they are opposed to abortion they are also opposed to alternative solutions. They are squeamish about sex education in the schools. They don't want teens to have contraceptives without parental consent. They offer little aid or sympathy to unwed mothers. They are the vigilant guardians of a narrow morality.

I wonder how abortion got to be the greatest of all sins? What about (11) poverty, ignorance, hunger, weaponry?

(12)   The only thing the anti-abortion groups seem to have right is that abortion is indeed the taking of human life. I simply cannot escape this one glaring fact. Call it what you will—fertilized egg, embryo, fetus. What we have here is human life. If it were just a mass of tissue there would be no debate. So I agree that abortion ends a life. But the anti-abortionists are wrong to call it murder.

(13)   The sad truth is that homicide is not always against the law. Our society does not categorically recognize the sanctity of human life. There are a number of legal and apparently socially acceptable ways to take human life. "Justifiable" homicide includes the death penalty, war, killing in self-defense. It seems to me that as a society we need to come to grips with our own ambiguity concerning the value of human life. If we are to value and protect unborn life so stringently, why do we not also value and protect life already born?

Mistakes

(14)   Why can't we see abortion for the human tragedy it is? No woman plans for her life to turn out that way. Even the most effective contraceptives are no guarantee against pregnancy. Loneliness, ignorance, immaturity can lead to decisions (or lack of decisions) that may result in untimely pregnancy. People make mistakes.

(15)   What many people seem to misunderstand is that no woman wants to have an abortion. Circumstances demand it; women do it. No woman reacts to abortion with joy. Relief, yes. But also ambivalence, grief, despair, guilt.

(16)   The pro-choice groups do not seem to acknowledge that abortion is not a perfect answer. What goes unsaid is that when a woman has an abortion she loses more than an unwanted pregnancy. Often she loses her self-respect. No woman can forget a pregnancy no matter how it ends.

(17)   Why can we not view abortion as one of those anguished decisions in which human beings struggle to do the best they can in trying circumstances? Why is abortion viewed so coldly and factually on the one hand and so judgmentally on the other? Why is it not akin to the same painful experience families must sometimes make to allow a loved one to die?

(18)   I wonder how we can begin to change the context in which we think about abortion. How can we begin to think about it redemptively? What is it in the trauma of loss of life—be it loved or unloved, born or unborn—from which we can learn? There is much I have yet to resolve. Even as I refuse to pass judgment on other women's lives, I weep for the children who might have been. I suspect I am not alone.

Black Men and Public Space

Brent Staples

Brent Staples has been a reporter for the Chicago Sun-Times *and an editor with the* New York Times Book Review *and the* Times *Metropolitan section. In addition, he has written a number of magazine articles. In "Black Men and Public Space," Staples describes a problem he often faces: because people perceive him as dangerous, he, himself, is at risk.*

The essay has a number of words that may be unfamiliar to you, so review the following vocabulary before you read.

affluent—wealthy

impoverished—poor

discreet—cautious

menacingly—threateningly

quarry—hunted animal

foyer—entrance way

errant—wrong

taut—tense

warrenlike—crowded

bandolier—belt that holds bullets, worn across the chest

perpetrators—people who cause something

lethality—deadliness

bravado—pretended courage

perilous—dangerous

ad hoc—formed for a specific purpose

labyrinthine—like a maze

constitutionals—walks

My first victim was a woman—white, well dressed, probably in her early (1) twenties. I came upon her late one evening on a deserted street in Hyde Park, a relatively affluent neighborhood in an otherwise mean, impoverished section of Chicago. As I swung onto the avenue behind her, there seemed to be a discreet, uninflammatory distance between us. Not so. She cast back a worried glance. To her, the youngish black man—a broad six feet two inches with a beard and billowing hair, both hands shoved into the pockets of a bulky military jacket—seemed menacingly close. After a few more quick glimpses, she picked up her pace and was soon running in earnest. Within seconds she disappeared into a cross street.

Source: Brent Staples. Brent Staples writes editorials for the *New York Times* and is the author of the memoir *Parallel Time: Growing Up in Black and White*.

(2)   That was more than a decade ago. I was twenty-two years old, a graduate student newly arrived at the University of Chicago. It was in the echo of that terrified woman's footfalls that I first began to know the unwieldy inheritance I'd come into—the ability to alter public space in ugly ways. It was clear that she thought herself the quarry of a mugger, a rapist, or worse. Suffering a bout of insomnia, however, I was stalking sleep, not defenseless wayfarers. As a softy who is scarcely able to take a knife to a raw chicken—let alone hold one to a person's throat—I was surprised, embarrassed, and dismayed all at once. Her flight made me feel like an accomplice in tyranny. It also made it clear that I was indistinguishable from the muggers who occasionally seeped into the area from the surrounding ghetto. That first encounter, and those that followed, signified that a vast, unnerving gulf lay between nighttime pedestrians—particularly women—and me. And I soon gathered that being perceived as dangerous is a hazard in itself. I only needed to turn a corner into a dicey situation, or crowd some frightened, armed person in a foyer somewhere, or make an errant move after being pulled over by a policeman. Where fear and weapons meet—and they often do in urban America—there is always the possibility of death.

(3)   In that first year, my first away from my hometown, I was to become thoroughly familiar with the language of fear. At dark, shadowy intersections, I could cross in front of a car stopped at a traffic light and elicit the *thunk, thunk, thunk, thunk* of the driver—black, white, male, or female—hammering down the door locks. On less traveled streets after dark, I grew accustomed to but never comfortable with people crossing to the other side of the street rather than pass me. Then there were the standard unpleasantries with policemen, doormen, bouncers, cab drivers, and others whose business it is to screen out troublesome individuals *before* there is any nastiness.

(4)   I moved to New York nearly two years ago and I have remained an avid night walker. In central Manhattan, the near-constant crowd cover minimizes tense one-on-one street encounters. Elsewhere—in SoHo, for example, where sidewalks are narrow and tightly spaced buildings shut out the sky—things can get very taut indeed.

(5)   After dark, on the warrenlike streets of Brooklyn where I live, I often see women who fear the worst from me. They seem to have set their faces on neutral, and with their purse straps strung across their chests bandolier-style, they forge ahead as though bracing themselves against being tackled. I understand, of course, that the danger they perceive is not a hallucination. Women are particularly vulnerable to street violence, and young black males are drastically overrepresented among the perpetrators of that violence. Yet these truths are no solace against the kind of alienation that comes of being ever the suspect, a fearsome entity with whom pedestrians avoid making eye contact.

It is not altogether clear to me how I reached the ripe old age of   (6)
twenty-two without being conscious of the lethality nighttime pedestrians attributed to me. Perhaps it was because in Chester, Pennsyl-
vania, the small, angry industrial town where I came of age in the
1960s, I was scarcely noticeable against a backdrop of gang warfare,
street knifings, and murders. I grew up one of the good boys, had perhaps a half-dozen fistfights. In retrospect, my shyness of combat has
clear sources.

As a boy, I saw countless tough guys locked away; I have since   (7)
buried several, too. They were babies, really—a teenage cousin, a
brother of twenty-two, a childhood friend in his mid-twenties—all gone
down in episodes of bravado played out in the streets. I came to doubt
the virtues of intimidation early on. I chose, perhaps unconsciously, to
remain a shadow—timid, but a survivor.

The fearsomeness mistakenly attributed to me in public places of-   (8)
ten has a perilous flavor. The most frightening of these confusions occurred in the late 1970s and early 1980s, when I worked as a journalist in Chicago. One day, rushing into the office of a magazine I was
writing for with a deadline story in hand, I was mistaken for a burglar.
The office manager called security and, with an ad hoc posse, pursued
me through the labyrinthine halls, nearly to my editor's door. I had no
way of proving who I was. I could only move briskly toward the company of someone who knew me.

Another time I was on assignment for a local paper and killing time   (9)
before an interview. I entered a jewelry store on the city's affluent Near
North Side. The proprietor excused herself and returned with an enormous red Doberman pinscher straining at the end of a leash. She stood,
the dog extended toward me, silent to my questions, her eyes bulging
nearly out of her head. I took a cursory look around, nodded, and bade
her good night.

Relatively speaking, however, I never fared as badly as another black   (10)
male journalist. He went to nearby Waukegan, Illinois, a couple of summers ago to work on a story about a murderer who was born there.
Mistaking the reporter for the killer, police officers hauled him from
his car at gunpoint and but for his press credentials would probably
have tried to book him. Such episodes are not uncommon. Black men
trade tales like this all the time.

Over the years, I learned to smother the rage I felt at so often being   (11)
taken for a criminal. Not to do so would surely have led to madness. I
now take precautions to make myself less threatening. I move about
with care, particularly late in the evening. I give a wide berth to nervous people on subway platforms during the wee hours, particularly
when I have exchanged business clothes for jeans. If I happen to be
entering a building behind some people who appear skittish, I may
walk by, letting them clear the lobby before I return, so as not to seem

to be following them. I have been calm and extremely congenial on those rare occasions when I've been pulled over by the police.

(12)   And on late-evening constitutionals I employ what has proved to be an excellent tension-reducing measure: I whistle melodies from Beethoven and Vivaldi and the more popular classical composers. Even merely New Yorkers hunching toward nighttime destinations seem to relax, and occasionally they even join in the tune. Virtually everybody seems to sense that a mugger wouldn't be warbling bright, sunny selections from Vivaldi's *Four Seasons.* It is my equivalent of the cowbell that hikers wear when they know they are in bear country.

WRITING ESSAY EXAMINATION ANSWERS

Essay examinations require you to respond to questions with answers that are paragraph length or longer. Because these examinations are an important part of a college student's life, you should learn to deal with them effectively.

How to Take an Essay Examination

Remembering information is not enough when you are taking an essay examination. You must also present that information in a clear, well-written answer. The following steps can help you.

Step 1

Read the directions before doing anything. The directions may tell you how many questions to answer and how long your answers should be, like this:

Answer three of the five questions. Each of your answers should be at least 150 words.

Step 2

Read all the questions before you begin. Part of your brain can work on question 2 while you are answering question 1 and so forth. Also, you may find clues to answers for later questions while you are working through the exam.

Step 3

Decide how to budget your time. If you must answer four questions in 60 minutes, then you know you can devote fifteen minutes to each answer. However, pay attention to how many points each question is worth. If you must answer 3 questions in 60 minutes and one question is worth 50 points and the other two are worth 25 points, you should spend 30 minutes on the 50-point question and 15 minutes on each 25-point question.

Step 4

Check the question for direction words. Words like these will direct the form your answer should take:

analyze—Break something down into its parts and discuss each part. Analyze the doctrine of manifest destiny.

classify—Group things according to their characteristics. Classify the most frequently occurring defense mechanisms.

compare—Technically, this means "show the similarities," but often *compare* is used to mean "show the similarities *and* differences." Compare the symbolism in the writings of Maxine Kumin and Margaret Atwood.

contrast—Show the differences. Contrast the foreign policies of Presidents George Bush and Bill Clinton.

define—Give the meaning of a term and include some information (often examples) to show you understand it. Define anomie.

describe—Give the significant features or tell how something works. Describe how plants convert carbon dioxide into oxygen.

discuss—Mention all the important points about a topic. Discuss the influences that led to the failure of the League of Nations.

evaluate—Give your view about the worth of something, being sure to support your opinions with detail. Evaluate competency testing as a way to ensure that students learn basic skills.

explain—Give the reasons for an occurrence. Explain the main causes of the Great Depression.

illustrate—Provide examples.

Illustrate the use of intermittent positive reinforcement to control behavior.

show—Explain or demonstrate something.

Show how hypnosis can improve the quality of daily life.

summarize—Briefly give the major points.

Summarize Jefferson's reasons for opposing the World Bank.

support—Give reasons in favor of something.

Support the plan to institute 12-month school years in grades kindergarten through twelve.

Step 5

Plan your answer. Jot down the points you will cover (on the back of or in the margin of your test sheet), and then number the points in the order you will write them. This planning will help you write a well-organized answer. Also, if you list your points, you need not worry about forgetting something in the heat of the moment. Organize simply—do not write introductions or conclusions; just give the information needed in the answer.

Step 6

Begin your answer with a sentence that reflects the question. For example, if the question is "Contrast the psychoanalytic views of Freud and Jung," you could begin with something like this: "The psychoanalytic views of Freud and Jung differ in several important ways."

Step 7

After writing your answer, revise and edit quickly. Pay special attention to clarity and completeness, but also look for serious mistakes in grammar and usage. Make changes directly on the original—you do not have time to recopy.

☐ TEST-TAKING TIPS ☐

1. *If you do not understand the directions or a question, ask the instructor.* You may not get help, but there is no harm in trying.

2. *Wear a watch* so you can keep track of the time and know when to move on to the next question.

3. *Leave generous margins and write on every other line* so you have ample space in case you must add something when you revise.

4. *Skip the questions you are unsure of and return to them after answering the ones you are more confident about.* In the course of answering other questions, you may think of the answers to a question you skipped.

5. *If you do not know, guess.* You may get partial credit.

6. *If you start to run out of time, list the points you would include if you had more time.* Although the answer is not in essay form, you still may get partial credit.

7. *Do not write more than you are asked for.* You will not get extra credit, and you are taking time away from answers that will give you credit.

8. *Never pad your answers with unrelated information to hide that you do not know the information requested.* Your instructor will recognize the stall.

Two Answers to Study

To understand the traits of an effective essay examination answer, study the two answers that follow. They were written in response to this question about Hayakawa's "How Dictionaries Are Made" (p. 459):

Describe how dictionaries are made.

The first answer is acceptable, but the second is not. Study the marginal notes that call your attention to the traits of each answer.

Acceptable Answer

The process of making a dictionary starts with the editors reading a tremendous volume of literature and recording on cards the words they encounter. Each card contains the word, the sentence the word appears in, and the work in which the sentence was found. That is, both the word and the context it appeared in are recorded. After each card is made, it is sorted and alphabetized. Each word can end up having hundreds of illustrative sentences, each on a separate card.

The answer opens with words that reflect the question.
Every sentence explains a step in the process.
No steps are left out.
No unrelated material

(padding) is included. Detail is arranged in a suitable order (in this case, chronological). There is no introduction or conclusion.

When it comes time to define a word, the editor studies the cards showing the various uses of the word and constructs definitions based on what the illustrations show to be the word's meanings. Editors cannot write what *they* think a word means. The cards are the sole basis of the definition.

Unacceptable Answer

The first two sentences stall; they contribute nothing, and they do not reflect the question. Sentence 3 provides information the question does not request. Sentence 4 responds to the question, but it is the only sentence that does. Thus, the response is incomplete. The last 2 sentences are padding.

Dictionaries are very important because we check them often and rely on them for spellings and definitions. Without dictionaries we would frequently be guessing about how to use and spell words, and the result would be chaos. Many people think dictionaries are authorities, but the truth is that dictionaries are just a record of the way people use words. Editors make dictionaries by collecting words and sentences they are used in, and then they present these usages in their definitions. People should understand this so they can use dictionaries properly. I know that now that I understand how dictionaries are made, I have a new respect for them.

Practice

Answering the following essay questions will give you valuable practice and help you become more skilled. In parentheses after each question is the essay the question is taken from.

1. Contrast what many people believe a dictionary is with what it *actually is*. ("How Dictionaries Are Made," p. 459).

2. What is Dick Gregory's view of eating meat? Explain why he believes as he does, and explain the connection between eating meat and segregation. ("If You Had to Kill Your Own Hog," p. 471)

3. Summarize Robert MacNeil's view of television and go on to agree or disagree with that view. ("The Trouble with Television," p. 437)

4. According to Ellen Goodman, teenage girls and their working mothers are caught in "that huge space between what we say and how we behave." Explain what this means and illustrate that meaning with examples from the essay and/or your own experience. ("What Mothers Teach Their Daughters," p. 476)

5. Rachel Richardson Smith is torn over the abortion issue because she sees right and wrong on both sides. Summarize what she sees as the chief elements of right and wrong in the pro-life pro-choice stands. ("Abortion, Right and Wrong," p. 478)

APPENDICES

APPENDIX

I

Personal Editing Profile

Careful editing is important because a reader loses confidence in a writer when errors in grammar, usage, spelling, capitalization, and punctuation appear. Thus, writers must be sensitive to the kinds of errors they make, so they can find and correct them. The Personal Editing Profile that follows will help you keep track of your mistakes so that when you edit you can look for your pattern of error.

Each time your instructor returns an evaluated writing, complete the profile by writing in the date and placing checkmarks in the column next to the errors your instructor marked. For example, if you made one error with sentence fragments, place one check in the sentence fragment column; if you made two errors in subject-verb agreement, place two checks in the subject-verb agreement column.

Each time you edit a draft, check your Personal Editing Profile. Edit one extra time, looking for the kinds of errors you have made in the past. Regular use of the Personal Editing Profile will make you aware of your errors so you can find and correct them.

If you notice certain errors keep occurring, study the pages given in parentheses. Learning to apply the rules will help you edit successfully.

Personal Editing Profile

Error and page reference	Symbol	Date	Date	Date	Date	Date	Date	Date	Date	Date	Date
sentence fragments (pp. 239–253)	frag										
run-on sentences (pp. 254–264)	R/O										
comma splices (pp. 254–264)	C/S										
double negatives (pp. 294–296)	d.n.										
spelling (pp. 296–304)	sp.										
verb forms (pp. 305–330)	vb										
subject-verb agreement (pp. 330–341)	S-V agr										
tense shifts (pp. 341–345)	T. shift										
pronoun-antecedent agreement (pp. 347–356)	P-Q agr										
pronoun reference (pp. 356–363)	ref										
subject & object pronouns (pp. 363–372)	pn										
person shift (pp. 372–376)	p. shift										
adjectives & adverbs (pp. 379–386)	adj/adb										
dangling modifiers (pp. 387–388)	d.m.										
misplaced modifiers (pp. 388–390)	m.m.										
capitalization (pp. 391–396)	cap										
end punctuation (pp. 397–400)	⊘/!/?										
commas (pp. 400–411)	∧										
semicolons (pp. 411–414)	;										
colons (pp. 414–418)	:										
parentheses (pp. 414–418)	( )										
dashes (pp. 414–418)	—										
apostrophes (pp. 418–426)	ᵛ										
quotation marks (pp. 426–430)	ᵛ⁄										

APPENDIX

‖

A Problem-Solving Guide

The following suggestions will not solve every writing problem, but when you are stuck, consult this guide. You may get the help you need.

Problem	Possible Solutions
1. "I don't know what to write."	A. Try listing, brainstorming, journal writing, clustering, or freewriting. If you have already tried one of these, try another.
	B. Go about your normal routine for a day, keeping your writing task in mind. Ideas may occur to you, and if they do, write them down so you do not forget them.
	C. Talk to people about your writing task. Their ideas will stimulate your thinking.

2. "I have some ideas, but I can't seem to get started."	A. Write your draft like a letter to a friend. You may feel more relaxed and able to write this way. B. Write your draft as if you were speaking to a friend. This may relax you enough to get started. C. Remind yourself that the first draft is supposed to be rough. You may be expecting too much too soon. D. Begin in the middle. If openings are hard, start with any idea you feel you can write; then go back to the beginning. E. Write your draft for yourself, not for another reader, so you are not blocked by thinking of a reader's criticisms. F. Do some additional brainstorming, clustering, listing, journal writing, or freewriting. You may not yet have enough ideas to begin.
3. "I don't like my draft."	A. Put the draft aside for a day. After some time away, you may feel better about the draft. B. Remember, a first draft is supposed to be rough, so do not look for polished material. Be accepting and look for raw material you can shape. C. Try to identify parts that can be salvaged. Ask someone else to read the draft and help identify what can be saved.

	D. If you decide to start over, do not despair. Many times a writer figures out what *not* to do before figuring what *to* do.
4. "I'm not sure what revisions to make."	A. Leave your draft for a day. When you return, you will be better able to decide what changes to make.
	B. Read your draft aloud to hear problems, or read your draft into a tape recorder and play back the tape.
	C. See p. 29 on using reader response to identify necessary changes.
	D. Study your draft in stages. First check for relevant detail; then check for adequate detail; next check your organization; finally, check your word choice. Breaking your evaluation into stages allows you to concentrate on the various aspects of your draft. As an alternative, evaluate your draft in stages by checking separately each item in the list of revision concerns on p. 28.
5. "I know what changes to make, but I'm having trouble making them."	A. Make the easier changes first and then go on to the harder ones. You will build momentum this way.
	B. See p. 29 on using reader response. Ask your reader for ways to make revisions.
	C. Take a break for a day to relax and then try again.
	D. Ask your instructor for advice.

6. "I need more detail."	A. Add examples for support. B. Tell a story to support a point. C. Try some additional idea generation. D. Check to see if your thesis or topic sentence is too narrow.
7. "My writing seems boring."	A. Circle all your general words and substitute specific ones to make your writing more lively. B. See p. 213 on sentence variety. C. Add specific examples and stories for vividness. D. Add description for vividness. E. Check your detail to be sure you are not stating the obvious. F. Revise clichés.
8. "My ideas do not seem related to each other."	A. Use transitions to show relationships between ideas. B. Use subordination and coordination to show how ideas relate to each other. C. Outline your draft *after* you have written it to be sure all ideas are logically placed. D. Check all your ideas against your thesis and topic sentences to be sure you do not have a relevance problem.
9. "I have trouble finding and correcting my errors."	A. Read your work aloud to listen for errors, or read your work into a tape recorder. Play back the tape, listening for errors.

B. Become sensitive to the kinds of mistakes you make by using the Personal Editing Profile on p. 489. Check the profile before you edit to remind yourself of your usual errors.

C. Edit a separate time for each kind of error you have a tendency to make.

D. Place a ruler under each line so you are not distracted by other words on the page.

E. Edit *very slowly.* If you go quickly, you will overlook errors.

F. Check the editing concerns on p. 32. Edit in stages, checking one or two of these concerns in each stage.

G. Learn the rules to be a confident editor.

H. When in doubt, check the rules in this book. If you are still in doubt, ask your teacher.

I. Trust your feelings. If you sense a problem, the chances are good that there is a problem.

APPENDIX
III

Answers to Pretests

p. 174—Finding Subjects and Verbs

Subjects	Verbs
1. mother	packed
2. Tuition	is
3. Marcos	has eaten
4. Mother	returned, studied
5. people	do know
6. Joan and her brothers	bought
7. carton	is
8. Jacques	has been studying
9. keys	are
10. excuse	will be
11. (you)	answer
12. holidays; all of us	are; can relax, recover
13. students	are making
14. accidents	can be
15. my parents and I	will move, buy

p. 240—Fragments

1. F	6. F
2. F	7. F
3. F	8. S
4. S	9. F
5. F	10. F

p. 255—Run-ons and Comma Splices

1. CS	6. CS
2. RO	7. C
3. RO	8. C
4. C	9. RO
5. RO	10. C

p. 306—Verb Forms

1. I	6. I	11. I
2. C	7. I	12. C
3. I	8. I	13. I
4. C	9. C	14. I
5. C	10. C	15. I

p. 330—Subject-Verb Agreement

1. means	6. decides
2. visits	7. are
3. plan	8. wants
4. likes	9. work
5. practices	10. sleeps

p. 342—Tense Shifts

1. TS	6. C
2. TS	7. C
3. C	8. TS
4. TS	9. TS
5. TS	10. C

p. 347—Pronouns

1. I
2. they
3. me
4. her
5. their
6. its
7. its
8. their
9. me
10. its

p. 378—Modifiers

1. no
2. yes
3. no
4. yes
5. no
6. no
7. yes
8. no
9. yes
10. no

p. 393—Capitalization

1. no
2. no
3. yes
4. yes
5. no
6. no
7. no
8. no
9. yes
10. no

p. 398—Ending Sentences

1. .
2. !
3. .
4. ?
5. .
6. . or !
7. ?
8. !
9. .
10. ?

p. 402—Using Commas

1. no
2. no
3. yes
4. yes
5. no
6. no
7. yes
8. no
9. no
10. no
11. yes
12. no

p. 413—Using Semicolons

1. yes
2. no
3. yes
4. yes
5. no
6. yes

p. 416—Using Colons, Parentheses, and Dashes

1. yes
2. yes
3. no
4. yes
5. yes
6. yes
7. no
8. yes

p. 421—Apostrophes

1. no
2. yes
3. no
4. yes
5. yes
6. yes
7. yes
8. yes
9. yes
10. no

p. 428—Using Quotation Marks

1. no
2. no
3. yes
4. no
5. yes
6. yes
7. yes
8. yes

INDEX